2001

When should I travel to get the best airfare?
Where do I go for answers to my travel questions?
What's the best and easiest way to plan and book my trip?

frommers.travelocity.com

Frommer's, the travel guide leader, has teamed up with **Travelocity.com**, the leader in online travel, to bring you an in-depth, easy-to-use resource designed to help you plan and book your trip online.

At **frommers.travelocity.com**, you'll find free online updates about your destination from the experts at Frommer's plus the outstanding travel planning and purchasing features of Travelocity.com. Travelocity.com provides reservations capabilities for 95 percent of all airline seats sold, more than 47,000 hotels, and over 50 car rental companies. In addition, Travelocity.com offers more than 2,000 exciting vacation and cruise packages. Travelocity.com puts you in complete control of your travel planning with these and other great features:

> **Expert travel guidance from Frommer's** - over 150 writers reporting from around the world!

> **Best Fare Finder** - an interactive cale͟ hen to travel to get the best airfare

> **Fare Watcher** - we'll track airf͟ destinations

> **Dream Maps** - a mapr͟ vel opportunities based

> **Shop Safe Guaran** days a week live customer service, and ͟

Whether traveling on a tight budget, ͟g for a quick weekend getaway, or planning the trip of a lifetime, Frommer's guides and Travelocity.com will make your travel dreams a reality. You've bought the book, now book the trip!

 Travelocity.com
A Sabre Company

 Frommer's

Also available from IDG Books Worldwide:

the Unofficial Guide® to California with Kids

2nd Edition

Colleen Dunn Bates and Susan LaTempa

Every effort has been made to ensure the accuracy of information throughout this book. Bear in mind, however, that prices, schedules, etc., are constantly changing. Readers should always verify information before making final plans.

IDG Books Worldwide, Inc.
An International Data Group Company
909 Third Avenue
New York, New York 10022

Produced by Menasha Ridge Press

UNOFFICIAL GUIDE is a registered trademark of IDG Books Worldwide, Inc.

ISBN 0-7645-6207-X

ISSN 1525-4992

Manufactured in the United States of America

10 9 8 7 6 5 4 3 2 1

Second edition

Contents

List of Maps

Acknowledgments

Thanks to literary agent Betsy Amster, for bringing us a wonderfully fun project. Thanks to Pam Brandon, author of *The Unofficial Guide to Florida with Kids,* who provided long-distance counsel, perspective, and laughs. Thanks to the publications that have sent us traveling with our families, especially *Westways, Avenues, Journey, the Los Angeles Times, Travel & Leisure, Food & Wine, Working Mother, Parenting, Family Fun,* and *Cooking Light.* Thanks to publisher Bob Sehlinger, associate publisher Molly Merkle, and editor Holly Cross at Menasha Ridge Press. They are surely the kindest souls in publishing. And, most importantly, thanks to our traveling companions: Daniel, Patricia, and Irene Milder; Pat Taylor; Darryl, Erin, and Emily Bates; Ellie Dunn; and the camping families at Sequoyah School.

Introduction

Our Families and Travels

From Colleen

My mother is never happier than when she's planning a trip, and I inherited that longing and joy. God knows it wasn't easy to take our brood anywhere—my parents had six kids in seven years, and I'm not sure how they ever got us dressed, let alone out of the house. But they did. From our Los Angeles home, we crammed into the station wagon and went to Yosemite, Palm Springs, Big Bear, and Disneyland. We rented an RV and camped the entire length of the state. We skied Mammoth and Tahoe. We flew to San Francisco, two at a time (the others stayed home with baby-sitters, awaiting their turn). And we went to the beach, from Malibu to San Onofre, chasing the waves that my father, then we kids, loved so much.

Now my husband, Darryl, and I are doing it with our two kids: fifth-grader Erin and second-grader Emily. We've rented a beach house, stayed in a fancy San Francisco hotel, taken Amtrak to San Diego, sledded in Big Bear, and camped in the Anza-Borrego desert. We've gone beyond California's borders, to Hawaiian beaches, a French country house, and Rocky Mountain ski towns. We've had mishaps, and stress, and a lifetime supply of whining, but we've never had a bad trip, and we've had lots of great ones. We've learned how to plan drives around Emily's essential rest times and set the stage to minimize Erin's fear of the unknown. And we've learned how to weave our grown-up desires and interests into those of our children, further fusing us as a family. (We've also learned how to take the occasional adult trip away from the kids . . . but that's another book.)

I will never tire of exploring California. My children are perpetually panting for a new outing in our home state. From the trail atop Half Dome to the splash at the end of Splash Mountain, California is a great gift to the traveling family.

From Susan

As I write this, I get up from the desk from time to time to check the laundry—an extra load this week because my daughter Irene and I have just returned from a trip to San Francisco and need some of our things for school and work tomorrow. Irene, 12, hasn't learned the joys of packing light yet, so I shake my head over the size of the pile of laundry. But even at 12, Irene has learned that travel is a special joy, that it's a great good fortune to substitute pictures in your head for place-names in a book. This trip brought forth her memories of previous family travels, and Irene shared with me her perspective on such adventures as our family's two-week car trip through Mendocino and the redwoods, or a more recent biking weekend in the Santa Ynez Valley. Her reminiscences this week reminded me again how children hold dear the most unexpected (and often unremembered by adults) moments of a vacation, and how, more than anything, travel is a kind of practice that allows a child to learn to face other new experiences and be free to explore in all parts of her or his life.

My own earliest memories of California are a child's images of giant pinecones and picnic tables at highway rest stops. But I have to admit that for the most part, I ignored my first chances to appreciate the state's spectacular scenery as I sat next to my brother in the back seat of the station wagon, bologna sandwiches floating in the ice chest at my feet. Today, my family travels frequently throughout the state, Irene and I being joined by my husband, Dan, and daughter Patricia, 16. We've summer-vacationed in Mammoth and Sequoia, in Oxnard and Mendocino. (Admittedly, we sometimes take two summer vacations!) We've had Christmas week or winter weekends away from home, and spring break has been a traditional time to travel with Grandma, once to La Jolla, once to Coronado. We've headed out to see natural wonders in Death Valley and to play on the water slides at Hurricane Harbor. We've seen and done enough for me (with a little help from the kids' sharper memories) to contribute half of the material in this book. But we haven't seen it all yet.

The Dynamics of Family Travel

Don't even think about planning a family trip until you answer this question: What does each member of the family want to get out of the vacation?

It seems like a simple question, but it'll take more time and thought to answer than you might realize. It means assessing your current relationship with your kids and your spouse. It means taking stock of your children's passions and fears, as well as your own. It means attaching a budget to everyone's wishes. And it invariably means compromise.

Start by asking yourself some questions. Is this vacation a time for togetherness, for time alone for you while the children are entertained, or for a little of each? Are you a single dad who doesn't get to see the kids much? Are you an at-home mom who never gets a break? Are you looking for exhilarating adventures or a laid-back getaway? Do you want intellectual stimulation for you and the kids? How well do your kids handle spontaneity?

Because your family's dynamics change with every birthday, the answers may surprise you. One child may be more ready for adventure than you've realized; another might be more ready for peace and quiet than you think.

THE PLEASURES OF PLANNING

It's best to decide what you want to do and come up with some options to start the ball rolling. Then call a family meeting and include your kids in the planning process. Let everyone ask questions. Show some brochures or books about the places you have in mind so they'll feel like they have enough information to be taken seriously. Pull out maps and a globe. Jump on the Internet. Teenagers in particular are quite vocal about expressing their choices, and they appreciate it when they can influence the planning process. The getaway is much more enjoyable when everyone wants to be there.

This shared planning time can be a great routine to continue as the trip itself gets under way. Remember, your kids may not be able to easily visualize your destination or the plane ride or cab ride you'll take on the way. And if you're traveling from place to place during your vacation, each new day dawns on the unknown. So keep the brochures and guidebooks handy, and break the itinerary down into manageable chunks. Offer an advance agenda every now and then, referring again to your original planning sessions ("Remember we thought that the Bubbling Brook Motel sounded like a good one?") and letting the kids develop anticipation rather than anxiety.

It's essential to be realistic when you plan a family vacation. Parents of young children may have to concede that the days of romantic sunsets are over for a while if there's a toddler tugging at their shorts. With infants and toddlers, the best vacations are the simple ones. They don't much need to see the sights; the idea is to be somewhere comfortable and intriguing for the adults, with a pleasant environment in which to relax and enjoy your children. In California, destinations like Mission Bay or Monterey are ideal for parents of the youngest group of kids. School-age kids revel in attractions created for their enjoyment—theme parks, amusement parks, arcades, rides. The metropolitan regions can also be a blast with elementary-age kids. Teens may seem reluctant, but if a pilgrimage to a special point of interest for them (a certain skateboard shop, a movie-star hangout) is included, the whole trip becomes "worthwhile." And they thrive in safe, explore-it-on-your-own situations like a tour of Alcatraz or a Gold Country town.

LESS IS MORE THAN ENOUGH

As you plan, we urge you to leave plenty of down time in the schedule. Some of our families' most memorable moments are simple breakfasts on the beach or early evening walks to nowhere, when the conversation naturally flows. Kids treasure moments, not places or days. Give your children plenty of room to run and play; a morning collecting seashells or an afternoon at the hotel pool can be more satisfying than standing in line at a crowded theme-park attraction.

A good rule of thumb may sound stringent: no more than two activities in a day. If you spend the morning at a museum, and plan to go to dinner at Universal CityWalk, go back to the hotel in the afternoon to rest and swim. If you're driving from San Francisco to Monterey, make your reservations for the aquarium the next day. Then you can stop on the way at the lighthouse and the artichoke fields and the funny little town that time forgot. Remember that travel itself is an activity.

Also, plan some activities that allow you to take a break from each other. The quarters get a little close after a week together in a hotel room, particularly if children are of significantly different ages. Schedule an afternoon where mom and dad split duties, giving each other a break; take advantage of child and teen programs offered in many resorts to make sure there's at least one evening alone with your spouse. Everyone benefits from a little elbow room.

Reconnections

Family vacations are a necessary indulgence in today's hurried-up world, a time for togetherness without the day-to-day distractions. Whether it's a car trip on a budget or a transcontinental flight, it's a time to reconnect with your family, especially teenagers. And the best times are the serendipitous moments—a heart-to-heart conversation on an evening hike, or silly "knock-knock" jokes while standing in line for the roller coaster. Roles are relaxed when schedules are flexible, and kids can have the opportunity to see their parents as interesting companions, not just bossy grown-ups. We all can learn from one another when there's time to listen and when we take the time to see the world through a loved one's eyes.

A seasoned traveler friend once scoffed at the notion of traveling with young children, "since they don't remember anything." We couldn't disagree more. Susan's children have often mentioned the hours spent sitting at the mouth of the Klamath River watching the incredible sight of sea lions, pelicans, Native American fishermen, and one ambitious, fast-swimming dog, all competing for the salmon swimming into the river from the ocean. When Colleen's daughter was seven, she struck up an intense friendship with a boy on a Hawaiian beach, and when they returned to their respective homes in Michigan and California, they kept in touch via e-mail. Given the open hearts and all the innocence of childhood, new impressions may sink in even more deeply with kids than with adults.

Our children have a greater understanding of the rest of the world as a result of travel to new places and experiencing new ideas. And siblings have formed a special bond from traveling together, a bond less likely to be formed at home, where they have separate classrooms, separate friends, separate rooms. As parents, it's up to us to be sure there's some fun in a trip for each member of the family. And as a family, we all need to remember to indulge our traveling companions from time to time. Remember, your responses to challenges on the road—delayed flights, long lines, unsatisfactory accommodations—will influence the way your children will deal with frustrations. Be patient, be calm, and teach your children these important lifelong skills.

Vacations are times for adventure, relaxation, shared experiences, time alone—whatever your family decides. Our goal with this book is to evaluate each destination with that in mind—recognizing that your family has needs, based on ages, backgrounds, and interests, that are quite different from any other family's—and provide you with some structure to analyze your family's needs and create a vacation that works.

We have traveled the world with our children, from France and Holland to the Hawaiian Islands and the Rocky Mountains. Yet some of our most wondrous trips have been in our own backyard: hopping a San Francisco cable car, body boarding on a Santa Barbara beach, playing hide-and-seek in a redwood forest. We can't imagine ever tiring of exploring our home state, whether we're stalking the newest amped-up amusement park or finding the next best beach.

This book is not meant to be a compendium of every family-priced hotel or every advertised attraction, though we have strived to cover a variety of interests for a variety of ages. Instead of compiling a family-travel yellow pages, we've edited out the less worthy places to better draw attention to the destinations that will make your trip a hit.

Dozens of families have contributed their opinions to this book; it is evaluative and opinionated, and it offers advice for the best ways for families to have fun together and further relationships.

Survival Guide for Little Kids

Think Small. Little ones love little pleasures: splashing in the hotel pool, playing hide-and-seek in the lobby, stacking up rocks on the beach. Don't overload them.

Seek Creative Transportation. For young children, getting there is often more fun than being there. When Emily was three years old, her greatest joy and memory from our gala two-week Hawaiian vacation was the open-air wiki-wiki shuttle at Honolulu Airport—she positively shook with excitement during the ride. Seek out the ferries, trolleys, shuttles, trains, surreys, and double-decker buses, and you'll be rewarded with a cheap thrill that's as fun for little ones as a Disneyland ride.

Limit the Shopping. Our rule at attractions is a firm one: No shopping, not even looking, until we are leaving the place. Young children can get consumed by and panicky about choosing a souvenir, and they'll enjoy the museum or theme park more if they can focus on the activities, not the trinkets.

Give Them a Voice. Even a four-year-old will benefit from feeling like he has some control over his vacation. When possible, let him make simple choices for the family—like "Should we walk to the beach or ride the trolley?"

Allow for Lots of Down Time. Bring books or quiet hobbies to amuse yourself during nap times or play times. Remember, children's ability to tackle the big world is much more limited than yours.

Accept Some Slowness. It's stressful enough to get a kindergartener out the door to school each morning, so don't keep up the stress on vacation. They need a break from being rushed, too. If they're happy playing in their pajamas for an extra half-hour, the museum can wait. Conversely, accept that the times you like to be more leisurely—like dinnertime—lead to impatience in children.

Survival Guide for School-Age Kids

Give Them Their Own Space. Whether it's a backpack, a carry-on train case, or one of those shoebag-like hanging pockets that fit over the car seat in front of them, each kid needs a portable room of his or her own in which to stow gum, cards, books, disposable cameras, and souvenirs.

Make a New Routine. At least until middle-school years, most kids do best with a certain amount of predictability, so it's a kindness to create little travel routines and rituals within your changed life. Knowing that his parents will always stop sight-seeing by 3 p.m. to swim (or will never check out without one last hour in the pool) is a comforting thought to many a fourth-grader. Knowing that you will have $5 spending money each day can do away with shopping anxiety. Having set turns as map reader can add some fun to a hundred-mile drive.

Avoid Eating Breakfast Out. Many savvy traveling parents never eat breakfast in a restaurant. School-age kids are at their brightest and best in the morning, and waiting for table service at a ho-hum restaurant can start the day on the wrong foot. We carry fruit, cereal, milk, and juices in coolers or to kitchenettes or pop for room service—it's the least expensive and most wonderfully indulgent time to do so.

Beware Befuddled Expectations. School-age kids are old enough to have some reference points, and young enough to have great gaping holes in their mental pictures of the world. Our kids have imagined that they'd find matzo ball soup instead of chocolate at Ghirardelli Square (thinking it was Jerry's Deli); they've worried that the car would tumble down the cliff on a winding mountain road; they've expected to see gold nuggets in the bottom of the creek in Gold Country. Ask what's going on in their minds. Listen. Don't overpromise.

Watch the Diet. It's fun to let vacation time be a time of special treats, but overindulgence in junk food, sweets, and caffeinated drinks may contribute to behavior changes in kids who aren't sleeping in their own beds and are full of adrenaline as it is.

Remember That Kids Hate Scenery. Drive them through it if you must, but don't make them actually look at too much of it.

Give Them a Ship's Log. A roll of tape and a blank book are all that's needed to turn ticket stubs, menus, brochures, and postcards from a clutter of trash into a wonderful scrapbook that's always ready to be shared and enjoyed.

Hotels and Motels Are Not Just for Sleeping. Allow time for getting ice, playing in the pool, reviewing all items and prices in the minibar, packing and unpacking, using the hairdryer, putting laundry into the laundry bags, trying out the vending machines, etc.

Hit the Playgrounds. Check your maps and ask ahead about public playgrounds with climbing and sliding equipment, and on days when you'll be sight-seeing, driving, or absorbing culture, allow for an hour's lunch or rest stop at the playground. Even on city vacations, try to set aside at least one day for pure physical fun at a beach or water park or ski slope.

Just Say Yes to Ranger Tours. These tours are often designed with schoolkids in mind. We'd never have tasted sand flies at Mono Lake or seen a tarantula up close at Anza-Borrego or understood about the Welsh miner's lunch pails if we hadn't checked the schedule at the state or national park information center and made a point to join the ranger walk.

Survival Guide for Teenagers

Don't Try to Fool Them. Don't try to tell them they'll have more fun with you than with their friends. They won't. But if you offer them the possibility of doing things they might want to tell their friends about later, they'll be interested.

Respect Their Culture. Let your teenager play an active role in planning the vacation. Ask her opinion of your arrangements. Often our daughter will offer a great suggestion or an alternative that we may not have considered. And look for pop culture landmarks—movie locations, palaces of fashion or music or sport. Add a ball game to the itinerary.

Night Moves. A vacation is a great time to go with your teenager to a music club or a midnight movie, or on a moonlight hike. Go to the theater or the ballet; check out a jazz club. If you have other kids needing earlier bed-times, let the parents switch-hit on going out at night with the older kids.

Give Them Options. You don't need to go everywhere with everyone. If your younger child wants to go see the dinosaurs at the museum, this is the time for a split plan: Dad and son see the dinosaurs, mother and daughter shop or take in a movie or a play. If you have a teenager who appreciates their sleep time, let them snooze late at least one morning. Slip out with younger siblings and take a walk or read a book. Also, set wake-up time before everyone says good night so that there are no grouchy morning risers (at least not because they've been awakened too early).

Give Them Freedom. Before age 12, kids are bound to parents, preferring to stay in your orbit; when adolescence hits, they're programmed to push away from you. Choose a vacation spot that is safe and controlled enough to allow them to wander or spend time with other teenagers. If you can't do that, look for an afternoon or evening at a controlled hangout place like Universal CityWalk or Pier 39. Give them the night to themselves at Disneyland or Knotts. Send them off to the ranger campfire by themselves at Yosemite; sign them up for an afternoon's photography workshop in Big Sur.

Compromise on the Headphone Thing. Headphones can allow teens to create their own space even when they're with others, and that can be a safety valve, but try to agree before the trip on some non-headphone parameters so you don't begin to feel as if they're being used to keep other family members and the trip itself at a distance. If you're traveling by car, take turns choosing the radio station or CD for part of the trip.

Don't Make Your Teenager the Built-in Baby-Sitter. It's a family vacation—a time for reconnecting, not for avoiding the kids. A special night out for parents also should be special for the children; let them order videos and room service, for example, or participate in age-appropriate hotel programs.

Make Peace with Shopping. Look for street markets and vintage stores; spend some time in surf shops and record stores. If you go with your teenager, you may find that the conversation in such an environment flows easily. Or hit the outlets—many a summer vacation has included a day of back-to-school shopping.

Just Say Yes to at Least One Big-Ticket Excursion. Teenagers will get a lot out of a half-day adventure. What look at first like expensive tours (often available through the hotel sports desk or concierge) have been memorable and important experiences for our kids that we, as parents, are simply not able to offer by ourselves. A raft ride, a desert jeep tour, a kayak and snorkel trip, a horseback trail ride—each took us far into the country we were exploring, and each was worth every cent. Or let the teenager sign up for a lesson: surfing, sailing, rock-climbing. One of our daughters took a remarkable rope-climbing course that had her swinging through the trees in Mammoth.

A Word on Homework

Both our elementary school and high school kids have faced a load of homework or a special project that had to be worked on during "vacation" time. If a surprise major assignment comes up, and plans can't be changed, there will be an unavoidable strain on the trip. Parents should consider strategies such as bringing along a laptop computer, scheduling vacation fun in half-day chunks so that the homeworked kid gets some work and some play, and/or a marathon session at a library at the vacation spot. You can also shamelessly beg the teacher for a reprieve, but make that a last resort.

The Secret to Visiting Art Museums

Room after room of paintings and sculptures are numbing to children. They need a focal point and a sense of adventure. Before your visit, find out what some of the major works on display are, and locate pictures of them (perhaps the museum will mail you a brochure with pictures, or you can look online or get an art book from the library). Let each child pick one or two works to sleuth out. They can learn a little about the artist and the work in question, and then when you visit the museum, they can go on a hunt for "their" artwork.

A Few Words for Single Parents

Because single parents generally are working parents, planning a special getaway with your children can be the best way to spend some quality time together. But remember, the vacation is not just for your child—it's for you, too. You might invite along a grandparent or a favorite aunt or uncle; the other adult provides nice company for you, and your child will benefit from the time with family members.

Don't try to spend every moment with your children on vacation. Instead, plan some activities for your children with other children. Look for hotels with supervised activities, or research the community you'll be visiting for school-vacation offerings at libraries, recreation centers, or temple or church day camps. Then take advantage of your free time to do what you want to do: read a book, have a massage, take a long walk or a catnap.

Tips for Grandparents

A vacation that involves generations can be the most enriching experience for everyone, but it is important to consider the needs of each family member, from the youngest to the oldest. Here are some things to consider.

- If you're planning to travel alone with your grandchildren, spend a little time getting to know them before the vacation. Be sure they're comfortable with the idea of traveling with you if their parents are not coming along.

- It's best to take one grandchild at a time, two at the most. Cousins can be better than siblings, because they don't fight as much.

- Let your grandchildren help plan the vacation, and keep the first one short. Be flexible and don't overplan.

- Discuss mealtimes and bedtime. Fortunately, many grandparents are on an early dinner schedule, which works nicely with younger children. Also, if you want to plan a special evening out, be sure to make the reservation ahead of time. Stash some crayons and paper in your bag to keep kids occupied.

- Gear plans to your grandchildren's age levels, because if they're not happy, you're not happy.

- Choose a vacation that offers some supervised activities for children in case you need a rest.

- If you're traveling by car, this is the one time we highly recommend headphones. Teenagers' musical tastes are vastly different from most grandparents', and it's simply more enjoyable when everyone can listen to their own style of music.

- Take along a nightlight.

- Carry a notarized statement from parents for permission for medical care in case of an emergency. Also, be sure you have insurance information.

- Tell your grandchildren about any medical problems you may have so that they can be prepared if there's an emergency.

- Many attractions and hotels offer discounts for seniors, so be sure you check ahead of time for bargains.

- A cruise may be the perfect compromise—plenty of daily activities for everyone, but shared mealtimes.

If planning a child-friendly trip seems overwhelming, try Grandtravel (800) 247-7651, a tour operator/travel agent aimed at kids and their grandparents.

For Travelers with Disabilities

Facilities for the physically challenged are plentiful in California. All public buildings have some form of access for those who use wheelchairs. In addition, many public buses are equipped with wheelchair lifts. Most of the state's attractions offer facilities and services for those with physical challenges, and many hotels have specially equipped rooms. The state's three most popular cities have guides for the physically challenged: in San Diego, call (858) 279-0704; in Los Angeles, call (323) 957-4280; and in San Francisco, call (415) 391-2000, TTY (415) 227-2619.

How the *Unofficial Guide* Works

ORGANIZATION

Our informal polls show that most families tend to choose a vacation spot based on geography—a place that's new and different, or familiar and comfortable. So we've divided California into eight regions, with family-friendly information in each region. The chapters are organized geographically, from south to north. For great places to stay within those regions—resorts, hotels, campgrounds—see the Family Lodging sections within each chapter; kid- and parent-pleasing restaurants are recommended in the Family-Friendly Restaurants sections found in each chapter.

The regions break down as follows:

- **San Diego County.** From Tijuana to Carlsbad, and inland to Anza-Borrego, this region centers on the San Diego metropolitan area and beaches.

- **Orange County.** From San Clemente in the south to Costa Mesa in the north, this region includes such beloved beach destinations as Newport, Laguna, and Dana Point, as well as Disneyland and Knott's Berry Farm.

- **Los Angeles and Vicinity.** This huge urban area centers on the nation's second-largest city and includes such satellite towns as Palm Springs, Pasadena, Redondo Beach, Big Bear, and Santa Monica, as well as such suburban amusements as Magic Mountain.

- **Central Coast.** North of L.A. lies this rich collection of beaches and small-town escapes, starting in Ventura, continuing through Santa Barbara and San Simeon (Hearst Castle), and going north through the wilds of Big Sur to the aquarium in Monterey.

- **Sierra Nevada.** Mountain fun awaits in this large region, from Yosemite's Half Dome to Sequoia's trees to sparkling Lake Tahoe. This region also includes Death Valley, on the Sierra's eastern boundary.

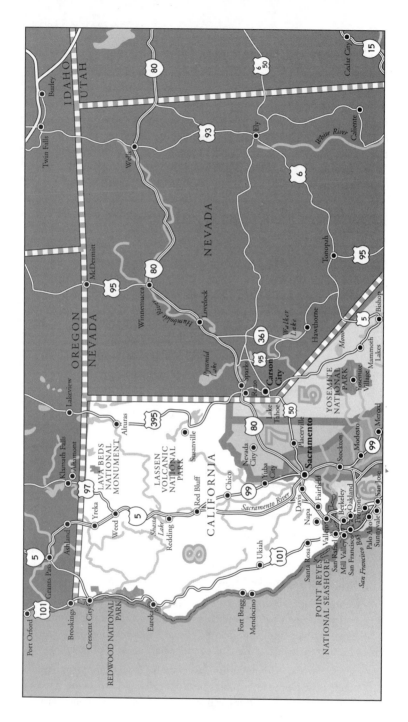

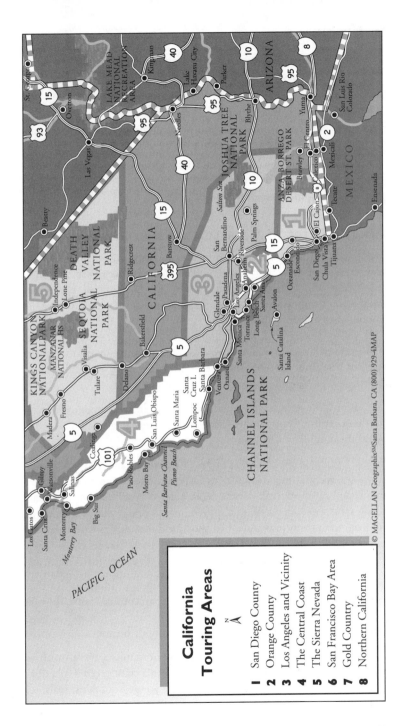

California
Touring Areas

N

1 San Diego County
2 Orange County
3 Los Angeles and Vicinity
4 The Central Coast
5 The Sierra Nevada
6 San Francisco Bay Area
7 Gold Country
8 Northern California

© MAGELLAN Geographix℠Santa Barbara, CA (800) 929-4MAP

- San Francisco Bay Area. Along with the great city by the bay, this region includes adventures in the East Bay (Berkeley) and Marin County, as far north as Point Reyes.

- Gold Country. Inland from San Francisco, this region encompasses the capital city, Sacramento, and wanders through the Gold Rush towns flanking the western Sierra Nevada.

- Northern California. This vast, rural region, rich in national and state parks, goes from Bodega Bay up through the redwoods to the Oregon border, and over to Mt. Shasta.

WHAT'S THERE TO DO BESIDES DISNEYLAND?

Each regional chapter recommends the best beaches, parks, family outdoor adventures, and attractions, ranging from theme parks to science museums. We've also included serendipitous sidebars on offbeat places that you'll want to know about, from children's theaters in L.A. to the old schoolhouses of the Gold Country.

If you're looking for some healthy family bonding, stretch beyond the man-made attractions. Have a sense of adventure, and plan some activities that are new and exciting—not necessarily strenuous, but memorable. Each region has specific spots for the following activities:

Camping. We've selected a few choice family-friendly campgrounds throughout the state. If it's your family's first experience, you might opt for a cabin; we list them in many state parks.

Biking. Cycling is one of the best ways to experience an area firsthand and can be enjoyed year-round in much of California. For beginners, we have recommended miles of paved bicycle trails; older kids will like the mountain biking spots we've found. You don't even have to bring your own bike; you can rent one at many resorts and bike shops, and many shops have trailers for rent for small children (5 and under) to travel safely behind you—they're much safer than bicycle seats. Know that helmets are the law for children, and it is strongly advised that all cyclists wear helmets.

Surfing. The wave is king (or queen) in many parts of California, so we've recommended the best surfing classes and camps for kids, as well as good beaches for wave riders of all kinds, including body boarders.

Whale-Watching. Wintertime visitors won't want to miss a whale-watching trip, which are offered up and down the California coast. Even if you don't spot one of the great gray whales, you'll surely enjoy dolphins, seals, sea birds, and an exhilarating ride on the Pacific Ocean.

Hiking. California is a hiker's paradise; we've concentrated on the easiest spots suitable for kids, from urban nature hikes to Sierra trails.

Kayaking and White-Water Rafting. From kayaking the coves of the north coast to rafting the wilds of the American River, these are wonderful bonding adventures for families with kids over 5 or 6 years of age.

The Unofficial Guide Rating System for Attractions

Our system includes an "appeal to different age groups" category, indicating a range of appeal from one star (★): don't bother, up to five stars (★★★★★): not to be missed.

WHAT'S "UNOFFICIAL" ABOUT THIS BOOK?

The material in this guide originated with the authors and researchers and has not been reviewed, edited, or in any way approved by attractions, restaurants, and hotels we describe. Our goal is to help families plan a vacation that's right for them by providing important details and honest opinions. If we've found a family-oriented destination to be dreary or a rip-off, we simply don't include it.

Readers care about the author's opinion. The author, after all, is supposed to know what he or she is talking about. This, coupled with the fact that the traveler wants quick answers (as opposed to endless alternatives), dictates that authors should be explicit, prescriptive, and, above all, direct. The *Unofficial Guide* tries to do just that—it spells out alternatives and recommends specific courses of action. It simplifies complicated destinations and attractions and allows the traveler to feel in control in the most unfamiliar environments. The objective of the *Unofficial Guide* is not to have the most information or all of the information, but to have the most accessible, useful information, unbiased by affiliation with any organization or industry.

This guide is directed at value-conscious, consumer-oriented families who seek a cost-effective, though not spartan, travel style.

Letters and Comments from Readers

We expect to learn from our mistakes, as well as from the input of our readers, and to improve with each book and edition. Many of those who use the *Unofficial Guides* write to us asking questions, making comments, or sharing their own discoveries and lessons learned. We appreciate all of the input, both positive and critical, and encourage our readers to continue writing. Readers' comments and observations are frequently incorporated into revised editions of the *Unofficial Guide* and will contribute immeasurably to its improvement.

How to Write the Authors

Colleen Dunn Bates and Susan LaTempa
The Unofficial Guide to California with Kids
P.O. Box 43673
Birmingham, AL 35243

When you write, be sure to put your return address on your letter as well as on the envelope—sometimes envelopes and letters get separated. And remember, our work takes us out of the office for long periods of time, so forgive us if our response is delayed.

Getting Ready to Go

WEATHER AND WHEN TO GO

California's climate varies tremendously from region to region, but in general it is a temperate state, suitable for year-round visiting. The deserts (Palm Springs, Anza-Borrego) are brutally hot in late summer, and the far north is rain-soaked in winter, so avoid those areas then. Otherwise, travelers have a lot of flexibility. You can always count on warmth and sun in Southern California from mid-June through October, though the coastal areas can get fogged in during early summer (the "June gloom"); the San Francisco Bay Area is more unpredictable, with its chill fog that's sent many a summer visitor scurrying to the Gap to buy a sweatshirt. (The average daily August temperature in L.A., for instance, is 82, while in San Francisco the average is just 69.)

We're most fond of visiting Los Angeles in May or October, when there's plenty of warm sun but not too much smog or blazing heat. If you're staying at the beach, know that May and June are often gray and overcast; the beach cities of San Diego, Newport, Laguna, Santa Barbara, and Santa Cruz shine in the peak of summer—July, August, and September are best—when days are long and the Pacific warms up. We like San Francisco best in winter, especially around the holidays, when it is festive and mildly brisk, or in September, when the fog is minimal. The mountains, from the southern Sierra to the Cascades, are wonderful year-round, from the ski days of February to the hikes of August.

In general, popular tourist sights are busier on weekends than weekdays, and Saturdays are busier than Sundays. Locals say the least crowded time to visit theme parks is on a rainy weekday in the winter.

Of course, family travel schedules often center around school holidays, which tend to be the busiest times to travel. But consider taking your children out of school for special family trips—a well-planned week of family travel is just as enriching as five days in a classroom. Make it clear that traveling is a privilege, and agree that all missed work must be made up upon return. Talk with teachers ahead of time.

PACK LIGHT

We limit ourselves to one carry-on bag each and a backpack, no matter what the duration of the trip or how we are traveling. (The exception is a ski or snow trip, which demands bulky clothes.) If you have small children, stashing an extra T-shirt and pair of shorts in your backpack comes in handy in emergencies. A California trip generally is casual, though you may want to pack one nice outfit for dressing up for a special evening out.

Make a list of necessities and let the kids pack their own bags (subject to your inspection). T-shirts, shorts, and bathing suits are perfect in the warmer regions, but never travel without a jacket or sturdy sweatshirt. California weather is fickle, and you may be surprised with cold. Take along a small bottle of detergent for hand-washing. The vacation is much more enjoyable if you don't have a bunch of bags to haul around busy airports or hotel lobbies.

Let your children pack their own backpack, then ask them to wear it around the house to test how comfortable it will be on a long trip. Our children have become savvy packers, aware that each piece counts. Of course, you should check their bags before departing, just to be sure the essentials are all there.

Finally, you may want to take along a "surprise bag" for young travelers. Sticker books, a card game, or a new book are perfect, lightweight diversions to bring out when everyone's patience is wearing thin.

WHAT TO TAKE WITH YOU: A CHECKLIST

No matter what your means of transportation, be sure you take along (and have handy at all times):

- Sunglasses and hats to protect you from the sun.
- Sunscreen, at least 15 SPF.
- Emergency information—who to contact at home in case of an accident or emergency, medical insurance cards, and your pediatrician's telephone number (they can often diagnose and call in a prescription by phone).
- A travel-size bottle of antibacterial gel (the kind that doesn't require water).

- Basic first-aid kit—children's aspirin and aspirin substitute, allergy medication, Dramamine for motion sickness, insect repellent, bandages, gauze pads, thermometer, cough syrup, decongestant, medication for diarrhea, antibiotic cream, tweezers, and fingernail scissors.

- Prescription medications.

- Unscented baby wipes that can be used for any clean-up.

- A small sewing kit with scissors.

- A small nightlight to ease fear of darkness.

- A couple of extra paperback books, especially for teenagers. My daughter fell in love with Agatha Christie novels when she was forced to read her first one on a trip after she finished her own book.

- A folding cooler. Perfect for carrying fruit, drinks, even sandwiches to theme parks, on walks, or in the car.

- Lightweight windbreakers for cool evenings at the beach.

- Inexpensive rain ponchos for surprise rainstorms.

- Comfortable walking shoes for nature trails, botanical gardens, and beachside strolls (as well as theme parks).

- Each child should bring along some cash of her own, even just a few dollars. Tell them it is theirs to spend on souvenirs or whatever they choose. When it's their money, they're much more judicious shoppers.

- A sense of humor. Traveling with children can be trying at times.

REMEMBERING YOUR TRIP

When you choose a destination, write or call for information (listed at the end of each chapter). The travel brochures can later be used as part of a scrapbook commemorating your trip.

Purchase a notebook for each child and spend time each evening recording the events of the day. If your children have trouble getting motivated or don't know what to write about, start a discussion; otherwise, let them write, or draw, whatever they want to remember the day's events.

Collect mementos along the way and create a treasure box in a small tin or cigar box. Months or years later, it's fun to look at postcards, seashells, or ticket stubs to jump-start a memory.

Add inexpensive postcards to your photographs to create an album, then write a few words on each page to accompany the images.

Cool Web Sites for California-Bound Kids

Elementary-age kids and teens will connect more with a trip if they're part of the planning. One of the best ways for them to plan is to explore the 'Net. Here are our favorite web sites to prepare for a trip within California.

Alcatraz Island/Golden Gate NRA: www.nps.gov/alcatraz

Birch Aquarium at Scripps: aquarium.ucsd.edu

California Division of Tourism: www.gocalif.ca.gov

California Heritage Digital Image Access Project: sunsite. Berkeley.EDU/calheritage

California History: www.geocities.com/Athens/Forum/1464

California History Review for 4th Grade: www.jspub.com/4thgrade.html

California State Parks: www.cal-parks.ca.gov/

Caltrans Driving Information: www.dot.ca.gov/onroad.htm

Channel Islands National Park: www.nps.gov/chis

Donner Party: members.aol.com/DanMRosen/donner/index.htm

Exploratorium: ExploraNet: www.exploratorium.edu

Gold Country Guide: www.malakoff.com/gctgfr.htm

Golden Gate Bridge: www.goldengate.org

Gold Rush sites: www.isu.edu/~trinmich/home.html, www.sfmuseum.org/hist6/masonrpt.html

Hearst Castle: www.hearstcastle.org

International Surfing Museum: www.surfingmuseum.org

Marine Mammal Center: www.tmmc.org

Monterey Bay Aquarium: www.mbayaq.org

National Park Service: www.nps.gov

Northern California Information: www.shastacascade.org

Redwoods: California's Redwood Canyons: redwoods.com/~ebarnett/redwood.canyons.html

San Diego Zoo and Wild Animal Park: www.sandiegozoo.org

Santa Cruz Beach Boardwalk: www.beachboardwalk.com/

Universal City: www.mca.com/unicity

Zeum: www.zeum.org

Give each child a disposable camera to record their version of the trip. Our five-year-old snapped an entire series of photos that never showed anyone above the waist—his view of the world (and the photos are priceless).

Nowadays, many families travel with a camcorder, though we don't recommend using one—parents end up viewing the trip through the lens rather than enjoying the sights. If you must, take it along, but only record a few moments of major sights (too much is boring anyway). Let the kids tape and narrate.

Even better, because it's more compact, carry a palm-sized tape recorder and let everyone describe their experiences. Hearing a small child's voice years later is so endearing, and those recorded descriptions will trigger an album's worth of memories, far more focused than what most novices capture with a camcorder.

GETTING THERE

By Car

Driving is certainly the most economical way to travel, but if you're covering a lot of miles, it's time-consuming and can try the patience of every passenger. For starters, don't pull any punches with your kids about just how long you'll be in the car.

If it's a long trip, leave before daylight. Take along small pillows and blankets (we use our children's baby blankets), and let the kids snooze. When they're fully awake a few hours down the road, stop for breakfast and teeth brushing.

Be sure there are books, crayons and paper, and a couple of laptop games (though not the electronic kind with annoying beeps). Parents can stash a few surprises to dole out along the way: sticker books, action figures, magazines. We take along a deflated beach ball to blow up, a Frisbee, or a Koosh ball for impromptu play times at rest stops.

Be sure you have maps, and chart your trip before you leave home. Share the maps with the children so that they'll understand the distance to be covered.

The most significant California highway is Interstate 5, which runs from the Mexican to the Oregon borders, connecting San Diego, Los Angeles, Sacramento, and Shasta. It's fast and convenient, but frequently dreary; the stretch from L.A. to San Francisco is particularly numbing. Highway 1 is the oceanfront road that starts and stops throughout the state; it's worth the detour and time to drive it through the Big Sur area. Highway 101 heads in roughly the same direction as Interstate 5, connecting L.A. to the Oregon border, but is far more charming (and slower), passing through farm and beach towns.

Traffic is a force to be reckoned with in California's urban areas, and you should plan around it. Don't even think about driving across L.A. or over San Francisco's Bay Bridge at 5:30 p.m.

Seat belts for front-seat drivers and passengers are the law in California. Child car safety seats are mandatory for children under four years of age or weighing less than 40 pounds.

Snacks are great, but leave the drinks (preferably water, since it doesn't stain or get sticky when spilled) until the last moment, or frequent rest room stops will prolong the journey. Rest areas can be found all along California's major highways, and most are open around the clock. Pack a picnic for mealtimes, and everyone can take a walk or stretch.

Small pillows and your own CDs or tapes make the journey peaceful. Take turns and let everyone choose a favorite. If kids fight over music, make them take turns choosing. To solve the seat fights, we rotate turns, either weekly or daily, for who gets to choose a seat first.

Don't forget to always lock your car, and never leave wallets or luggage in sight. Keep valuables locked in the trunk.

By Train

Amtrak brings Easterners to California via Chicago and Denver aboard the Zephyr; Northwesterners can train down on the Coast Starlight, which runs from Seattle to Los Angeles. Amtrak also runs popular commuter/vacationer trains from L.A. north to Santa Barbara and south to San Diego.

We have taken long train trips, and for youngsters, it's interesting for about the first hour of a many-hour trip. But with books, games, and activities to occupy the time, it's a leisurely and relatively inexpensive way to travel, with time to unwind and spend quality moments with your family. You can stand up and stretch, or go for a walk, and there's more legroom than in an airplane or car (and no traffic jams). Many trains offer sleeping and dining cars, but remember—some trips can be mighty long, and the fare is not much less than cut-rate airfares. If you opt for a longer trip, book first-class and a sleeping car.

Amtrak offers a children's discount—kids ages 2–15 ride for half-price when accompanied by a full-fare-paying adult. Each adult can bring two children for the discount; one child under the age of 2 rides free with every adult ticket purchased.

If you're arriving in L.A. by train, you'll need a car to get around, so reserve one in advance. It's entirely possible, however, to arrive in San Francisco, Santa Barbara, and San Diego and enjoy a stay without a car.

For reservations and information, call (800) USA-RAIL or log on the Internet at www.amtrak.com.

By Plane

Every part of California is served by major airlines, so choosing a flight is a matter of time and economics. Booking as far in advance as possible can save hundreds of dollars for a family of four. When you book your tickets, be sure to get your seat assignments. Request bulkhead for small kids who won't be entertained by a movie but might be able to move around a bit. Although far-front seats are preferred for the most part, be sure to inquire as to how the movie is shown; if you're more than a few rows back from a small screen, it can be hard to enjoy the film.

Take-off and landing bother some children's ears, particularly if they have a cold. Look for plastic earplugs designed to ease ear-pressure pain. They come in children's sizes and are available at travel stores, drug stores, and airport sundry stores. We've found them to be highly effective. One pair lasts for two plane flights at least; they cost two or three dollars per pair. You can also take along gum for older children or a bottle or sipper cup for babies and toddlers. A washcloth heated with hot water from a thermos and held to ears will also help the younger ones who can't tolerate earplugs. Most of your fellow passengers would agree that the best babies on airplanes are sleeping babies, so, if possible, book your flights around nap times, which assures a peaceful flight for you and a happy child as you land.

Pack a few nutritious snacks, like pretzels, dried fruit, or crackers, and a small bottle of water. Food and beverage service takes a while on a packed flight (and food isn't always served). If you or your child wants or needs a special meal, be sure to call the airlines at least 48 hours in advance to request.

Bring your own child safety seat; though airlines allow children under two years of age to fly free on a parent's lap, it's much safer if they're strapped in a safety seat (and they're much more likely to nap, giving you a break). A car seat must have a visible label stating it is approved for air travel.

IF YOU RENT A CAR

The car is king in California, so rental rates are competitive, and every major company is located at the larger airports. Recreational vehicles, four-wheel-drives, and convertibles also can be rented, though they are considerably more expensive. To rent a car, you will need a valid driver's license, proof of insurance, and a major credit card. Some companies have minimum age requirements.

Ask about extras. Many companies offer cellular phones, ski racks, area maps, and child safety seats (California law says that any child who is less than 40 pounds or under four years old must sit in a safety seat).

If there are more than four in your family, you might want to consider renting a minivan. They cost a little more, but the comfort is worth it.

Family-Friendly Lodging

HOTELS, MOTELS, AND RESORTS

In each regional chapter you'll find our favorite family-friendly hotels, motels, and resorts. Note that we said favorite *family-friendly* hotels, not favorite hotels—many wonderful retreats were excluded because they're aimed at romantics or businesspeople, and they'd make parents of an energetic four-year-old feel like lepers. We've reviewed only places that particularly catch our fancy or seem suitable for families, and we've strived to find places with character. If you don't see an accommodation in the region you wish to visit, call the 800 number of your favorite chain to find out what they offer.

Tips on Hotels, Motels, and Resorts with Kids

First, there has to be a pool. After that, you get some choices.

One room or two? Large or small? Upscale hotel or basic motel? Old or new? There are pros and cons with each of these overnight options, and we've found that on different days on the same vacation, we might make different choices.

Overall, one of the hardest things for some of us parents to adjust to is being awake when the kids are asleep but not wanting to leave them alone in the room. Although adjoining rooms are a good option in some hotels, they're not offered everywhere, and the choice between one or more rooms for a family always seems to come up.

So we try, on an extended family vacation during which we're moving from place to place, to book ourselves into several different kinds of facilities and have different solutions. In a hub city where we're not expecting to be in a picturesque setting, we look for a business-suite chain, especially on the weekends, when discounts are often offered (but check to see that all amenities, like breakfasts, continue). The price for a spacious suite may be the same as for a cramped room at the motel down the street, and it's great to be able to watch the late show while the little ones snooze.

Big landmark hotels or luxury hotels with character are worth the splurge for us if the location is workable, and they might come at the end of a road trip, when the only choices in small-town stops on the way have been inexpensive roadside motels. Our kids tell us they like the excitement of big hotels (it's almost like a theme park, they say) and even enjoy "the neat old stuff" in some establishments. And room service is God's gift to traveling parents. But we also always ask about the executive, concierge, or butler floor of this kind of establishment, because the lounge areas often offer breakfast, coffee, snacks, and wine at various hours. For one thing, it's convenient for grabbing a muffin for a kid in the room; for another, it's a place for parents to escape to, like a living room, without being far away.

The all-American motel is, of course, a favorite with families. No need to find a bellman—you park in front of your room and unload only what you need. Kids love roaming the corridors for ice, soda from the machines, and the spotting of other children. Lack of towel service poolside may be compensated for by the existence of a coin laundry. At this kind of hostelry, we might opt for one room, but we'd request a room near the pool with a patio or veranda. Proximity to the pool allows kids of a certain age to come and go; the patio extends the living space nicely.

CAMPING

We've included a small but choice collection of California campgrounds— ones that are easily accessible, fun for children, and not too demanding of parents (we consider bathrooms and running water, for instance, to be essential). Camping can be a wonderful family experience, slowing down the pace so you can all take pleasure in the small things, from fishing in a stream to chasing butterflies. And, of course, camping takes you to California's most beautiful places for very little money.

Nearly all of these campgrounds are state properties, and all are popular; for those that take reservations, make them early. Call Reserve America, (800) 444-7275.

Tips on Camping with Children

We've had wonderful family camping trips—and horrible ones. Basically, if you are regular campers and your children are used to it from birth, you'll be happy at any of the campgrounds we recommend. If you're not regular campers, we'd recommend the motel option while your children are between infancy and the age of at least three, maybe four. Our eight-year-old now rolls up her own sleeping bag, rinses her own cup, and hikes a couple of miles, but at age two she mostly ate rocks, cried, and slept about four hours a night (tent living can greatly upset the routines of a sensitive toddler).

Camping is a superb opportunity to teach children independence and self-reliance. If they're all expected to pitch in, and the adventure aspect is played up, they'll help prepare food, pitch tents, and do all the camp chores.

Our daughter's school organizes many camping trips, and we've adopted the school's camp rules in our families, because they maximize safety and comfort. They are as follows:

- No one is allowed to leave the campsite (even to go to the bathroom) without a whistle. Children wear the whistle around their necks; adults can carry it as they like. The whistle is blown only in an emergency, which can range from a twisted ankle to getting lost.

- Hats and sunscreen must be worn on all outings.
- Water must be carried on all outings.
- No playing, exploring, or hiking until the morning campsites are tidied and breakfast dishes are done.

Finally, recognize that camping is tiring, and after a few days of sleeping on the ground, tempers of both children and adults can get frayed. After two or three nights of roughing it, nothing cheers a family up like clean hotel sheets, a swimming pool, and a restaurant hamburger.

WHAT TO LOOK FOR IN A HOTEL

Some families want every moment planned; others just want advice on interesting hotels that other families recommend. Many of our recommendations are suites or apartments, since the best vacations give everyone a space of their own. Four in a hotel room may be economical, but adjoining rooms or an apartment or condominium may save your sanity and be worth the extra dollars.

Here are some important questions you might want to ask before booking a reservation:

- Do kids stay free?
- Is there a discount for adjoining rooms? How much?
- Can you rent cribs and rollaway beds?
- Does the room have a refrigerator? A microwave?
- Is the room on the ground floor? (Particularly important if you have small children.)
- How many beds in the room?
- Is there a swimming pool? Is there a lifeguard? Is it fenced?
- How close is the room to the pool?
- Are there laundry facilities on the premises?
- Is there a kid-friendly restaurant? A breakfast buffet? Other kid-friendly restaurants nearby?
- Is there a supervised children's program? What are the qualifications of the staff? How much does it cost? How do you make a reservation?
- Is there in-room baby-sitting? What are the qualifications of the caregivers? How much does it cost per hour? How do you make a reservation?

- Are the rooms childproofed? Can patio or balcony doors be securely locked and bolted?
- Is there an on-site doctor or medical facility nearby that the hotel recommends?

WHAT'S IN A ROOM?

Here are a few of the things we check:

Room Size. A large and uncluttered room is generally preferable for families, especially if you are taking advantage of the "kids stay free with parents" offered at many hotels. Ask if the hotel has suites, or if they will offer you a discount for an adjoining room for children.

Temperature Control and Ventilation. The guest should be able to control the temperature of the room. The best system, because it's so quiet, is central heating and air-conditioning, controlled by the room's own thermostat.

The vast majority of hotel rooms have windows or balcony doors that have been permanently secured shut. Though there are some legitimate safety and liability issues involved, we prefer windows and balcony doors that can be opened to admit fresh air.

Safety. Every room should have a fire or smoke alarm, clear fire instructions, and preferably a sprinkler system. Bathtubs should have a nonskid surface, and shower stalls should have doors that either open outward or slide side to side. Bathroom electrical outlets should be high on the wall and not too close to the sink. Balconies should have sturdy, high rails.

Noise. Most travelers have been kept awake by the television, partying, or amorous activities of people in the next room, or by traffic on the street outside. Better hotels are designed with noise control in mind. Wall and ceiling construction are substantial, effectively screening routine noise. Carpets and drapes, in addition to being decorative, also absorb and muffle sounds. Mattresses mounted on stable platforms or sturdy bed frames do not squeak, even when challenged. Televisions enclosed in cabinets, and with volume governors, rarely disturb guests in adjacent rooms.

Lighting. Poor lighting is an extremely common problem in American hotel rooms. The lighting is usually adequate for dressing, relaxing, or watching television, but not for reading or working. Lighting should be bright over tables and desks and alongside couches or easy chairs. If you're sharing a room with children, ask for a room with separate lights over the bed, so you can stay up reading after the kids have lights-out.

Furnishings. At bare minimum, the beds must be firm. Pillows should be made with hypoallergenic fillers, and, in addition to the sheets and spread, a blanket should be provided.

Childproof Your Room

When you arrive at the hotel, some childproofing may be in order. Be sure that both the front door and any patio or balcony doors and windows can be securely locked and bolted. Some hotels offer electrical outlet coverings if you have toddlers, and protective covers for sharp furniture corners. They also will remove glass objects or other knick-knacks that might be easy for a toddler to break. And if the mini-bar is stocked with junk food and alcoholic beverages, it should be locked.

With a family of four or more sharing a hotel room, you may not have enough dresser space to give everyone more than a drawer. You can request extra luggage racks if there is wall space to accommodate.

Many well-designed hotel rooms have a sleeper sofa, which is invaluable for families. Other family-friendly amenities to look for include a small refrigerator, a microwave, a digital alarm clock, and a coffeemaker.

Bathrooms. Two sinks are better than one, and you cannot have too much counter space. A sink outside the bath is a great convenience when families are bathing and dressing at the same time.

Overall Appearance. We recommend that you ask to be sent a photo of a hotel's standard guest room before you book, or at least get a copy of the hotel's promotional brochure. Be forewarned, however, that some hotel chains use the same guest room photo in their promotional literature for all hotels in the chain and that the guest room in a specific property may not resemble the photo in the brochure. When you or your travel agent calls, ask how old the property is and when the guest room you are being assigned was last renovated. If you arrive and are assigned a room inferior to that which you had been led to expect, demand to be moved to another room.

CHILDREN'S PROGRAMS

Many large hotels offer supervised programs for children, some complimentary, some with fees. We've included several hotels throughout California that offer exemplary activities.

If you decide to take advantage of the kids' programs, call ahead for specific children's events that are scheduled during your vacation. Ask about cost and the ages that can participate; the best programs divide children into age groups. Make reservations for activities your child might enjoy (you can always cancel after arrival).

After check-in, stop by and visit with the kid's program staff. Ask about counselor-child ratio and whether the counselors are trained in first aid and CPR. Briefly introduce your children to the staff and setting, which typically will leave them wanting more, thereby easing the separation anxiety when they return to stay.

Some hotels offer in-room baby-sitting, but if your hotel does not, there is a national, non-profit referral program called Child Care Aware that will help you locate a good, high-quality sitter. You can call (800) 424-2246, Monday–Friday, 9 a.m.– 4:30 p.m EST.

Be sure to ask if the sitter is licensed, bonded, and insured. To ease your children's anxiety, tell them how long you plan to be away, and be sure they feel good about the person who will be caring for them. Finally, trust your own instincts.

CHAIN HOTEL TOLL-FREE NUMBERS

This guidebook gives details on some of the hotels in California with outstanding children's programs. However, for your convenience we've listed toll-free numbers for the following hotel and motel chains' reservation lines:

Best Western	(800) 528-1234 United States and Canada
	(800) 528-2222 TDD
Comfort Inn	(800) 228-5150 United States
Courtyard by Marriott	(800) 321-2211 United States
Days Inn	(800) 325-2525 United States
Doubletree and Doubletree Guest Suites	(800) 424-2900 United States
Econo Lodge	(800) 424-4777 United States
Embassy Suites	(800) 362-2779 United States and Canada
Fairfield Inn by Marriott	(800) 228-2800 United States
Four Seasons	(800) 332-3442 United States
Hampton Inn	(800) 426-7866 United States and Canada
Hilton	(800) 445-8667 United States
	(800) 368-1133 TDD
Holiday Inn	(800) 465-4329 United States and Canada
Howard Johnson	(800) 654-2000 United States and Canada
	(800) 654-8442 TDD
Hyatt	(800) 233-1234 United States and Canada

Loew's	(800) 448-8355 United States and Canada
Marriott	(800) 228-9290 United States and Canada
	(800) 228-7014 TDD
Quality Inn	(800) 228-5151 United States and Canada
Radisson	(800) 333-3333 United States and Canada
Ramada Inn	(800) 228-3838 United States
	(800) 228-3232 TDD
Residence Inn by Marriott	(800) 331-3131 United States
Ritz-Carlton	(800) 241-3333 United States
Sheraton	(800) 325-3535 United States and Canada
Renaissance Hotels	(800) 468-3571 United States and Canada
Wyndham	(800) 822-4200 United States

Family-Friendly Restaurants

We love food and love to eat out, and our kids love to eat out, too, but rarely do we agree on what constitutes a good restaurant. We like comfort, good service, creative cooking, and a nice glass of wine. They like noise, cups with lids, and as much fried food as possible. Hence the challenge: to put together a roster of restaurants throughout the state that make both parents and children happy. We had more success in some areas than others; some parts of the state don't have much more than coffee shops and chains, so you'll have to make do. Other areas, however (especially the San Francisco Bay area, the Central Coast, and the L.A. area), are rich in kid- and parent-friendly dining.

You'll note that most major chain restaurants and all the chain fast-food restaurants are not found in the listings that follow. We encourage you to skip McDonald's whenever possible and make the effort to patronize local places—not only is it better for your health, but you're more likely to get a feel for an area when you sit with the locals and eat a burrito or dim sum or pancakes. As for the big chain restaurants, we find most of them to be soulless and dull. There are exceptions, especially in such smaller, regional chains as California Pizza Kitchen, Crocodile Cafe, and Rubio's, all of which are good family restaurants that have California flair.

The major tourist areas all seem to have Hard Rock Cafes and Planet Hollywoods, but we cover those rarely—after all, if you've been to one Hard Rock, you've been to them all. Your hotel in San Francisco, L.A., San Diego, or Orange County can steer you to one of them.

Tips on Dining Out with Children

Be Realistic about Age Limits. We ate at elegant restaurants when our children were sleeping infants in car seats. By the time toddlerhood hit, we restricted ourselves to quality fast food (like taquerias), child-friendly ethnic restaurants (Chinese, Cuban, Mexican, etc.), and takeout food enjoyed in park picnic areas. We began restaurant-training in earnest at about age four, the dawn of a years-long process of gentle reminding about napkins on laps, feet off chairs, and proper butter-knife etiquette. We expect to have achieved success around the junior year of college.

Don't Battle a Picky Eater. You'll never win this one. If everything looks yucky, get them some plain rice and plain bread. Enjoy your food with gusto, and if the kids get hungry enough, they'll break down and ask to try some.

Look Beyond the Children's Menu. The vast majority are monotonous and unhealthy, consisting mostly of burgers, deep-fried chicken, and french fries. Encourage experimentation in the grown-up menu, and ask if it's possible to order smaller portions of the "adult" food.

Remember the Tailgate. We had more fun eating on a tailgating vacation than perhaps any other. Grocery stores, delis, upscale gourmet shops, and mini-marts are all stocked with foods that seem almost too decadent to buy at home—but if you're tailgating, you have to go for the convenience foods. So we'd get takeout salads and chicken, made-to-order sandwiches, sushi, poached salmon, fresh baguettes, imported cheeses, and exotic fruits. The price was still less than a bad meal at a roadside coffee shop.

Watch the In-Betweeners. When they feel too old for (or don't like) the children's menu but can't really eat a big meal, some parental diplomacy is in order, or the in-betweener will be taking one bite from a huge order of whatever and then stopping, overwhelmed. Some kids will agree to splitting or sharing a meal, but let them choose most of it. Sometimes it's just a matter of ordering three meals for four people, so you avoid huge quantities of leftovers (which you can't take home when traveling) and yet allow for some tasting of different things.

Soup, Soup, Soup. Not only is it comforting and homey, but soup is often a tasty, nutritious, affordable basis for a kid's meal that needs only an appetizer to complete it.

Let Them Be Weird. One man we know is still grateful to his parents for letting him order hamburgers at breakfast, and conversely, how many people are cheered up by a nice breakfast at 7 p.m.? As much as possible, let your kids enjoy the get-what-you-want pleasure of restaurant eating as part of their vacation. Remember, they're also missing home, routine, and the certainty of their daily meal rituals.

Special Challenges to a Golden State Vacation

Most families with children visit California during the summer months, when school is out—and much of the state can get seriously hot, particularly in August and early September. So before starting off on a day of touring or a visit to the beach, parents should keep some things in mind.

Overheating, Sunburn, and Dehydration. Due to Southern California's desert and subtropical climates, parents with young children on a day's outing need to pay close attention to their kids. The most common problems of smaller children are overheating, sunburn, and dehydration. A small bottle of sunscreen carried in a pocket or fanny pack will help you take precautions against overexposure to the powerful sun. Be sure to put some on children in strollers, even if the stroller has a canopy. Some of the worst cases of sunburn we have seen were on the exposed foreheads and feet of toddlers and infants in strollers. To avoid overheating, rest at regular intervals in the shade or in an air-conditioned museum, hotel lobby, restaurant, or public building.

Don't count on keeping small children properly hydrated with soft drinks and water fountain stops. Long lines at popular attractions often make buying refreshments problematic, and water fountains are not always handy. What's more, excited children may not inform you or even realize that they're thirsty or overheated. We recommend renting a stroller for children six years old and under, and carrying plastic water bottles.

Blisters. Blisters and sore feet are common for visitors of all ages, so wear comfortable, well-broken-in shoes or sandals. If you or your children are usually susceptible to blisters, carry some precut "moleskin" bandages; they offer the best possible protection, stick great, and won't sweat off. When you feel a hot spot, stop, air out your foot, and place a moleskin over the area before a blister forms. Moleskin is available by name at all drugstores. Sometimes small children won't tell their parents about a developing blister until it's too late. We recommend inspecting the feet of preschoolers two or more times a day.

Sunglasses. If you want your smaller children to wear sunglasses, it's a good idea to affix a strap or string to the frames so the glasses won't get lost and can hang from the child's neck while she's indoors.

Beach Safety. To avoid a severe sunburn that can ruin a child's—and your—vacation, keep a lot of SPF 15 or 30 sunscreen on hand and reapply it a few times a day. Don't be lax on overcast days—UV rays are still plentiful, and the reflection caused by the sand and water makes them more potent. Splurge on a souvenir surf shirt, those stretchy, lightweight water shirts that can be found at any surf shop. All the cool California kids wear them, and they keep out the sun, as well as prevent rashes from body boards and surfboards. Finally, never let little kids swim alone, and encourage even teenagers to use the buddy system. The ocean can be fierce, even on seemingly calm days.

SAFETY

- Discuss safety with your family before you leave home.

- Discuss what to do if someone gets lost. If you are going to a crowded theme park or anywhere that there's a possibility you and your child could get separated, write your child's name on adhesive tape and tape it inside their shirt. Be sure that young children know their full name, address, and phone number (with area code).

- Carry photos of your kids for quick ID.

- Travelers' checks are the easiest way to protect your money.

- In emergencies, call 911 for assistance in reaching paramedics, law enforcement, or the fire department.

- Teach your children to find the proper authorities if they are lost. Tell them to approach a security guard, a store clerk, or "a grown-up who is working where you're lost."

- Before heading out for a stroll, if you are unsure about the safety of an area, ask the front desk manager or concierge in your hotel.

- Always lock your car when it is parked.

- Always try to keep your gas tank full.

- At night, try to park your car under a street light or in a hotel parking garage. Never leave wallets, checkbooks, purses, or luggage in the car. It's best to lock your luggage out of sight in the trunk.

- Keep your wallet, purse, and camera safe from pickpockets. A fanny pack, worn around the waist, is the most convenient way to stash small items safely.

- Leave your valuables at home, and if you must bring them along, check with your hotel to see if there is a safe.

- Be sure you lock sliding doors that lead to your hotel balcony or porch while you are in your room and always when you leave. Never open the hotel room door if you are unsure about who is at the door.

- Keep medicine out of reach of small children; it's easy to forget and leave it out in hotel rooms.

- Check with the front desk, hotel security, or guest services at attractions for lost property. Report lost or stolen travelers' checks and credit cards to the issuing companies and to the police.

- Crime can happen anywhere, so use common sense and take necessary precautions.

FREE CALIFORNIA PUBLICATIONS FOR VISITORS

For a destination and statewide visitors' information, contact the California Division of Tourism, 801 K Street, Suite 1600, Sacramento, CA 95814, (916) 322-2881; fax (916) 322-3402. For publications detailing the exceptional state park system, call or write the California State Park System, Department of Parks & Recreation, Box 942896, Sacramento, CA 94296; (916) 653-6995. To reserve a state campground, call (800) 444-7275; for a federal campground, call (800) 365-2267.

Fun California Facts

- California is the nation's most populous state.
- The state mineral is gold.
- The state tree, the redwood, is a prehistoric tree, and all trees are descended from the redwood.
- Within the state you'll find the largest, tallest, and oldest living trees in the world (giant sequoias, redwoods, and bristlecone pines, respectively).
- California has the largest population of Native Americans in the country.
- The lowest spot in the country is Death Valley, at 282 feet below sea level. The highest spot in the country outside Alaska is Mt. Whitney, at 14,494 feet. It's possible to visit them both in the same day, as they're just 85 miles apart.
- The state insect is the Dog Face Butterfly.
- The state flower is the Golden Poppy.
- The state mammal is the California Grizzly.
- California has the largest Armenian population outside of Armenia and the largest Mexican population outside of Mexico.
- Ribbon Falls in Yosemite is the highest waterfall on the North American continent.

Part One

San Diego County

What an interesting toehold San Diego County has on the continent—right at the edge, where travelers must choose between the ocean and a foreign country if they keep going. The inland part of the county is alternately desert and agricultural valleys, but the dominant characteristic of eastern San Diego County is parkland—notably **Anza-Borrego Desert State Park.** The coastal region is the population center, with the city of San Diego (second-largest in the state) dominating. The northern part of the county (before the huge military base Camp Pendleton takes over the map) is dotted with golf courses. To the south, of course, is Mexico.

Families will find San Diego County easy to like. It has all the California good stuff—palm trees, beaches, a multicultural population, unlimited outdoor recreation, sophisticated cultural offerings—with less of the bad stuff (high prices, congestion) that sometimes goes along.

We've taken our kids to San Diego County in all seasons and for lots of different kinds of vacations. We've taken the train from L.A. and stayed in downtown San Diego, riding the trolley to the zoo and shopping in **Horton Plaza.** We based ourselves in **Del Mar** to visit the **Wild Animal Park** and enjoyed a bonus of beach time and watching racehorse trailers come and go. We've lolled in a fancy **Coronado Island** resort's outdoor spa after biking all over the island and taking the ferry back and forth just for fun. And we've sat in the gentle tidal waters of **Mission Bay** while a happy toddler splashed next to us. You see where this is headed, of course. It'll take more than a single vacation to even begin to sample San Diego's charms.

If it's your first time to the San Diego area and you're arriving in summer, a four-day itinerary with a base at one of the Mission Bay resorts is ideal. **Sea World** is right in Mission Bay, so that's one day's outing. Pick among **the zoo, Wild Animal Park,** and **Old Town** for another two days of fun. Finish with a day dedicated to water sports and beach fun. Families traveling with convention-goers won't be disappointed with a more urban

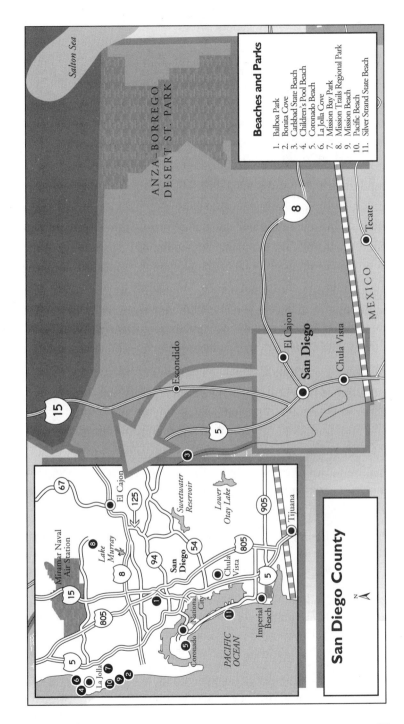

Salton Sea

ANZA–BORREGO
DESERT ST. PARK

Beaches and Parks

1. Balboa Park
2. Bonita Cove
3. Carlsbad State Beach
4. Children's Pool Beach
5. Coronado Beach
6. La Jolla Cove
7. Mission Bay Park
8. Mission Trails Regional Park
9. Mission Beach
10. Pacific Beach
11. Silver Strand State Beach

MEXICO

Tecate

Escondido

El Cajon

San Diego

Chula Vista

San Diego County

Miramar Naval
Air Station

Lake
Murray

Sweetwater
Reservoir

Lower
Otay Lake

El Cajon

San
Diego

National
City

Coronado

Chula
Vista

Imperial
Beach

Tijuana

PACIFIC
OCEAN

35

base and can try out the car-free itineraries described below. Visitors with another day should add a Borrego Springs overnight. The contrast between the coast and the dramatic desert is an eye-opener for all ages.

GETTING THERE

By Plane. Most major airlines serve San Diego International Airport; Lindbergh Field, (619) 231-2100, is located just a few miles northeast of the city.

By Train. Amtrak makes its final southbound stop in San Diego, delivering travelers from as far north as Seattle. From L.A., the train trip is about two hours on the popular, well-patronized San Diegan commuter line (frequent departures morning and afternoon). Excellent public transportation from the train station makes a trip without a car possible. Call (800) USA-RAIL.

By Car. Interstate 5, which runs from the Canadian to the Mexican borders, is the main freeway heading into San Diego. It's also reached from the north by Highway 15, which comes from the Riverside area and connects to Interstate 10, and by Interstate 8, which heads east to Arizona. A car is not necessary to enjoy central San Diego, but it's great to have if you want to explore the farther reaches.

Car-Free Sight-Seeing

Although San Diego and its suburbs are spread generously over many acres and motorists will find their way along good roads and modern freeways, the city has also created a network of public transportation that permits easy access to major attractions, many of which are in a comparatively concentrated geographic area. The weather's almost always sunny and mild, so the journey from place to place is a pleasant jaunt; and because the city does a brisk convention business, the various trams, trolleys, and ferries have enough patronage to justify frequent, convenient runs.

If you think you'd like to do San Diego without a car (arriving by train, for example), you'll need to stay downtown, in Coronado or near Old Town, in order to easily combine the attractions mentioned here into a network. You can also simply take a taxi or municipal bus to the first boarding point of the day.

Here's a sample no-car itinerary: Board the Old Town Trolley Tour bus at your hotel in Coronado and ride it (enjoying the guide's descriptions of passing sights) to Balboa Park. Enjoy a morning at the zoo, then take the free Balboa shuttle to the Space Museum, then reboard the Old Town Trolley and continue to Old Town. Save the historic buildings for another day, but enjoy a Mexican meal and some shopping, then take the San Diego Trolley to downtown, changing to another trolley to Seaport Village. At Seaport Village, let the kids play some games and get an ice cream cone, then get on the ferry to cross the water to Coronado and your hotel.

You might think the Old Town Trolley Tours bus (with narration and music) is corny, but it sure is convenient. It goes to most of the major attractions, and you can get on and off at eight stops, including Old Town, the Embarcadero, Seaport Village, Horton Plaza, Coronado, and Balboa Park. Call (619) 298-8687 for locations of stops and timetable. $24 adults, $12 ages 4–12, 3 and under free.

Metropolitan Transit Service's Transit Store, 102 Broadway, downtown San Diego, (619) 234-1060, is a center of information about buses, Coaster (Coastal Light Rail), and the San Diego Trolley. The Day Tripper Transit Pass, available as a one- ($5), two- ($8), three- ($10), or four-day ($12) pass, is sold here. There is no charge for children age 6 and under. One-day passes can also be purchased at trolley stations and the ferry landing.

The San Diego Trolley (phone (619) 233-3004; automated info line (619) 685-4900) operates daily from 5 a.m. to midnight, with service every 15 minutes most of the time. Tickets are dispensed from automated machines at each station. The Blue Line extends from Old Town through downtown to the Mexican border. The Bayside Line covers the Harbor Drive area and goes to Seaport Village, to the convention center, and through downtown and the Gaslamp Quarter. Another line heads for Padre Stadium via Mission Valley.

There is free daily tram shuttle service around Balboa Park.

The San Diego–Coronado Ferry, (619) 234-4111, runs between downtown San Diego's Broadway Pier (1050 N. Harbor Drive, at Broadway) and the Ferry Landing Marketplace on Coronado at 1st Street and B Avenue. The crossing is 15 minutes, and it leaves San Diego every hour on the hour from 9 a.m. to 9 p.m., returning from Coronado every hour on the half-hour. Fares are $2 per person and 50¢ per bike; reservations are not needed.

The San Diego Water Taxi (Fish Harbor Pier, Seaport Village, 891 W. Harbor Drive, (619) 235-8294) offers on-call service from 10 a.m. to 10 p.m. and transports people to various spots around the bay, including Shelter Island, Harbor Island, Coronado, and Chula Vista; fares vary by destination.

How to Get Information before You Go

Balboa Park Visitors Center; (619) 239-0512.

Border Station Parking and Tourist Information, San Ysidro, Mexican border; (619) 428-1422.

Carlsbad Convention and Visitors Bureau; (760) 434-6093.

Coronado Visitors Bureau; (619) 437-8788 or (800) 622-8300; http://www.coronado.ca.us.

San Diego Convention and Visitors Bureau; (619) 232-3101; http://www.sandiego.org.

CHILD CARE/BABY-SITTING

Kiddiecorp. 10455 Sorrento Valley Road, Suite 200, San Diego; (858) 455-1718. Onsite group child care and special events for kids.

Marion's Childcare. 4328 60th Street, San Diego; (619) 582-5029; (888) 891-5029; www.hotelchildcare.com. In-room child care from a licensed, bonded, insured service of 18 years.

The Best Beaches and Parks

Balboa Park. San Diego has taken the urban park to new heights, going beyond outdoor recreation to create a compact cultural hub that no other American city can rival (except, of course, Washington, D.C.). In the heart of the city, not far from downtown, it is home to 14 museums (many are reviewed later), the world-famous San Diego Zoo, and five theaters (including the Old Globe). Before you visit any of these places, hop on the free tram that cruises the park, both to get oriented and to give your kids a cheap thrill. You'll also find outdoor pleasures, including picnic areas, three playgrounds, and botanical gardens; and such amusements as a miniature train ride, a carousel, and butterfly rides for kids ages five and under. Visitors center: House of Hospitality building, 1549 El Prado, (619) 239-0512; open daily 9 a.m.–4 p.m.; free parking. The web site is www.sddt.com/features/balboapark.

Bonita Cove. Within Mission Bay Park, near Belmont Park and Mission Beach, you'll find this outdoor paradise for young children. The calm, shallow water is friendly even to toddlers, and there's a playground, a grassy picnic area, and sand to dig. (858) 694-3049.

Carlsbad State Beach. A broad sand beach with a wide concrete bike/skating path, this is a great summertime beach for families—there's typically enough surf to have fun in, but it's rarely rough. Just south of the beach is Agua Hedionda Lagoon, a calm, wave-free spot for swimming, fishing, and boating. Lifeguards, rest rooms, showers. (760) 438-3143.

Children's Pool Beach. Still known by the name given it by locals who brought kids to play in the quiet surf, this beach is now home to herds of sea lions. Families stop by to look down on the hundreds of huge, protected creatures from a viewpoint above. End of Jenner Street, La Jolla.

Coronado Beach. San Diego's widest beach, Coronado is so big that it absorbs even the largest crowds comfortably. Good for swimming, body boarding, people-watching, and basic beach fun, it is guarded by the looming Hotel del Coronado. There are volleyball courts, fire pits on the north end, changing rooms, lifeguards in summer, showers, and pay parking at hotel or free parking on streets. Beach information, (619) 435-4179.

La Jolla Cove. A drop-dead gorgeous jewel of a beach, in a cove protected by cliffs, La Jolla Cove seems smaller than ever in peak season, when crowds get intense. But don't let that keep you from enjoying the tide pools, the calm, clean water, the excellent snorkeling, and the grassy picnic areas. Next door is Boomer Beach, an expert body-surfing spot that's dangerous for most but great for pros, or for watching the locals put on a show. Changing rooms, lifeguard. Coast Boulevard to Scripps Park, La Jolla.

Mission Bay Park. Although there are major resorts and hotels lining Mission Bay, a calm-water tidal area that curls and curves for many acres, Mission Bay Park is a huge public playground, with grassy meadows and picnic areas sloping down to sandy beaches (many areas with no waves!), as well as several marinas servicing the 4,600-acre aquatic sports area. There are designated areas for each sport (swimming, sailing, windsurfing, kayaking, waterskiing, and fishing). And paved bike paths dot the grassy areas and run along the shore. Free parking lots adjacent, no overnight parking or camping. Fires allowed in designated fire containers on beaches. The playground at Tecolote Shores was especially designed for disabled children. For more information, call (619) 221-8900 or (858) 694-3049.

Mission Trails Regional Park. See Hiking in Family Outdoor Adventures, page 40.

Mission Beach. If you have older kids who want to be where the action is, head to this two-mile-long shoreline on the ocean side of Mission Bay. Teenagers are plentiful here, playing volleyball, skating on the boardwalk, body boarding in the sometimes-rough surf (riptides are common), and showing off the latest surf wear. On the boardwalk right in the center of the beach is Belmont Park amusement park (see page 49). Changing rooms, showers, lifeguards. Mission Boulevard, Mission Bay, (619) 221-8900.

Pacific Beach. Locals call it the Strand, and locals are plentiful on hot summer days, of which San Diego has many. (Consequently, parking is a challenge.) It has everything a big public beach should have, from a fishing pier, to a bike/skating path, to body board rentals, to lifeguards; surfers are limited to one area, so swimmers don't have to battle them for wave space. The many restaurants and shops of the neighborhood of Pacific Beach are a short walk away. Changing rooms, showers, rest rooms (but no public rest rooms between Pacific Beach Drive and Mission Beach). Mission Boulevard, San Diego, (619) 221-8900.

Silver Strand State Beach. Three things make this state park a good beach for families: The surf and riptides are fairly calm; parking is plentiful, unlike at the city beaches; and the shoreline sparkles with millions of tiny silver shells, which enchant many children. This two-mile-long beach connects the isthmus of Coronado (no, it's not really an island) to the mainland's Imperial

Beach, and it's quieter than the beach in front of the Del. The broad, shallow shoreline allows for lots of safe scampering in gentle waves (or in no waves on the bay side), as well as good clamming and surf fishing. If you visit in winter, know that the location invites wind and chill, so dress warmly. Parking is $6 per car, and a night at one of the nice first-come, first-served campsites is $16 (one-night stays only). Rest rooms, showers, lifeguards. Follow signs off Highway 75, (619) 435-5184.

Family Outdoor Adventures

Bicycling/Skating. On some bright summer days, it seems that every San Diegan is on skates, bikes, or skateboards, making good use of the endless paved paths that wend around Mission Bay and along the beaches. Mission and Pacific Beaches are particularly fun to cruise, but in season they can get intimidatingly crowded and speedy for the training-wheel set. For a quieter, beautiful, long ride, follow the path along the Coronado shoreline through Silver Strand State Park. The Mission Bay paths are also good for younger children. On Coronado Island, you can rent bikes and skates from Bikes and Beyond, Ferry Landing Marketplace, (619) 435-7180. In the Mission Bay area, get gear from Hamel's Action Sports Center, 704 Ventura Place, Mission Beach (in the castle near the roller coaster), (858) 488-5050.

Boating. Even novices can learn to sail in the calm waters of Mission Bay, and every weekend, they're out there doing it. Boats and lessons are offered at Mission Bay Sportcenter, 1010 Santa Clara Place, (858) 488-1004, and the San Diego Sailing Center, 1010 Santa Clara Point, Mission Beach, (858) 488-0651. At the San Diego Hilton, C.P. Watersports (phone (619) 226-8611) offers sailboats and lessons as well as kayaks, aqua cycles, and windsurfing gear.

Fishing. Oceangoing fishing charters are plentiful in San Diego, but with kids we prefer a cheaper, lower-key outing—we head for one of the several fetching piers, where licenses are unnecessary and fish are often caught. The piers at Pacific Beach and the Coronado Ferry Landing are good ones, and both have bait-and-tackle shops.

Hiking. Serious hiking opportunities abound in the region, but with kids in tow, our favorite destination is Mission Trails Regional Park (Father Junipero Serra Trail, San Diego, (619) 668-3275; visitors center open daily 9 a.m.–5 p.m.). This inland 5,800-acre urban park has 35 miles of trails for hiking, mountain biking, and horseback riding, and some of the trails are paved to accommodate strollers and wheelchairs. Pick up a map at the visitors center. If your kids are sturdy, tackle the trail to San Diego's highest peak, a 1,600-foot climb that pays off with a 360° view of the city.

Snorkeling. California's clearest waters are found in La Jolla Cove, a protected part of the San Diego–La Jolla Underwater Park. For swimming children old enough to manage a mask and snorkel (typically ages seven and up), a snorkeling adventure is mind-blowing, as interactive a nature experience as they'll ever experience. See La Jolla Cove listing in Best Beaches and Parks (page 39) for location details; if you don't have snorkel gear, you can rent it from Rent-a-Bike at the San Diego Hilton in Mission Bay, (619) 226-8611.

Surfing. Before you can make good use of San Diego's many fine surf breaks, you have to learn how to do it. The well-established San Diego Surfing Academy, (858) 565-6892, arranges private lessons for kids ages eight and up and adults; it also sponsors a good summertime surf camp as well as occasional surf safaris to Mexico. If you want to try it on your own, rent a soft foam longboard from the rental concessions at Pacific Beach and go for it.

Waterskiing/Windsurfing. On the ocean side of Mission Bay is some of the best windsurfing in California; on the bay side is superb waterskiing. For instruction and equipment for both sports, contact Mission Bay Sportcenter (1010 Santa Clara Place, (858) 488-1004), which can also get you started on a surfboard, Jet Ski, or kayak. Another good spot for waterskiing lessons and rentals is Seaforth Mission Bay Boat Rentals (1641 Quivira Road, (619) 223-1681); another windsurfing outfitter and instructor is Windsport Kayak and Windsurfing Center (844 W. Mission Bay Drive, (858) 488-4642).

Whale-Watching. The Pacific gray whale swims past San Diego from December through mid-March, and blowhole and breech sightings are common. In fact, so confident is one outfitter, H&M Landing (2803 Emerson Street, San Diego, (619) 222-1144), that it guarantees a whale sighting or your money back. Family trips are typically three hours long. If you'd rather scout whales from dry land, head to the Cabrillo National Monument on Point Loma (see Attractions, page 50).

Calendar of Festivals and Events

January

Whalefest, Birch Aquarium at Scripps, La Jolla. January–February. Special exhibits and hands-on activities teach kids about whales; (858) 534-FISH.

February

Wildflower blooms, Anza-Borrego. The blooms hit sometime between February and April, and they only last for a few weeks; (760) 767-4684.

Heritage Day Parade, San Diego. Late February. Celebrates the city's rich ethnic diversity; (619) 286-8887.

March

Ocean Beach Kite Festival, Ocean Beach. Sponsored by the Kiwanis for more than 50 years. Kite decorating and flying, as well as parade, food, and fun. Bring your own kite; (619) 531-1527.

April

Opening Day, San Diego Padres, Qualcomm Stadium; (619) 283-4494.

Gaslamp Quarter Easter Bonnet Parade, 5th and L Streets, San Diego. A charity event held the weekend before Easter. Hat-making workshop, Easter egg hunt, parade, and treats; (619) 233-5227; www.softtops.com.

San Diego Earthfair, Balboa Park. Earth Day festival with lots of activities for children; (858) 496-6666; www.earthdayweb.org.

May

Fiesta Cinco de Mayo, Old Town State Park, San Diego. A two-day party with music, entertainment, food, booths, and kids' activities; (619) 296-3161.

Pacific Beach Block Party, Garnet Avenue, Pacific Beach. A beachy street fair with a nice home-grown feel, featuring a farmers' market, children's activity area, and live music; (619) 641-5823.

June

American Indian Cultural Days, San Diego Museum of Man, Balboa Park. Native Americans from across the country gather to share tribal ceremonies, stories, music, foods, and crafts, with hands-on projects for children; (619) 239-2001.

Del Mar Fair, Del Mar. The county fair for San Diego, with carnival rides, flower shows, arcades, and nationally known musical performers; (619) 793-5555.

July

Various Fourth of July events. La Jolla: a free concert at Scripps Park followed by a fireworks show; (619) 454-1444. Coronado: a parade, free concert in Spreckels Park, U.S. Navy air/sea show, and fireworks; (619) 437-8788.

Annual Festival of the Bells, Mission Basilica. Weekend-long festival celebrating the anniversary of the founding of Mission San Diego de Alcala. Includes food, music and dance performances, llama rides, and games; (619) 283-7319.

U.S. Open Sandcastle Competition, Imperial Beach Pier. Sandcastles like you've never seen 'em, along with a parade and evening fireworks. Children have their own competition; (619) 424-6663.

August

World Body Surfing Championships, Oceanside Pier and Beach. Body surfers from around the world put on a show; (760) 966-4535.

Chula Vista Annual Downtown Lemon Festival. Food and crafts; (619) 422-1982.

September

Fall Apple Harvest, Julian. Fall foliage, apple cider and pie, apple picking, and more; (760) 765-1857.

October

Fleet Week. A week-long tribute to the military with many events, including ship and submarine tours, a ship parade, and an air show; (619) 236-1212; www.fleetweek.com.

Oktoberfest, Holiday Park, Carlsbad. Since Carlsbad was originally a German settlement named Karlsbad, this is the Oktoberfest event to attend; (760) 434-6093.

November

Mother Goose Parade, Main Street, El Cajon. Hundreds of thousands of spectactors jam into El Cajon for this decades-old parade honoring fairy tales, children, and Mother Goose rhymes; (619) 444-8712.

Del Mar Fairgrounds Holiday of Lights. Drive your car around the racetrack and view 250 holiday displays; (858) 793-5555.

December

La Jolla Christmas Parade and Holiday Festival, downtown La Jolla. Floats, marching bands, and Santa, followed by a carnival and street fair; (619) 454-1444.

Las Posadas and Luminarias, Old Town. Candlelit procession commemorating Mary and Joseph's journey, ending in a piñata-breaking fiesta; (619) 220-5422.

Mission Bay Christmas Boat Parade of Lights. Festively lit boats sail by, ending in the lighting of Sea World's Tower Tree of Lights; (619) 488-0501.

San Diego

San Diego is the one destination in California that combines an oceany resort feel with big-city culture and activities. You can lie on the beach at **Coronado** and 20 minutes later be downtown at a major rock concert. You can spend the morning in a museum as you might in other cities, but after lunch you'll be Rollerblading along **Mission Bay.** While you watch your little one ride the carousel at **Shoreline Village,** you'll admire the bay on one side and the skyscrapers of the financial district on the other.

More cosmopolitan than Santa Barbara, much easier to scope out than L.A., San Diego is an ideal introduction to Southern California. The big-deal attractions (**San Diego Zoo, Wild Animal Park, Sea World**) are indeed world-class; the historic areas (**Old Town, the Maritime Museum ships**) are colorful and inviting; there are wonderfully located concentrations of hotels and motels (Mission Bay, Coronado); north of town are some beautiful, laid-back beach towns for day trips or overnight escapes (**La Jolla, Carlsbad**); and the residents are relaxed and casual.

Family Lodging

Beach Bum Rentals

A long-established rental agency with a good supply of beach houses, apartments, and condos; if you'll be in San Diego for a week or two, this is the way to go. Almost all rentals are ideal for families, with full kitchens, living rooms, and home-like comfort; some condos have amenities like pools and spas. Locations include Mission Bay and Pacific Beach.

747½ San Fernando Place, Mission Beach; (858) 488-3100; fax (619) 488-3335. Weekly rentals in summer $350–3,000 per week for a small studio apartment.

Blue Sea Lodge

Families get a superb beach location for a reasonable tab at this 100-room Best Western, one of the chain's more upscale properties. The architecture is dreary but the setting can't be beat, facing the boardwalk and soft sand of Pacific Beach, with Mission Bay just around the corner and plenty of good restaurants close by. Many of the well-maintained rooms have kitchens, and the ocean-view suites can handle a family comfortably (other rooms are on the snug side). And though the pool is small, the ocean is vast. You can also rent bikes (bring your own helmets) and ride the boardwalk. Summertime visits typically require reserving two months in advance.

707 Pacific Beach Drive, San Diego; (858) 488-4700 or (800) BLUE-SEA; fax (858) 488-7276. Rates $109–161 off-season, $149–206 in summer; includes continental breakfast.

Catamaran Resort Hotel

This large Mission Bay resort has live parrots in the tropical-decor lobby, spacious rooms (many with sliding glass doors to patios and bayside), outside pizza delivery service, and a location convenient to Sea World. It's not as glitzy as some other San Diego area resorts, but it is a beach and watersports paradise—wear your bathing suits and board shorts and head for the hotel pier for rentals and lessons in kayaking, windsurfing, diving, and more, or go to the beach for swimming and volleyball. Brunch at the bayside restaurant is popular with locals, and breakfast and dinner at the restaurant make for fine people-viewing. Among the offerings for adventurous teens is sea cave kayaking.

3999 Mission Boulevard, Mission Bay; (858) 488-1081 or (888) 862-2442; fax (858) 488-1387. Rates $160–600; packages with Sea World or various sporting adventures offered.

Embassy Suites San Diego Bay

If you want to be downtown (not a first choice for beach-loving families, but it has its appeal), this is the place to stay. It has all the family comforts that the chain is known for (two-room suite, two TVs, sleeper sofa, refrigerator, microwave, free breakfast); it's close to the trolley line, Embarcadero, and Seaport Village; and it's not far from Balboa Park. There is a pool, but, curiously, it is indoors.

601 Pacific Coast Highway, San Diego; (619) 239-2400 or (800) EMBASSY; fax (619) 239-1520. Rates $103–300.

Hotel del Coronado

Incredibly popular with many travelers, this huge (692-room, six-restaurant) resort complex on Coronado Island offers lodgings from vintage/historic

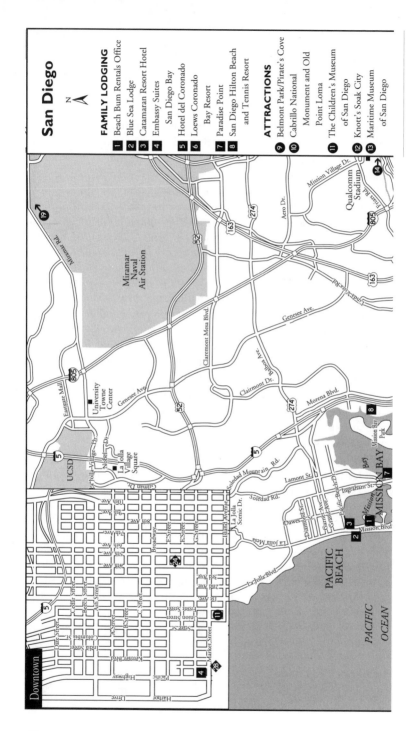

San Diego

N

FAMILY LODGING

1 Beach Bum Rentals Office
2 Blue Sea Lodge
3 Catamaran Resort Hotel
4 Embassy Suites San Diego Bay
5 Hotel del Coronado
6 Loews Coronado Bay Resort
7 Paradise Point
8 San Diego Hilton Beach and Tennis Resort

ATTRACTIONS

9 Belmont Park/Pirate's Cove
10 Cabrillo National Monument and Old Point Loma
11 The Children's Museum of San Diego
12 Knott's Soak City
13 Maritime Museum of San Diego

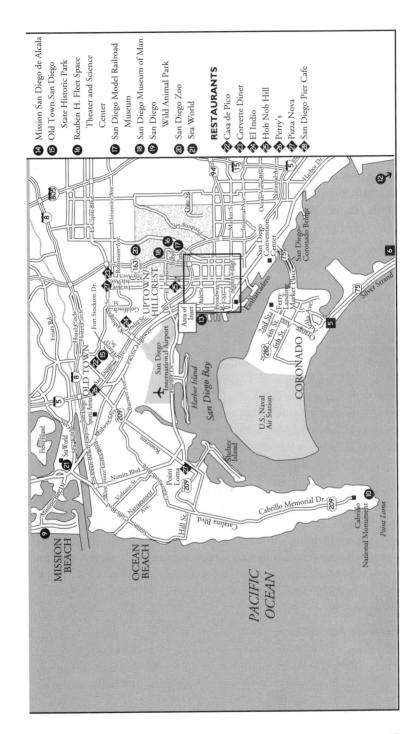

14 Mission San Diego de Alcala
15 Old Town San Diego State Historic Park
16 Reuben H. Fleet Space Theater and Science Center
17 San Diego Model Railroad Museum
18 San Diego Museum of Man
19 San Diego Wild Animal Park
20 San Diego Zoo
21 Sea World

RESTAURANTS

22 Casa de Pico
23 Corvette Diner
24 El Indio
25 Hob Nob Hill
26 Perry's
27 Pizza Nova
28 San Diego Pier Cafe

rooms to modern waterfront suites. Some kids find the main Victorian building kind of creepy, its dark hallways often crowded with busloads of day-trippers. And no kids under age six are allowed in the Prince of Wales restaurant. But there's plenty of sunshine out by the pool and the beach, where supervised kid's programs and activities (some free, most costing $5–45, depending on activity) are held in spring and summer and during the Christmas holidays. Activities for kids ages 5–12 include surfing, tennis, in-line skating, scavenger hunts, beach Olympics, sand-castle building, swimming, paddleboating, kite building and flying, s'mores on the beach, and music. The full line of sports and water equipment is available to rent, and there are two pools, tennis courts, and children's menus.

1500 Orange Avenue, Coronado; (619) 435-6611 or (800) 468-3533; fax (619) 522-8238. Rates $190–525, rooms $250, suites $600 in Victorian building.

Loews Coronado Bay Resort

This upscale, modern 403-room resort looks at first like a businessperson's hotel, but it is actually quite family-friendly. Located on its own little peninsula on Coronado Island, it's far from the taco bars and shops of Coronado Village, but there's enough to keep most families happy right at the resort. There's a nice pool area (three pools, one of which is adults-only) with a great snack bar; on Friday nights, a 9-by-12-foot screen shows family movies while kids float on inner tubes (and parents sip margaritas). You'll also find a playground, a game room, and sailboat and bike rentals. The Loews Loves Kids program for ages 4–12 ($40 a full day and $25 a half-day, with sibling discounts) offers arts and crafts, nature hikes, kite flying, pool games, sand-castle building, beach play, G-rated videos, playground and game-room play, swimming, snorkeling, and tennis. The resort offers babyproofing kits, and the casual restaurant and room service have kids' menus. Don't take the kids to the fine dining room—it is indeed fine and should be relished as a fairly formal experience. If needed, the Loews Loves Kids program offers in-room sitting at a rate of $36 for two children for three hours.

4000 Coronado Bay Road, Coronado; (619) 424-4000 or (800) 815-6397; fax (619) 424-4400. Rates $235–285.

Paradise Point Resort

This is no place for fans of intimate little hotels—462 rooms, six pools, tennis courts, a volleyball court, an 18-hole putting course, and much, much more are spread over a 44-acre island in Mission Bay. But it's a great place for an active family resort vacation. Despite the size of the place, it manages to seem serene, thanks to the low-lying cottage-style accommodations and the artful landscaping. Summertime brings the daily Kids

Camp, where kids ages 3–12 do everything from learn to Hula Hoop to make ice cream; the cost is $15 for a half-day and $25 for a full day, including lunch (the littlest ones have a morning program only). Teens get nighttime activities and lots to do on their own, from sunbathing at the beach to cruising the video arcade. Many rooms have kitchens; all have patios or terraces. Bike and paddleboat rentals, children's menus, sauna, fitness center, packages with local attractions.

1404 W. Vacation Road, San Diego; (858) 274-4630 or (800) 344-2626; fax (619) 581-5929. Rates $155–355 in summer, $135–335 off-season.

San Diego Hilton Beach and Tennis Resort

Part high-rise, part bungalow complex, this 357-room resort hotel on Mission Bay caters to families, with all sorts of kid-friendly amenities. Every day in summer, and on weekends during the rest of the year, Kids Klub offers children ages five and older treasure hunts, swimming, arcade games, and crafts; the program is free by day and $25 for the nighttime dinner activities. (It's less like day care and more like organized fun, so many kids just join in for an hour or two to take part in the activities that most attract them.) The over-11 set gets its own Teen Time program, which includes mixers. Kids can't possibly get bored here, what with the huge swimming pool, the little-kid wading pool, the biking and skating on the pathways (rentals available), the beach, the tennis, the water-sport rentals, the scuba-diving lessons, and the proximity to Mission Bay Park's playgrounds. Many of the large rooms have terraces or patios, and wet bars and refrigerators are common. Children's menus are available.

1775 E. Mission Bay Drive, San Diego; (619) 276-4010 or (800) 221-2424; fax (619) 581-5977. Rates start at $249 off-season, $279 in season; children stay free in parents' room.

Attractions

Belmont Park/Pirate's Cove

W. Mission Bay Drive and W. Mission Boulevard, Mission Bay; (619) 491-2988

Hours: In summer, Sunday–Thursday 11 a.m.–10 p.m., Friday–Saturday to 11 p.m.; off-season, Sunday–Thursday 11 a.m.–7 p.m., Friday–Saturday 11 a.m.–9 p.m.

Admission: Free to park; ride prices vary

Appeal by Age Groups:

Pre-school	Grade School	Teens	Young Adults	Over 30	Seniors
★★	★★★★	★★★★	★★★	★★	★★

Touring Time: Average 3 hours w/ swimming; minimum 1 hour

Rainy-Day Touring: Yes, for indoor facilities

Services and Facilities:

Restaurants Concessions	Lockers No
Alcoholic beverages No	Pet kennels No
Disabled access Limited on rides	Rain check No
Wheelchair rental No	Private tours No
Baby stroller rental No	

Description and Comments   Part old-fashioned seaside amusement park, part modern playground, this fun zone is particularly appealing to school-age kids and teens; many of the games and rides are too difficult or scary for young children, though there is a small kiddie area. The showpieces are the 1925 wooden roller coaster and the wooden replica of a Looff carousel; our kids particularly liked steering the little remote-control boats around the miniature harbor. The Plunge, a gigantic indoor saltwater pool, is worth a dip, if only to experience Wyland's impressive underwater whale mural. Arcades, video games, a movie theater, and shops ring the rides.

Next door is Pirate's Cove, home to more (indoor) kiddie rides, air hockey, video games, and a pirate-themed, Discovery Zone–style tunnel/ball pit/climbing structure that's perfect for a rainy day.

Cabrillo National Monument and Old Point Loma

Point Loma, south on Catalina Boulevard, San Diego; (619) 557-5450

Hours: Later in summer, daily 9 a.m.–5:15 p.m.

Admission: $5 per car, or $2 per person walk-in

Appeal by Age Groups:

Pre-school	Grade School	Teens	Young Adults	Over 30	Seniors
★★★	★★★★	★★★	★★★★	★★★★	★★★★

Touring Time: Average 2 hours; minimum 1 hour

Rainy-Day Touring: Not good

Services and Facilities:

Restaurants Vending machines	Lockers No
Alcoholic beverages No	Pet kennels No
Disabled access Yes	Rain check No
Wheelchair rental Yes, free	Private tours No
Baby stroller rental No	

Description and Comments   This falls under the scenery category, which typically bores kids, but ours enjoyed this outing as much as we did. Reached after driving past the airport through Shelter Island, a huge Navy base (some of which is operational and some abandoned), and Point

Loma, this point of land several hundred feet above the ocean seems like the end of the world. As you stand on the point's bluff, the Pacific stretches eternally to your right, while the whole of San Diego Bay spreads out straight ahead and to the left. The kids loved looking through the coin telescope for close-ups of the many incoming and outgoing military ships and planes, commercial planes, and pleasure boats (in winter and spring, this is also a great vantage to spot gray whales). Then we walked higher up the point to the tiny old 1856 lighthouse; what enthralled our eight-year-old was not the light itself, but the preserved (behind glass) living quarters of the lighthouse captain, his wife, and two sons. A steep trail down to tide pools is a worthy outing with older kids, and the visitors center has displays on the history of Juan Cabrillo's discovery of San Diego.

The Children's Museum of San Diego

200 W. Island Avenue, San Diego; (619) 233-5437 or (619) 233-8792

Hours: Tuesday–Sunday 10 a.m.–4 p.m., closed major holidays

Admission: $6; under age 3, free; workshops $3 extra

Appeal by Age Groups:

Pre-school	Grade School	Teens	Young Adults	Over 30	Seniors
★★★★	★★★★	★★	★	★	★

Touring Time: Average 2 hours; minimum 1 hour

Rainy-Day Touring: Yes

Services and Facilities:

Restaurants No	Lockers No
Alcoholic beverages No	Pet kennels No
Disabled access Yes	Rain check No
Wheelchair rental No	Private tours No
Baby stroller rental No	

Description and Comments Exhibitions change constantly at this inventive, hands-on museum, in which Mexican culture is given as much prominence as American culture. Art projects are always going on in the studio, where kids get to continually repaint a 1952 pickup truck, and dress-up play predominates in the Improv Theater. Temporary exhibits let kids experience everything from building a house to making candy. Note that the trolley stops here.

Knott's Soak City

20525 Entertainment Circle, Chula Vista; (619) 661-7373

Hours: Daily 10 a.m.–6 p.m., May, June, and September; daily 10 a.m.–8 p.m., July and August

Admission: $19.95 adults, $13.95 children ages 3–11, $11.95 after 4 p.m.; parking $4

Appeal by Age Groups:

Pre-school	Grade School	Teens	Young Adults	Over 30	Seniors
★★	★★★★	★★★	★★	★★	★

Touring Time: 4–6 hours; minimum 1 hour

Rainy-Day Touring: Yes

Services and Facilities:

Restaurants Snack bar	Lockers Yes
Alcoholic beverages No	Pet kennels No
Disabled access Yes	Rain check No
Wheelchair rental No	Private tours No
Baby stroller rental No	

Description and Comments   As we went to press, the former White Water Canyon waterpark was being transformed into a '50s-themed waterpark celebrating the surf-soaked California myth. The Coronado Express is the newest attraction, a family raft ride that rushes down almost 700 feet of twists and turns into a super splashdown pool. Among the 22 other rides are tube slides, body slides, speed slides, and a lazy river for folks who just want to kick back and float.

Maritime Museum of San Diego

1306 N. Harbor Drive, San Diego; (619) 234-9153

Hours: Daily 9 a.m.–8 p.m.

Admission: $6 adults, $4 ages 13–17, $2 ages 6–12, free ages 5 and under

Appeal by Age Groups:

Pre-school	Grade School	Teens	Young Adults	Over 30	Seniors
★★★	★★★★★	★★★★★	★★★★	★★★★★	★★★★★

Touring Time: Average 3 hours; minimum 1 hour

Rainy-Day Touring: Not a great idea

Services and Facilities:

Restaurants No	Lockers No
Alcoholic beverages No	Pet kennels No
Disabled access Limited	Rain check No
Wheelchair rental No	Private tours No
Baby stroller rental No	

Description and Comments   The picture in our minds of the cozy passenger cabin of the square-rigged *Star of India,* an 1863 merchant sailing ship, is as fresh as the day we stepped into the officers' and passengers' area. As we talked to the children about what it might have been like to sail across an ocean on a ship like this, the wooden floor beneath us gently rose and fell with the waves. *Star of India* is one of three moored vessels that together constitute the Maritime Museum; the others are an 1898 ferryboat and a 1904 steam-powered luxury yacht. Visitors walk or scramble up and down the ships, in and out of decks and holds, seeing ropes and engines and sailors' bunks. In summer, nautical film classics like *Captain Blood* are projected onto the ship's sail for an evening of unusual entertainment.

Mission San Diego de Alcala

10818 San Diego Mission Road, San Diego; (619) 281-8449

Hours: Daily 9 a.m.–5 p.m., except Thanksgiving and Christmas; mass: Saturday 5:30 p.m., Sunday 7, 8, 9, and 10 a.m., 11 a.m. (Spanish), noon, and 5:30 p.m.

Admission: $3 adults, $2 seniors, $1 children under 12

Appeal by Age Groups:

Pre-school	Grade School	Teens	Young Adults	Over 30	Seniors
★	★★	★★	★★	★★★	★★★

Touring Time: Average 1 hour; minimum 30 minutes

Rainy-Day Touring: Yes

Services and Facilities:

Restaurants No	Lockers No
Alcoholic beverages No	Pet kennels No
Disabled access Yes	Rain check No
Wheelchair rental No	Private tours Self-guided tape
Baby stroller rental No	tour

Description and Comments   This was the first of the California missions, and it still serves as an active parish church. It's a short stop for most families, because the museum area is small, but the grounds are lovely, and the church sanctuary is a fine example of the folkloric quality of mission architecture.

Old Town San Diego State Historic Park

Bounded by Wallace, Congress, Twigs, and Juan Streets; (619) 220-5422

Hours: Daily, beginning at 11 a.m. for historic houses; most shops open until 9 p.m.

Admission: Free; donations appreciated

Appeal by Age Groups:

Pre-school	Grade School	Teens	Young Adults	Over 30	Seniors
★★★	★★★★★	★★★★	★★★★★	★★★★★	★★★★★

Touring Time: Average a half-day; minimum 3 hours, with a meal and minimal shop browsing

Rainy-Day Touring: Not great; outdoor paths, unpaved areas

Services and Facilities:

Restaurants Surrounding	Lockers No
Alcoholic beverages In some restaurants	Pet kennels No; pets allowed on leash
Disabled access Yes	Rain check No
Wheelchair rental No	Private tours Yes
Baby stroller rental No	

Description and Comments   Shops and restaurants occupy many of the landmark buildings that surround the official historic state park part of Old Town, so the kids may never know they're being educated when you come here. The park showcases aspects of San Diego's past during the period from 1821 to 1872, when the area was first under the Mexican and then later the American government. The original town plaza is the focal point of the pedestrian-only zone; it is surrounded by restored homes with furnishings of the period, a smithy and stable, a courthouse, a schoolhouse, a dental museum, a drugstore museum, and a newspaper museum. Free tours are given daily at 11 a.m. and 2 p.m. by costumed docents at the visitors center in the Robinson-Rose House (4002 Wallace Street). The Bazaar del Mundo, shops and cafes surrounding a courtyard, often has mariachis and costumed dancers performing.

Reuben H. Fleet Space Theater and Science Center

1875 El Prado, near San Diego Zoo; (619) 238-1233

Hours: Sunday–Thursday 9:30 a.m.–5 p.m., Friday–Saturday 9:30 a.m.–9 p.m., later in summer

Admission: $6.50 adults, $5.50 seniors 65 and over, $5 children ages 3–12, free to children under 3, first Tuesday of month is free; Omnimax Theatre admission (includes Science Center): $9 adults, $7.50 seniors 65 and over, $6.50 children ages 3–12, free to children under 3

Appeal by Age Groups:

Pre-school	Grade School	Teens	Young Adults	Over 30	Seniors
★★★	★★★★	★★★★	★★★★	★★★★	★★★★

Touring Time: Average 2 hours; minimum 1 hour

Rainy-Day Touring: Yes

Services and Facilities:

Restaurants Yes	Disabled access Yes
Alcoholic beverages No	Wheelchair rental No

Baby stroller rental No   Rain check No
Lockers No   Private tours No
Pet kennels No

Description and Comments   Of the many, many fine museums in Balboa Park, this is the hardest to find—despite its tremendous appeal to families, it is not mentioned on any of the directional signs posted in the park. (Hint: It's across the fountain plaza from the Natural History Museum, en route to the zoo.) Newly expanded and refurbished, this is an excellent hands-on science museum, where kids can touch, feel, experiment, and explore. The special exhibits are always first-rate, and they sometimes stay for a long time; recent examples included interactive exhibits on mobile communication, high definition television, and eyesight restoration. Big-screen Omnimax (like IMAX) films, usually about nature and/or outer space, are shown daily in the adjacent theater, and they are invariably worth seeing—but note that the noise and special effects may scare small children. This place can get mobbed, so try to visit on a school day after lunch, when the field trips have all returned to school.

San Diego Model Railroad Museum

1649 El Prado, San Diego; (619) 696-0199

Hours: Tuesday–Friday 11 a.m.–4 p.m., Saturday–Sunday 11 a.m.–5 p.m.

Admission: $4 adults, $3 seniors, $2.50 students, free for children under age 15

Appeal by Age Groups:

Pre-school	Grade School	Teens	Young Adults	Over 30	Seniors
★★★★	★★★★	★★★	★★★★	★★★★	★★★★

Touring Time: Average 2 hours; minimum 1 hour

Rainy-Day Touring: Yes

Services and Facilities:

Restaurants Sandwich shop   Lockers No
Alcoholic beverages No   Pet kennels No
Disabled access Yes   Rain check No
Wheelchair rental No   Private tours No
Baby stroller rental No

Description and Comments   We've seen many a grown man get far more excited about model trains than any kid does, and this museum caters to both groups. The country's largest collection of model trains winds through elaborate miniature countrysides and towns, some of which represent historical periods in Southern California. This fascinates some kids but makes others insane, because they're not allowed to touch—so take them to the Toy Train Gallery, where they can work the controls of Lionel O Gauge toy trains and push Brio wooden trains on their tracks.

San Diego Museum of Man

1350 El Prado, Balboa Park; (619) 239-2001

Hours: Daily 10 a.m.–4:30 p.m.; closed Christmas, Thanksgiving Day

Admission: $6 adults, $3 children 6–17, $5 seniors 65+, free for children under 6

Appeal by Age Groups:

Pre-school	Grade School	Teens	Young Adults	Over 30	Seniors
★★	★★★★	★★★★	★★★	★★★	★★★

Touring Time: Average 3 hours; minimum 1 hour

Rainy-Day Touring: Yes

Services and Facilities:

Restaurants No	Lockers No
Alcoholic beverages No	Pet kennels No
Disabled access Yes	Rain check No
Wheelchair rental No	Private tours No
Baby stroller rental No	

Description and Comments If your kids aren't fascinated with the history of man and woman, they will be after a visit to this cool museum, home to mummies, skeletons, and life-size, very realistic (often naked) re-creations of our predecessors going back to early Africa. Weekends bring live demonstrations of crafts and cooking from cultures around the world, and the Children's Discovery Center offers changing hands-on displays keyed to the museum's collection, allowing kids to, for instance, dress up like ancient Egyptians.

San Diego Wild Animal Park

15500 San Pasqual Valley Road, Escondido; (760) 747-8702; TDD (760) 738-5067; www.sandiegozoo.org

Hours: In summer, daily 9 a.m.–6 p.m.; in winter, daily 9 a.m.–4 p.m. (grounds open until 5 p.m.)

Admission: $21.95 adults, $14.95 ages 3–11, free for ages 2 and under, $19.75 seniors; combination tickets for the Zoo and Wild Animal Park are $38.35 adults, $23.15 ages 3–11, parking $5.

Appeal by Age Groups:

Pre-school	Grade School	Teens	Young Adults	Over 30	Seniors
★★★★ (play area)	★★★★★	★★★★★	★★★★★	★★★★★	★★★★★

Touring Time: Average two-thirds of a day; minimum a half-day

Rainy-Day Touring: Some shows and exhibits close

Services and Facilities:

Restaurants Yes

Alcoholic beverages Yes

Disabled access Yes

Wheelchair rental Yes

Baby stroller rental Yes

Lockers Yes

Pet kennels No; yes for service animals

Rain check No

Private tours Photo Caravan, ages 8+, $85–105

Description and Comments Although it's actually in Escondido, about 45 minutes northeast of downtown, we're putting this in the San Diego section because San Diego heads up the name and it'd be confusing otherwise. This is a unique animal-viewing experience, designed to replicate the kind of viewing you'd do if you were visiting animal parks in Africa. The animals roam freely in herds over many acres of land similar to an African savannah, and the visitors observe from a monorail that travels through the park's 21,000 acres. The 55-minute ride (usually too long for ages two and under) departs from a theme park–like Nairobi Village and Mombasa Lagoon area, where more traditional exhibits as well as animal shows are presented in an African-village setting, and visitors can relax at cafes—and, of course, shop. A new walk-through exhibit, Condor Ridge, showcases endangered North American bird species. There's also a pleasant play area for younger kids, with slides and climbing equipment, also themed. For a more in-depth adventure, consider the special slumber-party offering called Roar and Snore, (760) 738-5049, an overnight family camping program for parents and children ages eight and over; the cost is $55–87.50, depending on age.

We like to sit on the right side of the monorail car, and we always bring binoculars, so when someone shouts "Look over there!" we can actually see the animal they're pointing to. We'd also advise that you watch little children carefully on some of the viewing platforms; one is a three-story-high circular platform with wood railings that attracts climbing kids like magnets.

If you're planning to visit both the San Diego Zoo and the Wild Animal Park more than once a year, consider a membership for yourself and your children—it's probably cheaper, and you get other benefits as well. For details, call or go to the web site.

San Diego Zoo

2920 Zoo Drive, Balboa Park, San Diego; (619) 234-3153 or (619) 231-1515; www.sandiegozoo.org

Hours: Daily 9 a.m.–4 p.m. (grounds open until 6 p.m.); in summer to 9 p.m., but animals generally go to sleep at dusk. Panda viewing schedule changes; call (888) MY-PANDA for current day's schedule

Admission: $18 adults, $8 ages 3–11, free ages 2 and under; deluxe admission $26 adults, $14 ages 3–11; includes bus tour and sky tram

Appeal by Age Groups:

Pre-school	Grade School	Teens	Young Adults	Over 30	Seniors
★★★★★	★★★★★	★★★★★	★★★★★	★★★★★	★★★★★

Touring Time: Average 6 hours; minimum 2 hours

Rainy-Day Touring: Some shows and exhibits close in the rain

Services and Facilities:

Restaurants Yes	Lockers Yes
Alcoholic beverages Yes	Pet kennels Service animals only
Disabled access Yes	Rain check No
Wheelchair rental Yes	Private tours (619) 685-3264 for
Baby stroller rental Yes	info on Kanagaroo Bus

Description and Comments   This legendary zoo has been exhibiting rare species since 1915 and now has more than 4,000 animals of 900 species. Unbarred enclosures and sensitive landscaping (Dr. Seuss used to sketch in the cactus gardens here) have been the norm at this 100-acre facility for many years, but trying to see everything means a lot of walking. We head right for the Children's Zoo built to a four-year-old's scale, where kids can pet some creatures and see the newborns. The narrated bus tour gives a good overview in just 35 minutes; best viewing is from the left side. The giant pandas, Bai Yun and Shi Shi, gave birth recently to Hua Mei, the first panda cub born in captivity in the West since 1990. The newest exhibit, Owens Rain Forest Aviary, is a walk-through bird habitat. Between June and September, the zoo opens at 7:30 a.m. (great if you have your own early birds) and stays open until 10 p.m. for nocturnal animal viewing and special entertainment programs.

Sea World

1720 S. Shores Road, Mission Bay; (619) 226-3901; www.seaworld.com

Hours: Fall–spring, daily 10 a.m.–dusk; summer, daily 10 a.m.–10 p.m.

Admission: $40 adults, $30 children ages 3–11; parking $7

Appeal by Age Groups:

Pre-school	Grade School	Teens	Young Adults	Over 30	Seniors
★★★★	★★★★★	★★★★★	★★★★★	★★★★★	★★★★★

Touring Time: Average 6 hours; minimum 3 hours

Rainy-Day Touring: So-so; most attractions are outdoors

Services and Facilities:

Restaurants Yes

Alcoholic beverages Beer garden

Disabled access Yes

Wheelchair rental Yes

Baby stroller rental Yes

Lockers Yes

Pet kennels Yes

Rain check No

Private tours Yes

Description and Comments   Part theme park, part zoo, part serious animal rescue and research program, Sea World has an appeal that cuts across age groups and interests—just try to find someone jaded and cynical enough to not be thoroughly wowed and charmed by the dolphin show, in which smiling dolphins perform amazing acrobatic feats and deliberately splash the audience. Over in Shamu's stadium, a huge crowd roars its approval when the killer whales leap far into the sky, ask for the extra-large bucket of fish, and serve as mammalian surfboards for trainers. New attractions are "Fools with Tools," a sea lion, walrus, and otter show, and "Pirates 4-D," a comic film-and-special-effects experience with Leslie Nielsen, Eric Idle, and surprise squirts of water. Our five-year-old loved adventuring through the aquarium tunnel under the shark tank, and the sight of our shivering but deliriously happy eight-year-old after a Shamu soaking will stay with us for years. (Her little sister, however, was shocked into shrieking tears by the coldness of the water, so don't forget a change of clothes for less tough little ones.) Even the less popular exhibits are worthwhile—we stopped at the bird show because the stadium was empty and we needed a rest, and were then dazzled by hawks and falcons dive-bombing into the audience from a 300-foot-high balloon blimp.

Sea World also gets points for going a little beyond the deep-fried, junk-food theme-park basics—over by the penguin house, you can get a tasty fresh-fruit smoothie for a cooling, healthy lunch that kids love.

In summer, the park stays open later and jazzes things up with live music, an ice show, and special night performances. But we prefer getting dolphin-splashed under a hot San Diego sun.

Family-Friendly Restaurants

CASA DE PICO

Bazaar del Mundo, Old Town; (619) 296-3267

Meals served: Lunch and dinner
Cuisine: Mexican
Entree range: $6–16.95 (lunch and dinner)

Children's menu: $3.25
Reservations: No
Payment: All major credit cards

Come early to snag a table at this lively restaurant, where mariachis and Mexican folk dancers entertain most evenings. The adobe-style setting is charming, especially the courtyard tables in Bazaar del Mundo. The food is typical Cal-Mex, fine but nothing special, with plenty to please kids, from chips to chicken fajitas. Full bar.

CORVETTE DINER

3946 5th Avenue, San Diego; (619) 542-1001 or (619) 542-1476

Meals served: Breakfast, lunch, and dinner
Cuisine: American
Entree range: $5.95–9.95 (lunch and dinner)
Children's menu: Yes
Reservations: Not accepted
Payment: All major credit cards

Hugely popular with local families, this 1950s diner camps it up with a live DJ, a magician, wisecracking waitresses, and blaring oldies rock. The decor is equally over the top: neon, chrome, a soda fountain, and an actual Corvette. The food is retro diner: meat loaf, chicken-fried steak, burgers, and, for kids, corn dogs, PB and Js, and root beer floats. Our kids beg to go back.

EL INDIO

409 F Street, Downtown; (619) 239-8151

3695 India Street, Old Town; (619) 299-0333

Meals served: Breakfast, lunch, and dinner
Cuisine: Mexican
Entree range: $6–8 (breakfast, lunch, and dinner)
Children's menu: Yes, at Old Town location
Reservations: Not accepted
Payment: MC, V, D

Tortilla chips are the claim to fame of this beloved chain—they're so good that people buy them as souvenirs and ship them home. Originally a tortilla factory in 1940, the Old Town location is the parent restaurant, and it's notable for its bare-bones outdoor seating, as well as its claim to have invented the word "taquito." Other than the fabulous chips, the food is solid Cal-Mex; try the carne asada, the vegetarian tamale, the nachos deluxe, and, of course, the handmade tortillas. Beer and wine only.

HOB NOB HILL

2271 1st Avenue, Downtown; (619) 239-8176

Meals served: Breakfast, lunch, and dinner
Cuisine: American
Entree range: $5.95–12.95 (breakfast, lunch, and dinner)
Children's menu: Yes
Reservations: Recommended
Payment: All major credit cards

Since 1944, Hob Nob Hill has been dishing out home cooking, and it still looks like it's 1944 inside: red Naugahyde booths, chintz curtains, glass pie cases, and waitresses who know their way around a coffeepot. The location is convenient to nowhere, but that doesn't stop this place from being San Diego's favorite breakfast restaurant, home to very good Western omelets, pancake sandwiches, roast beef hash, and cinnamon rolls. Dinner is of the turkey-croquette variety, and it's popular with the early-bird-special crowd.

PERRY'S

4610 Pacific Highway, Old Town; (619) 291-7121

Meals served: Breakfast and lunch
Cuisine: American/Mexican
Entree range: $3–5.50 (breakfast and lunch)
Children's menu: Yes
Reservations: Not accepted
Payment: D, MC, V

The best place in Old Town for breakfast, Perry's serves an odd but appealing mix of Mexican (huevos rancheros), Italian (frittatas), and American (French toast) cooking; the children's menu is the usual pancake–hot dog roster. The food is cheap, tasty, and generously served, and there's a crowd on weekends.

PIZZA NOVA

3955 5th Avenue, Downtown; (619) 296-6682

5120 N. Harbor Drive, Mission Bay; (619) 226-0268

Meals served: Lunch and dinner
Cuisine: Italian/Californian
Entree range: $5.95–9.50 (lunch and dinner)
Children's menu: Yes
Reservations: Advised
Payment: All major credit cards

Winner of *San Diego Magazine*'s Best Pizza award, this small chain makes very good wood-fired pizzas, ranging from classic pepperoni to ones with lox or Mexican lime chicken. Pastas, salads, and special-occasion desserts are also offered, along with kid-size pizzas. The original branch in Mission Bay has water views and an appealing funkiness.

SAN DIEGO PIER CAFE

865 W. Harbor Drive, Downtown; (619) 239-3968 or (619) 232-7981

Meals served: Breakfast, lunch, dinner, and Sunday brunch
Cuisine: Seafood/American
Entree range: $8–15 (lunch); $13–21 (dinner)
Children's menu: Yes
Reservations: Accepted only for 6 or more
Payment: MC, V, AE

It may look like a tourist trap, given the Seaport Village location, but the food is better than it needs to be at this family favorite. Perched on the end of a small pier next to an old boathouse, it's a wonderful place for watching seagulls fly past, with the Coronado Bridge in the background; try to snag an outdoor table, especially if you have restless kids. The clam chowder, fresh fish, and fish tacos are all tasty, and the all-American breakfasts are particularly good; the children's menu includes fish 'n' chips.

La Jolla

A sophisticated village perched above a dramatic public beach, La Jolla isn't the kind of place you'd hurry to take your kids—unless they are precocious, design-conscious jet-setters. But the cove (see page 39) is indeed spectacular, a couple of the low-key beach resorts are family-friendly, and the aquarium at **Scripps Institute** is worth a stop if you haven't seen one of the larger aquariums in Monterey or Long Beach. La Jolla is located a few miles north of San Diego, about a ten-minute drive.

Family Lodging

La Jolla Beach and Tennis Club

This is the sort of old-money beach retreat that Pasadena families have been summering at for decades. It's decidedly unglamorous, even frumpy, but once you get to know it, its charms are seductive. It has its own lovely private beach, close to but just far enough away from the mob scene at La Jolla Shores public beach, and a large pool is tucked into a wind-protected courtyard. Supervised activities are held throughout the summer for kids from ages three on up, including swim meets, treasure hunts, and craft making; with almost all 90 rooms filled with families, the kids make friends fast. The club can set you up so you can have your own beach barbecue. Other on-site fun includes tennis courts and a par-three golf course.

2000 Spindrift Drive, La Jolla; (858) 454-7126 or (800) 624-2582. Rates $215–359 off-season, $275–479 summer.

Sea Lodge on La Jolla Shores Beach

Sea Lodge doesn't have supervised children's activities, which is just fine with its many loyal patrons, who like to spend family time together. The tile-roofed, Spanish-style hotel, a sibling of the La Jolla Beach and Tennis

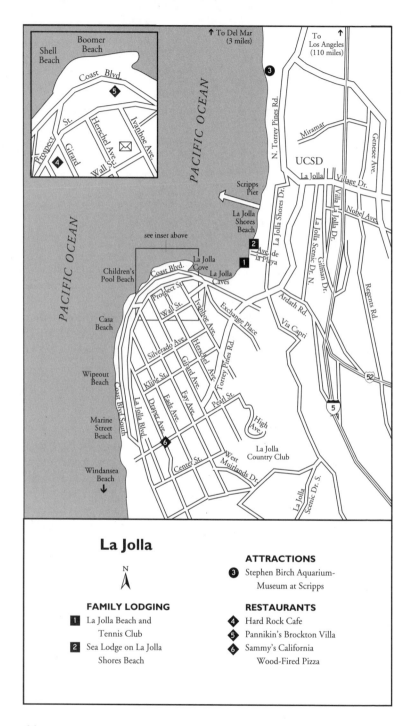

La Jolla

N

FAMILY LODGING

1 La Jolla Beach and
   Tennis Club
2 Sea Lodge on La Jolla
   Shores Beach

ATTRACTIONS

3 Stephen Birch Aquarium-
   Museum at Scripps

RESTAURANTS

4 Hard Rock Cafe
5 Pannikin's Brockton Villa
6 Sammy's California
   Wood-Fired Pizza

Club, is right on the very good beach (with boardwalk, good body boarding, a gentle shoreline for little kids, and lots of people—sometimes a few too many) and next door to a public park and playground; families also make good use of the pool, whirlpool, two tennis courts, Ping-Pong, and upscale restaurant, which has a children's menu. Wet, hungry kids can get a grilled-cheese sandwich delivered poolside. The 128 rooms have a no-frills, beachy-rattan decor, with refrigerators, coffeemakers, and wooden balconies; 19 of the larger rooms have kitchenettes. Be warned that rooms next to the public park can be noisy (scuba-divers arrive at 5 a.m.).

8110 Camino del Oro, La Jolla; (619) 459-8271 or (800) 237-5211. Rates $219–359 off-season, $239–459 in-season; children under 12 stay free.

Attractions

Stephen Birch Aquarium-Museum at Scripps

2300 Expedition Way, La Jolla; (858) 534-3474; www.aquarium.ucsd.edu

Hours: Daily 9 a.m.–5 p.m., except Thanksgiving, Christmas, and New Year's Day

Admission: $8 adults, $7 seniors, $6 students, $5 ages 3–17, under 3 free, parking $5

Appeal by Age Groups:

Pre-school	Grade School	Teens	Young Adults	Over 30	Seniors
★★★★	★★★★	★★★	★★★	★★★★	★★★★
(touch tank)					

Touring Time: Average 1½ hours; minimum 30 minutes

Rainy-Day Touring: Yes

Services and Facilities:

Restaurants Concession stand	Lockers No
Alcoholic beverages No	Pet kennels No
Disabled access Yes	Rain check No
Wheelchair rental Yes	Private tours Yes
Baby stroller rental No	

Description and Comments   The museum is perched on a bluff high above the blue Pacific, and the outdoor touch tank is on a balcony boasting one of the most extraordinary views ever. Parents will find themselves admiring their offspring as the strong sunlight glints on their heads while they concentrate on sea stars and the gulls circle overhead. Meanwhile, inside, dramatically dark hallways are lined with glowing aquariums, lit from behind to best showcase the jellyfish, lobsters, and other marine species. There's also a theme-park moment—a simulated submersible ride—but be warned that the ride might be too scary for kids under age six. If your kids want to prepare for a visit, have them go to the web site.

Family-Friendly Restaurants

HARD ROCK CAFE

909 Prospect Street, La Jolla; (858) 454-5101

Meals served: Lunch and dinner
Cuisine: American
Entree range: $8–15 (lunch and dinner)
Children's menu: Yes ($5.95)
Reservations: Not accepted; expect to wait
Payment: All major credit cards

If you've been to one Hard Rock, you've been to them all. But for a 12-year-old, there's no such thing as too many trips to the Hard Rock. Like the others, it's a loud place, perhaps too loud for the very young; the small patio is a bit quieter. The ribs, burgers, and chicken are tasty, but it's the T-shirts that most kids remember.

PANNIKIN'S BROCKTON VILLA

1235 Coast Boulevard, La Jolla; (858) 454-7393

Meals served: Breakfast, lunch, brunch, and dinner
Cuisine: American
Entree range: $5–12 (lunch); $15–30 (dinner)
Children's menu: Yes
Reservations: Advised; a day in advance
Payment: All major credit cards

The perfect funky beach restaurant, the Brockton Villa is pure San Diego. Breakfast or lunch at this 1894-vintage white clapboard beach house perched over La Jolla Cove will evoke beach summers of your childhood, or at least of your fantasy childhood. While you take in the ocean view you can feast on the city's best French toast, scented with orange; warming oatmeal; a great turkey meat-loaf sandwich; or fresh grilled albacore with ginger-cilantro butter.

SAMMY'S CALIFORNIA WOOD-FIRED PIZZA

702 Pearl Street, La Jolla; (858) 456-5222

Meals served: Lunch and dinner
Cuisine: Californian
Entree range: $9.95–16.95 (lunch and dinner)
Children's menu: Yes ($4.75)
Reservations: Not accepted
Payment: AE, DC, MC, V

This is the parent of a bright, yuppified San Diego chain dedicated to the California pizza: small pies flavored with things like goat cheese, grilled zucchini, and barbecued chicken. They are utterly delicious and can be paired with tasty Caesar salads. Kids have their own menu of mini-pizzas, and they can decorate a paper pizza with crayons. Come early to beat the considerable crowds.

Del Mar and Carlsbad

The racetrack at Del Mar is the famed adult draw here, but plenty of families frequent Del Mar and never place a bet. Instead, they head for the broad, white-sand **beach between 15th and 29th Streets,** and the quaint little downtown area. We've used it as a base for visiting the Wild Animal Park—still a half-hour's drive, but along scenic country roads from here. Downtown San Diego is a 15- to 20-minute drive south.

A half-hour north of San Diego, Carlsbad is a quiet community that has typically attracted the upscale golfing set (think George Bush), but it's changing fast now that **Legoland** has come to town. Between this major new theme park, the clean state beach, the new kid-friendly (if pricey) Four Seasons resort, and the fine children's museum, Carlsbad is turning into a lovely family destination away from the urban crowds. If you're in town in spring, don't pass up a quick trip to the flower fields at **Carlsbad Ranch,** (760) 431-0352, 50 ocean-view acres planted with thousands of ranunculuses.

Family Lodging

The Del Mar Inn

There's a snapshot of our kids in the pool area of this motel, and the brightness of their smiles is matched by the bright flowers everywhere around them—real home gardens, not institutional landscaping. A landmark along the Pacific Coast Highway, and a popular lodging for the horse professionals frequenting the racetrack (just count the trailers in the parking lot), this 80-room Tudor-style place has some unusual homey touches. Afternoon tea is served in real china cups by a woman with a genuine English accent; the pool area is splendid with flowers; decor is heavy on horse pictures and red plaid. It's not near the beach, but it's high enough up that some rooms have ocean views.

720 Camino del Mar, Del Mar; (858) 755-9765 or (800) 252-7466; fax (858) 792-8196. Rates $96–135.

Four Seasons Resort at Aviara

It may not have a beach—South Carlsbad beach is a couple of miles away—but this resort has just about everything else: a gorgeous golf course, tennis, a swimming pool, a health club, complete spa services, high-end restaurants, ocean views, walking/jogging trails around the neighboring Batiquitos lagoon and bird sanctuary, and luxuriously outfitted rooms. Like almost all Four Seasons resorts, this one is out to corner the upscale family market, and they're succeeding. Children are won over from the moment of check-in: waiting for them in the room are cookies and milk on customized plates, and their names are spelled out with sponges in the bathroom. The Kids for All Seasons program is free and first-rate, going far beyond the video-room basics—warm, well-qualified counselors take kids on nature walks and swimming in the pool; kids also enjoy storytelling in a teepee, make their own postcards, play board games, and pet and feed the program's mascot, Avie the frog. Available for kids ages 4–12, the program is offered daily in summer, weekends and school vacations in spring, and weekends the rest of the year. The children's menu is excellent, and the grown-up food is pretty wonderful, too.

7100 Four Seasons Point, Carlsbad; (760) 603-6800 or (800) 332-6801; fax (760) 603-6801. Rates $305–550, special packages sometimes available; children stay free in parents' room.

La Costa Resort and Spa

More old-money (meaning less posh) than the new Four Seasons, La Costa is heaven for the sporting family, what with its acclaimed golf, 21 excellent tennis courts, pool, gym, bikes, hiking trails, and famed spa facilities; the only thing it lacks is a beach, being an inland resort. While you're playing tennis, the kids (ages 5–12) can go to Camp La Costa (which runs daily) and do things like fly kites, swim, create art projects, and walk to the nearby fire station; the cost is $65 a day, including lunch. There's also a Friday and Saturday night dinner-and-activity program for school-age kids, and baby-sitting is available for younger ones; $45 per child includes dinner. The large, comfortable rooms, including many family-size suites and villas, are spread over many manicured acres.

El Camino Real off La Costa Avenue, Carlsbad; (760) 438-9111 or (800) 854-5000; fax (760) 438-3758. Rates $250–450.

San Elijo State Beach Campground

Located in spiffy Cardiff-by-the-Sea, just south of Carlsbad and about 20 minutes north of San Diego's Mission Bay, this campground is beautifully located on a small bluff above the beach, with most of the tent campsites

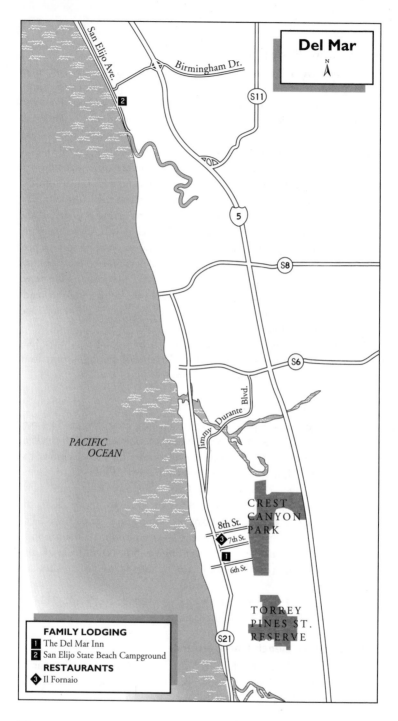

Del Mar

N

PACIFIC
OCEAN

San Elijo Ave.

Birmingham Dr.

S11

5

S8

S6

Jimmy Durante Blvd.

CREST
CANYON
PARK

8th St.
7th St.
6th St.

TORREY
PINES ST.
RESERVE

S21

FAMILY LODGING
1 The Del Mar Inn
2 San Elijo State Beach Campground
RESTAURANTS
◆ Il Fornaio

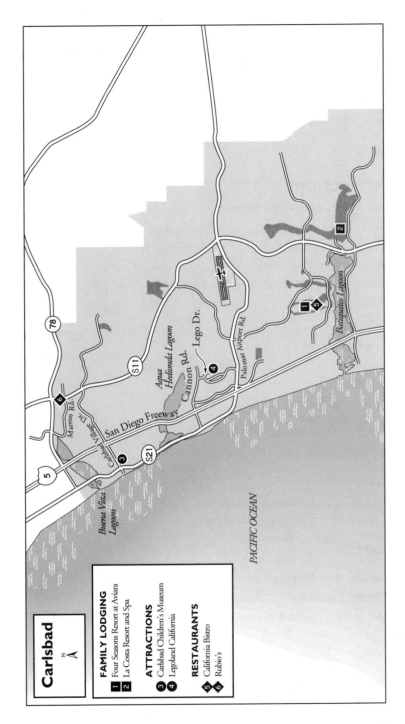

Carlsbad

N

FAMILY LODGING
1 Four Seasons Resort at Aviara
2 La Costa Resort and Spa

ATTRACTIONS
3 Carlsbad Children's Museum
4 Legoland California

RESTAURANTS
5 California Bistro
6 Rubio's

PACIFIC OCEAN

Batiquitos Lagoon

Palomar Airport Rd.

Lego Dr.

Cannon Rd.

Agua Hedionda Lagoon

San Diego Freeway

Carlsbad Village Dr.

Marron Rd.

Buena Vista Lagoon

78

S11

S21

5

overlooking the ocean. You won't get any privacy out here in the open, with the beachfront road running right by, but you'll get a lot of beach beauty and fun for very little money. Unfortunately, you can't reserve these popular sites, so spots go fast in summer. Hot showers, flush toilets, lifeguards, barbecues, lots of nearby restaurants.

On Highway 1, Cardiff-by-the-Sea; (760) 753-5091. Campsites about $16.

Attractions

Carlsbad Children's Museum

300 Carlsbad Village Drive, Suite 103, Carlsbad; (760) 720-0737

Hours: Tuesday–Friday noon–5 p.m., Saturday–Sunday 10 a.m.–5 p.m.; open Monday in summer only

Admission: $4, free for children age 2 and under

Appeal by Age Groups:

Pre-school	Grade School	Teens	Young Adults	Over 30	Seniors
★★★★	★★★★	★	★	★	★

Touring Time: Average 2 hours; minimum 1 hour

Rainy-Day Touring: Yes

Services and Facilities:

Restaurants No	Lockers No
Alcoholic beverages No	Pet kennels No
Disabled access Yes	Rain check No
Wheelchair rental No	Private tours No
Baby stroller rental No	

Description and Comments   This is a worthwhile, hands-on museum with a child-size grocery store, a castle complete with king and princess costumes, a toddler play area, and art and science projects for kids to do. A good rainy-day outing, or for when you've all had enough sun.

Legoland California

Palomar Airport Road, Carlsbad; (760) 918-5346

Hours: Daily 9 a.m.–9 p.m. mid-June through Labor Day; daily 10 a.m.–5 p.m. the rest of the year (extended hours on some holidays)

Admission: $34 adults, $29 children ages 3–16 and seniors; discounts for parents and/or Southern California residents are sometimes offered

Appeal by Age Groups:

Pre-school	Grade School	Teens	Young Adults	Over 30	Seniors
★★★★★	★★★★★	★	★★	★★	★★

Touring Time: Average 5 hours; minimum 3 hours

Rainy-Day Touring: Limited

Services and Facilities:

Restaurants Yes	Lockers Yes
Alcoholic beverages No	Pet kennels Yes
Disabled access Yes	Rain check No
Wheelchair rental Yes	Private tours No
Baby stroller rental Yes	

Description and Comments   Most theme parks try to be all things to all people, but not Legoland: unless your 14-year-old loves Legos, he'll be bored stiff. But 3- to 11-year-olds, and Legomaniacs of any age, will be in heaven. There are no grown-up-pleasing thrill rides, but there are lattes to drink and nice shady spots in which to sit while the kids play.

The theme here, of course, is Legos, the little primary-colored plastic bricks out of which children (and adults) make everything from houses to *Star Wars* vehicles. The showpiece is Miniland, which is perhaps the most appealing part of the park for adults and older Lego-loving kids, if a bit frustrating for little ones, who aren't allowed to touch. Five regions of the United States have been meticulously recreated with 20 million Lego bricks. Lego boats chug in the New England harbor, subway trains run under Rockefeller Center in Manhattan, and cars drive down the streets of Beverly Hills. It's pretty astounding.

Our kids' hands-down favorite attraction is the driving school, which takes Disneyland's Autopia to the next level. Your pint-size drivers attend a brief class on driving safety and rules of the road and are then rewarded with a driver's license (these are cherished by six-year-olds). In a Lego car they drive scaled-down city streets, stopping at signals and staying in their lanes like real drivers.

Otherwise, your child's favorite areas will depend on their age and interests. The littlest ones like the Duplo building area, while the oldest ones like Mindstorms in the Imagination Zone, where they can build robotics vehicles; in this same area, kids are often allowed to help the master builders with whatever they're currently creating. After a session of quiet building, head over to the Hideaways in Castle Hill, a terrific climbing/play structure.

Rides include the fairly tame Castle Hill roller coaster (an ideal thrill ride for five- to eight-year-olds), the very tame lake (great for preschoolers), and the fun Aquazone Wave Racer jet ski ride. We avoid the Kid Power Tower because of the unholy lines, but the recent addition of two more towers might improve things; kids pull themselves in a special chairlift to the top of a 30-foot tower and "freefall" back down. The Sky Cycle isn't worth the typically long wait, but if the line isn't bad, let the kids take a spin.

Allow time for some of the shows, which include nifty visiting ones (NASA was here recently) that skillfully combine education with entertainment. For sheer fun, don't miss the trampoline act.

Legoland gets huge kudos for making the food far more palatable and healthful than at any other theme park. Pastas, sandwiches, and salads (including a great fruit salad for kids) are made fresh to order, and the various restaurant spaces are inviting, with plenty of shade from the often-hot Carlsbad sun.

Our advice is to arrive right at opening time, do the driving school and rides first, wallow in some quiet building activities, have lunch, explore Miniland, and, finally, burn off lunch in the Hideaways and water-play area. If you leave at the hottest part of the day, in the early afternoon, you'll have time to drive back to the beach in Carlsbad for a refreshing family swim.

Family-Friendly Restaurants

IL FORNAIO

Del Mar Plaza, 1555 Camino del Mar, Del Mar; (858) 755-8876

Meals served: Lunch, dinner, and Sunday brunch
Cuisine: Italian
Entree range: $9.95–24.95 (lunch and dinner)
Children's menu: Yes
Reservations: Advised
Payment: All major credit cards

For an upscale family meal out with a sunset ocean view you won't soon forget, head to this accomplished chain. A different region of Italy is featured monthly, and those specials are always the best, but the regular menu of risotti, pasta, bruschetta, grilled fish, and salads is delicious, too. Children are welcomed and given their own menu, with things like an Italian-style macaroni and cheese.

CALIFORNIA BISTRO

Four Seasons Resort at Aviara, 7100 Four Seasons Point, Carlsbad; (760) 603-6800

Meals served: Breakfast, lunch, and dinner
Cuisine: Californian/American
Entree range: $9–14 (lunch); $12.50–22 (dinner)

Children's menu: Yes
Reservations: Advised
Payment: All major credit cards

A rare "nice" restaurant that's as comfortable for children as adults, the Four Seasons' more casual eatery is a real find for families seeking a relaxed dinner out. In a beamed, high-ceilinged, California-chic dining room with an ocean-view terrace, the staff dotes on kids, bringing them little frog key chains and even escorting them to the bathroom when necessary; babies and toddlers get a high chair, snack box of Cheerios, and spill mat. Our kids flipped for the Asian shrimp spring rolls from the grown-up menu, then returned to the safety of the children's menu for burgers and fries; we loved the lamb shank with lentils and the sandwich of chicken, Brie, and sprouts on toasted country bread.

RUBIO'S

2604 El Camino Real, Carlsbad; (760) 434-6298

Meals served: Lunch and dinner
Cuisine: Mexican
Entree range: $3.85–5.99 (lunch and dinner)
Children's menu: Yes
Reservations: Not accepted
Payment: V, MC

Born in San Diego, this order-at-the-counter chain is spreading like wild-fire, and for good reason: the food is fresh, healthy, cheap, and tasty, appeal-ing to kids and grown-ups alike. Known for its soft fish tacos, it also has a good grilled-chicken Caesar salad, peppery beans, and burritos and tacos filled with grilled mahi mahi, savory carnitas, and hearty *machaca* (beef and eggs). And unlike most fast-food places, the seating is comfortable, and you can get a cold Corona with your meal.

Side Trip: Anza-Borrego Desert State Park

Many Southern Californians manage to achieve middle age without even realizing that this 600,000-acre desert park is hiding right in their midst. Inland about two hours from San Diego, Anza-Borrego is a wilderness pre-serve, desert playground, and wildflower paradise in spring; the only town, Borrego Springs, still doesn't have a traffic signal, though it has a few hotels and amenities. Our favorite excursions are the extremes: either sleeping in relative luxury at La Casa del Zorro or sleeping under the stars at the fine state campground. Either way, pack a picnic (including lots of drinking water), have the kids wear swimsuits under their clothes, and spend a day hiking up the Palm Canyon trail, a most child-friendly outing that leads to lush palm oases with fun swimming holes and waterfalls. We visit every spring, and our kids scramble up the rocky trail a little farther each time, discovering a new swimming hole and secret grotto. Before your hike, pay a visit to the visitors center in Borrego Springs so your kids will know which sorts of cacti, birds, and wildflowers to hunt for. Avoid the area from July through September, when the heat can be brutal.

Family Lodging

Borrego Palm Canyon State Campground

Quiet campsites are scattered among the ocotillo, mesquite, and barrel cactus, close to the trailhead to Palm Canyon, an easy hike that kids love. When you're not on the trail, they can scramble up the hillside, hunt for lizards, and, at night, count the shooting stars. Hot showers, flush toilets, barbecues, fire pits, and drinking water are available.

2 miles north of Borrego Springs (check in at visitors center in Borrego Springs for directions), reservations through Reserve America, (800) 444-7275. Campsites $10–11, without hookups.

La Casa del Zorro Resort Hotel

More luxurious than the no-frills town and empty expanse of state park would suggest, this is a fine place to recover from a long, hot hike up Palm Canyon. Swim in the pool, play tennis, rent a bike, or stay cool in one of the large, handsome family-size villas or casitas, many of which have one or two bedrooms, refrigerators, and microwaves. Children's activities are sometimes scheduled on weekends. Rates plummet in the depths of summer. Good restaurant.

3845 Yaquie Pass Road, Borrego Springs; (760) 767-5323 or (800) 824-1884; fax (760) 767-4782. Rates $155–999.

Part Two

Orange County

Nationally, Orange County is best known as the home of **Disneyland Resort,** expanded with the addition of a new theme park (Disney's California Adventure) and a dining/entertainment complex called Downtown Disney. But while the Magic Kingdom is certainly one of the county's great draws, it's located in singularly unattractive Anaheim, which hardly epitomizes the California dream. The dream is here, however—you just have to get out of urban, motel-clogged Anaheim and head south to the beach towns. Traditionally a side trip for California visitors, the county is now a destination in and of itself, or a generous series of stops on the north-south coastal route.

Home to more than 2.6 million people, Orange County is exploding with suburban tract developments and strip malls. The lure is the county's 42 miles of coastline, peppered with lots of lively public beaches. On the north end of the county's coast is **Huntington Beach,** a.k.a. Surf City, a sun-bleached suburb known for its pier, its surf contests, and its relaxed friendliness. On the south end is **San Clemente,** located a bit too far from the business hubs of Irvine and San Diego to have become an affluent suburb—despite its prime oceanfront location, it remains a working-class, no-frills beach town. In between are such visitor meccas as mission-centric **San Juan Capistrano,** artsy **Laguna Beach,** and posh **Newport Beach,** along with beautiful, less-known beaches, endless family sporting adventures, and some way-cool attractions.

The one-two punch of Disneyland and Knott's mandates a few nights' stay at an Anaheim hotel and/or a Buena Park motel to provide you with a resting place and a chance to do the parks right. Otherwise, we'd advise parking your family as close to the beach as possible, in one of the areas described in this chapter. From campgrounds to luxury resorts to beach-house rentals, there are a lot of ways to hit the beach in the Big Orange.

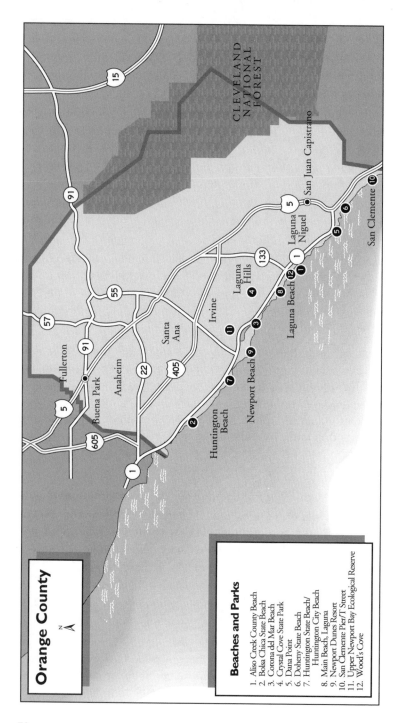

Orange County

N

Beaches and Parks

1. Aliso Creek County Beach
2. Bolsa Chica State Beach
3. Corona del Mar Beach
4. Crystal Cove State Park
5. Dana Point
6. Doheny State Beach
7. Huntington State Beach/
   Huntington City Beach
8. Main Beach, Laguna
9. Newport Dunes Resort
10. San Clemente Pier/T Street
11. Upper Newport Bay Ecological Reserve
12. Wood's Cove

If you've never visited Orange County, we advise spending a few days in the North County theme park area, then driving 20 to 45 minutes southwest to stay in one of the coastal towns described in this chapter (Newport, Laguna, Huntington, or the South County towns) for a few days. From any of these locations, you'll be no more than a 45-minute drive to **Wild Rivers** or the big shopping malls . . . or you can simply enjoy beach life closer to your home base.

GETTING THERE

By Plane. Orange County is served by John Wayne/Orange County Airport, (714) 252-5200, just off Interstate 405 in Irvine, inland from Newport Beach. Many major airlines fly into John Wayne; those that don't are served by Los Angeles International Airport, (310) 646-5252, located about 20 miles north on the 405 from Irvine.

By Train. Amtrak delivers passengers throughout Orange County, with stops in Fullerton, Anaheim, Santa Ana, Irvine, San Juan Capistrano, and San Clemente, connecting between Union Station in Los Angeles and downtown San Diego. If you're not doing Disneyland, one of the best possible day trips from L.A. is to take the train to the San Juan or San Clemente stations (there's also a stop at Anaheim stadium for an afternoon in the most family-friendly stadium in Southern California). The San Juan station is in the heart of the mission area of town, and between the station and the mission are shops and cafes. We had a mother-daughter day with friends this way and couldn't have had more fun. The San Clemente stop (only on selected trains) is at the beach and pier, so you really can wear your suits, bring a beach chair, enjoy a day at the beach and lunch at the pier, and then return to the big city. Call (800) USA-RAIL for details.

The same route is served during commuter hours by Metrolink, (800) 371-5465; it is considerably cheaper than Amtrak but lacks food service and weekend travel.

By Car. Two major freeways cut through Orange County. Interstate 5, which heads north to Canada and south to Mexico, runs right past Disneyland, San Juan Capistrano, and Dana Point; the 405, which splits off from the 5 and follows a coastal route north, will get you to Newport and Huntington Beach. Newly opened is the San Joaquin, Southern California's first toll road, which for $2 gives riders a fast, traffic-free route from Irvine to San Juan Capistrano, via Laguna. Note that while the Pacific Coast Highway can make for a pretty drive, it gets urban and slow in some areas and is not a good long-distance artery.

HOW TO GET INFORMATION BEFORE YOU GO

Anaheim/Orange County Visitor and Convention Bureau, 800 W. Katella Avenue, Anaheim 92803; (714) 765-8888; www.anaheimoc.org.

Huntington Beach Conference and Visitors Bureau, 417 Main Street, Huntington Beach 92648; (714) 969-3492; www.hbvisit.com.

Laguna Beach Visitors Bureau, 252 Broadway, Laguna Beach 92651; (800) 877-1115 or (949) 497-9229; www.lagunabeach info.org.

Newport Beach Conference and Visitors Bureau, 3300 W. Pacific Coast Highway, Newport Beach 92663; (800) 94-COAST or (949) 722-1611; www.newportbeach-cvb.com.

Orange County Tourism Council; (888) 276-7130.

GETTING AROUND

Although Orange County is a card-carrying member of the California car culture, it's proud of its new Orange County Connection bus shuttle service, which can be a godsend if you're stuck in Anaheim with no car and a desperate need to jump in the ocean. It links the Disneyland area with South Coast Plaza, John Wayne Airport, Fashion Island, Newport Beach, Laguna, and San Juan Capistrano. A one-stop, round-trip ticket is $12 for adults, $8 for children; discounts are offered for multiple stops and days. Call (714) 978-8855 for details.

CHILD CARE/BABY-SITTING

Baby Sitters (formerly *Blais-Bie*). This service was founded by Susan Blais 12 years ago to provide carefully screened sitters that match each family's needs; she'll even pair you up with a sitter to travel with you. Her sitters are located throughout Southern California, but Orange County is a specialty; (949) 494-6259.

The Best Beaches and Parks

Aliso Creek County Beach. Like its sister beach (Main Beach) to the north, Aliso Creek is so picturesque that it's beloved of film crews. The sand sweeps in a gentle golden arc, a tidy little pier adds charm, and kids frolic on the playground and in the waves. Barbecues, picnic tables, rest rooms, easy metered parking, and lifeguards in summer. 31131 Pacific Coast Highway, Laguna Beach, (949) 661-7013.

Bolsa Chica State Beach. A long, substantial, sometimes windy strip of sand between the ocean and Pacific Coast Highway, Bolsa Chica is between towns rather than in towns, and backing it on the other side of the highway is Bolsa Chica Nature Reserve, a bird sanctuary that's somewhat renowned. So families day-tripping or camping here can have some pretty pure all-nature days (bring binoculars). They are, however, within an easy bike ride of Huntington Beach's surf shops, movies, and taco joints, and both the overnight and day-use areas access a snack bar. The thrill of bonfires at night is available here, too. Barbecue pits, lifeguards in summer, camping, showers, concessions. Pacific Coast Highway between Warner and Golden West, (800) 729-6252.

Corona del Mar Beach. A.k.a. Big Corona, this is one of Southern California's prettier beaches, with cliffs behind, the sparkling Pacific ahead, and a rock pier into the sea. Lifeguards, bathrooms, a snack bar, volleyball courts, barbecues. Ocean Boulevard and Iris, Corona del Mar, (949) 644-3044. The neighboring beach is known as Little Corona, but its formal name is Corona del Mar Marine Life Refuge. When the tide is low, you can explore fascinating marine life pools; call for a schedule of kid-friendly ranger tours, (949) 722-1611.

Crystal Cove State Park. Developers have just begun to build on the heretofore unspoiled land surrounding these 2,200 acres of bluffs, chaparral canyon, and open land—not to mention the 3.5 miles of coastline—between Laguna and Corona del Mar; a new luxury hotel and golf course are planned, and a housing development on the inland side is under construction. For now, however, this is still one of the most amazing open stretches south of Santa Barbara. Inland are miles of trails beloved by mountain bikers and hikers; on the beach is superb tidepooling in the rocky stretches. Docents hold nature walks on Saturday and Sunday mornings. 8471 Pacific Coast Highway, between Laguna and Corona del Mar, (949) 494-3539. Parking is $6.

Doheny State Beach. Along with San Onofre, this is the best Southern California beach for kids (or adults) to learn how to surf, thanks to the long, gentle waves that break just south of the Dana Point Harbor breakwater. This is also a great beach for a day trip, especially if you reserve one of the extremely popular barbecue-equipped picnic sites in advance, through Reserve America (800) 444-PARK. Rolling green lawns studded with picnic areas are interwoven with pedestrian/bike paths; all this fronts a broad sand beach equipped with pro-quality volleyball courts, a snack bar, showers, and, in summer, both lifeguards and a concession that rents body boards, surrey bikes, in-line skates, and other amusements. Near the entrance to the beach is a small but worthy interpretive center with an indoor tidepool and 3,000-gallon marine aquarium system; call (949) 496-2704 for information on programs for children. 23500 Dana Point Harbor Drive, Dana Point, (949) 496-6171.

Huntington State Beach/Huntington City Beach. When the surf is really booming, your kids will need to stay out of the water, but they'll have a blast watching the surfers put on a show, especially on the north side of the magnificent 1,800-foot-long pier. Typically, however, the waves aren't too forbidding. The city and state beaches adjoin each other, with the Bolsa Chica wetlands (see listing page 81) connecting via a fun bike path from the State Beach. This is a classic white-sand California beach, great for everything from castle-making to body surfing to fishing on the pier. Summer lifeguards, a snack bar, bathrooms, a bike path, barbecue pits, concessions. State Beach is at Pacific Coast Highway at Magnolia, (800) 729-6232.

Main Beach, Laguna. This is the beach you've seen in a million commercials for everything from cars to sunscreen—it's the idealized California beach. A compact, gently sweeping arc in the heart of Laguna Beach, it's famed for its old-fashioned lifeguard tower (painted ad nauseam by local artists), its near–NBA level pickup basketball games, its volleyball courts, its swimming, and, most of all, its people-watching. At the north end you'll find the Glenn E. Vedder Ecological Reserve, which continues north to Crescent Bay Drive. Pick up a tide chart at the Visitors Center, visit at low tide, and discover wonderful tidepooling; make sure children understand before you start that this is a marine preserve, so nothing may be removed, not even a shell. Older kids may want to join you in a snorkeling tour of the reserve at higher tide. Take younger ones to the south end of the beach, where there's a nifty new playground. Summer lifeguard service, showers, and rest rooms. Restaurants, ice cream parlors, and shops are plentiful, but parking is not. Pacific Coast Highway at Broadway, Laguna Beach, (800) 877-1115.

Newport Dunes Resort. The Disneyland of beaches, this chic, RV-oriented, private campground is also a very fun day trip with young children. There's loads of clean, white sand, a wave-free lagoon in which sits a big fiberglass whale (the kids can swim to the whale), a good playground, and even decent shell hunting. A concession rents pedalboats, kayaks, and other watercraft, and you can even get a hot indoor shower. Snack bar, food shop, lifeguards, tent camping (but no stakes), RV camping. 1131 Back Bay Drive, Newport Beach, (949) 729-3863. Admission is $5 per car.

San Clemente Pier/T Street. A fine day-at-the-beach destination, T Street beach surrounds the San Clemente Pier; Amtrak trains stop right here a couple of times a day, making this a fun car-free trip from L.A. or Anaheim. It's a great beach for all ages—the shorebreak area is broad and shallow, with gentle waves that amuse toddlers to no end; farther out are some of the best body-surfing/body-boarding waves for miles (surfboards are banned after 10 a.m., to protect the kids). We like to stake out a spot north of the pier, closer to the rest rooms, showers, and snack bar. Avenida Del Mar and Avenida Victoria, San Clemente, (949) 361-8264; the Marine Safety Headquarters on the pier can be reached at (949) 361-8261.

Upper Newport Bay Ecological Reserve. Bring bikes or your sneakers to explore the 700 acres of pristine peace in the midst of developed Newport. The bird population is astounding; look for great blue herons and snowy egrets, and see how many different kinds of ducks you can spot. Back Bay Road off Jamboree, Newport Beach, (949) 722-1611.

Wood's Cove. If Laguna's Main Beach is too crowded, head over to this lesser-known gem, hidden by dramatic bluffs. Kids love climbing the many rocks and hunting for crabs and other sea critters. Bathrooms, summer lifeguards. Pacific Coast Highway at Diamond Street, Laguna Beach, (949) 494-1018.

Family Outdoor Adventures

Bicycling and Blading. Cycling or skating (or, suddenly, scootering) is a passion with countless Orange County families, and for good reason—the county is zigzagged with miles of easy, dedicated paths, especially near the beaches. One of our favorite family rides is the path between Huntington State Beach north to Bolsa Chica, where you can watch birds in the wetlands. Or you can ride south from Huntington all the way to Newport Beach, a beautiful ride for ten-and-ups who can pedal a few miles. Another great one is the Back Bay Drive bike path, which wanders through the Upper Newport Bay Ecological Reserve (see Best Beaches and Parks, above). Finally, you can ride along Balboa Peninsula in Newport, stopping to watch the gnarly bodysurfing waves at the Wedge on the south end of the peninsula. Then take your bikes over to Balboa Island on the ferry, explore the tiny island, have a snack, ferry back, and ride north along the peninsula to Newport Pier. You can get completely outfitted in rental skates, bikes, and protective gear at Ocean Front Wheel Works (105 Main Street, (949) 723-6510) on Balboa Peninsula; in Huntington Beach, try Team Bicycle Rentals (8464 Indianapolis Street, (714) 969-5480).

Mountain bikers will want to check out the trails in Laguna's Crystal Cove State Park (see Best Beaches and Parks, above) and in Laguna Canyon (see Hiking, below). If you need mountain bikes, you can rent them at Laguna Beach Cyclery (240 Thalia Street, (949) 494-1522).

Boating. Puttering around Newport Harbor in a rented boat can be big fun for young sailors. Pick up a small sailboat ($25/hour), electric boat, motorboat, or kayak at Balboa Boat Rentals in Newport Harbor, (949)

673-7200, and set out for a tour of the harbor's many nooks and crannies. Most of the smaller boats are not allowed out of the harbor.

Fishing. Fun, affordable seagoing fishing trips are run out of Dana Point Harbor by Dana Point Sportfishing (34675 Golden Lantern, (949) 496-5794). A half-day trip is $22 for adults and $17 for kids under age 12, with rods and reels renting for another $8; fishing licenses available for $7. The crew will help neophytes, and any fish you catch (there's calico bass, sand bass, rock cod, mackerel, even the occasional shark out there) will be filleted and packaged for you. Whale-watching trips are also offered in season. If you're based in Newport, try Newport Landing Sport Fishing (309 Palm, Suite F, Balboa, (949) 675-0550).

Hiking. There's more than beaches to Orange County's outdoors—there's also a surprising amount of high-quality hiking. The best ones for families are in the Laguna area; good trails are also found near San Juan, but fear of mountain-lion attacks sometimes forces rangers to prohibit children from the trails. Our favorite family hike, other than the tidepooling/rock-climbing adventures at Dana Point and Crystal Cove (see Best Beaches and Parks, page 81), is in the Laguna Hills, led by Nature Conservancy docents by reservation on weekends, (714) 497-8324. This easy, two-mile trek to "Orange County's Grand Canyon" is recommended for kids ages five and up. The Nature Conservancy also leads more difficult hikes for older families, as well as great mountain-biking rides in Laguna's backcountry. You'll find other trails to explore on your own at Crystal Cove State Park.

Parasailing. Adventurous teens (maybe you, too) will get a huge thrill out of a parasail trip—they'll be lofted up like a human kite, tethered to the deck of a boat, to soar over the ocean for a 12-minute ride that seems like much longer. And it's completely safe. The best place to try it is Marina Water Sports (Balboa Fun Zone, 1700 E. Edgewater, Balboa, (949) 673-3372, $60 per trip).

Surfing/Ocean Sports. Perhaps California's best, gentlest beach to learn to surf is Doheny; the position of the harbor jetties, reef, and shoreline make for long, friendly, small waves. Happily, the state's superb Junior Lifeguards program offers surfing lessons at Doheny, via the Dana Point Youth and Group Facility; call (949) 661-7122 for details. For week-long surf lessons, see the Surf Camp sidebar that follows. If your family wants to try Jet-Skiing, the best place to go is the calm waters of Dana Point Harbor; Capo Beach Watercraft Rentals (3412 Embarcadero Place, (949) 661-1690) rents good equipment and provides instruction.

Tidepooling. An afternoon spent scrambling over rocks hunting for crabs, anemones, shells, sea stars, and maybe even an octopus is often a highlight of a trip. Orange County has several great locations, so look under a specific beach heading for recommendations. See Corona del Mar Beach, Crystal Cove State Park, and Main Beach in Best Beaches and Parks, and see also the Orange County Marine Institute in South County Attractions, page 94. You can pick up a tide chart at any of the dozens of surf, fishing, or boat stores in any of the beach towns. Make sure your kids understand that if the tide pools are part of a preserve, nothing may be removed, not even an empty shell—a hermit crab may need it for a home later.

Whale-Watching. Much anticipated by local schoolchildren each year, and celebrated with a terrific festival in Dana Point (see Calendar of Festivals and Events, page 87), whale-watching season arrives each January and lasts through March. These boat trips are fun half-day outings for kids of all ages; even if you aren't lucky enough to spot a herd of migrating gray whales, you're sure to see dolphins and sea birds and get great views and a feel for the vast Pacific. Trips depart from the harbors in Dana Point (phone (949) 496-2274) and Newport (phone (949) 673-1434). The Dana Point trips are run by the Orange County Marine Institute with curious kids in mind.

SURF CAMP

Nothing symbolizes the California image more than surfing, yet few sports are more challenging to master. Enter the surf camp, which offers a week or more of intense instruction, along with a lot of camaraderie and fun. After a week at any of these Orange County camps, your kid will be a real surfer. And don't be afraid to try it yourself—it's one of the simplest, purest thrills in the sporting world.

Summer Fun Surf Camp. San Clemente (949) 361-9526. This popular, state-licensed program offers five- and seven-day summer sessions at San Clemente State Beach, an excellent campground and public beach. "Everybody leaves surfing" is the motto, and that "everybody" often includes moms and dads, who get their own campsite adjacent to the kids. When they're not in the water, kids can ride bikes, skate, and play volleyball or Ping-Pong; evenings bring rousing campfires and, for those who can't live without it, TV watching. A five-day day camp is also offered. Prices range from $595 to $895 per person for the sleep-away programs, including all meals, boards, lots of one-on-one instructor time, and a videotape analysis of each student's surfing progress.

Super Surf Camp. Huntington Beach (714) 680-4000; www.jrlifeguards.com. Part of the excellent California Junior Lifeguards Program, these one-week day camps (ages eight to adult) are offered during spring break and throughout summer. Based at such Orange County beaches as Sunset and Salt Creek (near Dana Point), this is a great way to get to know the ocean. Your kids (or your whole family) will learn not only how to surf or bodyboard, but also the essentials of first aid, CPR, lifeguarding, and ocean safety. The price is moderate, and it includes free loaner boards and wetsuits for those who don't have their own. If you have a daughter, take note that even though surfing seems boy-dominated, 35–40% of the camp participants are girls.

Paskowitz Surf Camp. San Clemente (949) 361-9283. The Paskowitzes are the first family of surfing, a sprawling clan of siblings who became surf stars as kids and are now mostly in their 30s. Surf base is San Onofre, where long, gentle, sweeping waves (reminiscent of Waikiki's) are superb for learning. The instructors here are good, led by former longboarding champ Izzy Paskowitz; sometimes celebrity pros teach as well. After spending all day at the beach, you crash at San Mateo State Park, a good beach campground with hot showers; evening activities include watching surf movies and telling tall tales around the campfire. Popular with entire families, or kids alone (including girls-only weeks), this is a solid week-long camp that will have you all surfing. It's not cheap, though, at $980 per person per week, all-inclusive.

Finding a Home in Orange County

RENTING A BEACH HOUSE

If you've got a week or more to spend in Orange County, a beach house is a great way to go. True, you have to do your own dishes and daily housekeeping, but the good news is that you can get plenty of room for a family right on the sand, for less than a comparably located hotel, and you can save more money by eating a meal or two a day in your house. From any of the locations below, you can make easy day trips to Disneyland, Knott's, Wild Rivers, or the other Orange County amusements—but your kids will have just as much fun on the beach and in the ocean, and you may be happiest staying put. If you have younger children, try sleepy Capistrano; if you have teenagers, you're better off in Newport or Laguna, where they'll find more close-by shops, amusements, and other teens.

Burr White Realtors. With 31 years of experience renting beach houses, this Newport firm is the best source for a beach house on the Balboa Peninsula; it has choices on the oceanfront, for wave fans; on the bay front, for gentler waters; and less expensive ones in between, for those on a budget who don't mind walking a block to the beach. August prices for a three-bedroom waterfront house range from $1,500 to $2,500 a week or more, depending on the property. The beach is less secluded and private than Capistrano, but there's more action for teens. 2901 Newport Boulevard, Newport Beach, (949) 675-4630.

Capistrano Realty. In between San Clemente and Dana Point lies one of Orange County's few private beachfront communities, perhaps the only one in which every house sits on the sand. This agency is the primary source for renting a house along guard-gated, 1½-mile Beach Road, which parallels Pacific Coast Highway just across the (frequently traveled) railroad tracks. Although hardly cheap, the houses rent for much less than in the Malibu colony or Del Mar: A high-quality three-bedroom, two-bath place might go for $2,200 a week in June and $4,000 in August. Cycling families note that you can ride from Beach Road all the way to Dana Point Harbor (about three miles) on a flat, protected, oceanfront route; a vendor at the public beach at the beginning of the road rents bikes, surreys, and skates. Houses on the north end of the road have the largest sand beach; those on the south end have the best swimming for children. 34700 Pacific Coast Highway, Capistrano Beach, (949) 496-5353. Summer rentals start at $1,000 a week.

Laguna Beach Oceanfront Rentals. This agency can get your family all sorts of weekly rentals in Laguna, from a tiny one-bedroom apartment for $750 a week up to a beachfront mansion for $18,000 a week (that's for July and August—prices are lower off-season). Beachfront houses are scarce in Laguna, and therefore they're prohibitively expensive, but there are plenty of adorable cottages a block or three from the ocean renting in the $1,500–2,000 a week range, which can be a good value compared to a week in a nice hotel. A cute two-bedroom, two-bath house (sleeps six) in chic North Laguna, for instance, with a fireplace, piano, and kid-friendly back-yard, rents for $1,750 a week in August. Laguna Beach Oceanfront Rentals, 900 Glennyre, Laguna Beach, (949) 494-8110. Weekly rates start at $600.

Calendar of Festivals and Events

February

Festival of Whales, Dana Point. Held the last two weeks of February. First-rate (and free!) open-air rock, blues, and jazz concerts; a film festival; and a street fair on the weekends. Loads of great kid activities, from the one-mile Little Whales Run to the 2K Wag-a-Thon pet walk, which raises money for animal causes. A parade features lobster jugglers, and at the ranger-led camp-fire, kids learn about whales and marine life. Whale-watching trips leave from the Dana Point Harbor. Call for details; (949) 496-1094.

March

Return of the Swallows, Mission San Juan Capistrano. In mid-March. They ain't what they used to be (some years it's just a handful of swallows), but that doesn't stop a good time from happening. Street fair, Mexican food, shows, live music; (949) 248-2048.

Glory of Easter, Crystal Cathedral. Late March/early April. A gala show with live animals, special effects, and a cast of 200 in a spectacular church; (714) 971-4019.

April

Mud-Slinging Festival, Mission San Juan Capistrano. In mid-April, celebrate the old adobe-making ways with a hilarious romp flinging mud at the old mission walls—it helps restore the mission as well as blow off some steam; (949) 248-2048.

May

Imagination Celebration, countywide. An arts festival for children, teens, and their parents, with lots of hands-on workshops, performances, and exhibits; (949) 833-8500.

July

Huntington Beach Fourth of July Parade and Fireworks, Main Street, Huntington Beach. Several hundred thousand people attend this all-American parade in the morning; most stick around for the beachfront fireworks show after dark; (714) 969-3492.

Old Glory Boat Parade, Newport Beach. July Fourth; (949) 673-5070.

Sawdust Festival, Laguna Canyon. The funkier cousin to the upscale Festival of Arts, this craft-oriented art festival is particularly appealing to teenagers; (949) 494-3030.

Orange County Fair, 88 Fair Drive, Fairgrounds, Costa Mesa. A classic county fair; (714) 708-3247.

Gotcha Pro Surfing Competition, Huntington Pier, Huntington Beach. In late July. If your kids are surfers (or wannabes), they'll want to check out this acclaimed surf contest; (949) 366-4584.

September

Tallships Festival, Orange County Marine Institute, Dana Point. Weekend after Labor Day. Grand old tall ships sail into the harbor; families can get aboard one of the ships and sail in the great parade (reservations are essential; call the number below). You can also tour old ships, learn how to sail a square-rigger, listen to live sea-chanty music, and see the work of nautical artisans; (949) 496-2274.

Pierfest, Huntington Beach. Live music, beach games, sports, and general festival merriment; (714) 960-3378.

Sand Castle and Sand Sculpture Contest, Corona del Mar Beach. Kids and adults (including professionals) create amazing works in sand; (949) 729-4400.

October

Korean Festival, Garden Grove. A three-day cultural fair with kiddie rides, a parade, and great food; (714) 638-7950.

December

Christmas at the Mission, Mission San Juan Capistrano. Early December. The season kicks off with Christmas music, entertainment, and refreshments; (949) 248-2048.

Christmas Boat Parade, Newport Harbor. Seemingly all of Newport turns out to watch some 200 decorated, Christmas-lighted boats parade by; (949) 729-4400.

South County: San Clemente, Dana Point, and San Juan Capistrano

Low on A-list amusements but high on beach fun, the towns in southernmost Orange County aren't well known to the tourist trade (with the exception of San Juan's fast-disappearing swallows). That's just fine by the locals, who get to enjoy clean, sunny beaches and small-town appeal without burdensome crowds. We have a number of friends who live within walking distance of Santa Monica Beach but who drive an hour or more south to **San Clemente's T Street** every Saturday in summer, because its water is cleaner, its beach more picturesque, and its surf better for both little kids and body surfers.

San Clemente is the southernmost town in this area, and it's a great place to spend a beach day. Amtrak trains stop right in front of the pier and beach, making it a fine car-free day trip from L.A. or Anaheim. It's a funky town, populated by lots of retirees and blue-collar folk, so don't expect lots of Starbucks or Santa Cruz charm—just a classic pier, a public beach with all the amenities, and a not-yet-gentrified downtown with a few interesting shops and Mexican restaurants.

Dana Point, a few miles north, is centered around a large pleasure-craft harbor, described in Attractions on page 93. The heart of town itself is a rather dispiriting collection of late-model storefronts along the Pacific Coast Highway (PCH), but if you look carefully you'll find a few shops that surf-fascinated kids will adore, including **Hobie's, Girl in the Curl** (for girl surfers), and **Killer Dana.** Along with the usual streets, a bike path follows San Juan Creek from its endpoint—the bird sanctuary/ estuary in between Doheny State Beach's campground and public park— about three flat miles into **San Juan Capistrano,** the handsome mission town in which even the fast-food restaurants have red-tile roofs. The mission is San Juan's main draw, and it's one of the state's loveliest and most interesting to children. From the mission, you can walk to the train depot

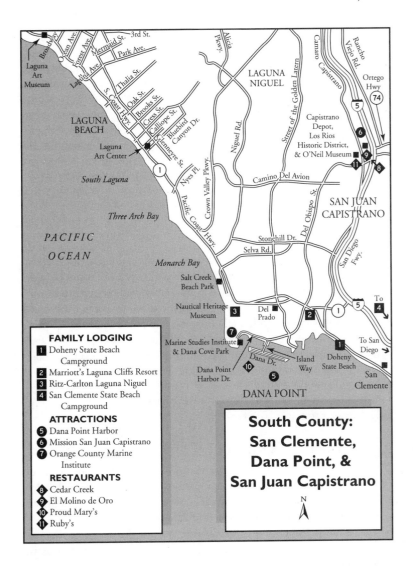

LAGUNA
NIGUEL

Ortego
Hwy
74

5

6

Capistrano
Depot,
Los Rios
Historic District,
& O'Neil Museum

Camino Del Avion

SAN JUAN
CAPISTRANO

Stonehill Dr.

Selva Rd.

San Diego Fwy.

Laguna
Art
Museum

LAGUNA
BEACH

Laguna
Art Center

South Laguna

Three Arch Bay

PACIFIC
OCEAN

Monarch Bay

Salt Creek
Beach Park

Nautical Heritage
Museum **3**

Del **2**
Prado

1

To
4

To San
Diego

1

To San
Diego

Marine Studies Institute
& Dana Cove Park **7**

Dana Point
Harbor Dr.

Dana Dr.
10

Island
Way

Doheny
State Beach

5

Doheny
State Beach

San
Clemente

1

DANA POINT

FAMILY LODGING

1 Doheny State Beach
   Campground
2 Marriott's Laguna Cliffs Resort
3 Ritz-Carlton Laguna Niguel
4 San Clemente State Beach
   Campground

ATTRACTIONS

5 Dana Point Harbor
6 Mission San Juan Capistrano
7 Orange County Marine
   Institute

RESTAURANTS

8 Cedar Creek
9 El Molino de Oro
10 Proud Mary's
11 Ruby's

**South County:
San Clemente,
Dana Point, &
San Juan Capistrano**

N

and let kids run through the old train cars that make up the station and
station restaurant; across the train tracks are a few of the town's oldest
houses, including some adobes, as well as a sweet little petting farm and
pony ride that local kids love.

Family Lodging

Doheny State Beach Campground

It's small, it has no RVs (no hookups), and it's right on one of the most family-friendly beaches in Southern California, so this tent campground is booked months in advance for weekends and summer. Because it's so compact, don't expect much peace and quiet, but do expect to find lots of other families skating and cycling the bike paths, playing volleyball, learning to surf the famed gentle waves, barbecuing, visiting the small indoor aquarium, and exploring the neighboring Dana Point Harbor.

23500 Dana Point Harbor Drive, Dana Point; (949) 496-6171; reservations through Reserve America, (800) 444-7275. Oceanfront campsites $19–22, other campsites $14–16.

Marriott's Laguna Cliffs Resort

A Cape Cod–style hotel that sprawls over a bluff with views from Dana Point to San Clemente, this newish resort has already had several changes in management, but it has remained a good family resort no matter who's in charge. From the extensive lawns, paths lead down to a pine-dotted city park above the harbor, with a children's playground, excellent basketball court, and lawns popular with kite flyers. On site are two pools and spas and lots of room to run around. The children's menu is available in both the restaurant and room service, and kids get a free breakfast when they eat with an adult.

25135 Park Lantern, Dana Point; (949) 661-5000 or (800) 533-9748. Rates $179–259 for rooms; $400 and up for suites.

Ritz-Carlton Laguna Niguel

This is paradise for kids and their parents, as long as they've got plenty of money and don't mind a setting that's more formal than California beachy. There are 393 guest rooms; elegant restaurants, lounges, lobbies, and meeting rooms are spread along a bluff overlooking a soft sand beach; everywhere are lawns and flowers and walkways, along with the expected pools, spas, a fitness center, spa facilities, and tennis courts (golf is adjacent). While you play tennis or get a facial, your 6–12-year-old children can join in the free Ritz Kids program, which includes swimming, beach games, arts and crafts, tidepooling, and trips to the Orange County Marine Institute; if you crave a grown-up meal, the hotel offers Kids' Night Out on Friday and Saturday, when they're served kid-friendly dinners and entertained with movies or live performances (such as puppet shows). The worthwhile Terrace Restaurant offers a good children's menu, which is also available through room service.

1 Ritz-Carlton Drive, Dana Point; (949) 240-2000 or (800) 241-3333. Rates are $355–495; four people allowed in a room ($50 per additional guest), and children under 18 stay free.

San Clemente State Beach Campground

Popular with surfers and beach-loving families, this is a well-equipped (hookups, fire rings, hot showers, flush toilets) campground on a bluff overlooking the beach; the trail down is easily manageable for kids, though the littlest may whine heading back up. A fine beach for body boarding, surfing, splashing, and general beach fun.

3030 Avenida del Presidente, San Clemente; (949) 492-3156; reservations through Reserve America, (800) 444-7275. Campsites are $19–22, plus $1 if you bring the family dog.

Attractions

Dana Point Harbor

Golden Lantern off Pacific Coast Highway, Dana Point; (949) 496-1094

Hours: Shops and restaurants open daily; hours vary

Admission: Free

Appeal by Age Groups:

Pre-school	Grade School	Teens	Young Adults	Over 30	Seniors
★★★	★★★	★★★	★★★	★★★	★★★

Touring Time: Average 4 hours including lunch or dinner; minimum 1 hour

Rainy-Day Touring: Not great

Services and Facilities:

Restaurants Many	Lockers No
Alcoholic beverages Yes	Pet kennels No
Disabled access Yes	Rain check No
Wheelchair rental No	Private tours No
Baby stroller rental No	

Description and Comments More an afternoon's destination than an attraction, the harbor is home to a fine museum (the Orange County Marine Institute, see page 94) and a kid-beloved outdoor cafe, Proud Mary's (see page 97). The harbor is also the place to head out for a whale-watching, fishing, or Jet-Skiing expedition (see Family Outdoor Adventures, pages 83–85). You can also skate, cycle, or walk the pedestrian paths linking the shopping, eating, and boating areas; tidepool and explore the little caves and rocky shoreline on the far west end of the harbor; and let little ones splash in safety at the wave-free little beach dubbed Stretchmark Shores by the local moms. On a sunny day, the hippest place to be is the terrace front of the Scoop Deck, an ice cream parlor next door to a coffee-house. Locals and their many dogs join visitors to sit and watch the passing parade of in-line skaters, sailors, and walkers.

Mission San Juan Capistrano

Visitors Center, 31882 Camino Capistrano, San Juan Capistrano; (949) 248-2048

Hours: Daily 8:30 a.m.–5 p.m.; except for Thanksgiving, Christmas, and New Year's Day

Admission: $6 adults, $4 seniors and children ages 3–12

Appeal by Age Groups:

Pre-school	Grade School	Teens	Young Adults	Over 30	Seniors
★★	★★★	★★★	★★★	★★★★	★★★★

Touring Time: Average 2 hours; minimum 1 hour

Rainy-Day Touring: Some; outdoors may be difficult

Services and Facilities:

Restaurants Off site, but convenient	Baby stroller rental No
	Lockers No
Alcoholic beverages No	Pet kennels No
Disabled access Yes	Rain check No
Wheelchair rental No	Private tours Docent tours $8

Description and Comments   Perhaps the most fully restored of the misson chain, with the most to see in the way of demonstrations and living, working, sacred, and exhibition areas, San Juan Capistrano is also an enclosed park-like setting that makes it an easy place to keep track of kids while they scramble and skip around a bit. The mission buildings are laid out around two enclosed courtyards, and the rooms you see are on the ground level with a simple step in and out of the adobe doorways. Parents of very young children don't even have to bother with the lectures; instead they can wander past the tables full of ancient tools and bits of leather and such that are set out especially for little ones to touch and examine. On the last Saturday of each month, the mission holds Living History Day, which is worth a visit—docents dress and act in character as Native Americans and missionary priests.

Orange County Marine Institute

24200 Dana Point Harbor Drive (far western end of harbor), Dana Point; (949) 496-2274

Hours: 10 a.m.–4:30 p.m. Saturday and Sunday only; weekdays are reserved for children on field trips

Admission: Free; prices for special excursions, $6–24

Appeal by Age Groups:

Pre-school	Grade School	Teens	Young Adults	Over 30	Seniors
★★★	★★★★	★★★	★★★	★★★	★★★

Touring Time: Average 30 minutes; minimum 30 minutes

Rainy-Day Touring: No problem inside; difficult near tide pools

Services and Facilities:

Restaurants Nearby	Lockers No
Alcoholic beverages No	Pet kennels No
Disabled access Yes	Rain check Excursions only
Wheelchair rental No	Private tours Yes
Baby stroller rental No	

Description and Comments   The name suggests an aquarium center, but while plans are afoot to add tank space, that's not what this place is about. It's a quirky, intriguing collection of marine-centered activities and sites, from the tide pools out on the shoreline to tours of a historic tall ship. Inside is a simple docent-manned touch tank, allowing kids to hold a sea star or tiny crab, along with a gift shop and such whale memorabilia as a fully reconstructed skeleton hanging overhead. Across the lawn outside is the home dock of *The Pilgrim,* site of overnight field trips for seemingly every fifth-grade class in Southern California; you can tour the ship on Sundays, which will bring your child's Captain Hook fantasies to life. Parent-child overnighters are offered sporadically in summer; call for information.

Even cooler, at least for the eight-to-teen set, is a trip aboard the *R/V Sea Explorer,* a state-of-the-art research ship complete with underwater remote cameras. Outings include the Marine Mammal trip (best during whale-watching season), and our favorite, the Bioluminescent Night Cruise, a 2 ½-hour trip in search of glowing fish, plankton, and glowworms.

Finally, the institute supervises (and sometimes leads tours of) the wonderful tidepooling preserve on its northern edge, at the base of the actual point. Our kids have spent many happy hours exploring the life here and hiking the rocky but easy trail that hugs the bluff, leading to several kid-size caves and even more tidepooling.

Family-Friendly Restaurants

CEDAR CREEK

26860 Ortega Highway, San Juan Capistrano; (949) 240-2229

Meals served: Lunch, dinner, and Sunday brunch
Cuisine: American
Entree range: $6.95–11.25 (lunch); $15.95–22.95 (dinner)
Children's menu: Yes; $3.95
Reservations: Not accepted
Payment: AE, MC, V

Ideally located across the street from Mission San Juan Capistrano, this place has the prettiest patio in town, all brick and greenery and mission-influenced, with a fireplace for chilly evenings. Unlike the Cedar Creek in Laguna, this one welcomes children with things like special menus and booster seats. The well-prepared food is solid American with a bit of modernity (there's a rare ahi sandwich as well as a burger). Later evenings often bring live music and what passes for a singles scene in San Juan, so families are best coming for lunch and early dinner.

EL MOLINO DE ORO

31886 Plaza Drive, San Juan Capistrano; (949) 489-9230

Meals served: Breakfast, lunch, and dinner
Cuisine: Mexican
Entree range: $4–6
Children's menu: No
Reservations: No
Payment: D, MC, V

Almost hidden in a strip center south of the mission (look for the Star-bucks to find it), this tortilleria/cafe makes the best Mexican food in town. There's always a line at the counter, and the plastic tables on the sidewalk fill up fast, thanks to the fresh homemade tortillas and hearty, cheap, delicious burritos, soft tacos, enchiladas, and more. My picky kids love the cheese quesadillas and fresh chips.

PROUD MARY'S

34689 Golden Lantern, Dana Point Harbor; (949) 493-5853

Meals served: Breakfast and lunch
Cuisine: American
Entree range: $2–8 (breakfast); $6–10 (lunch)
Children's menu: Yes
Reservations: Not accepted
Payment: AE, DC, MC, V

This is my ten-year-old's favorite restaurant in the world, for a host of reasons. For one, all lunches come with a small bag of potato chips. For another, the children's menus are great to color, and they can hang them on the inside wall when finished. Best of all, the patio tables overlook the fishing boats, coastline, and harbor walkway, which is always packed with kids, dogs, and adults on weekends. While waiting for their chicken fingers, they can watch crabs scurry on the rocks below and wave to departing fishing boats. We love it, too, because of the sunny patio, the view, and the really superb hamburger, Ortega chicken sandwich, and breakfasts. If you still have room, there's an ice cream shop farther along the harbor front.

RUBY'S

31781 Camino Capistrano, San Juan Capistrano; (949) 496-7829

Meals served: Breakfast, lunch, and dinner
Cuisine: American
Entree range: $5–8 (breakfast); $4.50–7.50 (lunch and dinner)
Children's menu: Yes
Reservations: Not accepted
Payment: All major credit cards

A local chain that grew out of the Newport Beach original, Ruby's is another rider on the 1940s-nostalgia bandwagon, and kids can't get enough of it. Booths are big, red, and shiny, children's cheeseburgers come in car-shaped cardboard boxes (complete with toy), and a model train chugs around the ceiling. The food is generic, inexpensive, and more fun for kids than parents, but it's guaranteed to make them happy.

Laguna Beach and Newport Beach

Laguna Beach is the antidote to the tract-house sterility of Orange County. This hilly, meandering town is funky, artistic, and utterly charming. It's known more as a beach-town retreat for artists, art lovers (including devotees of the bizarre Pageant of the Masters, when people dress in costume and re-create famous paintings), and couples (straight and gay) seeking a romantic weekend. But it's also an excellent base for a family beach vacation with teens and preteens, who will love the shopping (beads, tie-dyes, surfwear, locally made jewelry), the snack/coffee/yogurt vendors, the hip cafes, and the fellow teen–watching. Don't look for amusements like theme parks or kid-oriented museums, but do spend time exploring some of its 30 jewel-like beaches, many hidden at the base of steep bluffs. If you choose Laguna as a beachy base for exploring Orange County, know that Newport is only about a 15-minute drive north, Dana Point about a 15-minute drive south, and Disneyland/Knott's some 30 minutes inland. Add more time to the drives in July and August, when central Laguna can turn into a Gordian's knot of traffic.

Newport Beach is the nouveau-riche capital of California. It oozes prosperity, with seemingly more Mercedeses than in Germany. Although this can be irritating for less materialistic families, prosperity does have its advantages. Newport has miles of wide, clean, well-maintained beaches, a yacht harbor stocked with pretty boats, bike paths galore, some of the country's best shopping, good restaurants, and fetching little **Balboa Island,** almost a toy beach village.

In some social circles, families have rented Newport beachside cottages for generations, which can be a fine idea (see Renting a Beach House, pages 86–87). **Balboa Peninsula** is a particularly nice place to be, with its bay and ocean beaches, bike path, pier, pedalboats on the bay, ferry, and Fun Zone. Teens especially love Balboa and Newport, because there's always life

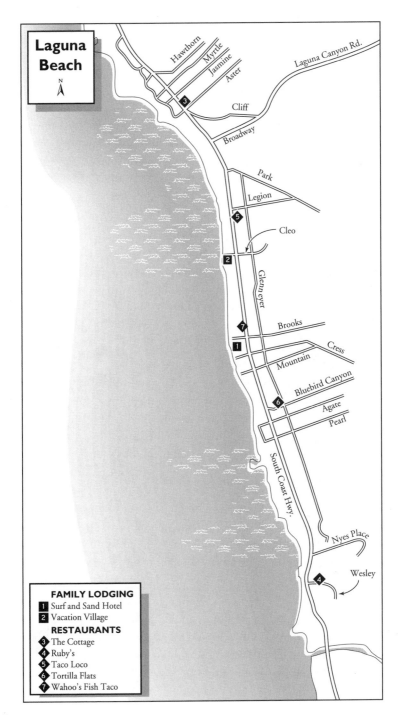

Laguna Beach

N

Hawthorn
Myrtle
Jasmine
Aster
Laguna Canyon Rd.
Cliff
Broadway
Park
Legion
Cleo
Glenneyer
Brooks
Cress
Mountain
Bluebird Canyon
Agate
Pearl
South Coast Hwy.
Nyes Place
Wesley

FAMILY LODGING
1 Surf and Sand Hotel
2 Vacation Village
RESTAURANTS
3 The Cottage
4 Ruby's
5 Taco Loco
6 Tortilla Flats
7 Wahoo's Fish Taco

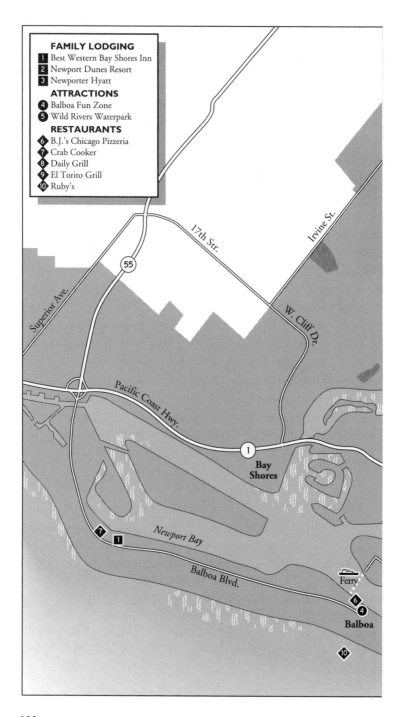

FAMILY LODGING
1 Best Western Bay Shores Inn
2 Newport Dunes Resort
3 Newporter Hyatt
ATTRACTIONS
4 Balboa Fun Zone
5 Wild Rivers Waterpark
RESTAURANTS
6 B.J.'s Chicago Pizzeria
7 Crab Cooker
8 Daily Grill
9 El Torito Grill
10 Ruby's

55

Superior Ave.

17th Str.

Irvine St.

W. Cliff Dr.

Pacific Coast Hwy.

1

Bay Shores

Newport Bay

Balboa Blvd.

Ferry

6
4
Balboa

10

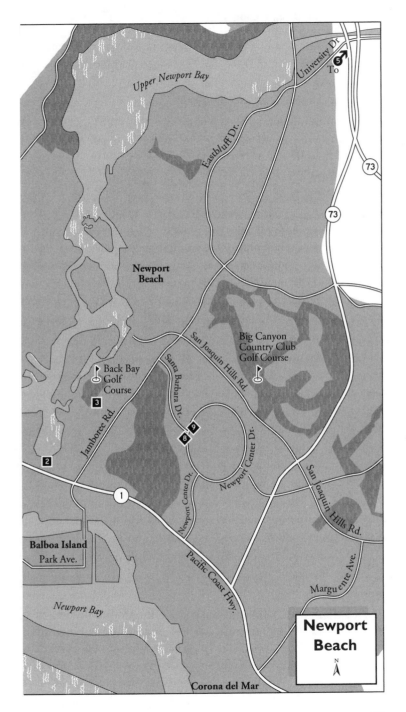

Upper Newport Bay

University Dr.

To ⑤

73

73

Eastbluff Dr.

Newport
Beach

Big Canyon
Country Club
Golf Course

San Joaquin Hills Rd.

Back Bay
Golf
Course

Santa Barbara Dr.

3

9
8

Newport Center Dr.

Newport Center Dr.

San Joaquin Hills Rd.

Jamboree Rd.

2

①

Balboa Island
Park Ave.

Pacific Coast Hwy.

Marguerite Ave.

Newport Bay

**Newport
Beach**

N

Corona del Mar

(and other teens) on the boardwalk and the beach. Don't miss a morning visit to the **Newport Pier** to watch the dory fishermen row in and unload their morning catch—kids find it enthralling. (They'll also like watching the Asian families from Westminster up on the pier, catching their dinners.) If you don't have a week or the inclination to rent a house, one of the hotels or the campground at Newport Dunes will also make a fun family base. The theme parks of the north county are only about 20 minutes away.

MALL MANIA

Two of the country's finest malls reside in Orange County: **Fashion Island,** in Newport Beach, and **South Coast Plaza,** in neighboring Costa Mesa. If you have shop-crazed preteens or teens, you'll want to hit one or both. We prefer the smaller Fashion Island, because it's open-air and visually appealing, with good restaurants; our favorite is the beautiful Tutto Mare, though it's really only appropriate for preteens and older (the Hard Rock Cafe is, of course, where kids want to go). See also reviews for Daily Grill and El Torito Grill under Family-Friendly Restaurants, page 109.

Many others prefer South Coast Plaza, a glitzy, huge mall that sells everything imaginable. Younger kids will want to ride the carousel and play in FAO Schwarz, the Disney Store, and the other toy stores; older ones can hit the Gap and the dozens of other fashion-oriented shops and department stores. A good on-site restaurant choice is the Wolfgang Puck Cafe, home to great salads, chic pizzas, and a children's menu; across the street is Planet Hollywood.

Middle-schoolers infatuated with skateboard culture will love **The Block at Orange,** home not only of all the best surf and swimwear shops in Southern California, but also of Van's Skate Park, an indoor facility where skateboarders and Rollerbladers can pay by the hour to skate the two "swimming pools" and the many ramps and other structures. There's also a movie megaplex, and adults can cool their heels at some surprisingly good cafes.

Older teens will want to head down the street to the **Lab Anti-mall,** a small, outdoor collection of teen/GenX shops—Urban Outfitters, a thrift shop, a skate shop, Tower Records—that sort of thing. Nose rings and pink hair are the norm here.

South Coast Plaza, 3333 S. Bristol Street, Costa Mesa, (714) 435-2000; Fashion Island, Newport Center Drive between Jamboree and MacArthur, Newport Beach, (949) 721-2022; The Block at Orange, City Drive off I-5 or the 22 freeway, (714) 769-4000; The Lab Anti-mall, 2930 Bristol Street, Costa Mesa, no phone (Urban Outfitters is (714) 966-1666).

Family Lodging

LAGUNA BEACH

Surf and Sand Hotel

The best hotel in Laguna Beach, this is a small-scale resort most notable for its exceptional location perched on the rim of the Pacific; from some rooms you might feel like you're shipboard. Although it is a quiet, sophisticated, subtly elegant place, it also manages to welcome families. Many of the rooms, from the least expensive ones with two queens to the oceanfront kings with pullout sofas, can handle a family of three or four; a bigger splurge are the large Catalina mini-suites, which can easily handle four. Along with the 500 feet of beautiful beach (which can all but vanish during highest tides), there's a pool, summertime children's activities, and Splashes, a marvelous Mediterranean restaurant (with children's menu) facing the beach, with big windows and open shutters that allow not only a view but also an experience of the sea air. Downtown Laguna is a few blocks' walk.

1555 S. Coast Highway, Laguna Beach; (949) 497-4477 or (800) 524-8621. Room rates $270–330; suites $435–635; children under 18 stay free.

Vacation Village

This older, family-run hotel is the beachfront location of choice for families who can't swing the steeper fares at the Surf and Sand or Ritz-Carlton—and many of these families have been returning for years. The 130-room, medium-rise hotel sits right on the sand, though that sand vanishes at high tide, when the waves lick the hotel's foundation and everyone moves camp to one of the two compact pools or walks a few blocks into downtown Laguna for a shopping expedition. Rooms come with coffee-makers, small refrigerators, and movie channels; the family suites have complete kitchens. Since this is an aging, moderately priced place, guests accept that some rooms are small, that bathrooms are basic, and that corridors and rooms bear traces of that motel-disinfectant smell.

647 S. Coast Highway, Laguna Beach; (949) 497-4477 or (800) 843-6895. Room rates $140–300; family suites start at $290.

NEWPORT BEACH

Best Western Bay Shores Inn

Location is king, say the realtors, and this modest motel has location in spades—it's one block to Newport Bay and, in the other direction, one block to the ocean-side beach. To make up for the lack of a pool, the motel supplies everything you need for the beach, including towels, body boards, chairs, and umbrellas. Other extras include a good breakfast buffet and in-room VCRs supplied with a free video library. The 21 rooms are basic and relatively small; four of you can fit in a room with two doubles, but just barely. But you don't come here to hang out in your room. If you have a big group, consider splurging on the two-bedroom suite, which has a full kitchen and a dining room.

1800 W. Balboa Boulevard, Newport Beach; (949) 675-3463 or (800) 222-6675; www.thebestinn.com. Summer rates start at $219 per room or $299 per suite; kids under 12 stay free in parents' room.

Newport Dunes Resort

This private campground is so fun for families that it rates its own listing under Best Beaches and Parks (see page 82). Along with all the amenities described there, it has RV and tent sites (free-standing tents only—no stakes allowed), windsurfing lessons, picnic facilities, barbecues, changing rooms, a restaurant, a market, and a boat launch. Reservations for the summer are taken from January 1 on, so call early for a prime time.

1131 Back Bay Drive, Newport Beach; (949) 729-3863; reservations (800) 765-7661. In summer, tent sites $39–44 weekday, $40–46 weekends; higher on holidays.

Newporter Hyatt

The nearby Four Seasons may be a bit more swank, but for families, this is the best resort hotel in Newport. It's attractive and upscale but not too fussy; the 410 rooms and suites are spread over 26 acres, surrounded by lawns, flowers, trees, and all sorts of amusements. Like the three pools, one just for kids. Or the tennis courts. Or the Ping-Pong table, shuffleboard court, and nine-hole golf course. Or the bike-rental shop, which will steer you to the path connecting to the superb Upper Newport Bay Ecological Reserve (see Best Beaches and Parks, page 83). On weekends, the Camp Hyatt program offers supervised activities for kids ages 3–15, ranging from poolside games, to arts and crafts, to Friday and Saturday night pizza-and-movie gatherings; prices vary, $25–30. The amusements at Newport Dunes (see Best Beaches and Parks, page 82) are just across the street, and shuttles will deliver your family to Balboa's Fun Zone and Fashion Island.

1107 Jamboree Road, Newport Beach; (949) 729-1234 or (800) 233-1234. Rates start at $224; half-price adjoining rooms are sometimes available.

Attractions

Balboa Fun Zone

600 E. Bay Avenue, Balboa; (949) 673-0408

Hours: Monday–Thursday, noon–8 pm; Friday, noon–9 pm; Saturday, 11 a.m.–10 p.m.; Sunday, 11 a.m.–8 p.m.

Admission: Free; rides are $1–2

Appeal by Age Groups:

Pre-school	Grade School	Teens	Young Adults	Over 30	Seniors
★★★	★★★★	★★★	★★	★★	★★

Touring Time: Average 3 hours, with ferry ride; minimum 1½ hours

Rainy-Day Touring: No

Services and Facilities:

Restaurants Yes	Lockers In Laser Tag
Alcoholic beverages Yes	Pet kennels No; pets on leash
Disabled access Yes	Rain check Yes
Wheelchair rental No	Private tours On the boats
Baby stroller rental No	

Description and Comments On the waterfront near the Balboa Pier and Balboa Pavilion is a little amusement park full of small-town, old-fashioned charm. There's a Ferris wheel, a merry-go-round, bumper cars, a moon bounce, arcade games, laser tag, and such art projects as spin paintings. One of the fondest memories of my childhood is getting a "Balboa bar," a precursor to the Häagen-Dazs bar, that's as popular as ever.

Almost as fun as the Fun Zone is a ride over to Balboa Island on the Balboa Island Ferry, (949) 673-1070, which leaves right near the Fun Zone. It's a short, picturesque, little-kid-size ride to the island; kids ages 5–11 ride for just 25¢, and adults ride for 50¢. The island itself doesn't have much for kids, but if you bring bikes over on the ferry, it's great fun to pedal around the Lilliputian streets.

Wild Rivers Waterpark

8770 Irvine Center Drive, Irvine; (949) 768-9453; www.wildrivers.com

Hours: Mid-June to early September, open daily 10 a.m.–8 p.m.; limited hours available from mid-May to the prime season and in the post-season through September.

Admission: $23, $18 for children 48" or shorter, $10 seniors 55+ and for all ages after 4 p.m. in summer

Appeal by Age Groups:

Pre-school	Grade School	Teens	Young Adults	Over 30	Seniors
★★★★★	★★★★★	★★★★★	★★★★	★★★★	★★★

Touring Time: Average 4 hours, 6 for school age and up; minimum 2 hours, 4 for school age and up

Rainy-Day Touring: No

Services and Facilities:

Restaurants Yes	Lockers $4 small, $6 large
Alcoholic beverages No	Pet kennels No
Disabled access Limited	Rain check No
Wheelchair rental No	Private tours No
Baby stroller rental No	

Description and Comments   When Anaheim starts to swelter, and the sand burns your feet at Balboa, consider a trip to this first-rate water park, which has something for every age group. At about a foot deep, Pygmy Pond keeps the little ones happy, with its small, not-scary water slides, inner-tube rides, gorilla swing, and climbing structure that shoots out water. Older, braver kids will go for Surf Hills, which they can belly-slide down; the swimming pool with a water-basketball hoop; and the wave pools, which generate real waves. The bravest of all can tackle the vertical drops, rapids, and enclosed tunnel slides. All in all there are more than 40 rides, along with two swimming pools. If you don't want to eat at the restaurants, there's a picnic area outside the entrance.

Family-Friendly Restaurants

LAGUNA BEACH

THE COTTAGE

308 N. Coast Highway, Laguna Beach; (949) 494-3023

Meals served: Breakfast, Sunday brunch, lunch, and dinner
Cuisine: American
Entree range: $5–10 (breakfast and lunch); $7–20 (dinner)
Children's menu: Yes
Reservations: Not accepted
Payment: All major credit cards

There's always a crowd at this handsome old Arts and Crafts bungalow in north Laguna, thanks to the family-style conviviality and generous, simple food. Breakfast is the real draw (and the most crowded), not because the waffles and eggs are that memorable (they're fine) but because it's hard to find a solid breakfast in this upscale town.

RUBY'S

30622 S. Pacific Coast Highway, Laguna Beach; (949) 497-7829

Meals served: Breakfast, lunch, and dinner
Cuisine: American
Entree range: $3–8 (breakfast); $4.50–12.50 (lunch and dinner)
Children's menu: Yes
Reservations: No
Payment: All major credit cards

South of the town center—which means parking is free and plentiful—this is the hottest kid restaurant in Laguna. The gleaming 1940s and 1950s cars in the parking lot set the stage for the neo-sockhop theme: oldies music, big vinyl booths, uniformed waitresses, old Coke ads, model trains, and shameless catering to children, who find the food to be way more delicious than their parents do.

TACO LOCO

640 S. Coast Highway, Laguna Beach; (949) 497-1635

Meals served: Lunch and dinner
Cuisine: Mexican
Entree range: $3–9.95 (lunch and dinner)
Children's menu: No
Reservations: Not accepted
Payment: All major credit cards

If your teen wants to hang with the coolest surfers, come to this sidewalk cafe, where you'll find the best Mexican street food in town, along with hip Southwestern and Californian dishes; you can have a calamari quesadilla while your kids try a carne asada burrito. The food is so good that regular customer Jimmy Buffett hired the owner to cater his road tours.

TORTILLA FLATS

1740 Coast Highway, Laguna Beach; (949) 494-6588

Meals served: Breakfast, lunch, and dinner
Cuisine: Mexican
Entree range: $6.95–11.95 (lunch and dinner)

Children's menu: Yes
Reservations: Not necessary
Payment: AE, MC, V

A sprawling, atmospheric hacienda, with tile floors, painted walls, splashing fountains, and lots of greenery, Tortilla Flats is a Mexican restaurant in the style of the Acapulco chain, only better. A great spot for a casually upscale family dinner out, with good service, tasty food, and a family atmosphere.

WAHOO'S FISH TACOS

1133 S. Coast Highway, Laguna Beach; (949) 497-0033

Meals served: Lunch and dinner
Cuisine: Mexican
Entree range: $3.25–6.95 (lunch and dinner)
Children's menu: Yes
Reservations: Not accepted
Payment: MC, V

Everybody loves Wahoo's: little kids, who get their own menu; big kids, who love both the food and the grunge surfer decor; parents, who can have fresh-fish (not fried) tacos or burritos and a cold Corona while the kids have quesadillas and fries; and Laguna's surfers, who would surely starve if not for Wahoo's tasty, cheap Mexican food with a Hawaiian accent (the "da plate" lunch specials are good). This is an order-at-the-counter, throw a T-shirt-over-your-bathing-suit kind of place, well located between Main Beach and the Surf & Sand Hotel.

Newport Beach

B.J.'S CHICAGO PIZZERIA

106 Main Street, Balboa Peninsula; (949) 675-7560

Meals served: Lunch and dinner
Cuisine: Italian
Entree range: $3.95–6.95 (lunch); $6.95–17.95 (dinner)
Children's menu: Yes
Reservations: No
Payment: AE, MC, V, DC

Tasty thick-crust pizza is the draw here, as is the great location a half-block from Balboa Pier. Other pluses are a pretty good salad bar, kid-size pizzas and pastas, and boisterous camaraderie. Expect a wait, especially on summer weekends.

CRAB COOKER

2200 Newport Boulevard, Newport Beach; (949) 673-0100

Meals served: Lunch and dinner
Cuisine: Seafood
Entree range: $8–26.95 (lunch and dinner)
Children's menu: No, but there is a "Light Eaters" plate
Reservations: Not accepted
Payment: AE, V, D

A classic beach dive, the Crab Cooker is beloved of locals and tourists alike. The plates are paper, the prices are rock bottom, and the food (mesquite-grilled fresh fish, clam chowder, crab legs, sourdough bread) is mighty fine. Expect to wait in line.

DAILY GRILL

Fashion Island, 957 Newport Center Drive, Newport Beach; (949) 644-2223

Meals served: Lunch, dinner, and Sunday brunch
Cuisine: American
Entree range: $12.95 (Sunday brunch); $7–12.95 (lunch); $8–16.95 (dinner)
Children's menu: Yes
Reservations: Yes
Payment: AE, DC, MC, V

Success came quickly to this small California chain of updated bar and grill restaurants, thanks in part to its recognition that baby boomers like to take their kids out to eat. Little kids get their own menu, big kids can get a chicken pot pie or turkey meat loaf, and parents can get a drink and wonderful crab cakes. Avoid the pastas.

EL TORITO GRILL

Fashion Island, 951 Newport Center Drive, Newport Beach; (949) 640-2875

Meals served: Lunch and dinner daily; Sunday buffet brunch
Cuisine: Southwestern
Entree range: $12.95 adults/$5.95 children (Sunday brunch); $8–14 (lunch); $10–16 (dinner)
Children's menu: Yes
Reservations: Accepted but not necessary
Payment: All major credit cards

More Southwestern than Mexican, this offshoot of the El Torito chain of Mexican restaurants is a bit more upscale than its parent, but it's still family-oriented. Colorful, noisy, and friendly, it's a good spot for nachos, fajitas, red-corn taquitos, great carnitas, and spicy chicken dishes. Parents get hand-shaken margaritas, and the kids get coloring supplies and their own burritos and tacos, as well as such standards as chicken fingers; children's meals even come with fresh fruit.

RUBY'S

#1 Balboa Pier, Newport Beach; (949) 675-7829

Meals served: Breakfast, lunch, and dinner
Cuisine: American
Entree range: $5–7 (lunch and dinner)
Children's menu: Yes
Reservations: Not accepted
Payment: All major credit cards

The original of the 1940s-diner chain (see reviews in Laguna and San Juan), and the best located, smack on the end of the Balboa Pier. Get a table outside, soak in the view, drink a chocolate shake, have a good time.

Huntington Beach

Miles from the freeways, **Huntington Beach**, the original Surf City and the archetypal beach town, is as lively as it gets because the pier and the commercial section of town are contiguous. This means beach-goers can roll up their towels and head across the street for a frozen yogurt or to shop for surfwear. It also means an ongoing sense of festivity, enhanced by the city's near-constant schedule of concerts and art fairs during the summer. Do you have kids who never want to come out of the water? You don't have to hassle them here. Huntington Beach is one of the few places where you can still build a fire on the beach (it's open until 10 p.m.), so grab a fire ring early in the day and bring hot dogs, marshmallows, guitars, and blankets for an unforgettable summer evening. To learn more about the beach, see **Bolsa Chica** and **Huntington State Beaches** under Best Beaches and Parks, pages 81–82.

Family Lodging
Waterfront Hilton Beach Resort
Its high-rise design doesn't suit low-key Huntington Beach, but otherwise this 290-room hotel is a convenient resort, across the highway from the beach, with pedestrian and bike access to the bike trails and sand. The rooms are attractive and comfortable, the views can be great, and between the beach and the pool, kids have plenty to do. In fact, kids are catered to. The summertime program, Vacation Station, is the basic (but free) roster of supervised crafts, pool games, and such, for kids ages 5–10; kids can attend Dolphin Youth Club on weekend nights, when for $10 they get dinner and supervised fun.

21100 Pacific Coast Highway, Huntington Beach; (714) 960-7873 or (800) 822-SURF. Rates $169–254; kids under 18 free.

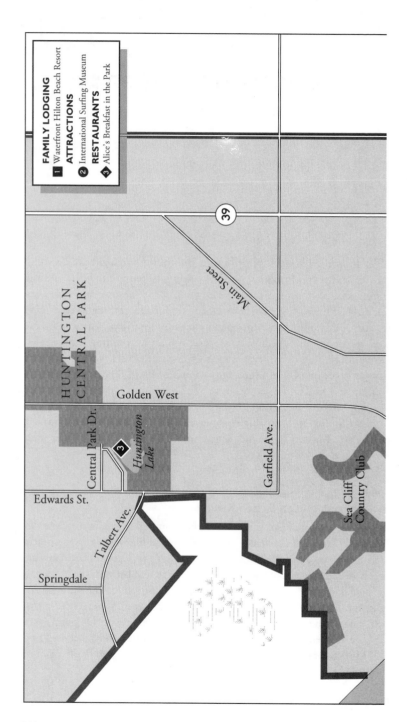

FAMILY LODGING
1 Waterfront Hilton Beach Resort
ATTRACTIONS
2 International Surfing Museum
RESTAURANTS
3 Alice's Breakfast in the Park

39

HUNTINGTON
CENTRAL PARK

Main Street

Golden West

Central Park Dr.

Huntington
Lake

3

Garfield Ave.

Edwards St.

Talbert Ave.

Sea Cliff
Country Club

Springdale

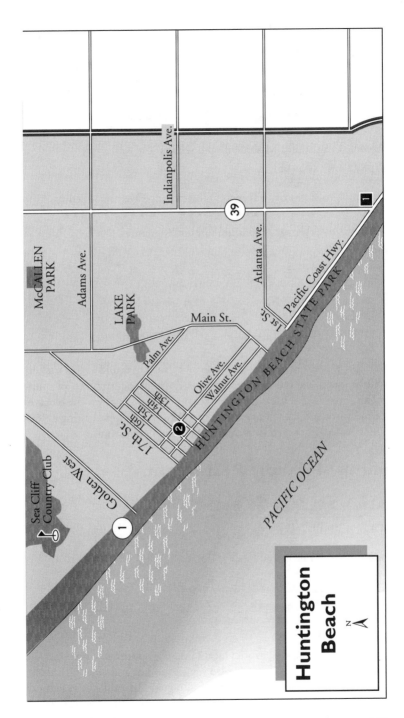

Huntington Beach

N

McCALLEN PARK

Adams Ave.

LAKE PARK

Indianpolis Ave.

Atlanta Ave.

39

Main St.

Palm Ave.

Olive Ave.

Walnut Ave.

1st St.

Pacific Coast Hwy.

17th St.

16th

15th

14th

13th

2

HUNTINGTON BEACH STATE PARK

Golden West

Sea Cliff Country Club

1

PACIFIC OCEAN

1

Attraction

International Surfing Museum

411 Olive Street, Huntington Beach; (714) 960-3483

Hours: June–September, daily noon–5 p.m.; October–May,
Wednesday–Sunday noon–5 p.m.

Admission: $2 adults, $1 students and seniors

Appeal by Age Groups:

Pre-school	Grade School	Teens	Young Adults	Over 30	Seniors
★	★★	★★★	★★★	★★★	★★★

Touring Time: Average 1 hour; minimum 30 minutes

Rainy-Day Touring: Yes

Services and Facilities:

Restaurants Many nearby	Lockers No
Alcoholic beverages No	Pet kennels No
Disabled access Yes	Rain check No
Wheelchair rental No	Private tours No
Baby stroller rental No	

Description and Comments   The history of surfing is told at this friendly
little museum, via old photographs, text, surf music, trophies, old surfboards, even Dick Dale's guitar. After your visit, walk down the block to
see the Surfer's Walk of Fame. Note that the Overall Appeal rating applies
only if you're interested in surfing; otherwise the museum's a snooze.

Family-Friendly Restaurant

ALICE'S BREAKFAST IN THE PARK

6622 Lakeview Drive, Huntington Beach; (714) 848-0690

Meals served: Breakfast and lunch
Cuisine: American
Entree range: $5–6.95 (breakfast and lunch)
Children's menu: Yes
Reservations: Necessary on weekends
Payment: No credit cards

Breakfast is often a kid's favorite meal to eat out, especially a breakfast like
this: huge cinnamon rolls, scrambled eggs, pancakes, and other such treats,
served on a patio next to the lake in Huntington Central Park, so kids can
run around and feed the ducks in between bites. After breakfast (or lunch),
spend a couple of hours exploring the lovely park and the excellent library.

North County: Anaheim, Buena Park, and Santa Ana

The inland area of northern Orange County would not be on any tourist's list if not for the ever-expanding **Disneyland/Knott's** nexus. It's a sprawl of several former agricultural town centers, now linked by residential areas that are generally more working-class than the expensive neighborhoods by the sea. It's an ethnically diverse region: Santa Ana is home to many Latino immigrants, and Westminister is known for its large Vietnamese community. But northern Orange County is not known for its natural beauty—**Anaheim** is notable for its 150-plus hotels, most of which are cardboard-box motels (although some now qualify as vintage examples of 1950s and 1960s kitsch architecture), and **Buena Park** is flat and featureless, an easy place to get lost under the glaringly reflective summer sun. But if you have kids, you will be forced to visit the north county, because that's where you'll find Disneyland Resort and Knott's Berry Farm, along with such lesser amusements as **Adventure City** and **Wild Bill's** theme restaurant.

By all means plan an overnight stay in Anaheim; Disneyland is best enjoyed over a two-day period, with a cool, quiet hotel room in which the family can retreat. Note that in season, Angels baseball games at Anaheim Stadium and Mighty Ducks hockey games at Anaheim Pond are nearby, and that the new water park at Knott's, Soak City, offers the contrast of a day of water play. Don't try (as some do) to fit **Universal Studios,** Disneyland, and Knott's into a sequential three-day period. Theme parks need the space of some nature days in between or it will all be a blur to your kids. If you have very young children, under age five, they will enjoy the woodsy atmosphere and gentle rides of Camp Snoopy at Knott's or the birthday-party-park feel of Adventure City more than a bewildering day in the crowds swirling through the hugeness of Disneyland.

Just know that the beach is a half-hour drive or more, and the fun here is man-made. After a couple of days doing the theme-park thing in the

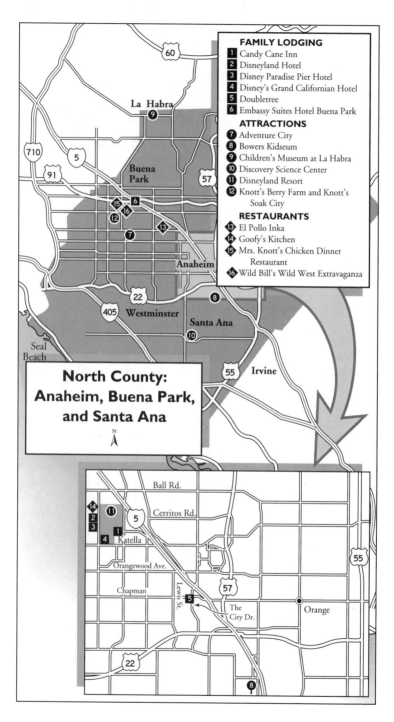

FAMILY LODGING

1. Candy Cane Inn
2. Disneyland Hotel
3. Disney Paradise Pier Hotel
4. Disney's Grand Californian Hotel
5. Doubletree
6. Embassy Suites Hotel Buena Park

ATTRACTIONS

7. Adventure City
8. Bowers Kidseum
9. Children's Museum at La Habra
10. Discovery Science Center
11. Disneyland Resort
12. Knott's Berry Farm and Knott's Soak City

RESTAURANTS

13. El Pollo Inka
14. Goofy's Kitchen
15. Mrs. Knott's Chicken Dinner Restaurant
16. Wild Bill's Wild West Extravaganza

North County: Anaheim, Buena Park, and Santa Ana

N

north county, head to the beach communities to experience another side of Orange County.

Family Lodging

Candy Cane Inn

A good bargain well located near Disneyland's parking lot, the Candy Cane is freshly spruced up. The rooms are motel basic; it's worth the $10 splurge for a deluxe room, which comes with a fridge and coffeemaker. One of the deluxe rooms can sleep five, if you pay an extra $10 for a rollaway. Rates include a continental breakfast and shuttles to Disneyland. Outside is a heated pool and a wading pool for little ones. Ask about packages including Disneyland tickets. Free parking.

1747 S. Harbor Boulevard, Anaheim; (714) 774-5284 or (800) 345-7057. Room rates $74 standard, $84 deluxe.

Disneyland Hotel

A gigantic annex to the park, connected by monorail (very nice for nappers), offering clean, comfortable, reasonably updated rooms in which to sleep off too many long lines. Younger children will enjoy a stay here as much as a trip across the street, thanks to the several pools, the little faux sand beach complete with pedalboats, the fish ponds, the gift shops, and Goofy's Kitchen (see page 133). Children under 17 stay free in parents' rooms; ask about hotel-park packages. And remember that most days, guests here are allowed into Disneyland an hour before the ordinary folk, which alone is worth a stay in busy times.

1150 W. Cerritos Avenue, Anaheim; (714) 778-6600 or (714) 956-6425. Rates $180–215.

Disney Paradise Pier Hotel

Like the Disneyland Hotel, this is officially part of the Magic Kingdom. We prefer it to its sibling, because it's less than half the size and is therefore quieter and less overwhelming, with more attractive rooms. The food is better, too. There aren't as many amusements, but you can make do with the pool, workout room, video games, several restaurants and lounges, and shops, as well as direct access to Disneyland.

1717 S. West Street, Anaheim; (714) 956-6425. Rates $180–215.

Disney's Grand Californian Hotel

Scheduled to open in January 2001, Disney's Grand Californian Hotel supplants the Disneyland Hotel as Disneyland's prestigious lodging property. The new 751-room luxury hotel is designed in the image of a rustic national park lodge and offers three swimming pools, a health club, and restaurants.

1600 South Disneyland Drive, Anaheim; (714) 956-6425. Rates $265–410.

Doubletree

This upper-mid-level hotel gives Disney-bound families a lot of bang for the buck. Aside from the nice but basic pool, there's a cool outdoor lagoon that's the size of several pools; other extras include two tennis courts, a fitness center, Nintendo in every room, free shuttles to Disneyland and local malls, in-room coffeemakers, and packages that include Disneyland tickets. The 454 rooms (and 11 suites) are well equipped and reasonably large.

100 The City Drive, Anaheim; (714) 634-4500 or (800) 222-8733. Rates are $89–130 (more with breakfast); kids under 18 stay free in parents' room.

Embassy Suites Hotel Buena Park

One of the best theme-park experiences we ever had was a day at Knott's with two nights here. This 202-suite facility is a four-story building surrounding a landscaped courtyard with pool and spa, and it's within walking distance of Knott's. We checked in the night before, enjoyed the cooked-to-order breakfast in the dining room (included in room rate), left the car in the (free) lot, and headed to Knott's. When we'd had our fill of the park, we got a chicken takeout dinner from Mrs. Knott's (far better than the restaurant, really), called the hotel shuttle, and returned to the hotel. We ate dinner in our dining area in the suite, then headed down (with bunches of other families) for a night swim and whirlpool soak.

7762 Beach Boulevard, Buena Park; (714) 739-5600; fax (714) 521-9650. Rates start at $119.

Attractions

Adventure City

10120 S. Beach Boulevard, Stanton; (714) 236-9300

Hours: In the off-season, Friday 10 a.m.–5 p.m., Saturday and Sunday 11 a.m.–7 p.m.; in summer, Monday–Friday 10 a.m.–5 p.m., Saturday 11 a.m.–9 p.m., Sunday 11 a.m.–8 p.m.

Admission: $11.95, $8.95 for seniors, free for children 1 and under; includes face painting, puppet shows, and theater

Appeal by Age Groups:

Pre-school	Grade School	Teens	Young Adults	Over 30	Seniors
★★★★	★★★	★	★	★	★

Touring Time: Average 3 hours; minimum 2 hours

Rainy-Day Touring: Not great

Services and Facilities:

Restaurants Yes, basic	Lockers Yes
Alcoholic beverages No	Pet kennels No
Disabled access Yes	Rain check No
Wheelchair rental No	Private tours Yes
Baby stroller rental No	

Description and Comments All it takes is that first visit to Disneyland with a three-year-old to understand that the Magic Kingdom is really for older kids—it can be an overwhelming and very scary place, overrun with huge mute cartoon characters and dark, fast rides. Enter this compact kiddieland in Stanton (next door to Anaheim), adjacent to the parent Hobby City, a retail center for collectors and hobbyists. It's designed with the three-year-old in mind, and while it's a dreadful bore for teens, it's heaven for little ones.

The roller coaster is small and not too intense, and the mini–Ferris wheel is so tame it's called the Giggle Wheel. In the 911 ride, they get to dress up in firefighter and police gear, climb in a kid-scaled fire truck, and listen to dispatcher calls. Trains are a big deal here, from the 1938 open-air choo-choo ride that circles the park to the new Thomas the Tank Engine play island. When it's time to sit down, head for a puppet show or one of the entertaining (to young ones) stage shows. Needless to say, this place is extremely popular for birthday parties. Be warned that there's an arcade, in the Chuck E. Cheese vein, so steer game-ticket-obsessed kids clear.

Bowers Kidseum

1802 N. Main Street, Santa Ana; (714) 480-1520

Hours: Thursday–Friday 2 p.m.–5 p.m., Saturday–Sunday 10 a.m.–
4 p.m.; hours may be expanded in summer

Admission: $8 adults, $6 senior/students, $4 children ages 5–12

Appeal by Age Groups:

Pre-school	Grade School	Teens	Young Adults	Over 30	Seniors
★★★	★★★★	★★	★★	★★	★★

Touring Time: Average 2½ hours hours; minimum 1 hour

Rainy-Day Touring: Yes

Services and Facilities:

Restaurants Yes	Baby stroller rental No
Alcoholic beverages No; only at Topaz Cafe	Lockers Items can be checked
Disabled access Yes	Pet kennels No
Wheelchair rental Yes, free	Rain check No
	Private tours By appt.

Description and Comments   A companion to the Bowers Museum of Cultural Art next door, this interactive museum brings to life the culture and art of Asia, Africa, and the Native Americans for elementary-school-age kids. They can try on masks, go into the Time Vault (an old bank vault), put on puppet shows in the theater, play strange musical instruments, and pretend to grind corn with an old stone mortar and pestle. Some of its best offerings are special events—storytelling, art classes, craft workshops—so call for a schedule before you plan a visit. These classes are geared for kids over age six, and they're especially good for ages 8–12; preschoolers will have fun in the interactive museum, but some of it will be above them.

The admission fee also includes the neighboring museum, so if your older kids are ready for more, browse through and look at its beadwork, carvings, sculptures, and costumes from around the world.

If you're touring at lunchtime be sure to stop in at the Topaz Cafe. *Gourmet* magazine has called it "one of the best restaurants in a museum in the country."

Children's Museum at La Habra

301 S. Euclid Street, La Habra; (562) 905-9793
Hours: Monday–Saturday 10 a.m.–5 p.m., Sunday 1–5 p.m.
Admission: $4 for ages 2 and older
Appeal by Age Groups:

Pre-school	Grade School	Teens	Young Adults	Over 30	Seniors
★★★★★	★★★★	★★	★	★	★

Touring Time: Average 2½ hours; minimum 1 hour
Rainy-Day Touring: Yes
Services and Facilities:

Restaurants Picnic area and restaurants nearby	Baby stroller rental No
	Lockers Cubbyholes
Alcoholic beverages No	Pet kennels No
Disabled access Yes (1 room not accessible)	Rain check No
	Private tours No
Wheelchair rental No	

Description and Comments   On more than one occasion I've loaded the kids in the car and headed to La Habra, bypassing the other children's museums closer to home. It occupies an old Union Pacific depot in a quiet neighborhood, and it's full of wonderful hands-on activities. My kids' favorite is the theater area, complete with lots of costumes, a stage, and a lighting booth for impromptu performances. They also love the front half of a city bus, to drive, ride, and scramble in; the full-size train caboose; the kid-scale supermarket; and the science experiments. There's always a new interactive temporary exhibit, and there's a separate play area for under-fives.

Discovery Science Center

2500 Main Street, Santa Ana; (714) 542-2823

Hours: Daily 10 a.m.–5 p.m.

Admission: $9.50 adults, $7.50 children 3–17 and seniors 55+; additional $1 for admission to 3-D Laser Theater; parking $3

Appeal by Age Groups:

Pre-school	Grade School	Teens	Young Adults	Over 30	Seniors
★★	★★★★	★★★★	★★★	★★★	★★★

Touring Time: Average 3 hours; minimum 1 hour

Rainy-Day Touring: No

Services and Facilities:

Restaurants Yes	Lockers Yes
Alcoholic beverages No	Pet kennels No
Disabled access Yes	Rain check No
Wheelchair rental No	Private tours No
Baby stroller rental No	

Description and Comments This new interactive science museum is packed with 100 of the latest and greatest in cool, hands-on, science-based exhibits and experiences. What better way than to lie on a bed of nails to learn that the larger the area over which a force is distributed, the less pressure is exerted on any one point? Kids can hoist themselves up with pulleys, redirect an eight-foot-tall tornado by walking through it, experience an earthquake in the Shake Shack, learn about waves by touching the spinning Lariat Chain, and make their hair stand on end by putting one hand on the Van Der Graaff Generator. Special exhibits have included such things as Par for the Planet, an 18-hole miniature golf game in which kids learn about the natural world, from butterfly metamorphosis to water pollution. And unlike at many science museums, the preschool set gets its own area, with age-appropriate science, art, and dress-up activities.

Food service is limited, alas, to a Pizza Hut Express and a Taco Bell Express, and there isn't an outdoor picnic area. But that's a small quibble, given that this place is such a wonderful new addition to Orange County.

Disneyland Resort
Includes: Disneyland Park, Disney's California Adventure Theme Park, and Downtown Disney

1313 S. Harbor Boulevard, Anaheim; (714) 781-4565

Hours: Year-round 10 a.m.–6 p.m.; hours extended as early as 8 a.m. and as late as 1 a.m. during busy seasons

Admission: One-day pass: $41 ages 10 and over, $39 seniors (60 and over), $31 ages 3–9, free ages 2 and under

Appeal by Age Groups:

Pre-school	Grade School	Teens	Young Adults	Over 30	Seniors
★★★	★★★★★	★★★★★	★★★★★	★★★★	★★★

Touring Time: Disneyland Park: average 16 hours/2 days; minimum 7 hours. Disney's California Adventure: average 8 hours/1 day; minimum 5 hours

Rainy-Day Touring: Yes—a mildly rainy day can be great at the parks, because the crowds disappear and many rides are indoors

Services and Facilities:

Restaurants Yes	Baby stroller rental $7
Alcoholic beverages At Disney's California Adventure only	Lockers $1
	Pet kennels $10; no overnight
Disabled access Yes	Rain check No
Wheelchair rental $7; electric carts $30	Private tours Yes

Description and Comments   In February of 2001 the Walt Disney Company will unveil its second theme park, Disney's California Adventure, on the Disneyland property. The opening caps an ambitious expansion of Disneyland that also includes new hotels and Downtown Disney, a dining, shopping, and entertainment complex. The entrances of Disneyland Park and Disney's California Adventure face each other across a palm-studded pedestrian plaza called the Esplanade. The Esplanade begins at Harbor Boulevard and runs west, passing into Downtown Disney, which you can visit without paying admission. From Downtown Disney the pedestrian thoroughfare continues to the new monorail station and to the Disneyland and Paradise Pier Hotels.

Disney's California Adventure, already known as "DCA" among Disneyphiles, is built on 55 acres (including a sizeable carve-out for the Grand Californian Hotel), quite a small park by modern theme park standards. The theme, celebrating all things (okay, okay, most things) Californian, is infinitely flexible, allowing Disney to offer diverse attractions that would not go well together under any other umbrella. Unfortunately, there's precious little new technology at work in Disney's newest theme park. Of the headliner attractions, only one, Soarin' Over California (a simulator ride), breaks new ground. All the rest are recycled, albeit popular, attractions from the Animal Kingdom and Disney-MGM Studios. When you move to the smaller-statured second half of the attraction batting order, it gets worse. Most of these attractions are little more than off-the-shelf midway rides spruced up with a Disney story line and façade.

Seen from overhead, Disney's California Adventure is roughly arrayed in a fan shape around the park's visual icon, Grizzly Peak (yet another of Disney's "mountains"). At ground level, however, the park's layout is not so obvious. From the Esplanade you pass through huge block letters spelling "California" and under a whimsical representation of the Golden Gate Bridge, over which the monorail passes. To your left and right you'll find guest services as well as some shops and eateries.

Comparable to Main Street at Disneyland Park, but not as long, the entranceway leads to a central hub where pedestrian thoroughfares branch like spokes to the various theme areas. "Lands" at DCA are called "districts," and there are three of them. A left turn at the hub leads you to the Hollywood Pictures Backlot district of the park, celebrating California's history as the film capital of the world. All other paths lead to the Golden State district of the park. Golden State is a somewhat amorphous combination of separate theme areas that showcase California's architecture, agriculture, industry, history, and natural resources. Within the Golden State district you'll find Condor Flats by taking the first right as you approach the hub. Grizzly Peak will likewise be to your right, though you must walk two-thirds of the way around the mountain to reach its attractions. The entrance to Bountiful Valley Farm branches off the central hub at about five o'clock, as does Golden Vine Winery. The remaining two Golden State theme areas, The Bay Area and Pacific Wharf, are situated along a kidney-shaped lake and can be accessed by following the walkway emanating from the hub at seven o'clock and winding around Grizzly Peak. The third district, Paradise Pier, recalls seaside amusement parks of the first half of the twentieth century. It is situated in the southwest corner of the park, across the lake from The Bay Area.

From a competitive perspective, Disney's California Adventure is an underwhelming shot at Disney's three Southern California competitors. The Hollywood section of DCA takes a hopeful poke at Universal Studios Hollywood, while Paradise Pier offers midway rides à la Six Flags Magic Mountain. Finally, the whole California theme has for years been the eminent domain of Knott's Berry Farm. In short, there's not much originality in DCA, only Disney's now-redundant mantra that "whatever they can do, we can do better."

We can't possibly do Disneyland and its two theme parks justice in this format; for the complete and inside scoop, pick up our sister book,

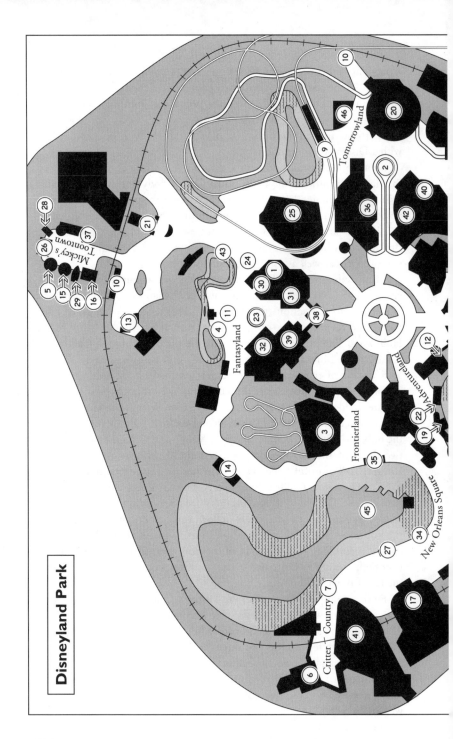

Disneyland Park

Mickey's Toontown

Tomorrowland

Fantasyland

Adventureland

Frontierland

New Orleans Square

Critter Country

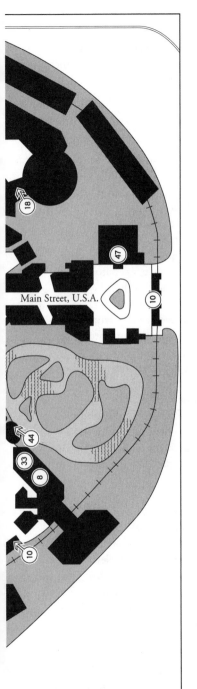

Main Street, U.S.A.

1. Alice in Wonderland
2. Astro Orbiter
3. Big Thunder Mountain Railroad
4. Casey Jr. Circus Train
5. Chip 'n' Dale's Treehouse
6. Country Bear Playhouse
7. Davy Crockett's Explorer Canoes
8. Disney Gallery
9. Disneyland Monorail
10. Disneyland Railroad
11. Dumbo, the Flying Elephant
12. *Enchanted Tiki Room*
13. Fantasyland Theatre
14. Festival of Fools
15. Gadget's Go Coaster
16. Goofy's Bounce House
17. Haunted Mansion
18. *Honey, I Shrunk the Audience*
19. Indiana Jones Adventure
20. Innoventions
21. It's a Small World
22. Jungle Cruise
23. King Arthur Carrousel
24. Mad Tea Party
25. Matterhorn Bobsleds
26. Mickey's House
27. Mike Fink Keelboats
28. Minnie's House
29. *Miss Daisy*
30. Mr. Toad's Wild Ride
31. Peter Pan's Flight
32. Pinocchio's Daring Journey
33. Pirates of the Caribbean
34. Rafts to Tom Sawyer Island
35. Riverboat and Sailing Ship
36. Rocket Rods
37. Roger Rabbit's Car Toon Spin
38. Sleeping Beauty Castle
39. Snow White's Scary Adventures
40. Space Mountain
41. Splash Mountain
42. Star Tours
43. Storybook Land Canal Boats
44. Tarzan's Treehouse
45. Tom Sawyer Island
46. Tomorrowland Autopia
47. *The Walt Disney Story*

125

The Unofficial Guide to Disneyland. If you have children and you're breathing, you know the basics of what Disneyland Park has to offer, from the atmospheric charms of Pirates of the Caribbean to the thrills of Splash Mountain, and the foregoing discussion of DCA should suffice as an overview of the new park. Therefore, instead of taking you through both parks in detail, we'll give you some tips and advice for how to best plan for the parks with each age group of kids.

1. Four-year-olds want to go to Disneyland Park only because their parents or their preschool friends tell them they want to go. Much of Disneyland Park is overwhelming, exhausting, and scary for kids under age six; in its research, *The Unofficial Guide to Disneyland* found that more than half of all kids that age are afraid of the characters (i.e., Mickey, Goofy, Pooh) that roam the park, which often catches parents by surprise. (But wouldn't you be alarmed if a mute, stuffed [but clearly alive] creature four times your size loomed near?) If your dream dictates that you take your little one to Disneyland Park, that's fine, but realize that the park is really designed for kids ages seven and older.

Disney's California Adventure is aimed at an even more mature audience. Though it offers several children's play areas, it has comparatively little to offer four-and-unders.

2. Consider a stay at a Disney hotel during busier seasons—on most days, you'll be granted early access to the parks as part of your overnight stay privileges, so you can do some of the most popular rides before the crowds descend. The monorail access back and forth (to Disneyland Park only) is also a fun and convenient way to break up the day. Kids object less strenuously to leaving for a few hours in the heat of the afternoon if it's to ride the monorail to take a swim (and of course a nap). The restaurants in the hotels and at Downtown Disney are less crowded than the food service areas in the parks during peak times, too.

3. Some 12 million people a year visit Disneyland, and on some days it seems like every one of them is waiting in your line. We locals know that the best time to visit is in the first three weeks of December. (Conversely, the parks' busiest season is the week between Christmas and New Year's.) The next best times to visit are from September to mid-November, January 4 through early March, and the week after Easter to Memorial Day (although we remember a particularly nasty crowd one early May weekday). Thursdays are the quietest day, and days that start with a drizzle (not pouring rain) are ideal. Visiting the Disneyland parks on a July weekend is a nightmare. Trust us. Don't do it.

4. Not all lines are created equal. Disneyland Park's oldest rides were built in the 1950s before it was known how huge the crowds of visitors would be, so they aren't set up to move large numbers of people through quickly. Although these Fantasyland rides are no longer popular with the

teen set, families (especially local parents who remember going on these rides as kids) often line up for Snow White or Peter Pan—and it can take forever to get in. Keep an eye out for when these lines are shortest. The rides built in the late 1960s—Small World, Pirates of the Caribbean, Haunted Mansion—have outdoor plaza areas built to accommodate lines that move more quickly. The newest rides—Indiana Jones, Splash Mountain, Tomorrowland rides—were built knowing that much of the ride time is spent in line, so the waiting areas are part of the ride structure itself (you won't see them from the entrance area), decorated and sometimes offering a bit of entertainment.

At Disney's California Adventure ride capacity and efficiency were sacrificed for eye appeal. Taking a step backwards, Disney loaded the park with midway rides, infamous for slow loading and long waits. Of 11 rides, only 2 move crowds efficiently. Fortunately, most of the shows and theater attractions can accommodate large numbers.

5. Here are our recommended sample days, by age group.

Under 6. To do Disneyland right with young children, think small and plan carefully. To avoid meltdowns, visit the park of your choice for a half-day and then return to your hotel for a swim and a nap, returning in the afternoon refreshed. Don't wander around the parks aimlessly, but head straight to the attractions best suited to young kids. At Disneyland Park with six-and-unders, we go right to Fantasyland and do Dumbo, Peter Pan, Pinocchio, Alice in Wonderland (usually twice, because there's no line), and, depending on their scary-tolerance, Mr. Toad's Wild Ride. Then it's lunch and a peaceful trip on It's a Small World, which is so cool and calm it makes for a good rest stop. Refreshed, we head to Mickey's Toontown to see Minnie's House, ride the dinky roller coaster, jump in Goofy's Bounce House, ride the trolley, and, if they aren't especially timid, do Roger Rabbit. (But if the crowds are bad we skip Toontown altogether, as it's impossible to understand its village setup when it's mobbed with people.) Then it's time for a cool drink and a souvenir stop near the exit gates, and the day is done. Any more with young kids is asking for trouble. Also with little ones, we establish a firm shopping policy. To prevent hours of panicked browsing through gift shops, we let our kids buy one toy or souvenir, but only at the very last stop before leaving. Before that, no shopping allowed.

Disney's California Adventure was not yet open at press time, but there is comparatively little of particular interest to the six-and-under crowd.

Early Elementary. For this age at Disneyland Park, we recommend a day alternating rides with shows and theme areas. Assuming that there's a too-scary limit for these kids but that they like a little thrill, we try to get them on Pirates of the Caribbean, Haunted Mansion, Indiana Jones, and Thunder Mountain as their "big" rides worth waiting in line for. In between the rides,

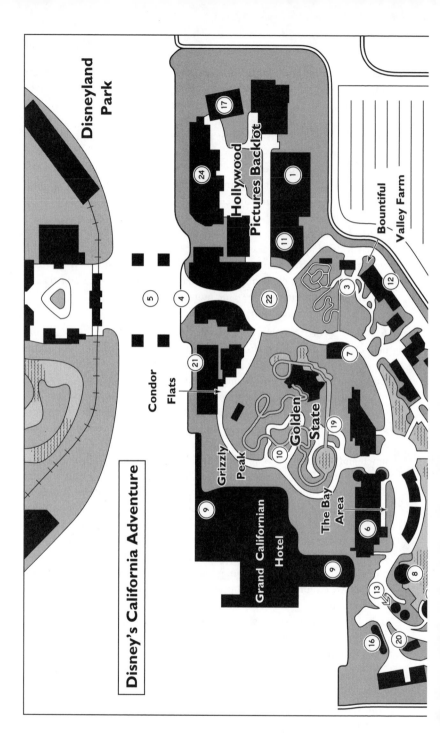

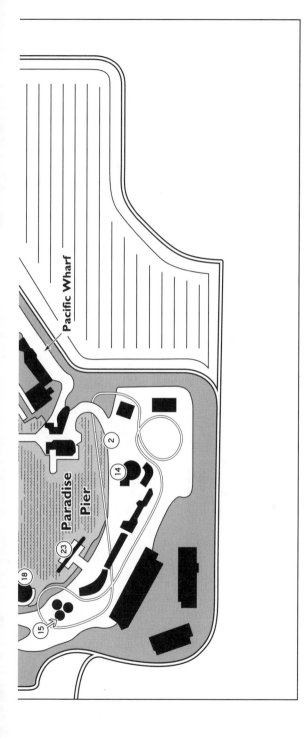

Pacific Wharf

Paradise Pier

1. Animation Building
2. California Screamin'
3. Demonstration Farm
4. Entrance
5. Esplanade
6. *Golden Dreams*
7. Golden Vine Winery
8. Golden Zephyr

9. Grand Californian Hotel
10. Grizzly River Run
11. Hyperion Theater
12. *It's Tough To Be A Bug!*
13. Jumpin' Jellyfish
14. King Triton's Carousel
15. Maliboomer
16. Mulholland Madness

17. *Muppet Vision 3-D*
18. Orange Stinger
19. Redwood Creek Challenge Trail
20. *S.S. Rustworthy*
21. Soarin' Over California
22. Sun Court (central hub)
23. Sun Wheel
24. Superstar Limo

we give them at least an hour for Tom Sawyer's Island (ride the raft over the water, run around the park-like trails, and see the fort) and take them to the Bear whatever-it-is Show, the Tiki Room, the Pocahontas show, Tarzan's Treehouse, and short-wait experiences like the excellent Honey, I Shrunk the Audience. We also schedule the nighttime parade and (if they're late stayeruppers) the unbelievably wonderful Fantasia spectacle over the waters in Frontierland. Getting good parade-type seats on the curbs, refreshments, and a chance to browse a souvenir shop while waiting (and while another family member saves places) make for a pretty good interlude. The park's live entertainment is excellent, and it imparts more of the Disney spirit this age group looks for than long hours in line for high-speed thrills.

At Disney's California Adventure, head for the Paradise Pier district of the park and sample the rides that appeal to your kids, then backtrack and catch the high-capacity rides. Save shows and theater attractions for last.

Older Elementary/Preteen. This age group, as is befitting, benefits from a half-and-half day. Kids ages ten and older with watches can be allowed to go off on their own in the parks for a few hours at a time, meeting parents (with younger kids to look after?) at designated times and places. When you first arrive at the park of your choice, discuss the park layout and the location of some key sites. Set early mealtime meeting places at a sit-down restaurant, and when you rendezvous, allow enough time for the kids to calm down and for you to assess their energy level. Let them have a half-hour leeway on the meeting time, so if they're in line for something, they don't have to get out in order to meet you; if you've picked a sit-down restaurant, you can relax comfortably while you wait for them. This age group can skip the parade and hustle off to the big-deal rides during that time, when the lines will be shorter. Another thing we've done with this group (because they like to go over and over again on a favorite ride) is bring a book and park ourselves on a bench while they do the rides and come check with us from time to time.

Teen. One of the few times when an ideal teen schedule fits into the world, a teen's trip to Disneyland should be almost the opposite of everyone else's. Don't make them get up early, but rather let them arrive at the park of their choice in late morning or early afternoon and stay until it closes (midnight and later in summer). Teens own the parks after dusk, and parents will love knowing that there's a safe place for kids this age to roam. (This is even more true of Knott's; see page 131.) If you have preteens and teens and you're staying at a Disneyland hotel, you can even retire with the preteens and let the teens walk or ride the last monorail back to the hotel.

6. *The Unofficial Guide to Disneyland,* also published by IDG Books Worldwide, offers in-depth information on both Disneyland Park and

Disney's California Adventure and provides step-by-step touring plans that will eliminate an average of three hours of waiting in line on a busy day. If you plan to visit during periods of moderate to high attendance, you'll find the guide indispensable.

Knott's Berry Farm

8039 Beach Boulevard, Buena Park; (714) 220-5220

Hours: October–May, Monday–Friday 10 a.m.–6 p.m., Saturday 10 a.m.–10 p.m, Sunday 10 a.m.–8 p.m.; in summer, Monday–Thursday 9 a.m.–8 p.m., Friday and Sunday 9 a.m.–10 p.m., Saturday 10 a.m.– 11 p.m..

Admission: $38 adults, $28 children ages 3–11 and seniors 60+

Appeal by Age Groups:

Pre- school	Grade School	Teens	Young Adults	Over 30	Seniors
★★★★	★★★★★	★★★★★	★★★★	★★★	★★★

Touring Time: Average 8 hours; minimum 4 hours

Rainy-Day Touring: Limited

Services and Facilities:

Restaurants Yes	Baby stroller rental Yes
Alcoholic beverages Yes	Lockers Yes
Disabled access Yes	Pet kennels No
Wheelchair rental Yes; call ahead for electric	Rain check No
	Private tours Yes

Description and Comments This really was a berry farm once upon a time, and today it takes pride in its claim to be the country's first theme park. The theme gets a little washed out from time to time, but in general the rides, shows, and amusements relate to early California and the Wild West.

Unlike Disneyland, Knott's can be great fun and not overwhelming for the 3–7-year-old set set, thanks to Camp Snoopy. Thoughtfully located close to the park's entrance, Camp Snoopy is a self-contained mini-park with rides scaled to little kids; my five-year-old is terrified of thrill rides, but she wanted to do this just-thrilling-enough little roller coaster over and over. She also loved the bumper cars, petting zoo, and Snoopy bounce. You can easily visit Camp Snoopy and then leave without dragging a cranky preschooler through other distractions.

If you have older kids, you'll want to explore the park's other areas, each of which has its own intense thrill rides. In Mexican-themed Fiesta Village, for instance, preteens and teens line up for Jaguar, a high-speed, 2,700-foot-long roller coaster; equally popular is Windjammer, a very intense dual-track roller coaster in the Boardwalk area. If you have timid kids, avoid Kingdom of the Dinosaurs; if you don't want to get wet, stay off the Roaring Rapids. If you have teens, they'll probably want to hang around the Boardwalk area, near some of the most intense thrill rides and full of midway games (which are too difficult, not to mention expensive, for younger kids).

What we most like about Knott's are the serendipitous items tucked around the park. Near Camp Snoopy, for instance, there's a trash can in the shape of a bear; when you walk by, it asks for trash, and when you put trash in its mouth, it thanks you. Our kids loved this bear so much that they went scavenging for trash. Elsewhere around the grounds you'll find a life-size great white shark; a ranger station (near Roaring Rapids) in which kids can hold insects and spiders; a one-room schoolhouse; informal blue-grass performances in the Old West Ghost Town; Native American artisans who will show kids how they make flutes, canoes, and jewelry; and a col-lection of Native American teepees and tents in which kids can play. And hokey though it is, they all love panning for gold, even jaded 15-year-olds. One daughter spent an hour watching in fascination as other visitors cracked open geodes with a hammer before finally deciding on which rock to select for herself and see what crystals lurked inside.

One caveat: Even though it's not as nationally famous as Disneyland, Knott's can also attract fearsome crowds. Camp Snoopy is labor-intensive, requiring you to help toddlers up and down steps; the lines don't move quickly when it's crowded, and it loses much of its appeal to four-year-olds who spend all their time waiting in line. If possible, visit on a weekday, first thing in the morning.

This is a very good park for teens, with music, dancing, and special shows and holiday events (sometimes requiring separate nighttime admis-sion). You really can drop 'em off and pick 'em up later.

Knott's Soak City

8039 Beach Boulevard, Buena Park; (714) 220-5220; www.soakcity.com

Hours: June 17–September 4 daily, September 9–24 weekends; June hours 10 a.m.–6 p.m, July–Labor Day 10 a.m.–8 p.m., September weekends noon–8 p.m.

Admission: $19.95 adults, $13.95 children ages 3–11; $7 parking; after 3 p.m. $11.95 all ages

Appeal by Age Groups:

Pre-school	Grade School	Teens	Young Adults	Over 30	Seniors
★★	★★★★	★★★★	★★★★	★★★★	★★

Touring Time: Average 4–6 hours; minimum 1 hour

Rainy-Day Touring: Limited

Services and Facilities:

Restaurants Snack bars	Lockers Yes
Alcoholic beverages No	Pet kennels No
Disabled access Yes	Rain check No
Wheelchair rental Yes	Private tours No
Baby stroller rental No	

Description and Comments Built on the site of Knott's Berry Farm's former parking lot, this 13-acre waterpark is themed to the '50s and '60s— the golden days of California beach and surf culture. Sixteen rides include various slides (including Banzai Falls, a collection of six high-speed slides), a third-mile long "lazy river" for folks who like to float, and a three-story fun house. There's a 750,000-gallon wave pool and a play area with nozzles, faucets, secret rooms, and surprise showers. For toddlers, there is a quiet lagoon with a submarine and an inactive octopus.

Family-Friendly Restaurants

EL POLLO INKA

400 S. Euclid Avenue, Anaheim; (714) 772-2263

Meals served: Lunch and dinner
Cuisine: Peruvian
Entree range: $4.75–16 (lunch and dinner)
Children's menu: Yes
Reservations: Accepted only Friday–Saturday
Payment: All major credit cards

If the blandness and sterility of the chain restaurants that clog Anaheim depress you, take the family on an adventure to this swell little joint, just a notch above a fast-food restaurant—it's home to superb roast chicken and interesting dishes involving french fries and other forms of potato (Peru is, after all, the birthplace of the potato). While a bit exotic, the food is simple enough for kids to enjoy, and the prices are hard to beat. Try to come on a weekend evening, when live Andean music is performed.

GOOFY'S KITCHEN

Disneyland Hotel, 1150 W. Cerritos Avenue, Anaheim; (714) 956-6755

Meals served: Breakfast, lunch, and dinner
Cuisine: American

Entree range: $15.95 adults, $8.95 children ages 3–12, $3.95 children ages 2 and under (breakfast and lunch); $24.95 adults, $8.95 children ages 3–12, $3.95 children ages 2 and under (dinner); all meals are all-you-can-eat
Children's menu: Yes
Reservations: Recommended
Payment: All major credit cards

If your 2–10-year-old isn't terrified of oversized, mute Mickeys and Cinderellas, bring them here for a meal and it will be one of the highlights of a trip to Disneyland. Perfectly tolerable food is served buffet style, which the kids adore, because they can have exactly what they want. Plan on a leisurely meal, so your kids will have time to hug, follow around, and get autographs from Goofy and the many other characters that wander the dining rooms.

MRS. KNOTT'S CHICKEN DINNER RESTAURANT

803 Beach Boulevard, Buena Park; (714) 220-5080

Meals served: Breakfast, lunch, and dinner
Cuisine: American
Entree range: $2.75–6.25 (breakfast); $4.95–6.95 (lunch); $10.95 (dinner)
Children's menu: Yes; entrees $1.95–4.95
Reservations: Not necessary
Payment: All major credit cards

Every evening, the front door to this legendary place is blocked by a line that stretches around the building, and that line helps further the restaurant's reputation. In truth, however, the family-style fried chicken dinner is not worth an hour's wait. If you time it right (early or late) and can get in quickly, your kids will enjoy the Jell-O, biscuits, chicken, corn, and ice cream, and you'll enjoy the low prices, but don't let the crowds get your hopes up for a memorable meal. However, the chicken takeout window just down the way from the restaurant entrance is a great option for folks staying nearby. The food's hot, hearty, and ready to go immediately, and you don't have to drive around looking for another stop to make.

WILD BILL'S WILD WEST EXTRAVAGANZA

7600 Beach Boulevard, Buena Park; (714) 522-6414

Meals served: Dinner nightly, as well as Saturday–Sunday afternoon
Cuisine: American/cowboy
Entree range: Set price of $37.95 adults and $23.95 children
Children's menu: No
Reservations: Strongly advised the day before
Payment: AE, DC, MC, V

If you blow into town in the late afternoon or evening and are looking for something to do in the way of entertainment, you could do worse than joining the bus tour groups at Wild Bill's. A brother facility to the better-known Medieval Times (where audiences eat chicken legs and watch knights joust and fair maidens faint), this is a family showroom with long tables set up to allow patrons to eat and watch the Wild West performance. The show is vaudevillian (singers, dancers, rope tricks) with a Western theme, the food is perfunctory but served in the kinds of themed accessories kids love (glasses shaped like boots, beans in a pot). All in all, if your kids are ages ten or under, you'll have a fine time. You're near Hollywood, remember, and the performers are Hollywood hopefuls and, as such, sometimes genuinely quite talented.

Part Three

Los Angeles and Vicinity: South Bay, Pasadena, Mountain Towns, Deserts, and Catalina

Despite its fabled sunshine and laid-back attitude, **L.A.** has not been an easy city to visit. But recent improvements and additions to the transit system make it easier to get around without a car, and the large number of new hotels has made it possible to stay and play in some good, family-friendly "home base" areas like Santa Monica, Universal City, and Long Beach. Because there is no compact city center, distances between destinations are sometimes considerable, so parents should select their home base carefully.

L.A.'s rewards are great. As residents (and natives), we tend to take for granted the diversity of experiences our families enjoy. You can sled in the local mountains and Boogie board at the beach in the same weekend. You can go from a Mexican street fair to an African-American art show to a Korean barbecue restaurant in the same day. You can wallow in Hollywood's illusions at **Universal Studios,** then decompress in a Japanese garden at Pasadena's **Huntington Gardens.** You can join the crowds exploring **Santa Monica's Third Street Promenade,** or ride a ferry to sleepy, sun-washed **Catalina Island.**

The secret to a successful visit to the greater L.A. area is twofold: careful planning and judicious editing. Make a list of everything you want to do, find a place you'd like to stay, review your wish list with a map in hand, and start cutting your list down. If you decide to stay in **Redondo Beach,** which is located south of LAX airport and a 30- to 60-minute drive from downtown L.A., accept that you may not be able to do Universal Studios, **Magic Mountain,** and **Hollywood** in the same weekend. Conversely, if Universal Studios and Hollywood are tops on your family's list, maybe you should save the beach for next time and stay in Universal City or Hollywood.

This chapter breaks the vast L.A. area into several geographical units, in the following order: the South Bay, composed of the beach towns of **Long**

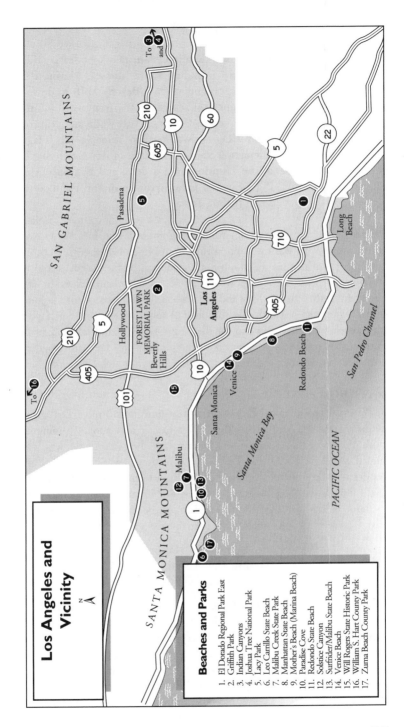

Los Angeles and Vicinity

N

Beaches and Parks

1. El Dorado Regional Park East
2. Griffith Park
3. Indian Canyons
4. Joshua Tree National Park
5. Lacy Park
6. Leo Carrillo State Beach
7. Malibu Creek State Park
8. Manhattan State Beach
9. Mother's Beach (Marina Beach)
10. Paradise Cove
11. Redondo State Beach
12. Solstice Canyon
13. Surfrider/Malibu State Beach
14. Venice Beach
15. Will Rogers State Historic Park
16. William S. Hart County Park
17. Zuma Beach County Park

Beach, Redondo, and **Manhattan; Catalina Island,** a two-hour ferry ride from San Pedro; L.A.'s Westside, including **Santa Monica, Marina del Rey,** and **West L.A.;** Central L.A., ranging from **Beverly Hills** to downtown and encompassing the majority of the attractions, from the new **California Science Center** downtown to **Universal CityWalk;** side trips to the suburbs of **San Dimas (Raging Waters)** and **Valencia (Six Flags Magic Mountain);** Pasadena, the city just northeast of downtown that is home to **Old Pasadena, the Huntington Gardens,** and **Kidspace;** the Mountains, including **Big Bear** and **Lake Arrowhead;** and the deserts, including **Palm Springs** and **Joshua Tree.**

Weather is rarely an impediment to L.A.-area travel, but contrary to New Yorkers' opinion, it is not summertime year-round. In fact, L.A. enjoys two seasons: spring and summer. Spring runs from November through May; in the early part of that season, rain is not uncommon, and it can get as cold as 50° near the beach, or even down in the 30s in the inland valleys. In late spring and early summer, May and June especially, be prepared for the June gloom, which can leave beaches shrouded in fog for weeks on end. If you crave beach sun, plan your trip for the period between mid-July and mid-October. Note that for the purposes of the summer-only lifeguard program at the beaches, summer is defined as Memorial Day through Labor Day.

GETTING THERE

By Plane. Almost all major airlines serve the region's main airport, Los Angeles International (LAX; (310) 646-5252), which is only about 15 minutes south of Santa Monica via the 405 Freeway—if there's no traffic, which is rare. If you'll be staying on the eastside—in downtown, Studio City, or Pasadena—you're better off flying via Burbank-Glendale-Pasadena Airport (2627 Hollywood Way, Burbank, (818) 840-8840), a pleasantly small-scale operation used heavily by commuter flights. Shuttle services, taxis, buses, and private car services link both airports to many locations across the region.

By Train. Amtrak delivers visitors from Northern California, the Pacific Northwest, and the Midwest to Union Station, a glorious, recently renovated mission-style building in downtown. Call (800) USA-RAIL.

By Car. The freeway rules in L.A., so there are major highways leading to the urban area from every which way. Visitors from the north and south arrive via Interstate 5, the artery connecting the Mexican and Canadian borders; the coastal route from the north into L.A. is the 101 Freeway, which travels via Santa Barbara. Travelers entering from almost anywhere east, from Palm Springs to Chicago, will arrive via Interstate 10. Once in the city area, the freeway numbers explode: There's the 210, and the 91, and the 110, and the 22, and the 60, and the 134—so do not arrive without a good map. (The Thomas Bros. map book is the bible, but a basic folding map will suffice for freeway navigation.)

How to Get Information before You Go

Beverly Hills Visitors Bureau, 239 S. Beverly Drive, Beverly Hills; (310) 271-8174.

Catalina Island Visitors Bureau, #1 Green Pier, Avalon; (310) 510-7649; www.catalina.com.

Long Beach Area Convention and Visitors Bureau, One World Trade Center, Suite 300, Long Beach; (800) 452-7829; www.golongbeach.org.

Los Angeles Convention and Visitors Bureau, 633 W. 5th Street, L.A. 90071; (213) 624-7300; www.lacvb.com.

Palm Springs Desert Resorts Convention and Visitors Bureau, 69-930 Highway 111, Suite 201, Rancho Mirage 92270; (800) 471-3529; (619) 770-1992; www.desert-resorts.com.

Pasadena Convention and Visitors Bureau, 171 S. Los Robles Avenue, Pasadena 91101; (626) 795-9311.

Santa Monica Convention and Visitors Bureau, 520 Broadway, Suite 250, Santa Monica 90401; (310) 319-6263; www.santamonica.com.

Child Care/Baby-Sitting

Babysitters (formerly Blais Bies). This service was founded by Susan Blais more than a decade ago to provide carefully screened sitters that match each family's needs; she'll even pair you up with a sitter to travel with you. Her sitters are located throughout Southern California; (949) 494-6259.

Sitters Unlimited. A licensed, bonded agency providing baby-sitters throughout the L.A. area; (800) 328-1191.

The Best Beaches and Parks

El Dorado Regional Park East. Your kids will have to try hard to be bored in this huge inland park in Long Beach. The 450 acres include four fishing lakes (stocked with trout, catfish, and bass), pedalboats, playgrounds, miles of level biking trails, an archery range used in the 1984 Olympics, and a fun, one-mile steam train ride (closed Monday in summer and Monday–Tuesday off-season). The biggest attraction here is the El Dorado Nature Center, which takes up 100 acres of the park. Its museum has cool stuff kids can touch and explore, like skulls and antlers, as well as insect and reptile houses, animal displays, and summer-camp programs. Outside are stroller-accommodating trails and a pond that's home to turtles and ducks. Call the Nature Center to reserve a spot in one of the guided family night walks or campfires. 7550 E. Spring Street, Long Beach, (562) 570-1745 (Nature Center) or (562) 570-1771 (park). Open daily 7 a.m.–dusk; closed Christmas. Parking $3 weekdays, $5 weekends and holidays.

Griffith Park. One of the country's great urban parks (it is, in fact, the nation's largest city park), Griffith Park is a world unto itself, home to many excellent amusements for children and worth a full day trip, if not two. It is drier and wilder than most city parks, notable more for its trail-etched hillsides than manicured gardens. On the park's eastern edge are the Los Angeles Zoo and the Autry Museum of Western Heritage (see Attractions, pages 183 and 178, respectively); smack in the middle is the landmark Griffith Park Observatory (see Attractions, page 180); a few miles east of there you'll find the pony rides and kiddie train ride, (323) 664-6788, loved by generations of L.A. children. On the northern, Burbank side is Travel Town, (323) 662-5874, a marvelous collection of old trains that kids can climb into and explore; a small-scale train ride circles the area. Children also love the old carousel (although the deafening music terrified our three-year-old), which is surrounded by playground areas and rolling lawns that are perfect for picnics. Extras include two golf courses, tennis courts, equestrian trails, a fern preserve, soccer fields, and woodlands. Many entrances: Zoo and Autry Museum from Zoo Drive off I-5; pony and train rides and carousel from Griffith Park Boulevard north of Los Feliz Boulevard; Travel Town from Victory Boulevard on Burbank side; Observatory, golf course, Greek Theatre, picnic areas, and trailheads from Vermont Avenue north of Los Feliz Boulevard, (323) 664-1191; open daily 6 a.m.–10 p.m.

The Indian Canyons. Some come for the tchotchke-filled gift shop, but we come for the hiking and the almost miraculously lush beauty of this desert oasis, a stream-fed, palm-rich hideaway in the mountain rocks. There's easy hiking near the base of the trails. If your kids are old enough to ride horses, a great way to see the canyons is on horseback; contact Smoke Tree Stables, (760) 327-1372. The Canyons are the property of the local Cahuilla Tribe, which maintains the land and charges admission for entrance. 38500 S. Palm Canyon Drive, Palm Springs, (760) 325-3400 or (800) 790-3398; admission $6 adults, $3.50 for seniors and ages 13–16, $1 ages 6–12, free for children under age 6.

Joshua Tree National Park. A desert unlike any other, Joshua Tree borders on the mystical. Gigantic boulders are strewn everywhere, like God's rough-hewn marbles; they're so awesome they almost seem alive. Add mysteriously soft and white sand and the armies of tall, prickly Joshua trees reaching their arms heavenward, and you have a place of great beauty, beloved by rock climbers, naturalists, hikers, and stargazers. Allow time to stop at the Oasis Visitor Center to get oriented and take the short nature walk to an oasis; ask for a map so you can find the fun one-mile trail in Hidden Valley and the cool Jumbo Rocks area. There are several campgrounds; one of the best is White Tank, where the boulders are grand and the sand soft. Visit in spring and fall only, and bring lots and lots of water—the entire park has none. If that makes camping sound too intense, Twentynine Palms motel will make a fine base. 74485 National Park Drive (off I-10), Twentynine Palms, (760) 367-5525; admission free, but $10 per vehicle for parking.

Lacy Park. One of the prettiest urban parks anywhere, Lacy is carefully hidden in the wealthy Pasadena suburb of San Marino. So skillful is its design that it seems to go on for miles, with the trees blocking any hint of residential development. It has an excellent, large playground, vast lawns, softball fields, a bike/skate path ringing the park, and complete picnic/rest room facilities. A popular day camp is held here in summer, and the Fourth of July festivities are legendary. This is a good play stop if you're staying either downtown or in the Pasadena area. 1485 Virginia Road (north of Monterey), San Marino, (626) 304-9648. There is a $3 parking fee on weekends

Leo Carrillo State Beach. Many a Southern California school goes field tripping to this Malibu beach, and for very good reason. Kids (and parents) adore it here, especially in the quieter fringe seasons, such as May and October. The tidepooling is the best in the L.A. area; everything is pro- tected, so kids can't take even a shell from the tide-pool preserve. There are sea caves to explore, rocks to climb, a sandy beach, good ocean swimming, a playground, nature trails, and a good campground with 300 sites for tents (no hookups for RVs). Lifeguards are on duty in summer. It can get chilly, so bring jackets. 35000 Pacific Coast Highway, between Point Mugu and Point Dume, Malibu, (818) 880-0350. Parking $6; campsites $17 midweek, $18 Friday–Saturday; for campsite reservations call Reserve America, (800) 444-7275.

Malibu Creek State Park. One of the many wonders of the Santa Monica Mountains, this park has lots to offer. You can ride mountain bikes, hike the Malibu Creek Trail (a beautiful hike, and not too challenging for school-age kids), fish for bass and bluegill in Century Lake, picnic, and swim in the rock pool near the visitors center. Parents take note that three miles in on the Malibu Creek Trail is the former set of the TV show *M*A*S*H*. Don't miss the visitors center, which has maps, children's infor- mation, and a little museum. There's also a nice campground. 125 Las Vir- genes Road, Calabasas, (818) 880-0367; parking $5 per vehicle per day.

Manhattan State Beach. Broad and long, this is a classic Southern California beach, with a bike path, volleyball courts, snack bars, summertime lifeguards, great people-watching, and lots of sunshine. The generally good waves for body-surfing, body boarding, and surfing make this a better beach for solid swimmers, usually kids over age eight. If you only have time to hit one good, all-around beach on an L.A. trip, this is the one to hit. The downside is the lack of parking—come early to find a metered spot. 1200 The Strand, Manhattan Beach, (310) 545-5621.

Mother's Beach (Marina Beach). So named for the plethora of moms and their young children, this wave-free beach in Marina del Rey makes for a pleasant beach morning or afternoon with children too young to brave ocean surf. Tucked among the pleasure craft of the marina, it's a small man-made beach with a sandy shore, shallow lagoon, playground, lifeguards, barbecues, nearby food stands, and rest rooms. Older kids will like the volleyball courts and summertime water-bike rentals. 4135 Admiralty Way (behind the Jamaica Bay Inn), Marina del Rey, (310) 394-3264. County parking lot is $5–7; street parking also available if you arrive early.

Paradise Cove. If you loathe giant, crowded beaches and want a nice family place—and if outrageous parking fees don't bother you—head for this lovely private beach fronting what must surely be the most attractive, upscale trailer-park community in the country. The sand is soft, the cove and small pier are picturesque, and the shallow shoreline lets kids have lots of wave fun without getting pounded. Extras include showers, rest rooms, and a summer lifeguard, but no snack bar; you can avoid the parking charge if you eat in the beachfront restaurant, a formerly terrible place recently taken over by the Gladstone's people—it should be an improvement over the previous owners. 28128 Pacific Coast Highway, Malibu, (310) 457-2511. Parking $15 if you aren't eating at the restaurant.

Redondo State Beach. A large, sweeping, sand beach complete with a pier, Redondo is popular with groups of teens and young families alike. The fishing from the pier is surprisingly good; down on the sand, there are waves, volleyball courts, a bike path, concession stands, lifeguards, and good rest room/shower facilities. On the King Harbor end of the beach you can sign up for a whale-watching trip in winter/spring, or a sportfishing trip in summer. In July and August, the pier is often home to free concerts and festivals. 1101 Esplanade, Redondo Beach, (310) 372-2166. Parking ranges from free to $7.

Solstice Canyon. A hike that's so easy you can do a major part of it with a stroller is the big draw here. A shaded, paved former ranch road leads through the canyon, often next to the babbling, rock-strewn creek, to an eighteenth-century adobe and several fine picnic areas, and on to the ruins of a house that was built almost into a rock grotto and falls. This is a perfect turn-around point, about an hour each way, although real hikers can continue. Make sure to allow time for playing in the grotto and in the creek along the way. We like to pick up gourmet picnic supplies in Malibu, take a hike here, then spend some time on the beach. Water, rest rooms, dogs allowed on leash. Off Corral Canyon Road, Malibu, (805) 370-2301; admission free.

Surfrider/Malibu State Beach. If you have a surfer in the family, or someone who thinks surfers are cool, head for these adjacent beaches on the north side of the Malibu Pier. The longboarding capital of L.A., Surfrider was one of the birthplaces of the California surfing scene in the 1940s and 1950s, thanks to its consistent (but rarely huge) cruiser waves. The International Surfing Contest is held here each September. The pier is a good fishing spot, and the state beach just north of Surfrider is home to a natural lagoon with great bird-watching, tide pools, a nature center, and easy little trails. Guided tours are offered; call (818) 880-0350 for details. 23000 block of Pacific Coast Highway (¼ mile south of Cross Creek Road), Malibu, (310) 457-9891. Parking $2–7, depending on season; limited parking available along PCH.

Venice Beach. When Angelenos host out-of-town visitors, they almost always bring them to Venice, but not to swim or sunbathe. The scene is the draw here, and what a scene it is: the boardwalk teems with merchants (T-shirts, jewelry, tie-dyes, junk of every description), tattooed acrobatic skaters, snake handlers, cycling musicians, chain-saw jugglers, street rappers, bodybuilders, and all manner of folk your Aunt Martha will never see in Topeka. Needless to say, teenagers adore it, and they'll want some spending money. (It may be too freakish and crowded for very young children, however.) Of the various food vendors, Jody Maroni's sausage stand is the hands-down winner. You might see some awesome basketball action (along with intense, often foul, street language) at the public courts, and famed Muscle Beach is still going strong. 2300 Ocean Front Walk, between Marina del Rey Channel and the Santa Monica city line, Venice, (310) 577-5700. Parking in the county lot is $2 on weekdays and $10 on weekends.

Will Rogers State Historic Park. The great storyteller's former house, still furnished as if he lived there, won't interest your kids in the slightest (Will who?), but they'll probably get a kick out of the visitors center video showing Will doing his rope tricks. After the video, head out for the one-mile (each way) hike to Inspiration Point, where the Pacific view is glorious, then return to the polo fields for a picnic or barbecue. Other trails link to Topanga State Park. 1501 Will Rogers State Park Road (off Sunset Boulevard), Pacific Palisades, (310) 454-8212; parking $6, $5 for seniors.

William S. Hart County Park. Animal-loving kids and cowboy fans will find a trip out here to the Santa Clarita Valley very worthwhile. Buffalo graze behind fences, you can often spot deer, and kids can feed the barnyard animals—sheep, horses, burros, ducks, chickens. When you're ready to move, you can hike a few of the 265 acres. The tour of the former home of cowboy–movie star William Hart can be frustrating for some kids, because they can't touch, but others like seeing some of the Western gear, especially the bear-skin rug and old guns. Also on site is a sweet little train station museum (open weekend afternoons only) with a steam locomotive out front and a nifty model train inside. 24151 N. San Fernando Road, Newhall, Santa Clarita Valley, (661) 259-0855; admission and parking free.

Zuma Beach County Park. L.A.'s coolest teens hang out at this northern Malibu beach, near the Ventura County line. Keep young children and inexperienced swimmers out of the water—strong riptides prevail—but enjoy the playgrounds, sandy beach, volleyball, and people-watching, especially if you have teens. Lifeguards, concession stands, rest rooms. 30000 block of Pacific Coast Highway, between Trancas Canyon Boulevard and Westward Beach Road, (310) 457-9891. Parking $5 weekdays and $7 weekends; limited free parking along PCH.

Family Outdoor Adventures

Bicycling/Blading. Cycling in this car-obsessed city isn't for the timid, but at the beach, the cyclist (and skater) is king. A smooth, paved bike path wends along the sand from the north end of Santa Monica Beach (in the Pacific Palisades) for more than 20 level miles, all the way south to Redondo Beach. The path gets pretty congested on warm-weather weekends, so consider a weekday outing. You can stop en route for a drink or lunch. Bike- and skate-rental shops are plentiful near the path in Santa Monica, in Venice, and down in the South Bay. Mountain bike trails also abound in the Santa Monica and San Gabriel Mountains; for information on how to find them, pick up *Mountain Bike! Southern California* (Menasha Ridge Press), or call the Santa Monica Mountains National Recreation Area, (818) 597-9192.

Boating. See the Catalina section later in this chapter, page 155.

Fishing. Surprisingly good fishing is found off the Redondo Beach and Malibu piers; both have tackle shops that can outfit you. If your family is ambitious enough for a seagoing fishing trip, try either Redondo Sport Fishing Company (233 N. Harbor Drive, Redondo Beach, (310) 372-2111) or L.A. Harbor Sportfishing (Berth 79, San Pedro Harbor, (310) 547-9916). Both offer half-day charters that are good for school-age children.

Hiking. Entire books have been published on the hiking opportunities in the L.A. area, so rich are the choices. With young children, we particularly like Solstice Canyon (see Best Parks, page 142) and the easy trails at Eaton Canyon (1750 N. Altadena Drive, Pasadena, (626) 398-5420), which offers wonderful Family Nature Walks every Saturday morning. Big Bear and Lake Arrowhead also offer lots of great family hiking; see Mountain Towns later in this chapter (page 205). You'll also find good trails in some of the parks described in Best Beaches and Parks (page 139), especially Will Rogers, Leo Carrillo, and Griffith Park.

Horseback Riding. One of our favorite outings in L.A. is the Friday-night sunset horseback ride through Griffith Park offered by Sunset Ranch (3400 Beachwood Drive, Hollywood, (323) 469-5450)—it's a wonderful evening to spend with teenagers. A guide takes you over the mountain and down into Burbank at sunset, with dusk settling on the wild scrub and scurrying jackrabbits; you tie up at a (pretty bad) Mexican restaurant in Burbank and ride back over after dinner, hopefully guided by a bright moon. Children as young as five are welcome on daytime rides; the stable is home to some very gentle horses. Another place to find high-quality horses and access to many park trails is the Los Angeles Equestrian Center (480 Riverside Drive, Burbank, (818) 840-8401). See also Indian Canyons (page 140).

Surfing/Ocean Sports. You're in the land of the Beach Boys, and you (or your kids) won't have experienced it fully if you don't get some wave action. The best place in town to learn to surf is at Malibu Ocean Sports (south side of Malibu Pier, (310) 456-6302). For beginners ages eight and up, it offers a two-hour private lesson, including equipment (board and wetsuit), for $94; lessons are usually held at famed Surfrider beach, in a spot away from the crowds, but if the waves are exceptionally large or small, they'll take you to another beach. The same company also has windsurfing lessons for the same fee. To try your hand at the easier sport of kayaking, head to Action Water Sports in Marina del Rey (4144 Lincoln Boulevard, (310) 306-9539).

If you just want to get into the surf without the cost and trouble of surfing lessons, rent a body board at any of dozens of concessions in Malibu, Santa Monica, Redondo, or any beach town, and ride the waves on your own. Know your swimming strength and ability, however, and if lifeguards have posted riptide or high-surf warnings, respect the power of the ocean and stay out.

Tidepooling. The best tidepooling in town is found at Leo Carrillo (see page 141). The snorkeling there is superb as well. You'll need to bring your own snorkeling gear, as there's no rental on site.

Whale-Watching. We've enjoyed the morning whale-watching expeditions offered by Redondo Sport Fishing Company (233 N. Harbor Drive,

Redondo Beach, (310) 372-2111), some of which have a Cabrillo docent on board to answer questions. On our last trip, we saw at least a half-dozen gray whales, along with dolphins and sea lions. On your way in or out of the Redondo harbor area, make sure to stop for a look at the gigantic Wyland whale- and sealife-mural on the side of the PG&E building. Another good whale-watching outfit is L.A. Harbor Sportfishing (Berth 79, San Pedro Harbor, (310) 547-9916).

KID CULTURE: THEATER, LITERATURE, AND THE ARTS

Forget the talk-show jokes about bubble-headed L.A.—contrary to popular opinion, Angelenos and their children are voracious readers and patrons of the arts. Here are our favorite pint-size cultural centers, for a civilized break from the theme-park sights.

Bob Baker Marionette Theater. Skillful puppeteers ply their craft, making their creations sing, dance, and interact with each other and the audience. An L.A. kid favorite since 1963. 1345 W. 1st Street, downtown L.A., (213) 250-9995; tickets $10 per person.

Children's Book World. If you're staying on the westside, head over here on Saturday morning for a generally captivating (and free) story time. Author signings are also sometimes offered. Call for schedules. 10580 W. Pico Boulevard, West L.A., (310) 559-2665; admission free.

Every Picture Tells a Story. We dare you to leave this gallery of children's art without spending way more than you should on a piece of art. Devoted to the best in illustrative work from children's books (think Babar, Roald Dahl, and Chris Van Allsburg), this gallery is one of the most enjoyable in town. There's a small bookstore as well. Call about artist open houses. 7525 Beverly Boulevard, L.A., (323) 932-6070; admission free.

Family Theater Musicals, Santa Monica Playhouse. Every Saturday and Sunday at 12:30 and 3 p.m., professional actors stage children's musical theater in a 92-seat playhouse, typically variations on popular fairy tales. Day-camp theater programs for kids are offered in summer. Come nighttime, the theater becomes a grown-up destination. 1211 4th Street, Santa Monica, (310) 394-9779; admission $8.50 per person.

Imagination Station Children's Theater, Morgan-Wixon Theater. Accomplished performances of children's theater are held on Saturdays and Sundays. 2627 Pico Boulevard, Santa Monica, (310) 828-7519; admission $7 adults, $5 children and seniors.

Los Angeles Philharmonic Symphonies for Youth. To introduce 6–12-year-olds to symphonic music, reserve early for one of the Philharmonic's Symphonies for Youth, typically held five times a year. The daytime weekend concerts start with hands-on, pre-concert activities, like art projects and instrument demonstrations; the concert features music that appeals to children. Preschool children get their own performances at the Open House Series. Dorothy Chandler Pavilion, Music Center, 135 N. Grand Avenue, downtown L.A., (213) 850-2000; admission $6–10.

Open House at the Hollywood Bowl. A superb summer program that combines hands-on activities (puppet making, folk-dancing lessons) with performances, aimed at children ages 3–16. After a jazz concert, for instance, children will make their own instruments. Performances 10 a.m. and 11:15 a.m. Monday–Friday from early July to mid-August; prices by event. Top of Highland Avenue, Hollywood, (323) 850-2000.

Serendipity Theater Company, Burbank Little Theater. One of the area's most respected Equity-waiver theaters is home to an excellent children's performing group. Plays are staged every weekend—Saturdays at 1 p.m. and Sundays at 1 p.m. and 4 p.m. Convenient for families staying on the eastside of L.A. 1100 W. Clark, Burbank, (818) 843-7944; admission $12 adults, $6 children, children under age 3 not admitted.

Storybook Theatre, Theatre West. Every Saturday at 1 p.m., this theater near Universal Studios puts on a lively, interactive musical play aimed at children ages 3–8. 3333 Cahuenga Boulevard West, Universal City, (818) 761-2203; admission $8.

Storyopolis. We know childless adults who hang out at this children's art gallery and bookstore—that's how wonderful it is. You'll find original works and limited-edition prints from the finest artists in children's literature, as well as high-quality books; on Saturdays, children gather for craft workshops, story hours, and author signings. 116 N. Robertson Boulevard, L.A., (310) 358-2500; admission $6 for Saturday events, otherwise free.

Calendar of Festivals and Events

January

Tournament of Roses Parade, Colorado Boulevard in Pasadena. January 1. Every year untold millions watch this parade on TV, and lots of them decide right then to move to L.A. If you've never been, get tickets—kids adore it; (626) 419-ROSE

February

Chinese New Year's Parade, Chinatown. Huge dragons snake through Chinatown's streets, and the costumes are great; (213) 617-0396.

Riverside County Fair and National Date Festival, Riverside County Fairgrounds, Indio. An extremely popular ten-day celebration of the desert and the sweet date, held not far from Palm Springs. Look for camel and elephant rides, camel races, a petting zoo, carnival rides, rodeo fun, and all the date shakes you can manage; (760) 863-8247.

March

Los Angeles Marathon, throughout L.A. The city becomes gripped with marathon fever, and everyone tries to find a spot to watch the runners, walkers, skaters, wheelchair-riders, and cyclists go by; (310) 444-5544.

April

Opening Day, Dodger Stadium. A festive, fun family outing; (213) 224-1500.

Blessing of the Animals, Olvera Street, downtown. Saturday before Easter. Hundreds of people bring their pets—from dogs to hamsters—to be blessed in this festive procession; (213) 628-1274.

Los Angeles Times Festival of Books, Dickson Plaza, UCLA. Includes a large children's area and lots of good storytelling events; (800) LA-TIMES, ext. 7BOOK.

Fiesta Broadway, Downtown. The last weekend in April kicks off Cinco de Mayo season when 36 downtown blocks are shut to traffic and thousands of revelers enjoy performances on several stages, with Latino pop stars headlining; (310) 941-0015.

May

Children's Day, Little Tokyo (downtown L.A.). A traditional Japanese celebration of the child, featuring footraces, games, arts and crafts; (213) 628-2725.

Valley Greek Fair, Northridge. Memorial Day party with music, food, etc.; (818) 886-4040.

June

Cajun and Zydeco Festival, Rainbow Lagoon, Long Beach. Rollicking music, dance lessons, Cajun food, and children's amusements; (562) 427-3713.

Noho International Theater and Arts Festival. A street fair in the burgeoning arts district; (818) 508-5155.

July

Fourth of July Celebration, Queen Mary, Long Beach. One of the best fireworks shows in L.A. County; (562) 435-3511.

Lotus Festival, Echo Park. In the park surrounding pretty little Echo Park Lake, home to a large lotus bed, is a terrific celebration of Asian food and arts, with dragon-boat races, kiddie rides, and pedalboat rides on the lake; (213) 485-1310.

August

African Marketplace and Cultural Faire, Rancho Cienega Park, L.A. Hundreds of booths, a Children's Village, and loads of live entertainment celebrating African cultures; (323) 734-1164.

September

L.A. County Fair, County Fairplex Fairgrounds, Pomona. An 18-day extravaganza of carnival rides, pie-eating contests, livestock shows, and live entertainment; (909) 623-3111.

October

Calabasas Pumpkin Festival, Paramount Ranch, Agoura. This Old West ranch, location for many a cowboy movie, hosts pumpkin sales, haunted houses, country music, and pumpkin seed spit-offs; (818) 222-5680.

November

Dia de los Muertos, Olvera Street, downtown. November 1 or 2. A lively, colorful celebration of the Day of the Dead, including a candlelit procession; (213) 624-3660.

Rosebud Parade, Lake Avenue, Pasadena. Sponsored by Kidspace Museum, this miniature version of the Rose Parade is a wonderful family event. Children parade in or on self-decorated wagons, bikes, trikes, and skateboards, and those who sign up in advance can take a float-making class at Kidspace; (626) 449-9144.

Doo Dah Parade, Old Pasadena. Saturday after Thanksgiving. A goofy, eccentric spoof of the Rose Parade; (626) 795-3355.

Hollywood Christmas Parade, Hollywood Boulevard. Sunday after Thanksgiving. A celebrity-studded parade with floats, marching bands, and the Big Guy himself; (323) 469-2337.

December

Christmas Boat Parade, Burton Chase Park, Marina del Rey. Come after dark to watch the decorated, colorfully lit boats parade by; (310) 821-7614.

The South Bay: Manhattan Beach to Long Beach

South of LAX is a string of beach communities linked by the 405 Freeway: **Manhattan, Hermosa, and Redondo Beaches, Torrance, San Pedro,** and **Long Beach.** They're better known for their suburbia than their tourist appeal, but if you're seeking a fun beach day, some of these towns make for fine day trips (see Best Beaches and Parks, page 139). We especially like Redondo, which has a lively pier popular with fishermen, a broad beach, and a harbor out of which run whale-watching trips. Although San Pedro is a fairly gritty port town, full of smokestacks and cargo containers, it has real visitor value, as the departing point for the Catalina ferries (see Catalina Island, page 155) and home of the hokey but amusing **Ports o' Call Village** (a shopping and seafood area on the waterfront) and the **Cabrillo Marine Aquarium.**

The largest city in this region, Long Beach is aiming to be a world-class family destination with the recent opening of the **Long Beach Aquarium of the Pacific.** (The *Queen Mary* has been here for years, but our kids find it a snooze.) Long Beach is also home to a miles-long beach popular with kite flyers, and the charming little villages of **Belmont Shore** and **Naples,** good walking neighborhoods with canals, boutiques, restaurants, and lots of summer street life. On the bay shore in Belmont Shore is a protected sand beach that's well used by young families, thanks to its shallow, warm, wave-free water.

Family Lodging

Crowne Plaza Redondo Beach Marina and Hotel

The massive saltwater aquarium in the lobby is a kid magnet, as is the heated outdoor pool. Overlooking Kings Harbor, this upscale hotel is well located for families interested in whale-watching, sportfishing, biking the beach

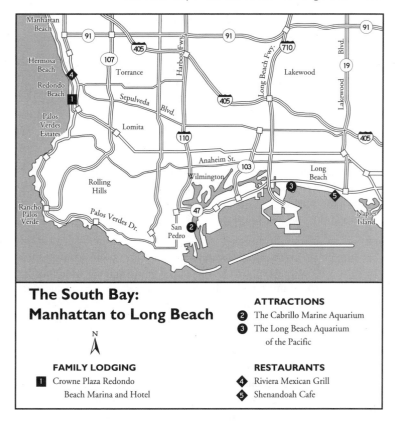

**The South Bay:
Manhattan to Long Beach**

N
ʌ

FAMILY LODGING
1 Crowne Plaza Redondo
   Beach Marina and Hotel

ATTRACTIONS
2 The Cabrillo Marine Aquarium
3 The Long Beach Aquarium
   of the Pacific

RESTAURANTS
4 Riviera Mexican Grill
5 Shenandoah Cafe

path, or enjoying summer days on Redondo Beach; it's also fairly close to LAX and the westside of L.A. Children under age 12 eat free in the restaurant when accompanied by a paying parent, and even room service offers a children's menu. The 339 newly renovated rooms, done in a subtle tropical style, are comfortable. Extras include a tennis court, gym, and spa.

300 N. Harbor Drive, Redondo Beach; (310) 318-8888 or (800) 368-9760; fax (310) 376-1930. Rates from $159; children under age 18 stay free.

Attractions

The Cabrillo Marine Aquarium

3720 Stephen White Drive (off Pacific Avenue and 36th Street), San
   Pedro; (310) 548-7562

Hours: Tuesday–Friday noon–5 p.m., Saturday–Sunday 10 a.m.–5 p.m.

Admission: $2 adults, $1 children and seniors

Appeal by Age Groups:

Pre-school	Grade School	Teens	Young Adults	Over 30	Seniors
★★★	★★★★	★★★	★★★	★★★	★★★

Touring Time: Average 1½ hours (more with beach visit); minimum 45 minutes

Rainy-Day Touring: Yes

Services and Facilities:

Restaurants No	Baby stroller rental No
Alcoholic beverages No	Lockers No
Disabled access Yes	Pet kennels No
Wheelchair rental Yes; call ahead for beach wheelchairs	Rain check No
	Private tours No

Description and Comments More modest than the grandiose Aquarium of the Pacific in nearby Long Beach, this collection of sea life is also much less crowded, which counts for a lot. To do this place right, bring a picnic lunch and plan on spending much of the day here. First, spend a couple of hours playing, exploring, and swimming at adjacent Cabrillo Beach. Then, after lunch, when the kids are ready for some inside time, head into the aquarium to delve deeper into local sea life. They'll see all the critters that share the Pacific with us, from corbina fish to moray eels to leopard sharks; they'll touch sea stars and anemones at the touch tank; they'll feel whale bones and shark skin; and they can marvel up close at the life-size models of a killer whale and dolphin. Ask about the seasonal grunion runs and the guided tours of the nearby marine refuge during very low tides.

The Long Beach Aquarium of the Pacific

100 Aquarium Way (off Shoreline Drive), Long Beach; (562) 590-3100

Hours: Daily 9 a.m.–6 p.m.; closed Christmas day

Admission: $14.95 adults, $7.95 children ages 3–11, under 3 free, $11.95 seniors 60+

Appeal by Age Groups:

Pre-school	Grade School	Teens	Young Adults	Over 30	Seniors
★★★	★★★★	★★★★	★★★	★★★★	★★★★

Touring Time: Average 3–4 hours; minimum 1½ hours

Rainy-Day Touring: Yes

Services and Facilities:

Restaurants Yes	Disabled access Yes
Alcoholic beverages No	Wheelchair rental Yes

Baby stroller rental Yes	**Rain check** No
Lockers No	**Private tours** Yes
Pet kennels No	

Description and Comments   This huge, impressive aquarium, part of the
Rainbow Harbor area of Long Beach, lies across the channel from the *Queen
Mary* and down the waterfront promenade from Shoreline Village, a charm-
ing collection of shops and restaurants. You can ride the $1 water taxi back
and forth to the *Queen Mary.* For visitors staying at any of the major Long
Beach hotels, it's all part of a convenient waterfront entertainment area.

Inside the dramatic aquarium building (its roof is designed to look like
waves), more than 12,000 ocean animals are on display. There is a huge
entry hall with a 142,000-gallon predator tank filled with leopard sharks
and giant sea bass. Passageways lead to three major underwater worlds,
each focusing on a different Pacific Rim marine habitat. The Southern California and Baja world is where you'll find Kid's Cove, with a touch tank
and an outdoor area devoted to up-close viewing of seals and sea lions. The
Northern Pacific section features exhibits of animals native to cold-water
areas of Canada, Alaska, Russia, and Japan, including puffins, sea otters,
and a giant octopus. The Tropical Pacific gallery has above- and below-
water viewing, a tube walkway that takes visitors right through the middle
of an enormous aquarium, and spectacular, colorful fish and coral. There
is also a new gallery devoted entirely to jellyfish.

Family-friendly extras include a kids-only register in the educational-
goodies-packed store; special overnight "Fishy Family" programs (must be
over five years old; $50 per person); and a changing roster of interactive,
staff-supervised activities throughout the facility.

Family-Friendly Restaurants

RIVIERA MEXICAN GRILL

1615 S. Pacific Coast Highway, Redondo Beach; (310) 540-2501

Meals served: Lunch and dinner daily
Cuisine: Mexican
Entree range: $4.95–8.95 (lunch); $6.95–12.95 (dinner)
Children's menu: Yes, $3.95
Reservations: Recommended on weekends
Payment: All major credit cards

Fresh, tasty, modern surfer-style Mexican food—shrimp tacos, creative
quesadillas—is the order of the day in this lively grill a block from
Redondo Beach. It's filled with surf photos and memorabilia, which
charms kids, and the patio is perfect for summer evenings.

SHENANDOAH CAFE

4722 E. 2nd Street, Long Beach; (562) 434-3469

Meals served: Dinner nightly, Sunday brunch
Cuisine: American
Entree range: $14–23 (dinner); $7–12 (brunch)
Children's menu: Yes, a verbal menu for $4.95
Reservations: Recommended
Payment: AE, DC, MC, V

A fantasy of what a Southern grandma's house looked like (or should have), Shenandoah has been a family favorite for years. This is generous, well-prepared American home cooking with a New Orleans flair: apple fritters, riverwalk steak, blackened fish, brownie sundaes. Ideal for a special-treat night out after a visit to the new Aquarium of the Pacific.

Catalina Island

Both a romantic's retreat and a hugely popular summertime family destination, this island is a great escape for two or three days. Centered around the dinky town of **Avalon,** life here is outdoors and active: swimming at the small beaches, snorkeling and diving in the crystal-clear waters, boating, fishing, cycling, and hiking or horseback riding into the rugged backcountry. You can wear shorts just about anywhere, and the kids never seem to get all the sand out of their hair. Once you get beyond the one square mile of Avalon, there's nothing but wilderness, except for the tiny village of **Two Harbors,** a popular campsite and boat harbor.

The fastest seagoing way to reach Catalina is on the high-speed ferries (75–90 minutes) run by Catalina Express, (310) 519-1212, out of San Pedro or Long Beach; a slower, two-hour ride is offered by Catalina Cruises, (800) 228-2546.

OUTDOOR ACTION

Catalina is a place to get moving. Here are some of the best ways to do that.

Boating/Jet-Skiing. You can rent every watercraft imaginable: kayak, Jet Ski, pedalboat, rafts, even paddleboards. Joe's Rent-a-Boat on the pier (310) 510-0455) is a good vendor; for Jet Skis try Catalina Jet Ski (310) 510-1922).

Cruises. Several one-hour cruises are good for families, including a cruise to the sea lion colony and a night cruise to see flying fish (both $9.75 adults, $5 kids). Tickets are available at mainland boat terminals and at the pier, boat landing, and Discovery Tours Center on the island; (310) 510-TOUR.

Cycling. Bikes are rented at concessions for riding around the small town. There's great mountain biking inland, but you have to spend $75 for an annual family permit from the Island Conservancy, (310) 510-1421.

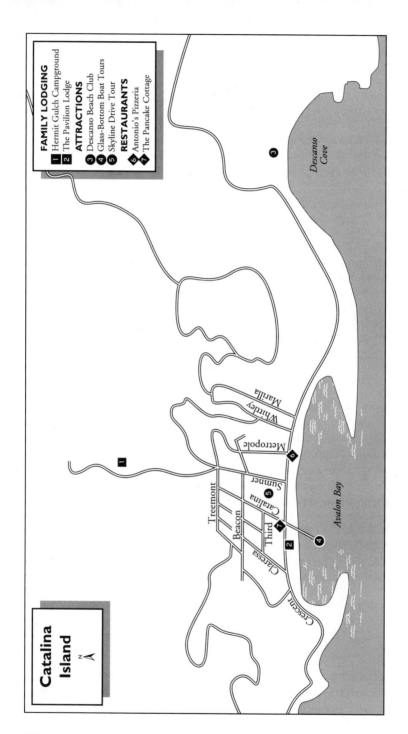

Catalina Island

N

FAMILY LODGING
1 Hermit Gulch Campground
2 The Pavilion Lodge
ATTRACTIONS
3 Descanso Beach Club
4 Glass-Bottom Boat Tours
5 Skyline Drive Tour
RESTAURANTS
6 Antonio's Pizzeria
7 The Pancake Cottage

Descanso Cove

Treemont
Beacon
Third
Claressa
Crescent
Catalina
Sumner
Metropole
Whitley
Marilla

Avalom Bay

Golf-Carting. Families with toddlers might enjoy a one-hour golf cart ride around Avalon, although there isn't a lot of territory to cover. You must be 25 or older to rent. Go to Cartopia Auto Rental, (310) 510-2493.

Hiking. The trails can be pretty intense here, so keep walks in the Avalon area with young children. But if you have sturdy walkers over age eight or so, pick up a map and free permit from the Island Conservancy, 125 Claressa Avenue, (310) 510-1421. When you get into the interior, you may see lots of wildlife (including bald eagles and wild boar).

Horseback Riding. Families with horse-knowledgeable children over age eight can join guided rides into the mountains above Avalon. Call Catalina Stables, (310) 510-0478.

Snorkeling/Diving. Catalina Divers Supply on the pier (phone (310) 510-0330) can outfit you with gear to snorkel at Lover's Cove, found on the other side of the boat landing area. The snorkeling here is superb, and the gentle water is accommodating to very young children. Teens and parents can consider a scuba-diving lesson.

Family Lodging
Hermit Gulch Campground
This privately owned campground is one of many fine family camping sites on Catalina; its selling point is its proximity to the town of Avalon, just a half-mile away. (So what it loses in isolation, it makes up for in convenience.) It's a pleasant, surprisingly quiet location in the hills overlooking the ocean; if you don't have your own tent, you can stay in a cabin or teepee. Barbecue pits, fire rings, picnic tables, hot showers, flush toilets, hiking trails.

A half-mile from Avalon, at the top of Avalon Canyon (transportation by shuttle bus, by taxi, or on foot); (800) 851-0217; www.catalina.com/camping. Rates $4–6 per night for children, $5–10 for adults.

The Pavilion Lodge
When the weather's fine, families pack into this 73-room motel a few feet from the beach. There are no suites, but rooms are large enough for a small family, and some rooms connect. Room rates include a basic continental breakfast, HBO and Disney Channel on the TV, and mini-refrigerators. Restaurants, shops, and the beach are a stone's throw away.

513 Crescent Avenue, Avalon; (310) 510-1788 or (800) 851-0217; fax (310) 510-2073. Rates $69–209, depending on season; children 11 and under stay free in parents' room.

Attractions

Descanso Beach Club

1 Descanso Way (just past casino building), Avalon; (310) 510-7400

Hours: Daily 11 a.m.–6 p.m.; Memorial Day–October, Friday and Saturday BYOB barbecue 6–9 p.m.; closed October–April

Admission: $2 for beach; everything else free

Appeal by Age Groups:

Pre-school	Grade School	Teens	Young Adults	Over 30	Seniors
★★★★	★★★★	★★★★	★★★	★★★	★★★

Touring Time: Average 3–4 hours; minimum 1 hour

Rainy-Day Touring: No, closed for rain

Services and Facilities:

Restaurants Yes	chairs available
Alcoholic beverages Yes	Lockers Yes
Disabled access Yes	Pet kennels No
Wheelchair rental No	Rain check No
Baby stroller rental No, but high	Private tours No

Description and Comments   If main Crescent Beach gets too crowded, consider a beach day at this private club on the other side of the casino. You can rent everything from beach chairs to rafts to kayaks to snorkeling gear, and kids will like the playground. The beach is large and pretty, with tiny waves and clear, clear water. Showers, changing rooms, lifeguards, and full food service (you can't bring your own food in).

Glass-Bottom Boat Tours

Green Pleasure Pier, Avalon; (800) 851-0217

Hours: Daily 10 a.m.–5 p.m.; conditional upon weather and visibility

Admission: $8 adults, $7.50 seniors 55+, $5 age 11 and under

Appeal by Age Groups:

Pre-school	Grade School	Teens	Young Adults	Over 30	Seniors
★★★	★★★★	★★★	★★★	★★★	★★★

Touring Time: 40–45 minutes

Rainy-Day Touring: Yes

Services and Facilities:

Restaurants No	Disabled access Yes
Alcoholic beverages No	Wheelchair rental No

Baby stroller rental No   Rain check No
Lockers No   Private tours No
Pet kennels No

Description and Comments   To get a glimpse of why Catalina is a diver's paradise, take this 45-minute boat tour to meet the local sea life. The water is amazingly clear, and when you get over to the kelp beds, you'll see vivid orange garibaldi, yellow giant kelpfish, bat rays, bass, maybe even a sea lion or some dolphins. The night cruise is cool, offering a look at nocturnal fish. The same company runs semi-submersible boat tours, but they aren't worth the substantial extra bucks.

Skyline Drive Tour

Leaves from Island Plaza, Avalon; (800) 851-0217

Hours: Summer, tours 11 a.m., 1 p.m., and 3 p.m.; fewer daily tours off-season

Admission: $21 adults, $18.50 seniors ages 55+, $10.50 ages 2–11; tickets available from kiosks around the island and at the mainland terminal

Appeal by Age Groups:

Pre-school	Grade School	Teens	Young Adults	Over 30	Seniors
★★★	★★★★	★★★	★★★	★★★	★★★

Touring Time: Average 3 hours; minimum 1 hour

Rainy-Day Touring: Yes

Services and Facilities:

Restaurants No   Lockers No
Alcoholic beverages No   Pet kennels No
Disabled access No   Rain check No
Wheelchair rental Yes   Private tours No
Baby stroller rental No

Description and Comments   First-timers to Catalina should make the effort to take this two-hour narrated tour. Not only does it introduce you to the natural environment, animal life, and geography of the island, but the ride itself is a thrill for children: the small bus climbs a steep grade for more than three miles, then drops 1,000 feet. Kids also love looking for wild boar and buffalo, and you'll love the views. Midway everyone gets out for a leg stretch, so kids can blow off steam and see the nature center at the Island Conservancy. Reservations are essential in the busy season.

Family-Friendly Restaurants

ANTONIO'S PIZZERIA

230 Crescent Avenue, Avalon; (310) 510-0008

Meals served: Breakfast, lunch, and dinner; call ahead because hours vary
Cuisine: Italian
Entree range: $6.95–12.95 (lunch and dinner)
Children's menu: No
Reservations: Accepted only for large parties
Payment: AE, MC, V

The food's a little on the leaden side, but it's messy, friendly stuff—dense pizzas, spaghetti with meat sauce, meatball sandwiches—and the setting couldn't be any more kid-friendly, with peanut shells on the floor and country music on the stereo.

THE PANCAKE COTTAGE

118–120 Catalina Street, Avalon; (310) 510-0726

Meals served: Breakfast and lunch; closed December–January
Cuisine: American
Entree range: $3.95–6.95 (breakfast); $4.95–8.50 (lunch)
Children's menu: Yes
Reservations: Not accepted
Payment: No credit cards, but personal checks okay

You name it, they'll make it: omelets and pancakes of any description, waffles, Mexican dishes, sandwiches—the menu is vast, and most of the food is just fine. The fresh-fruit pancakes are particularly good. Breakfast is served all day.

Los Angeles: Westside

It has considerably fewer attractions and museums than central L.A., but the westside is nonetheless our favorite family vacation base. In particular, we'd recommend choosing a Santa Monica hotel, where in this car-crazed city, you can actually stay quite happily without a car. Development in recent years has favored the pedestrian, so you can now stroll from your Ocean Avenue hotel to the **Santa Monica Pier** and its amusement park, to the beach, to the walking path along **Palisades Park,** the bluff overlooking the beach, and to a wealth of restaurants, shops, movie theaters, and small amusements, many of which are found on the car-free **Third Street Promenade** and the indoor mall across the street. The Tide Shuttle mini-bus (25 cents) operates every 15 minutes between downtown Santa Monica, the beach, and the promenade. Active families can hop on bikes and ride the bike path down to **Venice Beach** and even on to the South Bay. Although slightly less convenient, **Marina del Rey** is also a good base, with its own restaurants, shops, and beach areas.

From the Santa Monica area, downtown L.A. is 15 minutes by freeway, Disneyland is about an hour, and the Hollywood/Universal Studios areas are 20–30 minutes away. That's assuming that the freeways aren't congested, which seems increasingly rare, so factor in more time if you're traveling even remotely near rush hours. For a prettier drive, head north on the Pacific Coast Highway toward **Malibu** to explore some of the beaches and parks (see Best Beaches and Parks, page 139).

Family Lodging

Best Western Jamaica Bay Inn

Young families get an excellent location-price ratio here: This recently renovated motel is located right on Marina del Rey's Mother's Beach (see page

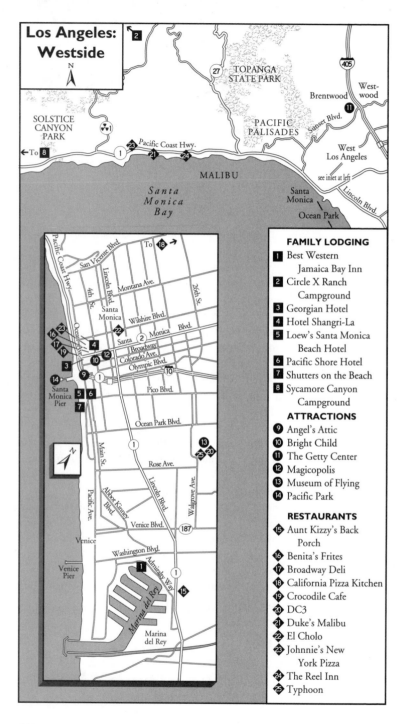

Los Angeles: Westside

N

TOPANGA STATE PARK

SOLSTICE CANYON PARK

←To 8

Pacific Coast Hwy.

MALIBU

Santa Monica Bay

Brentwood

West-wood

405

Sunset Blvd.

PACIFIC PALISADES

West Los Angeles

see inset at left

Santa Monica

Ocean Park

Lincoln Blvd.

27

Pacific Coast Hwy

San Vicente Blvd.

Lincoln Blvd.

4th St.

Montana Ave.

26th St.

Santa Monica

Wilshire Blvd.

Santa Monica Blvd.

Broadway

Colorado Ave.

Olympic Blvd.

Pico Blvd.

Ocean Park Blvd.

Rose Ave.

Abbot Kinney Blvd.

Main St.

Pacific Ave.

Walgrove Ave.

Venice Blvd.

187

Washington Blvd.

Admiralty Way

Marina del Rey

Venice

Venice Pier

Santa Monica Pier

To

FAMILY LODGING

1 Best Western Jamaica Bay Inn
2 Circle X Ranch Campground
3 Georgian Hotel
4 Hotel Shangri-La
5 Loew's Santa Monica Beach Hotel
6 Pacific Shore Hotel
7 Shutters on the Beach
8 Sycamore Canyon Campground

ATTRACTIONS

9 Angel's Attic
10 Bright Child
11 The Getty Center
12 Magicopolis
13 Museum of Flying
14 Pacific Park

RESTAURANTS

15 Aunt Kizzy's Back Porch
16 Benita's Frites
17 Broadway Deli
18 California Pizza Kitchen
19 Crocodile Cafe
20 DC3
21 Duke's Malibu
22 El Cholo
23 Johnnie's New York Pizza
24 The Reel Inn
25 Typhoon

142). Many of the 42 rooms in the low-slung, two-story motel have patios or balconies overlooking the marina, and the rooms with two queen beds are large enough to handle a family (some have microwaves and refrigerators). Outside are a playground, pool, spa, lawn, coffee shop, bike rental, and an excellent beach for young children.

4175 Admiralty Way, Marina del Rey; (310) 823-5333 or (888) 823-5333; fax (310) 823-1325. Rates $109–119.

Circle X Ranch Campground

A first-come, first-served hideaway in the Santa Monica Mountains, Circle X is more ranchlike than beachy, but it's popular with surfers, because the beach is a short drive away. Amenities include a swimming pool, basketball courts, drinking water, toilets, barbecues (charcoal only; no wood), and miles of hiking trails to wonderful locations, including grottos, subterranean caverns, and a waterfall; there's plenty of easy hiking for little ones.

12898 Yerba Buena Road, Malibu; (310) 457-6408 or (818) 597-9192, ext. 201. $6 per night. Only two vehicles and two tents per night allowed at each site.

Georgian Hotel

The pleasant, midsize (84 rooms) Georgian Hotel is much less formal than newer Santa Monica hotels. It's a family-friendly, moderately priced (given the neighborhood) place ideally located for walks to the Santa Monica pier, the beach, and the Third Street Promenade. Many rooms on the upper floors have ocean views. The restaurant only serves breakfast (a continental breakfast is free), but there are plenty of great places within walking distance. The TVs are stocked with Nintendo, and the 28 suites are big enough for a group.

1415 Ocean Avenue, Santa Monica; (310) 395-9945 or (800) 538-8147. Rates $210–475 January–June, $235–550 July–December.

Hotel Shangri-La

Long popular with artists and actors, the Shangri-La is a former apartment building that plays up its art deco heritage. What makes it notable for families are its neighborhood and its apartment-like amenities: Kitchens are common, and many of the 35 suites are big enough for four or more. A continental breakfast is included, and the beach, pier, and Promenade are all a short walk away. On the downside, there's no pool, no restaurant, and no other kid amusements.

1301 Ocean Avenue, Santa Monica; (310) 394-2791 or (800) 345-STAY. Rates start at $145 for a studio, $205 for one-bedroom suite, $310 for two-bedroom suite.

Loew's Santa Monica Beach Hotel

Children are actively courted at this newish atrium-style beachfront resort. From Memorial Day to Labor Day, counselors supervise free poolside activities, from craft making to games, for kids ages 3–12; parents need to be in the general vicinity, but they can read their book in peace by the pool while the kids are amused. The staff will also provide kids with everything from pacifiers to coloring books to sand toys. The pool is huge and kid-friendly, the concierge will provide baby-sitters, and the concession out front rents kid-size bikes (the great Santa Monica bike path is right out front). You'll also find a beach playground and children's menus in both the restaurant and room service. Rooms are modern, comfortable, and well equipped.

1700 Ocean Avenue, Santa Monica; (310) 458-6700 or (800) 23-LOEWS (235-6397). Rates $265–355, suites $625.

Pacific Shore Hotel

There's not much charm at this eight-story hotel, but there's a lot of convenience, value, and family amenities. Within a short walk are Santa Monica Beach, the pier and Pacific Park, lots of restaurants, and the Third Street Promenade. On site you'll find a large pool (complete with poolside food and drink service), a basic gym, laundry facilities, and in-room Nintendo and movies; children's menus are available in both the restaurant and room service, but there's better food to be had in the neighborhood. Rooms are cheerful, clean, and comfortable, if not exactly huge.

1819 Ocean Avenue, Santa Monica; (310) 451-8711 or (800) 622-8711; fax (310) 394-6657. Summer rates $149–189, winter rates less.

Shutters on the Beach

The only L.A.-area hotel that sits right on the sand, Shutters is a luxury hotel, its gray shingles and white trim and shutters evoking a grand Cape Cod beach house. It has ceded the kid's-club market to neighboring competitor Loew's, but many families still choose this place, willing to give up family amenities for Shutters' architecture, service, art collection, and location. There's a lovely ocean-view pool with poolside service, and a concession that rents adult- and kid-size bikes. The concierge can supply sand toys and baby-sitters, and the restaurant's children's menu is available for room service as well. Rooms are beautiful, done in pale ocean colors, with sliding shutters opening to small balconies.

One Pico Boulevard, Santa Monica; (310) 458-0030 or (800) 334-9000. Rates $355–550.

Sycamore Canyon Campground

A clean, safe, beautiful family beach retreat in the L.A. area, near multi-million-dollar movie-star houses—for $16 a night? Yes, that's the happy truth about this campground in north Malibu, on the ocean edge of the Santa Monica Mountains. The former Chumash Indian settlement sits at the mouth of a canyon, a site that keep visitors warmer in winter and cooler in summer. From the campsites, it's a short walk to a gorgeous white-sand beach, known for frequent visits from dolphins; in the canyon itself, you'll find sycamores, wild rose, monarch butterflies, a stream, and poison oak, so watch out on hikes. If you don't feel like cooking camp grub, drive a couple of miles south to Neptune's Net, a good ocean-side seafood shanty. Because of all this, the campground is extremely popular, so reserve very early. Best times are in spring wildflower season and in late summer after the June gloom burns off.

Point Mugu State Park (off Pacific Coast Highway just north of Deer Creek Road), Malibu; office is at 2860-A Camino Dos Rios, Newbury Park; (818) 880-0350; reservations through Reserve America, (800) 444-7275. Campsites $16–18.

Attractions

Angel's Attic

51 Colorado Avenue, Santa Monica; (310) 394-8331

Hours: Thursday–Sunday 12:30–4:30 p.m

Admission: $6.50 adults, $3.50 children, $4 seniors

Appeal by Age Groups:

Pre-school	Grade School	Teens	Young Adults	Over 30	Seniors
★★★	★★★	★★	★★	★★★	★★★

Touring Time: Average 1–2 hours; minimum 1 hour

Rainy-Day Touring: Yes

Services and Facilities:

Restaurants Tea on the veranda (reservations advised)	Baby stroller rental No
	Lockers No
Alcoholic beverages No	Pet kennels No
Disabled access First floor	Rain check No
Wheelchair rental No	Private tours No

Description and Comments Only a few blocks from the circuslike atmosphere of the shops and streetlife of the Third Street Promenade is this quaint museum located in a restored Victorian house. It's pleasantly small—just five rooms downstairs and another two upstairs comprise the galleries, where a changing selection of antique and vintage dollhouses is exhibited. Set on tables so that visitors peer right into the cunningly arranged rooms, the miniature habitats have included, on our visits, a grandly designed (and seasonally decorated) mansion for a rich English family (complete with chandeliers and garden boots by the back door); a Japanese country house with a serene rock garden; and a castle with soldiers on guard.

Tea (served by museum volunteers) is fun with even the youngest kids, because you sit on white wicker furniture and drink from real china cups, but the food and atmosphere aren't really fussy. There's a little store alcove that sells modern dollhouse supplies like teeny weenie Christmas presents and mini-TVs.

Bright Child Indoor Playground

1415 4th Street, Santa Monica; (310) 393-4844

Hours: Daily 10 a.m.–6 p.m.

Admission: $8 per child for two hours, $4 per child for each additional hour; one free adult with each paid child; $4 each additional adult. Adults must be accompanied by a child, and all children must be supervised by an adult.

Appeal by Age Groups:

Pre-school	Grade School	Teens	Young Adults	Over 30	Seniors
★★★★★	★★★★	—	—	—	—

Touring Time: Average 2 hours; minimum 1 hour

Rainy-Day Touring: Yes

Services and Facilities:

Restaurants Snack bar	Lockers No
Alcoholic beverages No	Pet kennels No
Disabled access Yes	Rain check No
Wheelchair rental No	Private tours Birthday parties
Baby stroller rental No	

Description and Comments An unusual new facility, this popular storefront playground combines elements previously available in preschools, kids' gyms, children's museums, and outdoor playgrounds. The overall idea is a safe, challenging, indoor environment for kids to explore while supervised by a parent. There's a huge play structure with slides and tunnels, a ball room, a basketball court with adjustable-height hoops, a putting green, an arts and crafts room, a keyboard area with musical keyboards set at many different heights, and a protected toddler area for climbing and exploring without getting run over by older kids. It's very popular for birthday parties and a great place for families staying in hotels to bring younger kids while older ones shop at the Promenade nearby.

The Getty Center

1200 Getty Center Drive, off 405 Freeway; (310) 440-7300

Hours: Tuesday–Wednesday 11 a.m.–7 p.m.; Thursday–Friday 11 a.m.–9 p.m.; Saturday–Sunday 10 a.m.–6 p.m.

Admission: Free, but parking is $5, and you must have parking reservations; college students with ID may enter at any time without reservations

Appeal by Age Groups:

Pre-school	Grade School	Teens	Young Adults	Over 30	Seniors
★★★	★★★★★	★★★★★	★★★★★	★★★★★	★★★★★

Touring Time: Average 3–4 hours; minimum 1 hour

Rainy-Day Touring: Yes

Services and Facilities:

Restaurants Yes	Lockers No
Alcoholic beverages Yes	Pet kennels No
Disabled access Yes	Rain check No
Wheelchair rental Yes, free	Private tours No; museum tours
Baby stroller rental Yes, free	daily

Description and Comments   When you visit the Getty Center, you really feel as if you are Somewhere. Even small children seem to absorb a sense of occasion. The dazzling setting is the main event. Perched like a Pacific Rim Parthenon on a ridge above the San Diego Freeway, the Getty Center commands a view of the ocean on one side and miles of metropolitan Los Angeles on the other. Its Richard Meier–designed buildings, too, signal that this is a Grand and Important Place. Because the plazas and balconies are filled with visitors from all over the world, speaking different languages, it really does feel like the center of something.

If the Getty Center offered just grandeur, we wouldn't recommend it for children (what's impressive to an adult can be merely big to a five-year-old), but the Getty aggressively courts kids and their parents. In part, this is to encourage the future museum-goers into an appreciation of the Getty's collection of paintings, photographs, scultpure, illuminated manuscripts, and decorative arts by a spectrum of artists—from unnamed ancients to Michelangelo to Van Gogh.

It's a kid-friendly place from the start. Upon arrival, patrons are whisked up the hill on a monorail, which, of course, delights children. As they disembark and enter the main plaza, kids are drawn to the outsides of buildings, which are sheathed in sand-colored Italian travertine and embedded with fossil prints (we've spotted shells, leaves, and fish). Sometimes we rent an audioguide, which we tune to the special family track that offers stories, fun facts, and sound effects related to the artworks (as opposed to the scholarly discourse on the main track). Sometimes, we head straight for the Family Room to check out "Perplexing Paintings" or "The Getty Art Detective" game box, so that moving through the museum becomes a treasure hunt. Before or after our tour, we snap photos of the kids posed in costumes and backdrops that re-create famous paintings.

With older kids, we stop in the Art Information rooms of galleries that intrigue them and spend time doing projects or playing with interactive exhibits. Weekend workshops that combine gallery visits with art projects are offered for children ages 5–13 accompanied by a parent (sign up at the information desk in the entrance hall).

There's no weirder place to let off steam than the Getty Center's garden, a circus of shapes and spaces, winding pathways, and odd plants designed by Robert Irwin. And there's no finer place in L.A. to have a muffin and a juice break than the balcony dining area of the cafeteria.

Magicopolis

1418 4th Street, Santa Monica; (310) 451-2241; www.magicopolis.com

Hours: Show times vary but are generally Tuesday–Sunday evenings with matinees on weekends

Admission: Ticket prices range from $15 to $20 depending on the show

Appeal by Age Groups:

Pre-school	Grade School	Teens	Young Adults	Over 30	Seniors
★	★★★★	★★★★	★★★★	★★★★	★★★★

Touring Time: Average 2 hours; minimum 1 hour

Rainy-Day Touring: Yes

Services and Facilities:

Restaurants Snack bar	Lockers No
Alcoholic beverages No	Pet kennels No
Disabled access Yes	Rain check No
Wheelchair rental No	Private tours Birthday parties
Baby stroller rental No	

Description and Comments   This theater has been welcomed heartily by young magic-lovers in L.A., because the other two showcases for the region's great pool of magic talent are nightclubs. And because a little magic appeals to everyone, Magicopolis is a good idea for any family looking for special-occasion live entertainment in a family atmosphere. Choose a show in either the 150-seat theater (with raked seating so that even the shortest audience member can see everything) or the 50-seat close-up theater.

Some famous and soon-to-be famous performers can be seen here, and performances range from the traditional approach to the more modern and innovative. Sometimes the theater mounts variety shows featuring several different performers.

Museum of Flying

2772 Donald Douglas Loop N., Santa Monica Airport, Santa Monica; (310) 392-8822

Hours: Wednesday–Sunday 10 a.m.–5 p.m.

Admission: $7 adults, $5 seniors/students, $3 ages 16 and under, free for children 3 and under

Appeal by Age Groups:

Pre-school	Grade School	Teens	Young Adults	Over 30	Seniors
★★	★★★	★★	★★	★★★	★★★

Touring Time: Average 1 hour; minimum 1 hour

Minimum Touring Time: 1 hour

Rainy-Day Touring: No

Services and Facilities:

Restaurants Next door	Baby stroller rental No
Alcoholic beverages In adjacent restaurant	Lockers No
	Pet kennels No
Disabled access Yes	Rain check No
Wheelchair rental Yes, free	Private tours Yes

Description and Comments A nice little museum within Santa Monica Airport, this place showcases restored vintage airplanes, models, historical exhibits, and some fun hands-on interactive things for kids to do: sit in an old military helicopter and work the cockpit controls, listen to the control tower on headphones, and ride in a flight simulator ($2 extra). Ask about workshops on model-plane building and other related crafts for kids ages five and up, and see the review of neighboring DC3 under Family-Friendly Restaurants on page 172 (kids can play here while parents dine).

Pacific Park

380 Santa Monica Pier, Santa Monica; (310) 260-8747

Hours: Summer, Sunday–Thursday 11 a.m.–9 p.m., Friday–Saturday 11 a.m.–midnight; after Labor Day, Friday–Saturday 11 a.m.–midnight, Sunday 11 a.m.–9 p.m.

Admission: Rides $1–3, $2–6 (depending on season) for parking on pier

Appeal by Age Groups:

Pre-school	Grade School	Teens	Young Adults	Over 30	Seniors
★★★★	★★★★	★★★	★★	★★	★★

Touring Time: Average 2 hours; minimum 1 hour

Rainy-Day Touring: No

Services and Facilities:

Restaurants Concessions only	Lockers No
Alcoholic beverages No	Pet kennels No
Disabled access Yes	Rain check No
Wheelchair rental No	Private tours No
Baby stroller rental No	

Description and Comments A new but old-fashioned amusement park on the planks of the Santa Monica Pier, Pacific Park is a fun beach excursion, if only for the coastline view from the Ferris wheel. If your children are under age ten, come as close as possible to opening time, when the crowds are minimal and the clientele is other young families; late afternoon and evening draws swarms of teens and young adults on dates. Its small size makes it not too overwhelming for little ones, who get their own area on the shore side of the pier: bumper cars, mini–Ferris wheel, imitation Dumbo ride, and such. Older kids get a short but fast roller coaster, a couple of other modest thrills, and arcade games. Everyone loves the Ferris wheel. Don't miss the wonderful old indoor carousel on the other end of the parking lot, and allow extra time for running around the vast sandy expanse of Santa Monica Beach.

Family-Friendly Restaurants

AUNT KIZZY'S BACK PORCH

Villa Marina, 4325 Glencoe Avenue, Marina del Rey; (310) 578-1005

Meals served: Lunch, Sunday brunch, and dinner
Cuisine: Southern
Entree range: $11.95 (brunch—all you can eat); $7.95 (lunch);
  $11.95–12.95 (dinner)
Children's menu: Yes, $7.95
Reservations: Not accepted
Payment: AE

Bursting with liveliness and conviviality, Aunt Kizzy's is a great place for a casual, hearty family meal: meat loaf, fried chicken, peach cobbler, and lemonade. The children's menu lets kids have the same good food the adults are having, only in smaller portions. Expect a wait on weekends.

BROADWAY DELI

1457 3rd Street Promenade, Santa Monica; (310) 451-0616

Meals served: Breakfast, lunch, and dinner
Cuisine: American/Californian
Entree range: $5.50–8.95 (breakfast); $7.50–15 (lunch and dinner)
Children's menu: Yes; $3.50
Reservations: Not accepted
Payment: All major credit cards

More a yuppie diner than a deli, this teeming place on the edge of the Promenade packs 'em in for everything from omelets and coffee to frou-frou California pizzas and Bordeaux wines. The huge booths can handle a big family, the noise level is forgiving, and the children's menu offers all the standards. The cooking is perfectly satisfying, if not memorable.

CALIFORNIA PIZZA KITCHEN

11677 San Vicente Boulevard, Brentwood; (310) 826-3573

Meals served: Lunch and dinner
Cuisine: Californian
Entree range: $8–11 (lunch and dinner)
Children's menu: Yes; $3.99
Reservations: Only for large parties
Payment: All major credit cards

There's something for everyone at this slick chain. We like the shrimp-pesto pizza, the field-green salads, the wine by the glass, and the modest prices. Our kids like the mini-pizzas, the coloring menus, the booths, and the kid's drinks in take-home cups, complete with lids and bendy straws.

CROCODILE CAFE

101 Santa Monica Boulevard, Santa Monica; (310) 394-4783

Meals served: Lunch and dinner
Cuisine: Californian
Entree range: $6–16.95 (lunch and dinner)
Children's menu: Yes; $3.25–3.95

Reservations: Only for large parties
Payment: AE, DC, D, V

This small regional chain competes with California Pizza Kitchen, except its menu is more varied, going beyond chic pizzas to Cal-Mex-Asian-Mediterranean: roast chicken with garlic mashed potatoes, spicy Mexican pastas, black-bean soup, crab cakes. Kids get a good cheese pizza or simple pasta, along with crayons and a menu that is particularly fun to color. This is a great location on the corner of Santa Monica and Ocean, close to the Promenade, the beach, and many hotels.

DC3

Santa Monica Airport, 2800 Donald Douglas Loop N., Santa Monica; (310) 399-2323

Meals served: Lunch and dinner; closed Sunday; no lunch Saturday
Cuisine: Californian/Modern American
Entree range: $17–26 (dinner)
Children's menu: Yes
Reservations: Essential
Payment: All major credit cards

Since they share a building with the spiffy little Museum of Flying, and since most of their customers are upscale baby boomers with kids, DC3's owner saw an opportunity a few years back, and it's been a big success. On Tuesday through Friday nights, from 6 to 9 p.m., parents can deliver their kids to "air-plane camp" at the museum. The kids eat Caesar salad, pasta, and ice cream with airplane cookies, supervised by pros from the Santa Monica Babysitters Agency; when they're not eating, they're busy making friends, building model airplanes, flying in a simulator, doing art projects, and watching flying movies. Meanwhile, mom and dad are upstairs, enjoying a peaceful, tasty dinner (shiitake mushroom salad, sesame-crusted ahi, chocolate soufflé).

DUKE'S MALIBU

21150 Pacific Coast Highway, Malibu; (310) 317-0777

Meals served: Lunch, dinner, and Sunday brunch
Cuisine: American/Seafood
Entree range: $8–13 (lunch); $14–35 (dinner); $16.95 (Sunday buffet brunch; $9.95 for children)
Children's menu: Yes; $5
Reservations: Recommended
Payment: AE, V, D, MC

If your kids are enamored of surf culture, bring them to this swell branch of the popular Waikiki original, devoted to the father of surfing, Duke Kahanamoku. Beautifully located right on top of the Malibu ocean, Duke's is a casual, lively place decorated with old surfboards and surf photos, offering modern surf 'n' turf fare: a mighty fine Caesar salad and straightforward grilled Hawaiian fish, with burgers and such for kids.

EL CHOLO

1025 Wilshire Boulevard, Santa Monica; (310) 899-1106

Meals served: Lunch and dinner
Cuisine: Mexican
Entree range: $7–20 (lunch and dinner)
Children's menu: Yes
Reservations: Necessary
Payment: All major credit cards

The original El Cholo, in the heart of central L.A., is loved by several generations of Angelenos for its tasty Cal-Mex food and margaritas; this sprawling new branch in Santa Monica continues the tradition honorably. Tilework, fountains, plants, and painted walls are the set, costumed waitresses are the performers, and families crowd in for the chips 'n' guac, saucy cheese enchiladas, fajitas, soft tacos, and other non-authentic but nonetheless delicious classics.

JOHNNIE'S NEW YORK PIZZA

1456 3rd Street Promenade, Santa Monica; (310) 395-9062

22333 Pacific Coast Highway, Malibu; (310) 456-1717

Meals served: Lunch and dinner
Cuisine: Italian/pizza
Entree range: $6.95–18.95 (lunch and dinner)
Children's menu: Yes; $2.95 at Santa Monica (no children's menu at Malibu location)
Reservations: Not accepted
Payment: AE, MC, V

Not only does Johnnie's make one of the best pizzas in L.A., it also has one of the best kid-menu deals in town at the Santa Monica location: $2.95 gets kids under age 12 a small pizza or spaghetti, a drink, and an ice cream sundae. This is traditional New York pizza, thin-crusted, herby, and cheesy, and it's really terrific. Both branches are noisy, casual, and New Yorkish, even if they are packed with tan Angelenos.

THE REEL INN

18661 Pacific Coast Highway, Malibu; (310) 456-8221

Meals served: Lunch and dinner
Cuisine: Seafood
Entree range: $5.95–14.95 (lunch); $7.95–25 (dinner)
Children's menu: Yes; $4.95
Reservations: Large groups only
Payment: AE, MC, V

Funky, affordable, and beach-adjacent, this is the sort of no-frills seafood joint found in every respectable beach town, an order-at-the-counter, share-big-tables sort of place. You can splurge on fresh lobster, but most people are perfectly happy with simple grilled ahi, wahoo, and snapper, with maybe a cup of chowder. The kids' menu is fine.

TYPHOON

Santa Monica Airport, 3221 Donald Douglas Loop S., Santa Monica; (310) 390-6565

Meals served: Lunch and dinner; closed Saturday lunch
Cuisine: Pacific Rim
Entree range: $7.95–15 (lunch); $12.95–20 (dinner)
Children's menu: No
Reservations: Advised
Payment: All major credit cards

At first glimpse, this might not seem a great family restaurant, what with the serious bar (featuring the sort of Technicolor drinks that have the word "killer" in their names) and preponderance of beautiful people. But take a second look, and you and your kids will love it. Request a table by the windows or on the balcony overlooking the runway of Santa Monica Airport, which still looks like it could be the set for the airport in Casablanca; the kids will love watching the small planes take off, and if you time it right, you might get a great sunset to boot. The menu wanders the Asian continent, offering everything from Thai mee krob to Japanese sushi to Korean barbecue, and it's all terrific; for kids who find such exotica yucky, there are simple noodles and delicious egg rolls.

Central Los Angeles

"Central" Los Angeles as we're describing it here is not a neighborhood in any way—in fact, we'll be touching on sights and attractions in **Hollywood, West Hollywood, Wilshire Center, downtown, Exposition Park, Griffith Park,** and **Universal City.** But all of these communities are geographically contiguous in a mostly flatland area best defined by freeway boundaries: the Santa Monica Freeway is to the south, the Ventura Freeway to the north, the Hollywood Freeway to the east, and the San Diego Freeway to the west. It's home to many of L.A.'s major museums and cultural centers as well as a multicultural triangle of eating/shopping districts: **Chinatown, Little Tokyo,** and **Olvera Street.** Finally, it contains one of California's premier theme parks, the movie lovers' **Universal Studios.**

Family Lodging

Beverly Plaza

This smallish (98 rooms), good-quality hotel is located a block and a half east of the Beverly Center shopping mall. It's not quite in Beverly Hills, but it's close enough for your luxury-loving shoppers, and yet near enough to the major streets that will carry you to other parts of town. The nearest attractions are the Petersen Museum, Farmer's Market, and Mann's Chinese Theatre, and there's plenty of walking and dining nearby. There's a nice outdoor pool and Nintendo on the TV.

8384 W. 3rd Street, L.A.; (800) 62-HOTEL (4-6835) or (323) 658-6600; fax (323) 653-3464. Year-round rates begin at $189.

The Clarion Hollywood Roosevelt

An oasis on oft-gritty Hollywood Boulevard, the historic Roosevelt is full of movie ghosts. A big celeb hangout in the 1930s, the hotel now honors the

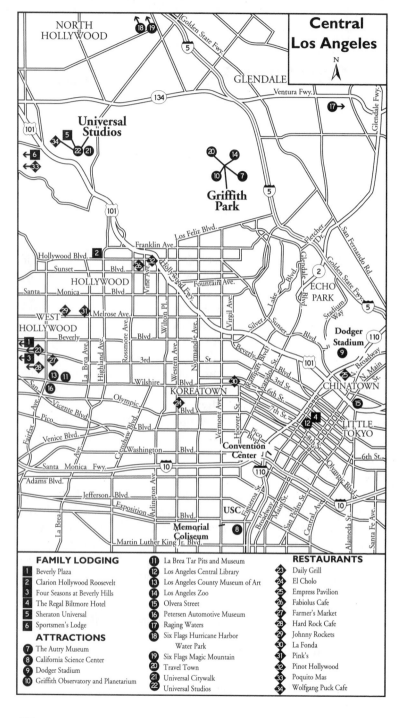

NORTH HOLLYWOOD

GLENDALE

Central Los Angeles

N

Universal Studios

Griffith Park

HOLLYWOOD

ECHO PARK

WEST HOLLYWOOD

Dodger Stadium

CHINATOWN

KOREATOWN

LITTLE TOKYO

Convention Center

USC

Memorial Coliseum

FAMILY LODGING
1. Beverly Plaza
2. Clarion Hollywood Roosevelt
3. Four Seasons at Beverly Hills
4. The Regal Biltmore Hotel
5. Sheraton Universal
6. Sportsmen's Lodge

ATTRACTIONS
7. The Autry Museum
8. California Science Center
9. Dodger Stadium
10. Griffith Observatory and Planetarium
11. La Brea Tar Pits and Museum
12. Los Angeles Central Library
13. Los Angeles County Museum of Art
14. Los Angeles Zoo
15. Olvera Street
16. Petersen Automotive Museum
17. Raging Waters
18. Six Flags Hurricane Harbor Water Park
19. Six Flags Magic Mountain
20. Travel Town
21. Universal Citywalk
22. Universal Studios

RESTAURANTS
23. Daily Grill
24. El Cholo
25. Empress Pavilion
26. Fabiolus Cafe
27. Farmer's Market
28. Hard Rock Cafe
29. Johnny Rockets
30. La Fonda
31. Pink's
32. Pinot Hollywood
33. Poquito Mas
34. Wolfgang Puck Cafe

past with a Hollywood Memorabilia Gallery. The pool is set in a tropical oasis within an oasis, encircled by popular "cabana rooms." The 320-room, 38-suite landmark hotel has changed hands many times, and service, food service, and amenities have varied widely in recent years, but it has few competitors in the heart of Hollywood. The Chinese Theatre and the home of the Academy Awards are across the street.

7000 Hollywood Boulevard, Hollywood; (323) 466-7000 or (800) 950-7667; fax (323) 466-9376. Rates start at $159; kids under age 18 stay free with parent.

Four Seasons Hotel Los Angeles at Beverly Hills

The Four Seasons people know how to cater to kids, and this elegant hotel succeeds in making both children and movie stars happy. The location, on the east border of Beverly Hills, is terrific, and the 284 rooms and 42 suites are first-class, appointed with every convenience and luxury. The recently remodeled pool area is one of the most glamorous in L.A., with a view over palm-tree tops across the prettier parts of the city. In spite of being a major power hangout, it's a great place for families ready to do the upscale thing. Gift bags are given to children upon check-in, and milk and cookies are served to them that night. Family-rated movies and VCRs can be rented for kids, a baby-sitter service is available, and not only does the very fine restaurant (as well as room service) have a kids' menu, but a beautiful kids' buffet table with kid-friendly foods is set up during the Sunday brunch.

300 S. Doheny Drive, L.A.; (310) 273-2222 or (800) 332-3442; fax (310) 859-3824. Rates range from $265 to $440.

The Regal Biltmore Hotel

The Biltmore is well located if you're bringing kids along on a downtown business/pleasure trip or if you want to focus on such cultural activities as theater at the Music Center and storytime at the Central Library. It sits in the heart of downtown, about 30 minutes east of Santa Monica beach and 20 minutes southeast of Universal Studios. We've found that kids actually enjoy the grand landmark hotels—the many differently decorated areas, the ornateness, and the various nooks and crannies seem to appeal to them. This beautifully restored 683-room, 46-suite dowager is, like many downtown hotels, a bustling center of activity, with locals and conventioneers streaming in and out of its many restaurants, bars, ballrooms, and meetings rooms, but the city-within-a-city feeling can be terrific for some kids. It's fun to dress up and take tea in the historic lobby-lounge, with its hand-painted beams overhead. Less formal settings are also around, including a cafe and an indoor pool. You may order half-price children's portions at the Italian trattoria, Smeraldi's.

506 S. Grand Avenue, downtown; (213) 624-1011 or (800) 245-8673; fax (213) 612-1545. Rates begin at $200.

Sheraton Universal

A well-run link in the Sheraton chain, this 442-room, 23-suite modern high-rise hotel is a good bet for families planning a Universal City visit, because its packages with the park offer savings and convenience. The packages ($199 for one night, $390 for two nights) include two Universal Studios passes (one and three days, respectively) with the room, plus discounts on additional passes that may be purchased at the hotel, so there's no waiting in the box-office line. That price is for two adults plus any kids using available bedding; rooms at this rate have two doubles or one king bed. Rollaways are $25 additional. Universal City and CityWalk are a free tram ride or a five-minute walk away. Game room, large heated pool, children's menus, and good-sized, comfortable, generic rooms, some with killer views of the Valley.

333 Universal Terrace Parkway, Universal City; (818) 980-1212 or (800) 325-3535; fax (818) 985-4980. Rates start at $149.

Sportsmen's Lodge

We're not sure what's so sportsmanlike about this comfortable, low-slung, garden-style hotel—the only thing people hunt for in this Studio City neighborhood is a good restaurant. Still, we like its subtly hokey charms, not to mention its large pool set in a protected courtyard, its little lagoon bedecked with swans, and its tiny tinkling waterfalls. The studio suites with patios are perfect for families. There's a children's menu in room service and the casual cafe, and there's also a lot of good eating along Ventura Boulevard. Universal City is only about five minutes away, Hollywood is just over the hill, and Pasadena's Old Town is about 15 minutes via freeway.

12825 Ventura Boulevard, Studio City; (818) 769-4700 or (800) 821-8511; fax (323) 877-3898. Rates start at $118; kids under age 18 stay free in parents' room.

Attractions

The Autry Museum of Western Heritage

4700 Western Heritage Way, Griffith Park; (323) 667-2000

Hours: Tuesday–Sunday 10 a.m.–5 p.m., Thursday until 8 p.m.

Admission: $7.50 adults; $5 seniors 60+; $5 students ages 13–18; $3 children ages 2–12; free for children age 2 and under

Appeal by Age Groups:

Pre-school	Grade School	Teens	Young Adults	Over 30	Seniors
★★★	★★★★	★★★	★★★	★★★	★★★★★

Touring Time: Average 2½ hours; minimum 1 hour

Rainy-Day Touring: Yes

Services and Facilities:

Restaurants Cafeteria-style cafe	Lockers No
Alcoholic beverages No	Pet kennels No
Disabled access Yes	Rain check No
Wheelchair rental Yes, free	Private tours Yes
Baby stroller rental Yes, free	

Description and Comments This is a perfect outing for grandparents and their 4–12-year-old grandchildren, or older parents and their kids. If you're over 50, chances are good that you idolized stars like Gene Autry and Tom Mix—and along with often-worthy exhibitions of paintings, sculpture, and other works from Western and Native American artists, you'll find great collections of Hollywood cowboy memorabilia, from costumes to posters. Our kids love the full-size jail cell, the dioramas reenacting the shootout at the OK Corral, the collections of sheriff's badges and pistols, and especially the hands-on re-creation of a Southwestern ranch house owned by generations of a Mexican-American family. Elsewhere in the museum is a "movie studio" in which kids are inserted via videotape into an old Western chase scene. But our kids' favorite stop is the gift shop. Weekends often bring free performances of cowboy music and/or children's art classes.

California Science Center

700 State Drive, Exposition Park; (213) 744-7400

Hours: Daily 10 a.m.–5 p.m.; closed Thanksgiving, Christmas, New Year's Day

Admission: Free, but $5 parking

Appeal by Age Groups:

Pre-school	Grade School	Teens	Young Adults	Over 30	Seniors
★★	★★★★★	★★★★	★★★★	★★★★	★★★

Touring Time: Average 3 hours; minimum 1½ hours

Rainy-Day Touring: No

Services and Facilities:

Restaurants Yes	Lockers Yes
Alcoholic beverages No	Pet kennels No
Disabled access Yes	Rain check No
Wheelchair rental Yes, free	Private tours No
Baby stroller rental No	

Description and Comments Los Angeles parents, teachers, and kids love this ambitious museum, which has revitalized the Exposition Park complex south of downtown. At first this popularity made for some pretty nasty crowds; when my daughter visited on a school field trip, she and her classmates couldn't even get near Tess, the 50-foot model woman with the see-through body that lets you see how the body's systems work. (What they missed was a 15-minute animatronic demonstration of a virtual soccer game that Tess plays; lights, sounds, and visual tricks help explain what's happening in her body while she runs and kicks.) But on a later visit, when the crowds had abated, some in our group did get a chance to operate the high-wire bicycle, and everyone experienced the simulated earthquake. The kids also enjoyed pulling, maneuvering, and playing with lots of hands-on science experiments and displays ("The magnetic boat was cool!"). The secret to visiting this place in relative peace is to come on a school day between 1 and 3 p.m. The field-trip kids will have left, and the after-school crowd hasn't hit yet. The exhibits are so dynamic, fun, and educational that they're worth our children missing a day of school.

Dodger Stadium Tour

Stadium, 1000 Elysian Park Avenue; (323) 224-1448; www.dodgers.com

Hours: Non-game days during baseball season, daily during off-season, 10 a.m., 11:30 a.m., and 1 p.m.

Admission: $8 adults, $4 children, seniors

Appeal by Age Groups:

Pre-school	Grade School	Teens	Young Adults	Over 30	Seniors
★	★★★	★★★	★★	★★★	★★★

Touring Time: Average 1–1½ hours; minimum 1 hour

Rainy-Day Touring: No

Services and Facilities:

Restaurants No, snackbars closed on non-game days	Baby stroller rental No
	Lockers No
Alcoholic beverages No	Pet kennels No
Disabled access Yes	Rain check No
Wheelchair rental No	Private tours Yes

Description and Comments   If you have a baseball nut in your family, this behind-the-scenes tour offers the kind of up-close experience so hard to come by in our electronic age. A guide takes you into the press box, clubhouse area, bullpen, and dugout, onto the field, and through the new Dodger Museum. Reservations required.

Griffith Observatory and Planetarium

2800 E. Observatory Road (off Vermont Avenue), Griffith Park; (323) 664-1191

Hours: In winter, Tuesday–Friday 2–10 p.m.; weekends 12:30–10 p.m.;
closed Monday; in summer, daily 12:30–10 p.m.; call to confirm hours

Admission: Hall of Science/telescope, free; Planetarium show $2 ages
5–12, $4 ages 13–64, $3 seniors, children under age 5 free for 1:30
p.m. show only; Laserium $8 adults, $7 children ages 5–12 and
seniors; for information call (818) 901-9405 or visit www.laserium.com

Appeal by Age Groups:

Pre-school	Grade School	Teens	Young Adults	Over 30	Seniors
★★	★★★★	★★★	★★★	★★★	★★★

Touring Time: Average 1 hour (planetarium show 1 hour long);
minimum 30 minutes

Rainy-Day Touring: Telescope closed during rain

Services and Facilities:

Restaurants Snack bar		Lockers No	
Alcoholic beverages No		Pet kennels No	
Disabled access Limited		Rain check No	
Wheelchair rental No		Private tours No	
Baby stroller rental No			

Description and Comments A clear, smog-free day is essential to making the
most of this revered L.A. landmark, perched in the Griffith Park hills a few
miles east of the Hollywood sign. Outside the curvaceous art deco planetarium building are coin-operated telescopes. These small telescopes fascinate
older kids but frustrate little ones, who can't see out of them very well—but
they're usually delighted to run up and down the curved stairways. Inside are
exhibits about planets, stars, and outer space, some a bit musty, some interactive and captivating. You can also take a peek at the really big telescope that
peeks out the planetarium's roof. The planetarium show is worthwhile for
school-age children, who can absorb a little of the space talk, and kids from
about age nine up to teenhood find the seven different Laserium shows really
cool, but they're too loud and intense for young ones.

La Brea Tar Pits and George C. Page Museum of La Brea Discoveries

5801 Wilshire Boulevard, Hancock Park; (323) 934-PAGE (7243)

Hours: Daily, 10 a.m. to 5 p.m.

Admission: $6 adults, $3.50 seniors/students, $2 children under 12; free
first Tuesday of every month

Appeal by Age Groups:

Pre-school	Grade School	Teens	Young Adults	Over 30	Seniors
★★★★	★★★★★	★★★★	★★★★	★★★★★	★★★★★

Touring Time: Average 1½ hours; minimum 30 minutes
Rainy-Day Touring: Yes
Services and Facilities:

Restaurants No	Lockers No
Alcoholic beverages No	Pet kennels No
Disabled access Yes	Rain check No
Wheelchair rental Yes, free	Private tours Yes
Baby stroller rental No	

Description and Comments   Every young Angeleno comes here at one time or another and pulls up on the poles suspended in tar-pit goo to get a feel for what it must have been like to be a prehistoric animal stuck in the bubbling ooze. This museum is architecturally interesting and pleasantly compact, with an inventive range of varied exhibits, from a film and holograms to models and a window through which visitors can watch paleontologists cleaning and studying bones. The exhibits are tightly focused—all pertain to fossils found on this very site. The Page is a standout, and it has the best museum shop in the city for kids.

Los Angeles Central Library

630 W. 5th Street, Downtown; (213) 228-7000
Hours: Monday–Thursday 10 a.m.–8 p.m., Friday and Saturday 10 a.m.–
   6 p.m., Sunday 1 p.m.–5 p.m.; closed major holidays
Admission: Free; parking in selected lots $2 with library card
Appeal by Age Groups:

Pre-school	Grade School	Teens	Young Adults	Over 30	Seniors
★★★	★★★	★★★	★★★	★★★★	★★★★

Touring Time: Average 2 hours; minimum 1 hour
Rainy-Day Touring: Excellent
Services and Facilities:

Restaurants Yes	Lockers Yes
Alcoholic beverages No	Pet kennels No
Disabled access Yes	Rain check No
Baby stroller rental No	Private tours Docent tours

Description and Comments   The hordes of office workers leave downtown L.A. on weekends, so parking is easier and cheaper than during the week, and the Central Library is a real treat. Children's programs (theater or puppets or video) on Saturday and Sunday give a shape and purpose to the outing, but it's great fun to simply browse the beautiful 1930s-era restored children's room, play on the computers in the room adjacent, ride the escalators through the glass-walled, four-story atrium, with its cartoonlike giant chandeliers, and get lunch at the Chinese buffet restaurant with terrace seating. There are docent tours that give insight into the wonderful artwork commissioned in all areas when the library was rebuilt after a fire (the elevator shafts are lined with the old card catalogue cards), but that's really an adult pleasure.

Los Angeles County Museum of Art

5905 Wilshire Boulevard, Miracle Mile; (323) 857-6000 or (323) 857-6010 (tickets)

Hours: Monday, Tuesday, Thursday noon–8 p.m.; Friday noon–9 p.m.; Saturday and Sunday 11 a.m.–8 p.m. Closed Wednesdays, Thanksgiving, and Christmas Day

Admission: $7 adults, $5 seniors/students, $1 children ages 6–17, free for ages under 5; some special-fee shows; free second Tuesday of every month

Appeal by Age Groups:

Pre-school	Grade School	Teens	Young Adults	Over 30	Seniors
★★★	★★★★	★★★★★	★★★★★	★★★★	★★★★

Touring Time: Average a half-day; minimum 2 hours

Rainy-Day Touring: Good

Services and Facilities:

Restaurants Yes	Lockers No
Alcoholic beverages Yes	Pet kennels No
Disabled access Yes	Rain check No
Wheelchair rental Yes, free	Private tours No
Baby stroller rental No	

Description and Comments This big-city art museum is a complex of buildings on the same park-like block as the La Brea Tar Pits and Page Museum. Don't try to see everything in a single visit—just pick a single period, floor, or section, enjoy it, and be done. Some strong holdings that might appeal to certain kids are the costume/fashion collection (try it on middle-schoolers), the photo collection (good for teens; too disturbing for little ones), the modern art wing (whose huge paintings and bright colors appeal to elementary-age kids), and the sacred art of India—stone sculptures are impressive at any age. A separate but related facility is the Japanese Pavilion, with a specialized collection not likely to be appreciated by many children.

Los Angeles Zoo

5333 Zoo Drive, off I-5 Freeway, Griffith Park; (323) 644-4200

Hours: Daily 10 a.m.–5 p.m.; closed Christmas

Admission: $8.25 adults, $5.25 seniors 65+, $3.25 ages 2–17, free for children under age 2

Appeal by Age Groups:

Pre-school	Grade School	Teens	Young Adults	Over 30	Seniors
★★★★	★★★★	★★★	★★★	★★★	★★★

Touring Time: Average 3 hours; minimum 1 hour

Rainy-Day Touring: Limited

Services and Facilities:

Restaurants Yes	Lockers No
Alcoholic beverages Yes	Pet kennels Yes
Disabled access Yes	Rain check No
Wheelchair rental Yes	Private tours Yes
Baby stroller rental Yes	

Description and Comments   A zoo membership is a must for many L.A. families—special events abound at this large, inviting attraction, and many are for kids. For visitors, this means you'll find plenty of entertainment in addition to looking at animals. There are excellent demonstrations and shows (schedules available at gate), as well as fun educational installations at various points (What Does a Bear Smell?). The children's zoo and adjacent baby-animal nursery are so comfortable for many that families with the youngest kids hardly wander from this area. Overnight camps and family camping nights are occasionally offered in the summer.

Olvera Street

125 Paseo de la Plaza, downtown; (213) 628-1274

Hours: Daily 10 a.m.–7 p.m.; summer, until 10 p.m.

Admission: Free

Appeal by Age Groups:

Pre-school	Grade School	Teens	Young Adults	Over 30	Seniors
★★★	★★★★	★★★★	★★★★	★★★★	★★★★

Touring Time: Average 2½ hours, with meal; minimum 1 hour

Rainy-Day Touring: Limited

Services and Facilities:

Restaurants Yes	Lockers No
Alcoholic beverages Yes	Pet kennels No
Disabled access Limited	Rain check No
Baby stroller rental No	Private tours No

Description and Comments   When we first came to L.A., we thought Olvera Street was corny, but when we worked downtown, we started to hang out here, and we came to appreciate its fine sidewalk cafes and strolling mariachis, its varied shops with colorful, often seasonal goods, and its lively street scene. Our daughter was enthusiastic after a school field trip that included a tour of the historic adobe and the vintage fire station. And everybody loves the shopping, which is every bit as good as on the main tourist strip in Ensenada. We've been happy with purchases of blankets, purses, silver jewelry, piñatas, paper flowers, and jumping beans.

Petersen Automotive Museum

6060 Wilshire Boulevard, Miracle Mile; (323) 930-2277

Hours: Tuesday–Sunday 10 a.m.–6 p.m.; Discovery Center closes at 5 p.m.

Admission: $7 adults, $5 seniors and students, $3 ages 5–12, free under age 5

Appeal by Age Groups:

Pre-school	Grade School	Teens	Young Adults	Over 30	Seniors
★★★	★★★★	★★★★★	★★★★	★★★★	★★★★

Touring Time: Average 2½ hours; minimum 1 hour

Rainy-Day Touring: Limited

Services and Facilities:

Restaurants	Mini-mart	Lockers	No
Alcoholic beverages	No	Pet kennels	No
Disabled access	Yes	Rain check	No
Baby stroller rental	No	Private tours	No

Description and Comments California's car culture is honored and explored in this unusual museum. More than 150 classic cars, hot rods, Indy cars, trucks, motorcycles, and custom vehicles are displayed in settings that bring the period or use of the car to life. It won't feel like a museum as you and the kids walk through settings from the horse-and-buggy era to the space-age future, each with motor vehicles of the period. Some visitors will like the vintage signage and other historically accurate parts of the environments (complete in some cases with sounds) as much as the gleaming motor vehicles. The second-floor exhibits are more traditional but include some favorites like hot rods and celebrity cars. The new Children's Discovery Center brings welcome interactivity to the museum.

Travel Town

5200 W. Zoo Drive, Griffith Park; (323) 662-5874

Hours: Monday–Friday 10 a.m.–4 p.m.; Saturday–Sunday, holidays 10 a.m.–5 p.m.; closed Christmas

Admission: Free

Appeal by Age Groups:

Pre-school	Grade School	Teens	Young Adults	Over 30	Seniors
★★★	★★★	★★	★★	★★	★★

Touring Time: Average 1 hour; minimum 8 minutes for the ride only

Rainy-Day Touring: No

Services and Facilities:

Restaurants No	Lockers No
Alcoholic beverages No	Pet kennels No
Disabled access Yes	Rain check No
Wheelchair rental No	Private tours Yes
Baby stroller rental No	

Description and Comments   A fond memory from our own childhoods, Travel Town is now enchanting a new generation of young train lovers, who can climb into old engines, scramble through cabooses, and ride a miniature train around the park. Our Thomas-obsessed nephew wants to come here every weekend. It's basically just a bunch of old train cars and engines, but that's enough for fun.

Universal CityWalk

1000 Universal City Plaza, Universal City; (818) 622-4455

Hours: Sunday–Thursday 11 a.m.–9 p.m.; Friday–Saturday 11 a.m.– 11 p.m.

Admission: Free (parking $6)

Appeal by Age Groups:

Pre-school	Grade School	Teens	Young Adults	Over 30	Seniors
★★	★★★★	★★★★	★★★★	★★★	★★★

Touring Time: Average 2 hours; minimum 1 hour

Rainy-Day Touring: So-so; mall area is outdoors

Services and Facilities:

Restaurants Yes	Lockers No
Alcoholic beverages Yes	Pet kennels No
Disabled access Yes	Rain check No
Wheelchair rental Yes	Private tours No
Baby stroller rental No	

Description and Comments   Newly expanded, CityWalk is even more aggressively courting the family (and date-night) market, and by the size of the crowds, it is succeeding beautifully. Now, in addition to the movie theaters, magic club, B.B. King's Blues Club, restaurants, and shops, there's an IMAX theater, a NASCAR virtual-racing experience, a rock 'n' roll bowling alley, a bunch more restaurants, and even more of the CityWalk shops that sell such quintessential inessentials as wind-up toys, nostalgic clothing, science-fiction memorabilia, magic tricks, and hair-braiding accessories. Of course, the entire place is as phony as a three-dollar bill (there's no actual *city* here!), and it's shamelessly shallow and commercial, but there's no denying that it's fun. You'll have to pry teenagers out of here with a crowbar.

Universal Studios

1000 Universal City Plaza, Universal City; (818) 508-9600

Hours: Mid-April–September, daily 9 a.m.–7 p.m. (box office open 8:30 a.m.– 4 p.m.); October–March, 9 a.m.–6 p.m.

Admission: $41 adults, $36 seniors 60+, $31 children ages 3–11

Appeal by Age Groups:

Pre-school	Grade School	Teens	Young Adults	Over 30	Seniors
★	★★★★	★★★★★	★★★★	★★★★	★★★★

Touring Time: Average 8 hours; minimum 4 hours

Rainy-Day Touring: None

Services and Facilities:

Restaurants Yes	Lockers Yes
Alcoholic beverages Yes	Pet kennels Yes
Disabled access Yes	Rain check Yes
Wheelchair rental Yes	Private tours Yes
Baby stroller rental Yes	

Description and Comments If your children are younger than eight you might want to postpone a trip here—it costs a fortune to get in, and the money is mostly wasted on the very young, for whom most of the special-effects rides are too scary. Although several new attractions for younger kids have been added, kids under age eight are too young to be impressed by the behind-the-scenes moviemaking aspect of the park, the main point of the place.

That said, a trip to Universal Studios can be a tremendously enjoyable day for the right group, especially older elementary-school kids, teenagers, and adults who haven't experienced it before. Although sometimes hokey, the one-hour, often-updated tour-bus ride is essential for first-timers, both for its backlot peek at sets from many popular movies and TV shows and for its thrills—the parting of the Red Sea isn't as cool as it used to be, but the simulated earthquake is impressively realistic (and scary for Angelenos!). As for the rides, their thrills come from special effects, not roller coaster speed, and those thrills are remarkable. Back to the Future and Jurassic Park are amazing feats of movie-ride technology, not to mention

Universal Studios Hollywood

1. Animal Actors Stage
2. Back to the Future
3. *Backdraft*
4. Backlot Tram Tour
5. *Beetlejuice's Rockin' Graveyard Revue*
6. E.T. Adventure
7. Jurassic Park—The Ride

big fun. Backdraft—not a ride, really, but a close-up view of special effects used in that fire-fighting movie—is also breathtaking, but if you take a fearful kid on this one, you'll be sorry. Instead, head for the Animal Actors Stage or the new Curious George interactive playground.

We recently brought a pack of elementary school boys here, and what they really remembered wasn't the rides but the spectacular Waterworld show.

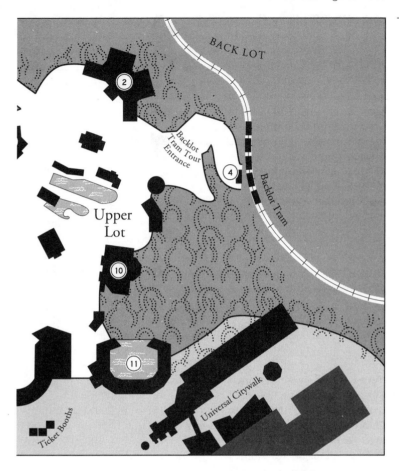

8. Lucy, A Tribute
9. *Terminator 2 3-D*
10. Rugrats Magic Adventure
11. Waterworld

12. *Wild, Wild, Wild, West
    Stunt Show*
13. *World of CineMagic*

What flopped on the screen is great fun on an outdoor stage—stuntmen and stuntwomen in fabulous rags fighting on jet skis and diving from towers. The Wild West stunt show is also a winner, and there's an Alvin and the Chipmunks revue for the little ones; in fact, any show is worth a look, because the studio connection attracts talented producers and performers.

Family-Friendly Restaurants

DAILY GRILL

Beverly Connection, 100 N. La Cienega Boulevard, L.A.; (310) 659-3100

Meals served: Lunch, dinner, and Sunday brunch
Cuisine: American
Entree range: $8.95–12.50 (lunch); $9.95–20.95 (dinner)
Children's menu: Yes
Reservations: Not necessary
Payment: AE, DC, MC, V, D

This spin-off of Beverly Hills's swank The Grill is popular with families catching a movie or shopping at the Beverly Connection or the looming Beverly Center across the street. It's a yuppie copy of an old New York or San Francisco bar and grill, with tile floors, wooden booths, chicken pot pie, and turkey meat loaf. Our kids adore the food, and they can color on the paper tablecloths.

EL CHOLO

1121 S. Western Avenue, Mid-Wilshire; (323) 734-2773

Meals served: Lunch and dinner
Cuisine: Mexican
Entree range: $6.95–19.95 (lunch and dinner)
Children's menu: Yes
Reservations: Advised
Payment: All major credit cards

Since 1921, El Cholo has been home to the city's best margaritas and green-corn tamales—and the enchiladas, chiles rellenos, taco tray, carnitas, and guacamole are pretty swell, too. A multiethnic cross-section of L.A. folk fills the maze of painted, tiled, adobe-style dining rooms, served by waitresses in flouncy costume. The children's menu has a burger, but they're better off with the junior quesadilla or enchilada. The location is midway between downtown and the La Brea Tar Pits.

EMPRESS PAVILION

988 N. Hill Street, Chinatown; (213) 617-9898

Meals served: Breakfast (dim sum), lunch, and dinner
Cuisine: Chinese
Entree range: $1.50–4 (dim sum plates); $7–15 (dinner)

Children's menu: No
Reservations: Accepted for dinner only
Payment: DC, MC, V

The problem with visiting the best dim sum restaurant in Chinatown is that everyone in L.A. knows it's the best dim sum restaurant, so the wait is an hour long by noon on weekends, and the good stuff is gone by 12:30. So arrive at this Chinatown mini-mall by 10:30 on weekends to share with your kids the spectacle of a vast, teeming dining room being serviced by surly women pushing metal steam carts of superb dumplings and buns of every possible description (ask for bao buns, potstickers, and shui mai, which are the most agreeable to children). Come nighttime, the dim sum vanishes and some very good Cantonese cooking takes over, from excellent seafood to Peking duck.

FABIOLUS CAFE

6270 Sunset Boulevard, Hollywood; (323) 467-2882

Meals served: Lunch and dinner, daily
Cuisine: Italian
Entree range: $8.95–17.95 (lunch and dinner)
Children's menu: No
Reservations: Accepted but not necessary
Payment: All major credit cards

If you're doing the Tinseltown tourist thing, skip the Hollywood Boulevard greasy spoons and head over to this friendly, inexpensive trattoria a few doors east of the Cineramadome. The pastas and salads are delicious, the setting casual, and though there's no children's menu, the kitchen is happy to make a plain pasta or pizza. There's another fine location next to Paramount Studios (5255 Melrose Avenue; (323) 464-5857).

FARMER'S MARKET

6333 W. Third Street, L.A.; (323) 933-9211 or (323) 931-3773

Meals served: Breakfast, lunch, and early dinner (closes between 5 p.m. and 7 p.m. depending on day and season)
Cuisine: All sorts
Entree range: Varies, but rarely over $7
Children's menu: Yes, at some stands
Reservations: Not accepted
Payment: Varies by stand

One of the city's great meeting spots and melting pots, Farmer's Market is beloved of senior citizens and children alike. Area retirees meet to chat, nosh, play cards, and shop for high-quality produce, meat, seafood, and specialty foods; children love to cruise the open-air merchants, looking for candy vendors and seeking kid paradise: Bob's, home of the best dough-nuts in town. Come early to snag a good table strategically located between the most interesting food vendors, so everyone can get what they want—a slice of pizza for one, a corned-beef sandwich for another (Magee's is superb), a bowl of gumbo for another. On your way out, pick up supplies for a picnic dinner in a park or on the beach.

HARD ROCK CAFE

Beverly Center, 8600 Beverly Boulevard, L.A./Also at Universal CityWalk; (310) 276-7605

Meals served: Lunch and dinner
Cuisine: American
Entree range: $7–17.99 (lunch and dinner)
Children's menu: Yes; $5.99
Reservations: Not accepted
Payment: AE, DC, MC, V

Located on the ground floor of the great hulking Beverly Center, this is typically the first place a first-time visitor to L.A. wants to go. Of course, it looks like every other Hard Rock in the country, and a real rock or movie star would never set foot inside, but that won't bother star-struck preteens and teens. They'll love the rock memorabilia, the throbbing music, the people-watching, the burgers and ribs, and the chance to buy a T-shirt. Where you will see stars, especially on quiet weekdays, is in the shopping mall upstairs: We've seen tons of them, often just catching a movie or buying shoes. If you have a teen, by all means allow time for a cruise of the mall.

JOHNNY ROCKETS

7507 Melrose Avenue, L.A.; (323) 651-3361

Meals served: Lunch and dinner (open late)
Cuisine: American
Entree range: $2.95–4.75 (lunch and dinner)
Children's menu: Yes; $1.75–2.95
Reservations: Not taken
Payment: AE, D, MC, V

Melrose isn't quite as hip as it once was, but teens will still find it worth a gander, and this chain is well located in the heart of the action. Basic burg-ers, fries, and shakes are served in a blindingly lit red-and-white diner to a soundtrack of rock oldies.

LA FONDA

2501 Wilshire Boulevard, Mid-Wilshire; (213) 380-5055

Meals served: Dinner
Cuisine: Mexican
Entree range: $12–17 (dinner)
Children's menu: No
Reservations: Essential
Payment: AE, DC, MC, V

One of the city's greatest cultural treasures is the mariachi group that is resident at this long-established supper club. The music is authentic, moving, memorable, and loud enough (seven or eight musicians include several brass players) to get the attention of usually jaded teens. (One 16-year-old boy removed his headset, and the next day mentioned, without prompting, that the music was "good, huh?") Every table holds an office party group, a birthday celebration, or a group of tourists, and the mariachis oblige with "Happy Birthday" in French and Japanese. But remember, you're seeing the real thing. And the food ain't bad, either. Remarkably priced for the experience, too.

PINK'S

709 N. La Brea Avenue, L.A.; (323) 931-4223

Meals served: Daily 9:30 a.m.–2 a.m.
Cuisine: Hot dogs, turkey dogs, turkey burgers
Entree range: $2–4 (lunch and dinner)
Children's menu: No
Reservations: Not accepted
Payment: No credit cards

A landmark of vernacular architecture, this hot dog–shaped roadside stand is considered by many to serve the best chili dog in town. Kids can get plain dogs, of course, and sloppy burgers as well. Be warned that the chili is likely to wreak havoc on your stomach, though you'll be loving it while it's going down. The clientele can get bizarre in the wee hours.

PINOT HOLLYWOOD

1448 N. Gower Street, Hollywood; (323) 461-8800

Meals served: Lunch and dinner
Cuisine: French/American
Entree range: $12–19 (lunch); $14–26 (dinner)
Children's menu: Yes; 10 and under free with an adult

Reservations: Suggested
Payment: All major credit cards

When we have an occasion to celebrate, we dress up and head here for dinner. Part of a small local chain linked to Patina, one of L.A.'s top restaurants, Pinot is one of the few upscale restaurants to actively court families—children under age 10 eat free (from an excellent, fairly sophisticated children's menu) with a paying adult. That's completely free, including a drink and dessert. The adult menu is a chic hybrid of French bistro classics (chicken with mustard sauce, onion soup) and modern American dishes, skillfully served in a setting of comfort and style. Since it's located next to Sunset-Gower and Paramount Studios, Pinot is an excellent star-spotting place. Full bar and good wine by the glass.

POQUITO MAS

3701 Cahuenga Boulevard W., Studio City; (818) 505-0068

Meals served: Lunch and dinner
Cuisine: Mexican
Entree range: $1.99–6.95 (lunch and dinner)
Children's menu: Yes; $2.75
Reservations: Not accepted
Payment: AE, D, V

For a taste of what Angelenos really eat, skip the tourist traps in Universal City and travel a mile or so to this strip-mall joint. You order at the counter and sit on plastic tables in the parking lot, and you're as likely to see a star here as in the studio. The carnitas (juicy pork) are among the best in town, the fish tacos are delicious, and the burritos are generous. You can also get takeout to eat in your hotel up the hill.

WOLFGANG PUCK CAFE

Universal CityWalk, 1000 Universal Center Drive, Universal City; (818) 985-9653

Meals served: Lunch and dinner
Cuisine: Californian
Entree range: $9–16.95 (lunch and dinner)
Children's menu: Yes
Reservations: Not accepted
Payment: AE, DC, MC, V

You have to reserve three months ahead and spend a car payment to have dinner at Wolfgang Puck's flagship Spago in Beverly Hills, but at this colorful, loud cafe, you can put your name in, browse CityWalk for awhile, then enjoy affordable modern American boomerfood: duck sausage pizzas, baby-green salads, homey desserts. Kids get a fine coloring menu of their own.

Where to Find the Real Hollywood

The glamour is coming back to landmarks of the movie business, as studios and vintage movie theaters in Los Angeles are restored and renovated, and proud owners show them off to the public. Just remember that visiting Hollywood doesn't mean simply exploring the neighborhood of that name, but rather wandering through working studios (there are now four different tours), TV show tapings, museums, and restored movie palaces throughout the city. Most tours and tapings have age restrictions, but the younger kids won't appreciate those experiences anyway. Even if they're not movie-mad, however, most junior-high kids and older kids have seen and heard enough about show business to enjoy a look behind the scenes. And don't forget, Universal Studios is a real studio as well as a theme park, and its backlot tram tour often features a glimpse of moviemaking in progress.

Audiences Unlimited   To obtain free tickets to tapings, call (818) 753-3470, or go to tutickets.com for show schedules, maps and directions, minimum age requirements, and other information. Peak taping season is August–March. Tickets are available for shows taped at production facilities in Hollywood, Burbank, Culver City, and Universal City/North Hollywood.

Hollywood Boulevard Movie Palaces: Mann's Chinese Theater, El Capitan, and the Egyptian Theater   The best, most recent Hollywood re-development effort has been the restoration of the Egyptian Theater by the American Cinematique, a film-appreciation society. This makes three movie-palace jewels on the crown of Hollywood Boulevard (a fourth is the legit house, the Pantages Theater) and allows visitors to really understand what the hoopla was all about in the '30s and '40s, when these movie palaces were the scene of grand premieres. Begin, if you can, at the **Egyptian Theater**, 6712 Hollywood Boulevard, Hollywood, (323) 466-FILM, www.egyptiantheater.com, which offers several daily screenings of a one-hour film ($5). A compilation of golden-age documentaries, classic movie clips, and interviews with current Hollywood celebrities, this movie is the perfect way to give your kids some background before they look at the footprints in the court of **Mann's Chinese Theater** at 6925 Hollywood Boulevard, Hollywood (no phone). Most of the stars who've left their marks here will otherwise be unfamiliar to your kids. There are often studio representatives passing out free tickets to TV show tapings at Mann's, so you might keep your itinerary flexible in case something appeals to your group. If you have younger kids, the highlight of Hollywood Boulevard is **Pacific's El Capitan** at 6838 Hollywood Boulevard, Hollywood, (323)

467-7674, gloriously renovated in a joint venture with Disney, and the location of premiere showings of the latest Disney releases. Local kids line up to see the latest Disney animated films here because there's glittering curtains and spotlights and special stage shows and sometimes souvenirs, interactive exhibits, and other extras.

Hollywood Walk of Fame   Hollywood Boulevard between Gower and La Brea and on Vine from Yucca to Sunset Boulevard, (323) 469-8311 (Hollywood Chamber of Commerce). Just ignore the Movieland Wax Museum (unless you're way into kitsch), Ripley's Believe It or Not, and the Hollywood Entertainment Museum (a so-far unsuccessful attempt at a showbiz museum) as you walk along, reading the names on the stars embedded in the sidewalk.

Museum of Radio and Television   465 N. Beverly Drive, Beverly Hills, (310) 786-1025, www.mtr.org, ($6 adults, $4 students). Another good pre-Chinese theater stop is this museum, where you can view a tape of the classic *I Love Lucy* in which Lucy visits the Chinese Theater and gets her foot stuck in a bucket of wet (quick-drying) cement. This small, ultramodern facility is heavily supported by the Industry, because it's really an archive that collects and preserves tapes of radio and TV shows, many of which had been previously preserved only by individuals. Your visit can include a stop in the screening room to see a scheduled show of select TV clips, settling back in the living room–like "radio listening room" with headsets and access to a vintage radio show, or visiting the TV library. In the library, visitors select footage choices from the museum's computer database, then move to private consoles to view their choice of vintage or historic TV clips (from episodes of *Welcome Back, Kotter* to footage of the moonwalk).

NBC Studio Tour   3000 W. Alameda Avenue, Burbank, (818) 840-3537 (tours leave weekdays between 9 a.m. and 3 p.m.; $7 adults, $3.75 kids ages 6–12, free under 12).This isn't a big movie studio with entire streets built as sets, but rather an indoor TV taping facility with several separate stages, including the one where the *Tonight* show has been filmed for decades. It isn't glitzy, but the tour is geared for kids, and the studio's real—we walked past "hot" prop tables, coiled cables, and "live" sets. The 70-minute walking tour includes a video, an NBC sports presentation, and a look at wardrobe, makeup, and set construction.

Paramount Studios Tours   860 N. Gower Street, Hollywood, (323) 956-4848 ($15 per person, weekdays departures every half-hour 9 a.m.–2 p.m.; must be over ten years old). Paramount has a terrific lot, with a New York Street, a Western town, a cement sky, and lots of sound stages, where, especially from mid-January through mid-March and from mid-August through mid-December, you might manage to plant yourself in the audience of a game show, talk show, or sitcom. You may make reservations by phone (call (323) 956-5000) a week before the taping (which will usually be on a Tuesday or Friday night; arrive by 6 p.m.).

Silent Movie Theater 611 N. Fairfax Avenue, (323) 655-2520, www.silentmovietheater.com ($8 adults, $6 children and seniors). This unique theater is adored by locals for its lovely presentation of pristine prints of the classics. It's a tiny theater, showing movies primarily on weekends (evenings and matinees), with personal touches that make attending a movie here as old-fashioned an experience as the Charlie Chaplin, Mary Pickford, and Laurel and Hardy movies (among many others) it screens.

Sony Pictures Entertainment Studio Tour 10202 Washington Boulevard, Culver City, (310) 244-3695 ($20 per person, several departures a day, weekdays only; no children under 12 permitted). The former MGM Studios was once the most glamorous of all the movie lots, and Sony has worked hard to restore the Art Deco and age-old buildings (there are some '20s-era window-walled buildings that are among the earliest movie industry buildings anywhere). The two-hour walking tour weaves in and out of sound stages and onto some working sets as the workers go about their jobs. Highlights include a stroll through wardrobe and a peek at artists at work in a backdrop studio with a seven-story high canvas in front of them. The tour begins with a video and ends on a street of picturesque facades, where participants can get an ice cream cone and shop in the studio store. Call Audiences Unlimited (see listing above) to arrange to attend a taping at Sony or nearby Culver Studios to coincide with your tour day.

Warner Bros. Studios VIP Tour 4000 Warner Boulevard, Gate 4, corner of Olive Avenue and Hollywood Way, Burbank (818) 954-1744 ($32 per person, all ages; children under 8 not permitted) Small group tours of this famous lot leave every half-hour between 9 a.m. and 4 p.m. weekdays; reservations are required. The tour lasts two hours with some walking and wanders through sound stages, past historic dressing rooms and offices, and through working studio areas.

Side Trips

ATTRACTIONS

Raging Waters

111 Raging Waters Drive (off 210 Freeway), San Dimas; (909) 592-2739; www.ragingwaters.com

Hours: Late April–May, Saturday–Sunday 10 a.m.–6 p.m.; June and September, Monday–Friday 10 a.m.–6 p.m., Saturday–Sunday 10 a.m. –7 p.m.; July, Monday–Friday 10 a.m.–8 p.m., Saturday–Sunday

9:30 a.m.–9 p.m.; August, Monday–Friday 10 a.m.–9 p.m., Saturday–Sunday 9:30 a.m.–9 p.m.; park typically closes at end of September

Admission: By height—over 4' tall $23.99, under 4' tall $14.99, under age 3, free; parking $6

Appeal by Age Groups:

Pre-school	Grade School	Teens	Young Adults	Over 30	Seniors
★	★★★	★★★★★	★★★★	★★	★

Touring Time: Average 6 hours; minimum 2 hours

Rainy-Day Touring: No

Services and Facilities:

Restaurants Yes	Lockers Yes
Alcoholic beverages No	Pet kennels No
Disabled access Yes, rate $14.99	Rain check Half-price coupon for another visit
Wheelchair rental No	Private tours No
Baby stroller rental No	

Description and Comments   One of the biggest and best of the water parks, Raging Waters is worth a side trip to hot-and-smoggy San Dimas if you have preteens and teens and the weather's hot. (It's a solid 45-minute drive from the westside and 20 minutes from Pasadena.) Plan on an all-day excursion, and be prepared for crowds and wild thrill slides. If your kids are younger, there's plenty for them to enjoy, but the real target audience is anyone crazy enough to slide down steep, wet slides in the dark after climbing hundreds of stairs for the privilege. Tickets are sold in advance, so call ahead to make sure the park hasn't been bought out before you arrive.

Six Flags Hurricane Harbor Water Park

Magic Mountain Pkwy. (off I-5), Valencia; (818) 367-2271 or (805) 255-4527

Hours: Weekdays 10 a.m.–6 p.m., weekends 10 a.m.–8 p.m.

Admission: $19.99, $12.99 for children under 48" tall, ages 2 and under free

Appeal by Age Groups:

Pre-school	Grade School	Teens	Young Adults	Over 30	Seniors
★★★★★	★★★★★	★★★★★	★★★★	★★★	★★

Touring Time: Average 4–6 hours; minimum 2 hours

Rainy-Day Touring: Not a good idea

Services and Facilities:

Restaurants Yes	Baby stroller rental Yes
Alcoholic beverages No	Lockers Yes
Disabled access Yes, but no	Pet kennels Yes
assisted slides	Rain check No
Wheelchair rental Yes	Private tours No

Description and Comments This water park is so much fun in the summer that we recommend it over Magic Mountain (next door and more expensive), unless you have roller-coaster-loving teens. And even then, why not let the older kids do Magic Mountain by themselves, while you relax on a chaise lounge while the younger kids either play at Castaway Cove, a toddler wading area; ride tubes around an island; roll with the waves in a giant cement sea; or hit the water slides. It's not as crowded as Magic Mountain, either, and the tropical jungle theme is played out in nice landscaping. Note that swimwear with metal ornamentation or rivets is not allowed on some rides. Valencia is located north of L.A., about a half-hour drive from downtown or 45 minutes from Santa Monica (much longer at rush hour).

Six Flags Magic Mountain

26101 Magic Mountain Pkwy. (off I-5), Valencia; (661) 255-4111

Hours: From mid-spring to late fall, open daily 10 a.m. (closing times vary with season and weather); rest of the year, Saturday–Sunday opens at 10 a.m.

Admission: $39.99 for adults, $19.99 for children 48" and under and seniors over 55, free for under age 2

Appeal by Age Groups:

Pre-school	Grade School	Teens	Young Adults	Over 30	Seniors
★★	★★★★	★★★★★	★★★★	★★★	★★

Touring Time: Average 5 hours; minimum 3 hours

Rainy-Day Touring: No

Services and Facilities:

Restaurants Yes	Lockers Yes
Alcoholic beverages No	Pet kennels Yes
Disabled access Yes	Rain check In some instances
Wheelchair rental Yes	Private tours No
Baby stroller rental Yes	

Description and Comments This cornucopia of hyper-intense roller coasters (it seems as if a new one opens every year) is heaven for teens and preteens, but it could be hell for younger ones. But if you do have under-tens, remember that the park offers a full slate of fun and enticing shows (a dolphin and whale show, for instance, and various themed music and dancing acts), and you can happily move from show to show with an occasional milder ride to spice things up. The Bugs Bunny World for small children offers tamer rides, like a mini-coaster and Daffy Duners, miniature dune buggies, along with concessions and a nearby petting zoo. Valencia is located north of L.A., about a half-hour drive from downtown or 45 minutes from Santa Monica (much longer at rush hour).

Pasadena

The Little Old Lady From Pasadena isn't much in evidence anymore—these days, Pasadena is packed with families, both ones who live on its stately old tree-lined streets and ones who are visiting this L.A. satellite city, just ten minutes north of downtown. In the last decade, formerly seedy **Old Pasadena** has become one of the hottest outdoor mall/restaurant/nightlife areas in southern California, beloved by Suburban-driving moms and tattooed teens alike. On weekends, street musicians, balloon-animal makers, and magicians amuse passers-by. Other family fun includes two movie-theater complexes, teen-haven stores, candy and frozen-yogurt shops, two good bookstores with children's areas, a virtual-reality game club, excellent restaurants, and a plaza with climb-on-me sculptures.

Elsewhere in town are a bounty of museums and parks, the most family-friendly of which are listed below; see also Lacy Park under Best Beaches and Parks (page 141).

Attractions

Kidspace

390 S. El Molino Avenue, Pasadena; (626) 449-9143

Hours: Wednesday–Friday and Sunday, 1–5 p.m., Saturday 10 a.m.–5 p.m.

Admission: $5 adults and children over 2, $3.50 seniors and ages 2 and under

Appeal by Age Groups:

Pre-school	Grade School	Teens	Young Adults	Over 30	Seniors
★★★★	★★★★	★	★	★	★

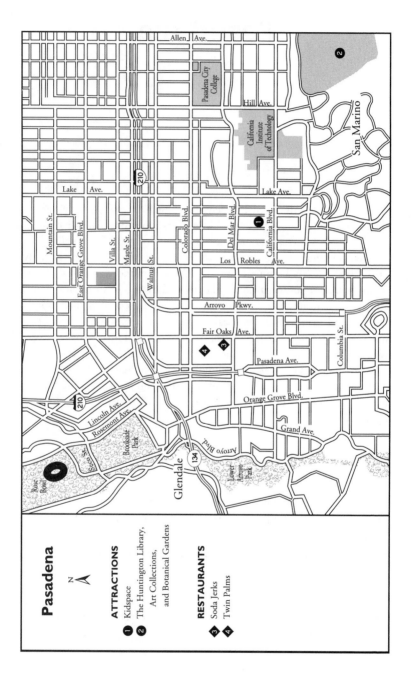

Pasadena

N

ATTRACTIONS

1 Kidspace
2 The Huntington Library,
   Art Collections,
   and Botanical Gardens

RESTAURANTS

3 Soda Jerks
4 Twin Palms

Allen Ave.

Pasadena City
College

Hill Ave.

California
Institute
of Technology

San Marino

210

Lake Ave.

Lake Ave.

Mountain St.

East Orange Grove Blvd.

Villa St.

Maple St.

Colorado Blvd.

Del Mar Blvd.

California Blvd.

1

Walnut St.

Los Robles Ave.

Arroyo Pkwy.

Fair Oaks Ave.

Columbia St.

4   3

Pasadena Ave.

210

Orange Grove Blvd.

Lincoln Ave.

Rosemont Ave.

Seco St.

Brookside
Park

Grand Ave.

Arroyo Blvd.

134

Lower
Arroyo
Park

Rose
Bowl

Glendale

Touring Time: Average 2 hours; minimum 1 hour

Rainy-Day Touring: No

Services and Facilities:

Restaurants No

Alcoholic beverages No

Disabled access Yes

Wheelchair rental No

Baby stroller rental No

Lockers No

Pet kennels No

Rain check No

Private tours No

Description and Comments One of the region's best children's museums, with a strong community presence, Kidspace combines usual kid-museum stuff with a vibrant array of special events and arts and crafts projects. The weeklong summer classes are superb. Each Earth Day in April, Kidspace holds an incredible program in which kids watch caterpillars become butterflies, then release the butterflies in unison; near New Year's, it sponsors the kids-only Rosebud Parade.

The Huntington Library, Art Collections, and Botanical Gardens

1151 Oxford Road, San Marino; (626) 405-2100

Hours: Tuesday–Friday noon–4:30 p.m., Saturday–Sunday 10:30 a.m.–4:30 p.m.; from June through August, Tuesday–Sunday 10:30 a.m.–4:30 p.m.; closed major holidays

Admission: $8.50 adults, $8 seniors, free for children age 12 and under; free first Thursday of month

Appeal by Age Groups:

Preschool	Grade School	Teens	Young Adults	Over 30	Seniors
★★★	★★★	★★★	★★★★	★★★★	★★★★

Touring Time: Average 2 hours; minimum 1 hour

Rainy-Day Touring: Yes, but you'll get wet

Services and Facilities:

Restaurants Cafe, tea room

Alcoholic beverages No

Disabled access Yes

Wheelchair rental Free, reserve

Baby stroller rental No

Lockers Yes

Pet kennels No

Rain check No

Private tours Arranged for mornings

Description and Comments A treasure found in sleepy San Marino, a wealthy suburb just south of Pasadena, this cultural center has appeal to both preschoolers and teenagers. The little ones love to run through the extraordinary gardens: world-class roses, a desert garden, a Zen garden, a jungle garden, and much more. Older children, especially bookworms, will be wowed by some of the venerable books in the library, including a Gutenberg Bible and first editions of Shakespeare. In-between kids will have fun searching for Gainsborough's Blue Boy in the art gallery.

Family-Friendly Restaurants

SODA JERKS

219 S. Fair Oaks Avenue, Pasadena; (626) 583-8031

Meals served: Breakfast, lunch, and dinner
Cuisine: American
Entree range: $4.25–7.50 (breakfast, lunch, and dinner)
Children's menu: Yes
Reservations: Not necessary
Payment: AE, MC, V

Our kids beg to come to this re-creation of an old-fashioned soda shop. They love to toot the pull-cord horn, spin on the counter stools, drool over the glass candy case, examine the antique toys hanging overhead, and sip sodas in tall glasses. The food is basic pancakes–burger–ice cream stuff, with something for everyone. You can get a good latte as well.

TWIN PALMS

101 W. Green Street, Old Pasadena; (626) 577-2567

Meals served: Lunch, dinner, and Sunday buffet brunch
Cuisine: Californian
Entree range: $6–18 (lunch); $10–28 (dinner); $21.95 (buffet brunch; $9.95 for children)
Children's menu: Yes; $2–5
Reservations: Advised
Payment: All major credit cards

You can dine under the stars and the namesake palms, or on a fetching covered patio overlooking the central plaza, or even in a dining room—but the point is to be outside. The food is first-rate casual modern-American cuisine, featuring chicken and meats cooked on the open-air rotisserie; the children's menu even includes a fruit-and-cheese plate, blessed relief from the deep-fried basics. Musicians take the stage in the later evening; music-loving families come for the Sunday brunch, fired up by great live gospel music.

The Mountains: Big Bear, Lake Arrowhead, and Ski Mountains

Local skiing is one of the great luxuries of Southern California life. It means that locals can be enjoying a sunny day in their hometown, drive two hours "up the hill," and get in a day of skiing. And the local ski resorts are especially nice for introducing kids to the sport. But these charming mountain retreats are equally appealing in the summer.

A popular weekend getaway for L.A. residents, **Big Bear** is less pretentious and easier for the casual visitor to negotiate, because the entire north shore of the lake is public land (so there's boat launching, bike trails, and picnic areas), and a combination of private and city concessions offer lake access on the southern side of the lake through a public swim beach, boat docks, and fishing sites. There are many modest vintage motels and cottages in Big Bear, as well as two conference resort hotels and some bed-and-breakfasts. It's also a ski center, five minutes from Southern California's largest ski mountain, Snow Summit.

Lakefront property in nearby **Lake Arrowhead,** on the other hand, is almost entirely in private hands, and unless you rent a house on the shoreline (not a bad option for a family), your only access to the lake is by boat, by staying at the Lake Arrowhead Resort, or in the shopping area known as the Village.

Meanwhile, **Idyllwild** is in another mountain range, about two hours from L.A. near Palm Springs, and it offers a much-less-trafficked locale for mountain hiking in the summer or snow play in the winter, weather permitting.

Family Lodging

Grey Squirrel Resort

Beloved of many L.A. families for weekend retreats, this cabin compound in the woods along Big Bear's main drag is an excellent value. Our favorite

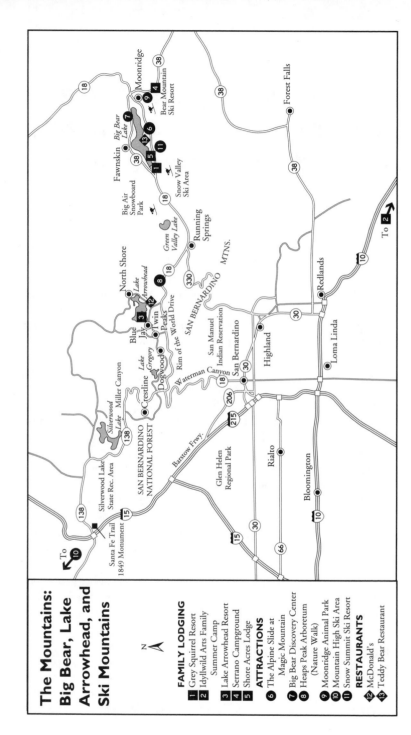

The Mountains: Big Bear, Lake Arrowhead, and Ski Mountains

FAMILY LODGING

1. Grey Squirrel Resort
2. Idyllwild Arts Family Summer Camp
3. Lake Arrowhead Resort
4. Serrano Campground
5. Shore Acres Lodge

ATTRACTIONS

6. The Alpine Slide at Magic Mountain
7. Big Bear Discovery Center
8. Heaps Peak Arboretum (Nature Walk)
9. Moonridge Animal Park
10. Mountain High Ski Area
11. Snow Summit Ski Resort

RESTAURANTS

12. McDonald's
13. Teddy Bear Restaurant

is the Raccoon Cabin, a 73-year-old, two-bedroom house with a stone fireplace, wood paneling, a roomy kitchen, beds for six, and comfortable country furniture. The ten cottages and two small motel units share outdoor barbecue facilities, a laundry area, and a heated pool. Even the family dog is welcome. This friendly, well-maintained place is a great base for hiking, sledding, and fishing down at the lake, a short walk away.

39372 Big Bear Boulevard, Big Bear; (909) 866-4335; fax (909) 866-6271. Rates start at $75.

Idyllwild Arts Family Summer Camp

When school is out at the Idyllwild Arts School in the cool, sleepy San Jacinto Mountains above Palm Springs, families move into the dorms for week-long arts-oriented camp fun. While young children enjoy playtime and day care and older children take part in supervised swimming, crafts, theater games, art projects, and sports, parents divide their time between their choice of arts classes—everything from ceramics and dance to writing and acting—and such outdoor pursuits as hiking and mountain biking. Everyone sleeps in modern, new Pearson Hall, with private bathrooms and daily maid service, and all meals are included.

52500 Temecula Road (off Highway 243), Idyllwild; (909) 659-2171; fax (909) 659-5463. One-bedroom unit with 3 people, $1,595 per week including all classes, activities, and meals; price varies with number of people and room configuration.

Lake Arrowhead Resort

Perfectly sited if you're not a real outdoorsy family but want to spend some time in the mountains, the 177-room Lake Arrowhead Resort is part of lakefront Arrowhead Village, a collection of shops and restaurants. The views are spectacular in the summer, and Christmas card–like in the winter. The resort has its own beach for swimming in the (cold) lake, as well as a (heated) pool. The adjacent marina offers watercraft rentals. A kids' club (fishing, arts and crafts, pizza party) for 4–12-year-olds is offered daily in the summer and on weekends in the off-season. The morning and afternoon sessions are $20 each, and they can be combined for $35.

27984 Highway 189, at entrance to Lake Arrowhead Village; (909) 336-1511 or (800) 800-6792; fax (909) 336-1378. Rates $139–399, depending on season and day of week.

Serrano Campground

A pleasant campground in the pines, close to Big Bear Lake and the town conveniences, this national forest campground allows some of its sites to be reserved, which is always a good bet when camping with kids. It's only open when the snow is gone, usually mid-May to mid-September. Shower, flush toilets, fire rings, firewood, and ranger interpretive programs, as well as lake access for boating and fishing.

Off Highway 38, Big Bear Lake; (877) 444-6777; reservations (877) 444-6777. Campsites, $17.

Shore Acres Lodge

Not quite a motel, more a collection of housekeeping cabins, this lodge is well located on a quiet stretch of Big Bear Lake, and it offers good value without the hassle of working through a private-home rental agency. The choices include 11 cabins with kitchens, ranging from studio-sized to a cabin that sleeps 12. All are near the shore, and some are directly on the lake. In the summer, the office also offers additional rental units in private homes. The lodge area has a playground, pool, Jacuzzi, and boat dock; there are VCRs in the cabins. Most have a several-night minimum stay.

40090 Lakeview Drive, Big Bear Lake; (909) 866-8200 or (800) 524-6600; fax (909) 866-3248. Rates are based on the number of people occupying the cabin. Rates for three people, $115 and up with a four-night minimum.

Attractions

The Alpine Slide at Magic Mountain

800 Wildrose Lane, Big Bear Lake; (909) 866-4626

Hours: Alpine Slide: Summer, Sunday–Thursday 10 a.m.–6 p.m., Friday–Saturday closes 9 p.m.; fall, Saturday–Sunday 10 a.m.–6 p.m., Monday 11 a.m.–4 p.m.; winter, Saturday–Sunday 10 a.m.–dusk, Monday–Friday 11 a.m.–4 p.m.; spring, Saturday–Sunday 10 a.m.–5 p.m. *Water Slide:* mid-June–mid-September, daily 10 a.m.–5 p.m. *Snow Play:* November–Easter, daily 10 a.m.–4 p.m.

Admission: Single ride on Alpine Slide $3.50; $15 water-slide or snow-play unlimited day pass; children ages 6 and under ride free with adult; various ride packages available

Appeal by Age Groups:

Pre-school	Grade School	Teens	Young Adults	Over 30	Seniors
★★	★★★	★★★	★★	★★	★

Touring Time: Average 1 hour; minimum 20 minutes
Rainy-Day Touring: No

Services and Facilities:

Restaurants Yes, snack bar	Lockers No
Alcoholic beverages No	Pet kennels No
Disabled access Yes	Rain check No
Wheelchair rental No	Private tours No
Baby stroller rental No	

Description and Comments This modest family attraction has been the highlight of a couple of winter-spring weekends in Big Bear. There was enough snow left to slide ourselves into exhaustion on the inner-tube slide, climbing up the small hill with giant inner tubes and flying right back down again (big kids can grab hold of a rope tow, but not the under-eight set, so we hoofed it). Then, since there wasn't too much snow, we had a ride on the curving, luge-like concrete slide, a little kid on our lap and the bigger kids steering their own, which was quite a thrill. Also open at various times are a go-kart track and waterslide. Not for the very young.

Big Bear Discovery Center

North Shore of Big Bear Lake on Highway 38 between Fawnskin and Stanfield Cutoff; (909) 866-3437

Hours: Daily, 9 a.m.–5 p.m., closed Christmas and New Year's Day

Admission: Free; some activities have fees or require a Park Service "Adventure Pass"

Appeal by Age Groups:

Pre-school	Grade School	Teens	Young Adults	Over 30	Seniors
★★	★★★	★★★	★★★	★★★	★★★

Touring Time: Average 1–4 hours; minimum 15 minutes

Rainy-Day Touring: Yes

Services and Facilities:

Restaurants No	Baby stroller rental No
Alcoholic beverages No	Lockers No
Disabled access Yes, into center, varies with different programs	Pet kennels No
	Rain check No
Wheelchair rental No	Private tours Yes

Description and Comments Big Bear Discovery Center is a wonderful new environmental education facility resulting from a partnership between the federal San Bernardino Forest and the San Bernardino National Forest Association, a private nonprofit organization. Because budget cuts decreased the number of forest rangers available to educate, guide, or entertain the public, the Discovery Center was created to take up the slack. More than 100 volunteers (among whom are two former Big Bear mayors and two former college presidents) staff the center's exhibits and displays seven days a week, and also develop and participate in programs such as campfire talks, interpretive hikes, and history tours. The Adventure Outpost store offers educational and nature-related merchandise.

After looking over the center's exhibits about local flora and fauna, families can sign up for activities like guided hikes, campfire programs with music and storytelling (fees vary, reservations required), or in the winter months, the center's Eagle Tours, which take participants by vans into bald eagle habitat areas closed to the general public.

Heaps Peak Arboretum (Nature Walk)

Highway 18 (2 miles from Lake Arrowhead turnoff); (909) 337-2444 (Ranger Station)

Hours: Daily dawn–dusk

Admission: Free, but parking "Adventure Pass" necessary to park ($5 for day or $30 for year); purchase from Arrowhead Ranger Station off Highway 18 or vendors around Lake Arrowhead

Appeal by Age Groups:

Pre-school	Grade School	Teens	Young Adults	Over 30	Seniors
★★	★★★	★★	★★	★★★	★★★

Touring Time: Average 1½ hours; minimum 20 minutes to stretch and look but not do whole trail

Rainy-Day Touring: No

Services and Facilities:

Restaurants No	Lockers No
Alcoholic beverages No	Pet kennels No; pets not allowed
Disabled access Some trails are	on trail
limited	Rain check No
Wheelchair rental No	Private tours Yes; call Ranger
Baby stroller rental No	Station

Description and Comments Located in an Arrowhead-adjacent site that makes a good first stop upon reaching the top of the mountain, this nature trail is a great place to walk after being in the car for a little too long. Your kids can stretch their legs and get acquainted with the forest on an easy one-mile loop that meanders through dogwood groves (blooming in May) and wildflower meadows, across a stream or two, and through pines and chaparral. The brochure that identifies various points to stop and learn a thing or two is geared beautifully to kids.

Moonridge Animal Park

Near Bear Mountain Ski Resort; Moonridge Road to Clubview to Gold-
mine Drive; (909) 866-0183

Hours: April–October, daily 10 a.m.–5 p.m. (weather permitting);
November–March, weekends and holidays only, 10 a.m.–4 p.m.

Admission: $2.50 adults, $1.50 children ages 3–10, ages 3 and under free

Appeal by Age Groups:

Pre-school	Grade School	Teens	Young Adults	Over 30	Seniors
★★★	★★★	★★	★★★	★★★	★★★

Touring Time: Average 1–2 hours; minimum 1 hour

Rainy-Day Touring: Open during light rain, but closes during snow-
storms

Services and Facilities:

Restaurants No	Lockers Yes
Alcoholic beverages No	Pet kennels No
Disabled access Yes	Rain check No
Wheelchair rental No	Private tours No
Baby stroller rental No	

Description and Comments   As we gazed at the fierce, dignified bald eagle
here, our daughter spotted a fallen feather. The docent gently took it from
her, explaining to the kids that any feathers shed by the eagles are given to
Native American groups for sacred use. Founded in 1959, the animal park
shelters orphaned and injured animals native to the San Bernardino mountains, releasing the recovered ones into the wild.

Visitors will see coyotes, bears, wolves, cougars, raccoons, foxes, and
birds of prey. There's a gift shop and a few educational exhibits. Its pine-
shaded enclosures offer kids a close-up look at the species inhabiting the
woods beyond. On weekends and in summer there are animal presentations at noon and feeding programs at 3 p.m. In October, there are special
Friday-night (6:30 p.m.) nocturnal programs.

Mountain High Ski Area

24510 Highway 2, Wrightwood; (760) 249-5808

Hours: Mid-November–mid-April 8:30 a.m.–10 p.m. (opens at 8 a.m.
Saturday–Sunday)

Admission: $35 adults, $29 ages 13–22 and seniors age 60+, $10 ages 12
and under, under age 10 free with paying adult

Appeal by Age Groups:

Pre-school	Grade School	Teens	Young Adults	Over 30	Seniors
★★	★★★	★★★	★★★	★★	★

Touring Time: Average 8 hours; minimum 6 hours

Rainy-Day Touring: No

Services and Facilities:

Restaurants Yes	Lockers Yes
Alcoholic beverages Yes	Pet kennels No
Disabled access Yes	Rain check Vouchers under cer-
Wheelchair rental No	tain conditions
Baby stroller rental No	Private tours Yes, classes

Description and Comments   Tucked into a sparsely populated community in the mountains north of L.A., an easy 90-minute drive from downtown, this working-class ski mountain is typically filled with local teens snowboarding, skiing, and hanging out on the big wooden deck of the lodge, checking each other out. Kindly instructors give reasonably priced lessons to younger children, but the facilities are minimal, with a little too much uphill walking for the littlest ones. The snow can get pretty wet at the bottom, not to mention thick with out-of-control beginning snowboarders, but if you stay on the lifts to the top of the mountain, you might be surprised at the quality of the snow, much of which is man-made. A good day-skiing location for kids ages 7–17.

Snow Summit Ski Resort

880 Summit Boulevard (just south of Big Bear Village); (909) 866-4621; www.snowsummit.com

Hours: Midweek 8 a.m.–4:30 p.m.; weekends 7:30 a.m.–4:30 p.m., sometimes open until 6 p.m. for night sessions on weekends in peak season; ski season is mid-November–mid-April; mountain biking and hiking available in off-season

Admission: In winter, $34 adults, $10 ages 7–12, ages 6 and under free when accompanied by an adult; in summer, lift prices are $7 adults, $3 kids for a round-trip, $5 adults, $2 kids for 1-way, $7 adults, $3 kids for 1-way with bike; all-day pass with a bike is $19 for adults, $8 for kids

Appeal by Age Groups:

Pre-school	Grade School	Teens	Young Adults	Over 30	Seniors
★★★	★★★★	★★★★	★★★	★★★	★★

Touring Time: Average 1 day; minimum a half-day

Rainy-Day Touring: Depending on conditions, resort may close

Services and Facilities:

Restaurants Yes, 4	Lockers Yes
Alcoholic beverages Yes	Pet kennels No
Disabled access Yes	Rain check Vouchers under cer-
Wheelchair rental No	tain conditions
Baby stroller rental No	Private tours Private lessons

Description and Comments By far the poshest of the local ski mountains, this is also the best for younger families. The children's center/ski school is professionally staffed and fun, with a bright indoor area well stocked with crafts, games, and toys, and a lesson/snow-play area outside. If your five-year-old gets wet and miserable and doesn't want to ski anymore, he can come inside, have some juice, and play with the toys. But that's not to say older kids aren't tended to—our late-elementary-age nephews enjoyed their snowboard lessons here, and after a morning's intro they were boarding down the slopes with other cool kids in the separate snowboard park. It only has a fraction of the runs that the major Sierra resorts have, and the snow is often man-made, but there's plenty to keep a novice or experienced skiing family happy for a two- or three-day trip. In summer, the runs become the turf of mountain bikers, often the same teens who were snowboarding here just a few months earlier.

Family-Friendly Restaurants

MCDONALD'S

28200 Highway 189, Bldg. G, Lake Arrowhead (Lake Arrowhead Village, lower level); (909) 337-0558

Meals served: Breakfast, lunch, and dinner
Cuisine: American fast food
Entree range: 75 cents–$4.99
Children's menu: Yes
Reservations: Not accepted
Payment: No credit cards

This may be the best-view McDonald's in California. It is indeed lakefront dining, and you won't see a bluer sky or more sparkling water from any of the terraces at the pricier restaurants down the way. So go ahead, let the kids get their favorites; just insist on getting a terrace table and put on plenty of sunscreen.

TEDDY BEAR RESTAURANT

585 Pineknot Avenue, Big Bear Lake; (909) 866-5415

Meals served: Breakfast, lunch, and dinner
Cuisine: American
Entree range: $4–7 (breakfast and lunch); $7–11 (dinner)
Children's menu: Yes
Reservations: Not accepted
Payment: AE, MC, V

One of our favorites in a town with pretty undistinguished dining, this coffee shop does a fine BLT, some great pancakes, and such local mountain specialties as warm hot chocolate on a chilly fall morning.

On the Lakes

You don't have to own or even rent a ski or fishing boat to spend some time on the water. We've made a point of taking the tour boats around both Big Bear Lake and Lake Arrowhead, and we recommend it as a family excursion. For one thing, if you take an afternoon tour, as we did, of Big Bear Lake, your fretful preschooler may nap the time away (as ours did) in the fresh mountain air, with the hum of the boat's engine to lull him or her. For another, the view from the lake is unique, and whether you're interested in gazing at celebrity vacation homes, geological formations, or the spectacular granite slopes of San Gorgonio Mountain against a bright blue sky, you'll see it from the boat. Big Bear's scenic boat tour leaves from Pine Knot Landing at the foot of Pine Knot Avenue for an 80-minute narrated excursion, April through November departing every two hours 10 a.m.–6 p.m.; fare is $8.50 adults, $6.50 over 52, $5 ages 4–12; call (909) 866-2628. The *Arrowhead Queen* can be boarded at Arrowhead Village for a 45-minute tour; boats leave at regular intervals daily 11 a.m.–5 p.m. year-round; fare $10, $9 over 59, $6.50 ages 3–12; they're sold at LeRoy's Sports, (909) 336-6992.

Palm Springs

The desert communities are loved by retirees, of course, and driving through super-quiet Palm Springs on a hot day, with its empty streets (everyone's indoors) punctuated by golf courses, can make parents panic— what will we do with the kids? But real kids live here, and there are a growing number of activities for young people. Resorts include kids in the mix, especially as parents are tending to bring kids along for a weekend added to a meeting or conference. Beloved as a weekend getaway in winter for sun-lovers (it's a two-hour drive east of downtown L.A.), Palm Springs can turn hellish in July and August, when temperatures sometimes hit 115°— but those months bring incredible deals at the family-oriented resorts. If you're going midweek or weekends, plan to include a Thursday night in your stay. The lively street fair and market (6–10 p.m. in the winter, 7–10 p.m. in the summer) offers fun food, booths (selling everything from vintage celebrity photos to a one-minute massage), and entertainment.

Family Lodging

Desert Springs Marriott Resort and Spa

This gigantic (more than 900 rooms and suites) resort hotel is loads of fun, because it offers entertainment and luxury without pretensions. There are, for example, little motorboats to take you to the restaurants and club— although you can walk perfectly well down the corridors to get there, too. The hundreds of people lounging poolside are serenaded by a reggae surf band playing Jimmy Buffett tunes, and the isolation of the place is not an issue, because it's got everything from a cappuccino bar to a hot dog stand. We took our kids to the golf course coffee shop for breakfast, sat in the Jacuzzi and watched colorful hot air balloons glide overhead, then spent some time playing badminton near the tennis courts. The year-round Kid's

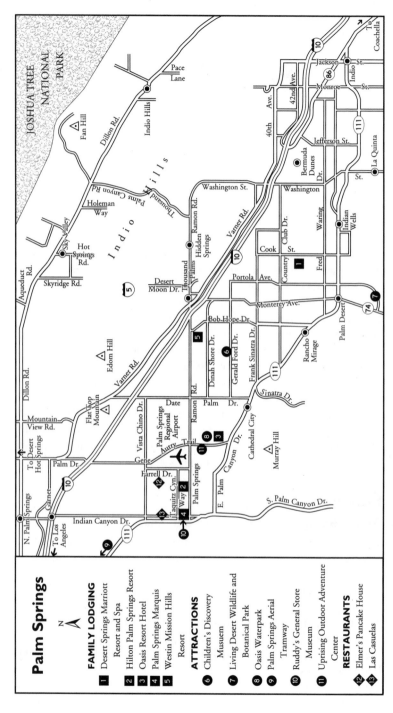

Palm Springs

N

FAMILY LODGING

1. Desert Springs Marriott Resort and Spa
2. Hilton Palm Springs Resort
3. Oasis Resort Hotel
4. Palm Springs Marquis
5. Westin Mission Hills Resort

ATTRACTIONS

6. Children's Discovery Museum
7. Living Desert Wildlife and Botanical Park
8. Oasis Waterpark
9. Palm Springs Aerial Tramway
10. Ruddy's General Store Museum
11. Uprising Outdoor Adventure Center

RESTAURANTS

12. Elmer's Pancake House
13. Las Casuelas

Club, featuring organized lawn games, rock-wall climbing, arts and crafts, pizza parties, swimming parties, cartoons, and movies, is billed for ages 4–12; as is so often the case, it's really better for ages 4–8 or so. The cost is $60 a day and $35 a half-day. There's also miniature golf, pottery painting (for a fee), an arcade, and children's menus in Lakeview restaurant and from room service.

74855 Country Club Drive, Palm Desert; (760) 341-2211 or (800) 228-9290; fax (760) 341-1872. Rates $199–439; substantial discounts in summer.

Hilton Palm Springs Resort

Perfectly located for walking around the downtown Palm Springs area with its museums and weekly street fair, the Hilton is also a casual motor hotel, less pretentious than some of the other hotels. You drive to a parking space near your room, for example, dispensing with bellmen and valets at every turn. There are no special programs for children, but if you have late-elementary age kids who'd be restless in a hotel daycare, this hotel is compact enough to allow easy access to pools and a game room.

400 East Tahquitz Canyon Way, Palm Springs; (760) 320-6868. Rates $79–89 in summer, $119–185 October–May.

Oasis Resort Hotel

This is a good choice for families from March through October, when the nearby water park is open. Your water-park admission is included in your room cost, and a tram will whisk you to the park entrance. But this isn't a hotel, really, it's the overnight rental arm of a time-share condo complex. Two- and three-bedroom condos are available, and the eight pools of the complex are open to overnight guests. The air-conditioned, fully furnished units are luxurious for the price, and although there is neither restaurant nor room service, we were happy to order pizza and relax.

4190 E. Palm Canyon Drive, Palm Springs; (760) 328-1499; www. oasiswaterresort.com. Rates start at $165 weekdays and $205 weekends for two-bedroom condo (sleeps 6).

Palm Springs Marquis, a Shadowrock Resort

We first chose this hotel because the price and location were right—it was cheaper than the luxury resorts and was right in the heart of old Palm Springs, an easy walk to shops, restaurants, and movies. The surprise was the quality of the free afternoon children's program, Kamp Wannakombak, for ages 2–12. We expected the basic drab room with a VCR and some coloring books, but instead found a fun basement play area with a caring staff, lots of toys, an indoor basketball hoop, playhouses, lots of room for arts and crafts, and even a sweet pet bunny that hops around the floor. Our kids had a ball. (But it's really best for 2–8-year-olds.) Also on site are two swimming pools, spas, tennis courts, and a restaurant (but there's better fare within walking distance). Bedrooms are large enough for a family of three or four; even roomier are the family suites, complete with full kitchens. An excellent family choice if you want to be right in town.

150 S. Indian Canyon Drive, Palm Springs; (760) 322-2121 or (800) 223-1050; fax (760) 322-2380. Rates start at $130 in summer (sometimes less with special offers) and $250 in winter.

Westin Mission Hills Resort

It was hard to be comfortable with a family of four in one of the small rooms at this 552-room resort, but the kids were happy in the daytime with the pool area, which includes misters at the bar and a wonderful 60-foot water slide into the pool. Because of the many conference attendees, the Cactus Kids program is pretty active for ages 4–12 (though kids over age eight might find it a little silly), offering a year-round program with daily morning and/or afternoon sessions ($30 each) featuring nature walks, swimming, arts and crafts, and movies. Family movies and a Sony Play Station are available in the rooms. In the summer, two kids dine for free when accompanied by a parent.

7133 Dinah Shore Drive, Rancho Mirage; (760) 770-2160 or (800) WESTIN1; fax (760) 321-2955. Rates start at $169 in summer, $350 in late fall and winter.

Attractions

Children's Discovery Museum

71–701 Gerald Ford Drive, Rancho Mirage; (760) 321-0602

Hours: Tuesday–Saturday, 10 a.m.–5 p.m.; open Monday November–April only

Admission: $5 per person ages 2 and up. All children must be accompanied by an adult.

Appeal by Age Groups:

Pre-school	Grade School	Teens	Young Adults	Over 30	Seniors
★★★★	★★★★	—	—	★	★

Touring Time: Average 2 hours; minimum 1 hour

Rainy-Day Touring: Yes

Services and Facilities:

Restaurants No	Lockers No
Alcoholic beverages No	Pet kennels No
Disabled access Yes	Rain check No
Wheelchair rental No	Private tours For groups, special
Baby stroller rental No	events

Description and Comments A hands-on activity center where kids can paint a car, play in a grocery store, and rummage in an "attic." Special Handworks programs are available and include arts and crafts from clay to Native American gourd art. A highlight is an archaeological dig, which simulates a dig for Cahuilla Indian artifacts. Picnic area and museum store.

Living Desert Wildlife and Botanical Park

47900 Portola Avenue, Palm Desert; (760) 346-5694

Hours: September 1–June 15, daily 9 a.m.–5 p.m.; in summer, call for special touring hours; closed Christmas Day

Admission: $8.50 adults, $7.50 seniors 62+, $4.25 ages 3–12, free for children ages 2 and under

Appeal by Age Groups:

Pre-school	Grade School	Teens	Young Adults	Over 30	Seniors
★★★	★★★★	★★★★	★★★★	★★★★	★★★★

Touring Time: Average 3 hours; minimum 50 minutes, for tram ride only

Rainy-Day Touring: No

Services and Facilities:

Restaurants Yes	Lockers No
Alcoholic beverages No	Pet kennels No
Disabled access Yes	Rain check No
Wheelchair rental Yes, free	Private tours Yes
Baby stroller rental Yes, free	

Description and Comments To dispel any myths about deserts being barren wastelands, bring the family to this wonderful 1,200-acre preserve. The elusive bighorn sheep clamber on hillsides as you wander through the pathways, along with the even rarer oryx, which the park is helping to save from extinction. The kids will meet coyotes, great horned owls, tortoises, mountain lions, and golden eagles of unspeakable grandeur. Inside is the Discovery Room, where kids can touch and feel. The desert botanical gardens will bore the kids, but sneak a peek if you can. If the day's too hot for walking, consider taking the 50-minute guided tram tour; in general, arrive right at opening time to beat the heat, unless you're visiting in winter.

Oasis Waterpark

1500 Gene Autry Trail, Palm Springs; (760) 325-7873

Hours: Mid-March–Labor Day, daily 11 a.m.–5 p.m., Labor Day–October, Saturday–Sunday 11 a.m.–6 p.m.; closed November–mid-March

Admission: $19.95 adults, $12.95 for children 3'–5' tall and seniors 55+, free for children under 3' tall; parking $3

Appeal by Age Groups:

Pre-school	Grade School	Teens	Young Adults	Over 30	Seniors
★★★	★★★★	★★★★	★★★	★★	★★

Average Touring Time: 3–4 hours

Minimum Touring Time: 1½ hours; there may be lines for some of the 13 slides

Rainy-Day Touring: No

Services and Facilities:

Restaurants Yes	Lockers Yes
Alcoholic beverages Yes	Pet kennels No
Disabled access Yes	Rain check No
Wheelchair rental Yes	Private tours Yes; call in advance
Baby stroller rental Yes	

Description and Comments   This may be among the smallest of the water parks we mention in this book, but you can believe that in the 100°+ temperatures of the desert, it's among the most loved. It has most of what a water park needs: a wave pool, slides, a tube river. But it's short on shade. Please take our advice and pay for a "cabana," which is actually a tent with chairs, tables, and indoor/outdoor carpeting. Otherwise, you'll fry every time you leave the water, and your kids'll get sun-addled brains.

Palm Springs Aerial Tramway

1 Tramway Road at Highway 111, Palm Springs; (760) 325-1449 or (760) 325-1391

Hours: Weekdays, 10 a.m.–9:45 p.m.; weekends 8 a.m.–8 p.m

Admission: $19.65 adults, $17.65 for seniors age 55+, $12.50 for children ages 3–12, under age 3 ride free.

Appeal by Age Groups:

Pre-school	Grade School	Teens	Young Adults	Over 30	Seniors
★	★★★	★★★	★★★	★★★	★★★

Touring Time: Average 4 hours; minimum 2 hours

Rainy-Day Touring: No

Services and Facilities:

Restaurants Yes	Lockers Yes
Alcoholic beverages Yes	Pet kennels No
Disabled access Yes	Rain check No
Wheelchair rental No	Private tours Yes
Baby stroller rental No	

Description and Comments New gondola cars that rotate 360 degrees give you dizzying views as they whisk you off the desert floor and swoop you up the side of Mount San Jacinto, delivering you to a cool (sometimes even snow-filled) mountain park at 8,500 feet, with pines, trails, and picnic areas. The ride is a very big thrill for kids age ten and under (maybe a little too much for squeamish ones), and when the heat is wilting, it's a lovely escape. Just remember to bring a sweatshirt, because temperatures often drop 40° or more. There's a restaurant up top, but we much prefer to bring a picnic.

Ruddy's General Store Museum

Village Green, 221 S. Palm Canyon Drive, Palm Springs; (760) 327-2156

Hours: October–June, Thursday–Sunday 10 a.m.–4 p.m.; July–September, weekends only 10 a.m.–4 p.m.

Admission: 50 cents per person, children 12 and under free

Appeal by Age Groups:

Pre-school	Grade School	Teens	Young Adults	Over 30	Seniors
★	★★	★★★	★★★	★★★	★★★★

Touring Time: Average a half-hour; minimum 15 minutes

Rainy-Day Touring: Yes

Services and Facilities:

Restaurants No	Lockers Yes
Alcoholic beverages No	Pet kennels No
Disabled access Yes	Rain check No
Wheelchair rental No	Private tours No
Baby stroller rental No	

Description and Comments Of the three small museums that make up Village Green in downtown Palm Springs, this one-room general store is the only one that will appeal to kids—and it's a fun and unique way to introduce them to everyday life of yesteryear. It's a facsimile general store, circa 1930s, and it's crammed with vintage packages of every imaginable product, all part of an extensive private collection. More than 6,000 unused items—from shirt collars to cigars, from soda pop bottles to straw boater hats, from kites to toy trains—line the shelves and display cases.

Uprising Outdoor Adventure Center

1500 S. Gene Autry Trail, Palm Springs; (760) 320-6630; www.uprising.com

Hours: Winter: daily except Monday 10 a.m.–8 p.m., Wednesday until 9 p.m.; summer: Tuesday–Friday 8–11 a.m. and 5–9 p.m..; Saturday and Sunday 10 a.m.–6 p.m.

Admission: Packages vary in price depending on the number of people and extent of climbing activity. Family rates are 10% off lessons with 3 or more participants.

Appeal by Age Groups:

Pre-school	Grade School	Teens	Young Adults	Over 30	Seniors
—	★★★	★★★★	★★★	★	★

Touring Time: Average 2 hours (includes preparation time); minimum 1 hour

Rainy-Day Touring: The climbing rock is covered and shaded; a mister operates in summer.

Services and Facilities:

Restaurants No		Lockers No	
Alcoholic beverages No		Pet kennels No	
Disabled access No		Rain check No	
Wheelchair rental No		Private tours Group programs	
Baby stroller rental No			

Description and Comments   This climbing rock with several faces is adjacent to Oasis Waterpark, and although accessible from Oasis, it has separate fees. It's a good bonus activity for older kids to enjoy for an hour during the family's day at the waterpark.

Family-Friendly Restaurants

ELMER'S PANCAKE HOUSE

1111 Sunrise Drive, Palm Springs; (760) 327-8419

Meals served: Breakfast, lunch, and dinner
Cuisine: American
Entree range: $6–10 (breakfast, lunch, and dinner)

Children's menu: Yes; $2.50
Reservations: Not accepted
Payment: All major credit cards

Popular with seniors and young families alike, this long-standing coffee shop does a booming breakfast business. Booths are roomy, service is friendly, and the pancakes really are good.

LAS CASUELAS

368 N. Palm Canyon, Palm Springs; (760) 325-3213

Meals served: Lunch and dinner
Cuisine: Mexican
Entree range: $4.95–6.25 (breakfast); $6.25–12 (lunch and dinner)
Children's menu: Yes; $5 limited choice of a hamburger, taco, or eggs
Reservations: Recommended
Payment: AE, DC, MC, V

Las Cas (as the locals call it) has been serving nachos, enchiladas, and tostadas to the desert for a couple of generations. This is the slightly more downscale original, which we like for its coziness and feel of local authenticity. A block away is the larger, fancier Las Casuelas Terraza, with a pretty sidewalk terrace and good margaritas (beer and wine only at the original location). The food at both is solid, tasty, and comforting; try the *mojo de ajos* (garlic shrimp).

Part Four

The Central Coast

Best known as the home of the most celebrated stretch of California Highway 1, the Central Coast region of California has come into its own in recent years—it's nobody's drive-through or fly-over territory anymore. The southern part of the Central Coast, from **Ventura** to **San Simeon,** is within easy reach of the Los Angeles metropolitan area, and the northern part, from **Big Sur** through the **Monterey Peninsula,** is weekend-getaway distance from San Francisco. Both sections of the Central Coast share a characteristic lack of urban sprawl: These are distinct and very different communities, with boundaries defined by agricultural or forest landscapes.

Small and medium-sized businesses relying on skilled employees are well established in each of these areas, anchored by their employees' desire to live in a part of the state where the quality of daily life is excellent. For family travelers, this means that the museums, restaurants, entertainment, and attractions are often as high in quality as in the big cities, but they're so much less crowded as to feel sinfully indulgent. In fact, the Central Coast's tourism industry seems to be based on sharing with outsiders the pleasures that locals have created or discovered for themselves.

A visit to the **Santa Barbara Zoo** or an afternoon on the **Santa Cruz Boardwalk** is no small-town experience, but it has an intimacy and ease that would be unthinkable in California's more heavily populated areas. (An exception to this rule is the internationally popular and crowded **Monterey Bay Aquarium.**) And the national restaurant or fast-food chain is not king here—many cafes are locally owned, use local produce, and create regional specialties for their menus.

We have explored the area with our children in a number of ways: by renting a beach house, by staying for the weekend during a soccer tournament, by adding time to an overnight business trip, by visiting friends and relatives. Highlights for our kids have included the unique and impressive

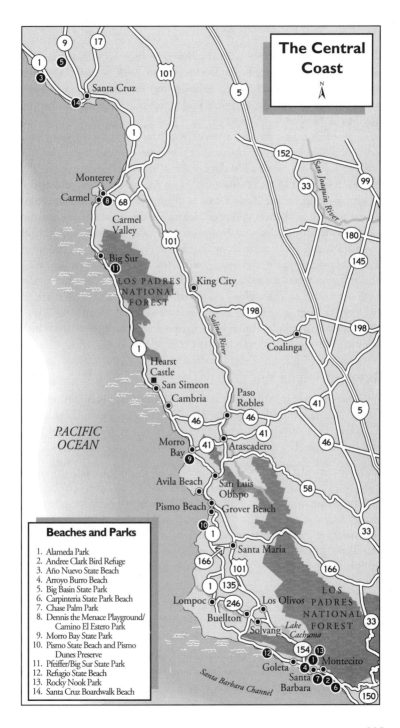

The Central Coast

N

Beaches and Parks

1. Alameda Park
2. Andree Clark Bird Refuge
3. Año Nuevo State Beach
4. Arroyo Burro Beach
5. Big Basin State Park
6. Carpinteria State Park Beach
7. Chase Palm Park
8. Dennis the Menace Playground/
   Camino El Estero Park
9. Morro Bay State Park
10. Pismo State Beach and Pismo
    Dunes Preserve
11. Pfeiffer/Big Sur State Park
12. Refugio State Beach
13. Rocky Nook Park
14. Santa Cruz Boardwalk Beach

PACIFIC OCEAN

Santa Cruz

Monterey
Carmel
Carmel Valley
Big Sur

LOS PADRES NATIONAL FOREST

King City

Hearst Castle
San Simeon
Cambria

Morro Bay
Avila Beach
Pismo Beach
San Luis Obispo
Grover Beach

Santa Maria

Lompoc
Buellton
Solvang
Los Olivos

Goleta
Santa Barbara
Montecito

Coalinga

Paso Robles
Atascadero

San Joaquin River
Salinas River

Lake Cachuma

LOS PADRES NATIONAL FOREST

Santa Barbara Channel

Monterey Aquarium, Santa Barbara's charming little zoo, camping at El Capitan State Beach, playing in the clear, cold creek at Big Sur, apple-touring in the **Santa Ynez Valley,** getting a wax impression of one's hand on Santa Cruz Boardwalk, and, amazingly, enjoying classical music at the **Ojai Music Festival.**

To give this region its due, a week's visit is only fair. If you only have two or three days, focus on one end or the other. On the Southern California end, you can spend a few days based in Santa Barbara, exploring the beaches, the zoo, **Lake Cachuma, Solvang,** the playgrounds, and parks. Or set up camp in **San Luis Obispo,** from where you can venture to **Morro Bay, Pismo Beach,** and even **Hearst Castle.** If you're coming from the northern end, you can easily devote three days to Monterey, with its aquarium and other attractions, or spend a day in Big Sur and a couple of days in Monterey. In summertime, Santa Cruz also makes a fine base for a minitrip, with lots of beach-oriented activities and a great boardwalk. You won't get a whit of the region's cherished intimacy and relaxed charm if you zoom through it all in a few days, so pick a couple of spots and focus, allowing time to wander through a farmers' market or have a picnic by a waterfall. The rest will wait for another trip.

GETTING THERE

By Plane. Monterey Peninsula Airport is serviced by seven airlines: Air Alaska, American Eagle, British Airways, Skywest/Delta, Northwest, United, and US Airways. Arrivals are to and from San Francisco and L.A., with connections beyond. To reach the Airport Department for the City of Santa Barbara (hours 8 a.m.–5 p.m. Monday–Friday), call (805) 967-7111. For San Luis Obispo Airport information, call (805) 781-5205.

By Train. Amtrak's Coast Starlight from L.A. to Seattle permits up to three stopovers, and it does stop in Santa Barbara and San Luis Obispo. Otherwise, there are commuter trains several times daily from L.A. to Santa Barbara. Trains to the Santa Cruz or Monterey areas originate in Oakland and only get as far as Salinas. Call (800) USA-RAIL.

By Car. The Central Coast area as we're defining it stretches from Ventura to Santa Cruz; it is best accessed from the north by California Highway 1 and from the south by US Highway 101. Tour this region by enjoying some part of its famous coast drive.

We recommend driving US 101 from L.A. to Santa Barbara (about a two-hour drive) and from Santa Barbara to San Luis Obispo (another two hours). From SLO to San Simeon, take Highway 1, allowing about an hour with no stops. You'll continue on the same road for about the same amount of time to drive from San Simeon to Big Sur. Allow at least 3½ hours total from San Luis Obispo to Monterey.

Heading south, from San Francisco, take Highway 1 through Half Moon Bay to Santa Cruz (about an hour and a half). Monterey is an hour's drive from Santa Cruz in light traffic on Highway 1.

Between Monterey and San Luis Obispo, US 101 runs roughly parallel to California Highway 1, but inland through the Salinas Valley. Between San Luis Obispo and Santa Barbara, California Highway 1 is not exactly on the coast (Vandenberg Air Force Base controls that land) but is west of 101 and goes through the little towns of Lompoc and Guadeloupe.

HOW TO GET INFORMATION BEFORE YOU GO

California State Parks, P.O. Box 942896, Sacramento 94296; (916) 653-6995; http://ceres.ca.gov/parks/.

Central Coast Tourism Council, (805) 544-0241.

Monterey Visitor and Convention Bureau, 380 Alvarado Street, Monterey 93942-1770; (831) 649-1770; fax (831) 648-5373.

Morro Bay Chamber of Commerce; (805) 772-4467.

Ojai Chamber of Commerce and Visitors Bureau, 150 W. Ojai Avenue, Ojai 93023; (805) 646-8126.

Pismo Beach Chamber of Commerce; (805) 773-4382.

San Luis Obispo County Visitors and Conference Bureau; (800) 634-1414 or (805) 541-8000.

San Simeon Chamber of Commerce; (805) 927-3500.

Santa Barbara Conference and Visitors Bureau; (805) 966-9222 or (800) 676-1266. Santa Barbara Visitors Center, 1 Santa Barbara Street; (805) 965-3021.

Santa Cruz County Conference and Visitors Council, 701 Front Street, Santa Cruz 95060; (408) 425-1234; fax (408) 425-1260; http://scccvc.org. Santa Cruz Visitor Information; (800) 833-3494. Santa Cruz Boardwalk; (408) 426-7433.

Solvang Chamber of Commerce, 1511 Mission Drive, Solvang 93464; (805) 688-0701 or (800) 468-6765.

Ventura Visitors Bureau, 89 S. California Street, Ste. C, Ventura 93001; (805) 648-2075; fax (805) 648-2150; www.venturausa.com.

The Best Beaches and Parks

Alameda Park. Santa Barbara's kids designed the Kid's World playground in this lovely mid-city park, and their parents built it. The result is a playground worth a detour, with such creations as an eel-shaped slide, a giant shark, and a really cool treehouse-style climbing structure. 1400 Santa Barbara Street, Santa Barbara, (805) 564-5418.

Andree Clark Bird Refuge. An easy bike or surrey ride along Santa Barbara's oceanfront path from Stearns Wharf, this lagoon is just past the zoo. Bring some bread crumbs for the kids to toss to the birds. 1400 E. Cabrillo Boulevard, Santa Barbara.

Año Nuevo State Beach. This one-of-a-kind animal refuge is found on the coast north of Santa Cruz. In the winter, by reservation, (800) 444-4445, rangers bring visitors along a roped path right into the breeding rookery of the remarkable elephant seals. These enormous sea mammals (bulls can get up to 20 feet long and some weigh in at four tons) can be seen up close, lying in the sand with their pups or bellowing at each other. In some frightening cases, visitors witness the bulls attacking each other in the waves. Sea otters are also within camera range. Visitors must be able to walk for two and a half hours on a three-mile round-trip trail that is sandy and uneven. Hwy 1/New Creek Road, Pescadero, (415) 879-2025 or (415) 879-0227; www.anonuevo.org. Wildlife viewing offered December 15–March 31. Individual exploration allowed during other parts of the year, but sensitive areas are controlled by rangers. Open 8 a.m. to sunset.

Arroyo Burro Beach. Santa Barbara locals with kids skip city-center Cabrillo Beach and head to this fine beach park, where whales and sea lions are sometimes spotted. The surf is usually calm enough for younger kids, and the creature comforts—rest rooms, showers, snack bar, lifeguard—are good. 2981 Cliff Drive, Santa Barbara, (805) 687-3714.

Big Basin State Park. More than 100 miles of trails lead visitors on explorations of the cool groves of towering 2,000-year-old redwoods in this acclaimed coastal park north of Santa Cruz. The short Redwood Nature Trail takes you into a grove of ancient trees, including the Mother of the Forest, a 330-foot monster. If your kids are over eight or nine years old, you should hike the Sequoia Trail, which leads past lush ferns and azaleas to Sempervirens Falls. There are several wonderful campgrounds, including a cluster of tent cabins for those who only want to rough it to a point (see page 286). 21600 Big Basin Way, Boulder Creek (Highway 1 north of Santa Cruz), (831) 335-3174. Open sunrise to sunset; $6 day-use fee.

Carpinteria State Park Beach. Named by the Spanish for the Chumash canoe-building carpentry shop once located here, Carpinteria has been called the world's safest beach. It has a natural breakwater that makes the surf exceptionally peaceful and allows for a mile of great swimming with lots of shallow water and no riptides. There's also a lagoon and tide pools. An area of the beach not protected by the offshore shelf offers surfing. There are 261 developed campsites, 120 with RV hookups; camping fees are $17–28 per night, and the day-use fee $5. Ranger walks include topics from tide-pool life to maritime history, and campfire programs include Chumash Indian lore. Restaurant, groceries, rest rooms, showers. At the bottom of Linden Avenue, Carpinteria (via Highway 224 off US 101), 12 miles south of Santa Barbara, (805) 684-2811 or (805) 968-3294. To make reservations, call (800) 444-7275

Chase Palm Park. Santa Barbara's newest city park is a Pacific Coast jewel. Across the street from the ocean and the city's beach volleyball courts, this meticulously crafted and landscaped public space is comprised of grassy knolls, ponds, a lavish fountain, perfectly situated benches, a vintage carousel, murals painted by local artists, an unobtrusive snack bar, clean rest rooms, picnic tables, and a superb playground that reflects the style and history of the region. Climb-on-me whales, half-submerged in the sand, spout real mist throughout the day. A mock mission is great for pretend play, as are ship-themed climbing structures. We took a gang of ten-year-olds who couldn't get enough of the stand-up slide. Bring a picnic lunch and hang out for awhile. East Cabrillo Boulevard at Santa Barbara Street, Santa Barbara, (805) 564-5418.

Dennis the Menace Playground/Camino El Estero Park. We have vivid childhood memories of playing on the locomotive here, so on a recent visit to Monterey, we took the kids on a pilgrimage. Time hadn't faded the park's charm for toddlers and preschoolers in particular, although it seemed modest to the over-four-footers. Designed by cartoonist Hank Ketcham, it does indeed still have the train engine, as well as slides, a bridge, and a maze. In the park at Camino El Estero, Monterey, (831) 646-3866. Open 10 a.m.–dusk Tuesday–Saturday; admission free. A little lake in the same park offers paddleboats; call (831) 375-1484 for times and charges.

Morro Bay State Park. This is one of the most varied-use state parks around, with a golf course (featuring a tree planted in the 1930s by the Civilian Conservation Corps), museum (see Natural History Museum under Morro Bay Attractions, page 269), a boat harbor with launch and rental facilities, a bayside restaurant, a bird sanctuary that protects peregrine falcon nesting sites, and campgrounds. You can rent a boat or kayak, fish in the surf or from a boat, go clamming, picnic, and hike. State Park Road, 1 mile south of Morro Bay, (805) 772-7434; campground reservations through Reserve America, (800) 444-7275. Open daily; free day use. Campsites with electricity and water are $23, and sites for a tent or self-contained vehicle are $17.

Pismo State Beach and Pismo Dunes Preserve. This huge (eight-mile) beach runs through the towns of Oceano, Grover City, and Pismo Beach. At the turn of the century, Pismo Beach was a tourist mecca, with visitors coming to dig clams and play in the sand. Nowadays, the monarch butterflies are the greater wildlife attraction—the largest colony to winter in the United States is found in and around a grove of pine and eucalyptus south of North Beach campground between November and March. Ironically, the sand dunes of this beach are known on the one hand for dune buggies and other off-road riding (see Family Outdoor Adventures below), and on the other hand for the Pismo Dunes Preserve, a protected area with unique and rare vegetation as well as archeological sites. You'll find the Dunes Preserve via Oso Flaco Lake Road, at the end of which is a parking lot that is open from 8 a.m. to 6 p.m.; the dunes may be reached after a ten-minute walk. Passenger vehicles may drive along the beach from Grand Avenue in Grover City and Pier Avenue in Oceano. The state park has two campgrounds, food service, a visitors center, exhibits, and programs. Pismo State Beach information is (805) 489-8655. Campground reservations through Reserve America, (800) 444-7275.

Pfeiffer/Big Sur State Park. Every campsite in this park is taken during the summer and over holiday weekends, when Californians bring their kids here to relive their own childhood memories of making dams in the cool, clear creeks under the canopy of redwoods, sycamores, and willows. Adults will remember the spectacular drive to and from the park on the often-photographed stretch of Highway 1 that winds on cliffs above the rugged shoreline. But kids will remember the canyon, whether you stop for a picnic (at least), an overnight in the park's motel-like lodge, or several quiet days of riverside camping. Junior Ranger programs, guided walks, ranger programs. See also the campsite listing on page 274. Off Highway 1, Big Sur, (831) 667-2315, camping reservations through Reserve America, (800) 444-7275. Day-use fee $7.

Rocky Nook Park. Nineteen acres in the heart of Santa Barbara near the mission and the Museum of Natural History, this park is great for a picnic with need-to-run kids after too much touring. No grassy lawns, but rather boulders for climbing along Mission Creek, as well as picnic and barbecue areas and playground equipment. 610 Mission Canyon Road, Santa Barbara, (805) 568-2460.

Refugio State Beach. About 20 minutes north of Santa Barbara lies this lovely, palm-rimmed cove nestled below Highway 101 and the train tracks. Campsites are tough to come by; if you can't score one, visit for the afternoon. The sand is soft, the swimming and bodyboarding great, and the tide-pools on the north end are stunning. Bring bikes to ride the 2.5-mile path to neighboring El Capitan State Beach; our kids also loved riding bikes in Refugio's paved areas. Lawns, barbecue facilities, showers, rest rooms, summer lifeguard. Highway 101 at Refugio Road, Goleta, (805) 968-1033.

Santa Cruz Boardwalk Beach. Why not spread your towel on the sand, with the sparkling Pacific before you and the colorful roller coasters and sky buckets of the boardwalk as a backdrop? There's a lot of sense in breaking up the hours spent on rides with a dip in the sea and a nap in the sun. In Santa Cruz, (800) 833-3494.

Family Outdoor Adventures

ATV Driving on the Sand Dunes. All-Terrain Vehicles are welcome at Pismo State Beach Vehicular Area. All off-road vehicles must be transported by street-legal vehicles to the off-road area, from which they may explore almost 2,000 acres of sand. Drivers under 18 years of age may operate ATVs on public land only if they have an ATV Safety Certificate of Completion. All riders are advised to wear helmets and protective clothing; vehicles must have an adequate roll bar and other safety features. For dune driving information call Pismo Dunes State Vehicular Recreation Area at (805) 549-3433. There are ATV rental companies in Grover City and Oceano, including BJ's ATV Rentals, 197 Grand Avenue, Grover Beach, (805) 481-5411, and Sand Center, 1163 Strand Way, Oceano, (805) 489-0395.

Eagle Cruise at Lake Cachuma. The personable and regionally famous ranger Neal Taylor was our guide when we took the 75-minute boat tour of Lake Cachuma, a man-made reservoir with camping areas about 18 miles northeast of Santa Barbara. He enthralled grandmother and five-year-old alike as he pointed out and identified birds for us, then pulled up to the shoreline and clipped a piece of "miner's lettuce" for us to see, and held open the palm of his hand to show us how a particular seed "walked." In winter months, visitors cruise to see eagle nesting areas as well as migratory birds like Canada geese. Summer cruisers see other birds (over 275 species, both year-round and migratory), including great blue herons, osprey, hawks, and woodpeckers.

Amenities for campers include yurts (tent-like cabins sleeping six) to rent, 500 campsites, a general store, laundry facilities, showers, a snack bar, a marina, bait and tackle shop, picnic tables, barbecues, corrals for campers on horseback, fireside theater programs, summer movies, and weekend nature walks. Access available for travelers with disabilities. Cachuma Lake Recreation Area, Santa Barbara County Park Dept., Star Route, Highway 154. Boat tour reservations, (805) 688-4040; cost $8 adults, $6 children under age 12. Camping and yurt reservations, (805) 686-5050.

Kayaking or Cruising. Before or after learning about the special marine ecology of the huge and magnificent Monterey Bay (with Santa Cruz on the north end and Monterey on the south), school-age and older kids can sign up for an outing in the Monterey Bay National Marine Sanctuary (phone (831) 647-4201; interpretive center at Santa Cruz Harbor), a stellar ocean-kayaking site thanks to its sheltered waters and remarkable wildlife (otters, sea lions, gray whales). Adventure Sports Unlimited (303 Potrero #15, The Old Sash Mill, Santa Cruz, (831) 458-3648) offers an intensive but not-too-long combination that includes training in sit-on-top kayaks and an excursion to the sanctuary. You begin in the evening with classroom and heated-pool instruction, then, the next day, enjoy an outing to the Sanctuary, complete with a "cooperative" brunch and an end-of-the-day Jacuzzi soak. Kayak Connections sets off from two locations in the Monterey Bay Sanctuary, at Santa Cruz Harbor (413 Lake Avenue, Santa Cruz, (831) 479-1121) and in Moss Landing, 20 miles south of Santa Cruz, at Elkhorn Yacht Club (2370 Highway 1, Moss Landing, (831) 724-5692). Rentals, guided tours, and instruction. The Monterey Bay Sanctuary tour is Sundays at 9 a.m., and private tours are held by request.

Non-paddlers can take a two-hour guided natural history tour on an easy-riding 27-foot pontoon boat. Called the Elkhorn Slough Safari, the tour takes you ten miles into the coastal wetlands of the Monterey Bay National Marine Sanctuary. Fares are $24 adults and $18 children, including binoculars, guide, and refreshments; tours depart from Moss Landing. Call (831) 633-5555, or look up www.elkhornslough.com.

Hiking. If you never do any other outdoor activities in California, we urge you to get out of your car and take a few hikes or nature walks while in Central California. There are several good trails for children in this area.

To reach **Cold Springs Canyon** in Santa Barbara (for older kids), off Highway 101 south of the San Ysidro Road exit, take San Ysidro east to Mountain Drive, turn left and continue 1.25 miles to the trailhead, where a creek crosses the road. Walk on trail for a quarter-mile, then head right at the main (east) fork, which leads to lovely pools in the creek.

To reach **Rattlesnake Canyon Trail** in Santa Barbara, take the Mission Street exit north from Highway 101 and continue past Mission to Foothill Road. Turn right on Foothill, left on Mission Canyon, and right on Las Canoas Road; the trailhead is about a mile from the turn at a stone bridge in Skofield Park/Rattlesnake Canyon Wilderness Area. Leads to pools and small waterfall.

Aliso Canyon Nature Trail is three miles from the Santa Barbara District Rangers Office at Sage Hill Campground. Call (805) 967-3481 for directions.

Nojoquoi Falls County Park Trail is located seven miles southwest of Solvang on Alisal Road. This easy trail travels alongside a creek under the California coastal oaks and comes to the 164-foot falls. Park open 8 a.m. to dusk, admission free.

Big Basin State Park in Santa Cruz offers the four-mile Sequoia Trail through the big trees, which culminates at a waterfall. See park in Best Beaches and Parks, page 228. Call (831) 338-8860.

Even the little ones can handle **Pfeiffer Falls Trail**—a less than half-mile loop up to see the waterfall. In Pfeiffer Big Sur State Park, (831) 667-2315.

Surf Sports. Certain beaches of the Central Coast are prime areas to try or enjoy surf sports, from Boogie boarding to body-surfing to surfing.

In Santa Barbara, instruction and rentals may be found at: Morningstar Surf and Sport, (805) 967-8288; Rincon Designs Surfboards, (805) 684-2413; Sundance Ocean Sports, (805) 966-4400. At the East Beach/ Cabrillo Pavilion, on Cabrillo Boulevard in Santa Barbara, the Cabrillo Bathhouse rents equipment and sells sunscreen, towels, Boogie boards, and such; call (805) 965-0509. Lifeguards are on duty daily in summer, and there's a children's play structure.

In Santa Cruz, the place to learn to surf is at Club Ed Surf Schools and Camps, established by "the Professor of Surfing" at U.C. Santa Cruz, Ed Guzman, a third-generation Santa Cruz surfer (his grandmother learned to surf in 1915!). The school offers lessons, rentals, excursions, and camps; it's located on Cowell's Beach in front of the West Coast Santa Cruz Hotel in Santa Cruz, (800) 287-SURF or (408) 459-WAVE; fax (831) 427-9283; www.club-ed.com. Private lessons are $70 an hour; two-hour group lessons are $70 for the first lesson, with follow-ups at $50 an hour, including equipment. You can also try Richard Schmidt Surf School, 236 San Jose Avenue, Santa Cruz, (831) 476-5200.

Noshing through the Central Coast

Agriculture is as important as surfing (maybe even more so!) in the Central Coast, so the food is often wonderful. Here are the edible souvenirs to look for:

Tub of butter cookies from Solvang (year-round). Available from several bakeries, but we like the quality of the cookies and other goods at Solvang Bakery (call (805) 688-4939) near the big visitors' parking lot on the mission side of town. Layers of different kinds of butter cookies (marble, cherry-in-center, chocolate crescents) are packed between sheets of baker's paper in a plastic tub with a handle. We always think it'll take a week to empty, but it's never made it past two days.

Bag of apples bought from streetside apple stand in Santa Ynez Valley (September and October). Farmers in the area grow several varieties, and fresh-picked ones are available from card tables in driveways and other roadside stands. We usually stop by Mr. Dittmar's stand at Greenhaven Orchard, 2275 Alamo Pintado Road (call (805) 688-3141) near the little town of Ballard, just down the way from the miniature horse farm. The startling superiority of fresh Fujis and Granny Smiths makes it easy for kids to enjoy a healthy snack from a bag carried along on your travels.

Strawberries and corn from roadside stands in Oxnard/Ventura (May and June). The corn is possible only if you have a kitchen, but a basket of strawberries is a wonderful addition to a picnic or tailgate lunch. Stand locations vary but can often be found alongside the 101 after descending the big grade heading north. Check by the Las Posas exit or in Ventura at the end of Telephone Road at Olivos Park.

Central Coast tri-tip sandwich from an outdoor barbecue stand at the Thursday night farmers' market in San Luis Obispo (year-round). The essence of Central Coast cowboy culture (formerly nineteenth-century *rancho* culture) is carried in the aroma of barbecued beef that emanates from competing barbecues set up during this weekly farmers' market and street fair. Tri-tip is the locally favored cut of beef (the top portion of choice sirloin), and it makes for a tasty sandwich. For the ultimate picnic, stop by El Rancho Market near Solvang (2886 E. Highway 246, (805) 688-4300), where, on the weekends, a barbecue wagon is set up outside the market and whole tri-tips, chicken, sausage, ribs, and turkey breast are grilled over oak and sold by the pound.

Pismo Beach clam chowder. In the late nineteenth century, Pismo Beach visitors would come for the sweet, succulent shellfish, so numerous then that it's said they could be dug with the toes (the earliest limits were for 200 a day per person). Today, visitors with a fishing license and a clamming fork can try to bag the current limit of ten clams per person a day, but they're not as easily found. If you're not the hunter-gatherer type, be sure to order some chowder at one of the beach shanty cafes in town.

Pick your own olallaberries at Avila Valley Barn (late May or early June). Call (805) 595-2816. Located at 560 Avila Beach Drive, ½ mile west of US 101 near San Luis Obispo. If you're too late for berry season, you can pick peaches, apples, or pumpkins. There's also a bakery and gift shop here, and a place to picnic. The overall season is approximately Memorial Day through Thanksgiving.

Fresh steamed artichokes. Eastern Monterey Peninsula borders on the rich agricultural lands of the Salinas Valley. Wineries abound, as do a variety of farms, but the area is most famous for its artichokes. Locals will be bagging produce here, but you can stop and eat fresh steamed artichokes at the Pezzini Farms stand off Highway 1 three miles from Castroville, north of Monterey. Open year-round at the corner of Nashua and Molera, (408) 757-7434.

Apple juice. Young apple-juice guzzlers will delight not only in drinking the fresh-squeezed apple juice from Gizdich Ranch in Watsonville near Santa Cruz (see page 289), but also in watching it made.

Calendar of Festivals and Events

January

Santa Cruz Fungus Fair. Displays of more than 200 varieties of mushrooms; (408) 429-3773.

Whalefest, Monterey. Special exhibits, art shows, children's activities; (408) 644-7588.

February

Whale Festival, Santa Barbara. The annual migration of the gray whale is honored in this fine festival, which includes live music, whale memorabilia, and a duck race; (805) 966-4426.

Migration Festival, Natural Bridges State Beach, Santa Cruz. Exhibits, slide programs, music, and crafts in celebration of "the fantastic journeys of migrating animals"; (408) 423-4609.

John Steinbeck Birthday Festival, Monterey. At Cannery Row, with tours, entertainment, refreshments; (408) 372-8512.

March

Solvang Century Bike Ride. A huge event open to participants ages ten and up, who take part in a 100-mile ride; (213) 943-9440.

April

Santa Maria Strawberry Festival, County Fairgrounds, Santa Maria. Locals celebrate the kick-off of the typically bounteous strawberry season with a lively carnival and festival that's great for kids; (805) 925-8824.

Old Monterey Seafood and Music Festival. Music on two stages, arts and crafts fair; (408) 655-8070.

May

Children's Festival, Alameda Park, Santa Barbara; (805) 969-7235.

Adobe Spring Celebration. Candle-making, bread-baking, and other period crafts at Santa Cruz Mission; (831) 425-5849.

Santa Cruz Longboard Club Invitational. Western surf clubs compete in this amateur competition; (408) 684-1551.

José Cuervo Volleyball Tournament, East Beach, Santa Barbara. School-age kids and their parents will love watching these beach gods and goddesses do their thing; (805) 564-5422.

California Strawberry Festival, Oxnard. Multi-event celebration includes soccer tournaments, arts and crafts, entertainment, and special events; (805) 385-7578.

Great Monterey Squid Festival, Monterey Fairgrounds. Cooking demonstrations, exhibits on commercial fishing industry, touch tanks, entertainment, arts, and crafts; (408) 649-6544.

June

Summer Solstice Celebration, central Santa Barbara, with music festival in Alameda Park. The antidote to overblown theme parks. No motorized floats, no amplified music, just one of the most joyous, free-wheeling parades you'll ever see; (805) 965-3396.

Live Oak Music Festival, San Luis Obispo. A three-day family-style festival of music including traditional, blues, Cajun, and classical. Concerts, barn dance, food, crafts, camping; (805) 541-8000.

Lompoc Valley Flower Show, Lompoc. Kids will go for the floral floats, marching bands, and carnival; gardening parents will love the tours of the region's great flower fields; (805) 735-8511.

July

Fourth of July Celebration, Monterey. Music, parade, and fireworks; (831) 646-5648.

Santa Barbara County Fair, County Fairgrounds, Santa Maria. An A-list county fair with everything from pie-eating contests to concerts by some of the country's best musicians; (805) 925-8824.

Old Spanish Days Fiesta, held at sites throughout Santa Barbara. Many activities include Children's Parade and Tardes de Ronda, a children's variety show; (805) 962-8101.

Pacific Grove Feast of Lanterns. For more than 90 years, this small community next to Monterey has celebrated with a week of activities; concludes with a pageant, barbecue, boat parade, and fireworks on the city beach; (408) 372-7625.

August

Mid-State Fair, Paso Robles; (805) 238-0506.

Shakespeare Santa Cruz. Outdoor theater festival at U.C. Santa Cruz; (408) 450-2121.

Russian Festival, Santa Cruz. Booths, food, crafts, music of Russia and the Ukraine; (408) 662-3761.

September

Danish Days, Solvang. Parade, special events to celebrate the town's Danish heritage. Always held the third weekend in September; (800) 468-6765.

Capitola Begonia Festival. An unusual and appealing flower boat parade — floats are constructed of flowers wired onto pontoons and sailed down Soquel Creek and under Stockton Bridge while onlookers gaze from banks. Also a sand-castle contest; (408) 475-6522.

Carmel Mission Fiesta. At the lovely site of the mission, a farmers' market, art fair, children's games, and entertainment; (408) 626-4567.

Shark Festival, Santa Cruz Municipal Wharf. Shark exhibits, live shark tanks, and everything shark; (831) 420-5273.

Festa Italia, Monterey. Outdoor mass, parade, blessing of the fleet, entertainment, arts and crafts, food; (408) 649-6544.

October

Harvest Festival and Draft Horse Days, Wilder Ranch State Park, Santa Cruz. Showcases antique tractors, historic farming techniques; celebrates local produce harvest. Food, games, children's activities; (408) 426-0505.

Welcome Back Monarchs, Natural Bridges State Beach, Santa Cruz. The butterflies return to Santa Cruz. Music, food, games; (831) 423-4609.

Clam Festival, held in the downtown pier parking lot and other locations, Pismo Beach. Always the third weekend in October. Clam digging for prizes, clam chowder cook-off, fishing derby. Parade featuring Pam and Sam Clam walking along and greeting kids. Admission $2, children under age 12 free; (805) 773-4382 or (800) 443-7778.

Harbor Festival, Morro Bay. Various events and locations, including entertainment, boat rides, and seafood fair; (805) 772-1155.

December

Caroling under the Stars, Santa Cruz. Rain or shine, families gather on successive weekends to carol at Lighthouse Point and Municipal Wharf; (408) 429-3477.

First Night, New Year's Eve, Santa Cruz. Annual non-alcoholic event features 3 p.m.–midnight performances and concerts, a grand procession, and midnight finale at landmark Town Clock; (408) 425-7277.

Ventura

If you're taking a coast vacation in short stages, Ventura offers a nice enough balance of beach, marina areas, agricultural landscapes, and suburban shopping to keep a family busy for a day or two, and it's a dandy half-day stop as well. As you approach the area from the south, the first thing you may notice is an expansive farming setting: On roads just off the freeways, there are orange groves as full of fruit and blossoms as on any picture postcard. The downtown area east of the freeway has a fun mid-century main street with vintage storefronts in various stages of renovation and re-use. The **courthouse** where Erle Stanley Gardner (author of the Perry Mason murder mysteries) once pleaded cases as a lawyer himself is the most prominent landmark. On the other side of the freeway (but accessible by foot) is a wide, sandy beach, with a pedestrian and bike path on a rise above the beach. It's great for walking, people-watching, and admiring vendors' wares when mini–arts fairs are set up. A few miles away, the **Ventura Harbor** area has shops, restaurants, boat slips, and the **Channel Islands Visitors Center.**

Family Lodging

Embassy Suites Resort Mandalay Beach

Another resort that's been run by one chain after another, this little-known all-suite (two-bedroom, two-bath) hotel has a choice on-the-beach location—but beware, it doesn't get sunny in this region until July. The 249 suites are roomy and comfortable, and the oceanfront ones could make a family happy for several days. Other rooms overlook a landscaped courtyard. Children are greeted with a welcome gift, and each adult meal in the restaurant buys a free kid's meal. Rates include full breakfast.

2101 Mandalay Beach Road, Oxnard; (805) 984-2500 or (800) EMBASSY. Weekend rates $214–259; family package, with minimum of two-night stay; weekday rates start at $174.

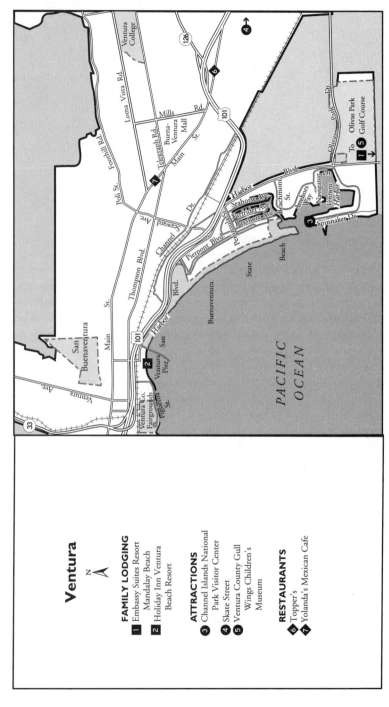

Ventura

N

FAMILY LODGING

1 Embassy Suites Resort
Mandalay Beach

2 Holiday Inn Ventura
Beach Resort

ATTRACTIONS

3 Channel Islands National
Park Visitor Center

4 Skate Street

5 Ventura County Gull
Wings Children's
Museum

RESTAURANTS

6 Topper's

7 Yolanda's Mexican Cafe

Holiday Inn Ventura Beach Resort

The people's beach resort, this high-rise hotel has a terrific location and affordable rooms. That means it is very popular, and although there are 260 rooms and 16 suites, it's often sold out in summer. There's a pedestrian walkway to a plaza with shops and cafes adjacent; the pool overlooks the public beach promenade and sands. You just walk across the sidewalk to reach the beach. There are no kids' programs or children's menus, but there is a game room.

450 E. Harbor Boulevard (off California and Harbor Boulevard), Ventura; (805) 648-7731 or (800) 842-0800; fax (805) 653-6202. Rates start at $109 in winter, $119 in summer.

Attractions

Channel Islands National Park

1901 Spinnaker Drive, Ventura Harbor; (805) 658-5730;
www.nps.gov/shis/

Hours: Visitors Center open daily, 9 a.m.–5:30 p.m. from Memorial Day–Labor Day, and 8:30 a.m.–4:30 p.m. the rest of year; closed Thanksgiving, Christmas, and New Year's Day

Admission: Free to Visitors Center. The all-day boat excursion and guided hike to Anacapa Island is $37 adults, $20 children. Contact Island Packers, authorized park concessionaire, (805) 642-7688; www.islandpackers.com for boat excursion information.

Appeal by Age Groups:

Pre-school	Grade School	Teens	Young Adults	Over 30	Seniors
★★	★★★★★	★★★★★	★★★★★	★★★★★	★★★

Touring Time: All day trip to Anacapa takes 7–8 hours; the half-day trip to Anacapa takes 3–4 hours; minimum touring time 30 minutes to walk through Visitors Center only and see nature exhibits

Rainy-Day Touring: Yes, to Visitors Center; boat excursions are weather permitting

Services and Facilities:

Restaurants No	Baby stroller rental No
Alcoholic beverages No	Lockers No
Disabled access Yes, to Visitors	Pet kennels No
Center	Rain check No
Wheelchair rental No	Private tours No

Description and Comments   Ever wanted to visit the Galapagos Islands? A visit to Channel Islands National Park is easier, way cheaper, and offers similar amazing wildlife experiences. The park includes five islands and their surrounding one nautical mile of ocean with its kelp forests. The ocean for six miles around each island is designated as a National Marine Sanctuary, and the isolation of the islands has resulted in many unique plant and animal species. The park is home to more species of seals and sea lions (pinnipeds) than anywhere else in the world; between 180,000 and 200,000 individuals live on and around the islands. Pelicans, seagulls, and other sea birds nest here, and the ocean around the islands often teems with dolphins. For families, the day trips to Anacapa Island are potentially wondrous. Sometimes, seagulls are nesting along the one-mile path the ranger leads you on; sometimes schools of dolphins surround your boat; sometimes whales are spotted along the way. You have to be able to climb a ladder (or be carried in a backpack) and a few flights of stairs; otherwise, the 1½-mile island is easily accessible. Landlubbers can stop by the visitors center, located in a waterfront complex of shops and cafes, and combine a look at the island exhibits and indoor tidepool with a ride on the carousel and stop for lunch. In the center store, you can pick up a copy of *The Island of the Blue Dolphins,* required reading in many fifth-grade classrooms, and based on a true story of the Channel Islands.

Skate Street

1990 Building B, Knoll Drive, Ventura; (805) 650-1213; www.skatestreetusa.com

Hours: Skate sessions are offered in three-hour increments at various times throughout the week, depending on camp and lesson schedules

Admission: $12 for entire session; $7 for last 90 minutes; parents must sign a liability waver; helmets and pads required and can be rented on-site

Appeal by Age Groups:

Pre-school	Grade School	Teens	Young Adults	Over 30	Seniors
—	★★★	★★★	★★	—	—

Touring Time: Average 3 hours; minimum 1 hour

Rainy-Day Touring: Yes

Services and Facilities:

Restaurants Snacks		Lockers Yes	
Alcoholic beverages No		Pet kennels No	
Disabled access No		Rain check No	
Wheelchair rental No		Private tours Birthday parties	
Baby stroller rental No			

Description and Comments   A 29,000-square-foot skateboard/inline skate/BMX facility, this is not your grandfather's roller rink, but rather a cavernous setting with an array of bowls, ramps, and specialty areas (like a water-wall), as well as a beginner's area (there are contests and events for children under six). Open sessions of three hours are scheduled around lessons and camp time, and in the evenings beginning at 7 p.m., skating gives way to all-ages concerts.

Ventura County Gull Wings Children's Museum

418 W. 4th Street, Oxnard; (805) 483-3005

Hours: Tuesday–Sunday, 10 a.m.–5 p.m.; closed Mondays

Admission: $3.50 adults, free for children under age 2

Appeal by Age Groups:

Pre-school	Grade School	Teens	Young Adults	Over 30	Seniors
★★★★★	★★★	★	★	★	★

Touring Time: Average 3 hours; minimum 2 hours (no point in rushing the little ones)

Rainy-Day Touring: Yes, excellent

Services and Facilities:

Restaurants No	Lockers No
Alcoholic beverages No	Pet kennels No
Disabled access Yes	Rain check No
Wheelchair rental No	Private tours No
Baby stroller rental No	

Description and Comments   An excellent, homegrown, low-tech children's museum, best for kids under age six. Our little ones spent happy hours with the bubble exhibit, puppet theater, pretend campground with tent, pretend farmers' market, and fossils to touch. Not glitzy like the big-city children's museums, but not overwhelming for the little ones in any way, so for some families it will be actually more fun and hands-on.

Family-Friendly Restaurants

TOPPER'S

3940 E. Main Street, Ventura; (805) 385-4444

Meals served: Lunch and dinner
Cuisine: American
Entree range: $3.11–4.88 (lunch); $6–17.75 (dinner)
Children's menu: No
Reservations: Not necessary
Payment: MC, V

This small local chain (five restaurants in Ventura County) is a good, reliable eat-in, takeout, or deliver-to-your-hotel-room restaurant. The pizzas are fine, and the six-inch sandwiches are fresh and tasty. If you eat in, there's a salad bar, games, and a big-screen TV.

YOLANDA'S MEXICAN CAFE

2753 E. Main Street, Ventura; (805) 643-2700

Meals served: Lunch, dinner, and Sunday brunch
Cuisine: Mexican
Entree range: $6.50–11(lunch); $7.75–15 (dinner)
Children's menu: Yes, $3.50
Reservations: Advised
Payment: AE, D, MC, V

One of the best Mexican restaurants in Southern California, Yolanda's is nevertheless completely kid-friendly. You'll find terrific homemade food here, made from the freshest ingredients, some obtained from local farms. Try the veggie combo plate, the enchiladas rancheras, and the flautas.

Santa Barbara

Santa Barbara is considered by its residents to be an unparalleled paradise of perfect weather, fine restaurants, and beautifully maintained residential neighborhoods. Strict zoning laws have kept the city's famous red-tile roof building style so predominant that even major shopping malls are discreetly tucked into the traditional Mediterranean silhouette (and in some cases into the historic buildings themselves).

For some families, the lack of theme parks and glitzy attractions will make Santa Barbara look like a sleepy, ho-hum sort of place, but we think that whether you're making a day trip up from L.A., stopping for a couple of nights en route north or south, or making a week-long vacation of it, Santa Barbara is a great place for a family trip. The trick is to focus on the area's unbeatable outdoor attractions: glorious beaches, beautiful hiking trails to rock-strewn waterfalls, pastoral agricultural areas of horse ranches and apple orchards. Making these outdoor pleasures family-friendly is easy to do—rent a bike, sign up for Boogie-board lessons, hang out at the kiddie wading pool on a sunny afternoon, or pack a picnic and look for the trailhead. Overnight options range from retro-appealing, postwar motels with kitchenettes near the main city beaches to full-service, five-star resorts to a vintage ranch resort.

Family Lodging

Casa del Mar

Built as a courtyard apartment building, this 1930s Spanish charmer offers a lot of comfort and location for the price. The downside for kids is the lack of a pool, but the large spa is lovely. Cabrillo Beach is just around the corner, and the 20 apartment-style accommodations are ideal for a family, offering kitchens, fireplaces, and plenty of room for everyone. A continental breakfast

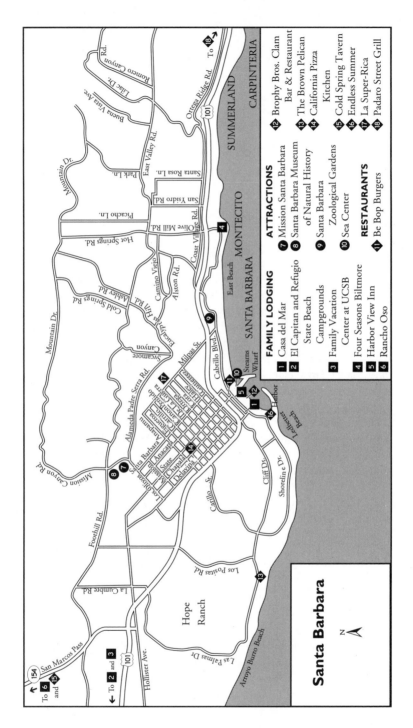

Santa Barbara

N

FAMILY LODGING

1. Casa del Mar
2. El Capitan and Refugio State Beach Campgrounds
3. Family Vacation Center at UCSB
4. Four Seasons Biltmore
5. Harbor View Inn
6. Rancho Oso

ATTRACTIONS

7. Mission Santa Barbara
8. Santa Barbara Museum of Natural History
9. Santa Barbara Zoological Gardens
10. Sea Center

RESTAURANTS

11. Be Bop Burgers
12. Brophy Bros. Clam Bar & Restaurant
13. The Brown Pelican
14. California Pizza Kitchen
15. Cold Spring Tavern
16. Endless Summer
17. La Super-Rica
18. Padaro Street Grill

is included in the price, and it's an easy walk to the beach, Stearn's Wharf, and the shops and restaurants of lower State Street.

18 Bath Street, Santa Barbara; (800) 433-3097 or (805) 963-4418; fax (805) 966-4240. Rates start at $114–149 but change according to the season.

El Capitan and Refugio State Beach Campgrounds

Very popular with locals seeking a simple beach vacation, El Capitan and Refugio are located about 20 minutes north of Santa Barbara. At El Capitan, you camp in a grassy, oak-shaded area on a bluff overlooking the sea, with a good beach below; request a campsite as far away from Highway 101 and the train tracks as possible, or you'll be up all night. Refugio is a wonderful spot, a little farther from the train and highway; the campground has less privacy than El Capitan, but a beautiful beach right in front. Fire rings, showers, flush toilets, picnic tables, lifeguard on beach in summer.

Highway 101 between Santa Barbara and Gaviota; (805) 968-1033; reservations through Reserve America, (800) 444-7275. Sites $17–18.

Family Vacation Center at UCSB

Are you jealous of kids who get to go off to summer camp and have more fun than grown-ups? Then check out this beachy summer camp for families, run by the alumni association at the University of California at Santa Barbara. For a week in July or August, you can stay on campus in a dorm suite (including daily maid service and all meals, better than our dorm-food days) and play your days away. Many activities are designed to enjoy together, from hikes and beach campfire sing-alongs to carnivals and tennis matches, while others are just for parents (golf, casino night, wine tastings). There are tournaments for everything from chess to tennis. While parents are otherwise occupied, kids of all ages (even infants) have a ball with the superb counselors, drawn from the education and child-development programs at UCSB.

Alumni Association, University of California at Santa Barbara; (805) 893-3123; fax (805) 893-4918. Weekly rates about $620 for adults, $540 ages 8–12, $510 ages 4–7, and $345 ages 1–3; alums receive discount.

Four Seasons Biltmore

To find the California dream, look no further than this famed luxury hotel facing the Pacific. From the spectacular flowerbeds to the enveloping king-size beds, every detail is perfect. The arches, tiles, and thick stucco walls evoke the romance of old California, but the amenities are thoroughly modern—like the free children's program, which keeps kids happily swimming, exploring, and making crafts while parents play tennis, get massages, or nap on the beach. You name it, they've got it: full spa services, health club, free bikes, Olympic pool, great food, hidden gardens, and the vast Pacific. Only the beach is a bit lacking—on the small side—but that's a small quibble in paradise.

1260 Channel Drive, Montecito; (800) 332-3442 or (805) 969-2261; fax (805) 969-4682. Rates start at $435.

Harbor View Inn

This handsome red-tile Spanish motel was renovated recently, and the results show. It has a large pool, wading pool, and whirlpool, as well as the breadth of Cabrillo Beach right across the street, with Stearns Wharf a three-minute walk. The newest of the cool, well-appointed rooms (coffeemakers, fridges, movies) are relatively large, so even though there are no suites, you may fit comfortably in one room. Rates include a good continental breakfast and afternoon refreshments.

28 W. Cabrillo Boulevard; (805) 963-0780 or (800) 755-0222; fax (805) 963-7967. Rates start at $180; no charge for children under 16.

Rancho Oso

Just up the San Marcos Pass from downtown Santa Barbara lies a rustic family retreat that offers a lot of fun for not much money. Originally a riding stable, Rancho Oso has evolved into a small guest ranch, with five simple cabins (each sleeps four) and the kids' favorite, ten covered wagons, which are fitted with army cots to sleep four. Luxuries are few—bathrooms are outside—but the fun quotient is high. Kids ages eight and up (and their parents) can head out on the several daily horseback rides; littler ones enjoy escorted pony rides. When you're not riding, you can swim in the two pools, soak in the spa, play in the playground, fish in the creek, and head out for nature hikes. A chuckwagon feeds guests hearty cowboy fare.

3750 Paradise Road (off Highway 154); (805) 683-5686. Wagons are $33 a night, cabins $56.

Attractions

Mission Santa Barbara

E. Los Olivos and Laguna Street, Santa Barbara; (805) 682-4149

Hours: Daily 9 a.m.–5 p.m.; closed Easter, Thanksgiving, and Christmas Day

Admission: $4 adults, free for children ages 12 and under

Appeal by Age Groups:

Pre-school	Grade School	Teens	Young Adults	Over 30	Seniors
★	★★	★★	★★★	★★★★	★★★★

Touring Time: Average 2 hours; minimum 1 hour

Rainy-Day Touring: Not recommended

Services and Facilities:

Restaurants No	Baby stroller rental No
Alcoholic beverages No	Lockers No
Disabled access Limited; some	Pet kennels No
steps	Rain check No
Wheelchair rental No	Private tours No

Description and Comments   We don't list all the California missions in this book because we think they're pretty confusing for the youngest kids and more interesting to adults than to even many school-age kids. But Santa Barbara's mission is well-preserved and restored and quite kid-friendly in the exhibits. Completed in 1820, this mission now features a self-guided tour with stops including a padre's bedroom, a Chumash Indian room, and the chapel and cemetery.

Santa Barbara Museum of Natural History

2559 Puesta del Sol Road (behind the Mission), Santa Barbara; (805) 682-4711

Hours: Monday–Saturday 9 a.m.–5 p.m.; Sunday and holidays 10 a.m.–5 p.m.; closed Thanksgiving, Christmas, and New Year's Day

Admission: $6 adults, $5 seniors and teens, $4 children

Appeal by Age Groups:

Pre-school	Grade School	Teens	Young Adults	Over 30	Seniors
★★★	★★★	★★	★★	★★★	★★★

Touring Time: Average 1½ hours; minimum 45 minutes

Rainy-Day Touring: Yes

Services and Facilities:

Restaurants June to September	Lockers No
Alcoholic beverages No	Pet kennels No
Disabled access Yes	Rain check No
Wheelchair rental Yes, free	Private tours No
Baby stroller rental No	

Description and Comments   A graceful, elegant complex of red-tile buildings, this museum prides itself on programming that focuses on the local environment, so it makes for an enlightening stop for visitors unfamiliar with California's ecology. Native animal and bird species are shown (stuffed) in dioramas and with models, like the full-size (33-foot) one of a giant squid. Other highlights are the Chumash Indian Hall, a planetarium, and an observatory.

Santa Barbara Zoological Gardens

500 Ninos Drive (off Cabrillo Drive), Santa Barbara; (805) 962-6310 or (805) 962-5339

Hours: Daily 10 a.m.–5 p.m.; closed Thanksgiving and Christmas

Admission: $7 adults, $5 seniors and children ages 2–12, children under 2 admitted free

Appeal by Age Groups:

Pre-school	Grade School	Teens	Young Adults	Over 30	Seniors
★★★★★	★★★★	★★	★★	★★★	★★★

Touring Time: Average 3–4 hours; minimum 2 hours

Rainy-Day Touring: Yes, but you'll get wet

Services and Facilities:

Restaurants Yes	Lockers No
Alcoholic beverages No	Pet kennels No
Disabled access Yes	Rain check No
Wheelchair rental Yes, free	Private tours No
Baby stroller rental Yes, $2.50	

Description and Comments   Neatly hidden on the west end of town, between Cabrillo Beach and the bird refuge, this gem of a zoo fits a lot into a compact space. The skillful wending of paths and exhibits through the former private estate makes this a wonderful place for even the littlest kids, who might get overwhelmed at huge, crowded animal parks and theme parks. The elephants, giraffes, and lions are a big hit, as is the reptile house. My preschool nephew insisted on three rides on the miniature train; other extras include a playground, an excellent gift shop, and a lovely picnic area. A unique gorilla-viewing area is a replica of Dian Fossey's African field station and allows kids to walk into a room with desk, hammock, and everyday objects left as if the famous scientist were just outside.

Sea Center

211 Stearns Wharf (base of State Street), Santa Barbara; (805) 962-0885

Hours: Winter, Monday–Friday noon–5 p.m., Saturday–Sunday 10 a.m.–5 p.m.; touch tank hours, Monday–Friday noon–4 p.m., Saturday–Sunday noon–5 p.m.; summer (Memorial Day-Labor Day), daily 10 a.m.–5 p.m.; touch tank noon–5 p.m.; closed Thanksgiving and Christmas Day

Admission: $3 adults, $2 ages 13–17 and seniors 62+, $1.50 ages 2–12, free for children ages 2 and under

Appeal by Age Groups:

Pre-school	Grade School	Teens	Young Adults	Over 30	Seniors
★★★	★★★★	★★★	★★★	★★★★	★★★

Touring Time: Average 1 hour; minimum 30 minutes

Rainy-Day Touring: Not very comfortable

Services and Facilities:

Restaurants No	Baby stroller rental No
Alcoholic beverages No	Lockers No
Disabled access Only to touch	Pet kennels No
tank	Rain check Yes
Wheelchair rental No	Private tours No

Description and Comments This mini-museum makes a walk on the land-mark (1872) Stearns Wharf (parking $2 an hour, two hours free with valida-tion) have a mini-purpose, and even if you're just driving through Santa Barbara, you can stop, walk the pier, grab a snack, and pop into the Sea Cen-ter to peer into the aquariums and look at the exhibits of local marine life and model of a gray whale and her calf. The touch tank is a highlight if you're not visiting the larger aquariums (Monterey, Long Beach, Scripps) in the state.

SANTA BARBARA FINDS

Not quite attractions, but well worth knowing about.

One Thousand Steps Beach. An unbelievably long staircase to the beach from Mesa on Santa Cruz Boulevard below Shoreline Drive. There's a landing midway so you can stop to enjoy the view and catch your breath.

Santa Barbara Arts and Crafts Show. Held Sundays and holidays year-round at Chase Palm Park between Cabrillo Boulevard and the ocean, this permanent arts show attracts vendors of all kinds and is patronized by locals for gift shopping. The sales are direct and the prices often very rea-sonable. We've walked our bikes along the path here, stopped to purchase some pottery (wrapped in newspaper and tucked into the backpack), and admired the paintings of regional scenery.

Santa Barbara Trolley Tour. Five times a day (10 a.m., 11:30 a.m., 1 p.m., 2:30 p.m., 4 p.m.), the Santa Barbara trolley leaves from Stearns Wharf. The 90-minute tour ($11 adults, $7 children under 12) gives a pleasant overview of the town, pointing out landmarks such as the bird refuge, zoo, Moreton Bay Fig Tree, mission, and so forth. Call (805) 965-0353.

Family-Friendly Restaurants

BE BOP BURGERS

111 State Street, Santa Barbara; (805) 966-1956

Meals served: Lunch and dinner, breakfast Saturday–Sunday only
Cuisine: American
Entree range: $4–6.95 (lunch and dinner)
Children's menu: Yes
Reservations: No
Payment: D, MC, V

Kids adore this neo-1950s diner, with its shiny red vinyl booths, loud 1950s and 1960s rock, photo booth, and standard-issue burgers, shakes, and fries. They especially love posing on the surfboard set inside a wave backdrop; bring a camera for a fun photo. On the third Friday of the month, classic car collectors fill up the parking lot with their showpieces.

BROPHY BROS. CLAM BAR & RESTAURANT

119 Harbor Way, Santa Barbara; (805) 966-4418

Meals served: Lunch and dinner
Cuisine: American/Seafood
Entree range: $4–15 (lunch); $13–17 (dinner)
Children's menu: Yes
Reservations: No
Payment: AE, MC, V

For the best waterfront seafood in town, head to this informal, family-friendly harborfront restaurant, where the locals flock to get the tastiest clam chowder, calamari, cioppino, and oyster shooters this side of Monterey. Kids love the views of the seagulls and boats as much as parents. There are plenty of kid-pleasing choices. Come early to avoid a long wait.

THE BROWN PELICAN

Hendry's Beach, 2981-1/2 Cliff Drive at Arroyo Burro County Park, Santa Barbara; (805) 687-4550

Meals served: Breakfast, lunch, and dinner
Cuisine: American
Entree range: $10–20 (lunch and dinner)
Children's menu: Yes

Reservations: Accepted
Payment: AE, MC, V

A television fantasy of California beach life come true, this restaurant is on the sand in an isolated cove beach. Park the car, spend time on the beach, and come up to the restaurant for a meal, or just stop for lunch and revel in the sun and surf and families playing in the waves. You'll eat basic seaside burger and bistro fare: huevos rancheros, omelets, seafood, sandwiches, crab cakes, lots of appetizers for the wine-and-tidbit crowd, espresso drinks, and rich desserts.

CALIFORNIA PIZZA KITCHEN

71 Paseo Nuevo, State Street, Santa Barbara; (805) 962-4648

Meals served: Lunch and dinner
Cuisine: California
Entree range: $3.99–11 (lunch and dinner)
Children's menu: Yes
Reservations: Not accepted
Payment: All major credit cards

A chain, yes, but a great one for families, well located in the Paseo Nuevo center. The vegetarian soups, field-green and Caesar salads, designer pizzas, and California wines keep parents happy, and the simpler pizzas and pastas are perfect for younger kids.

COLD SPRING TAVERN

5995 Stagecoach Road, Santa Barbara; (805) 967-0066

Meals served: Lunch and dinner, breakfast Saturday–Sunday only
Cuisine: American
Entree range: $6.95–11.95 (lunch); $16–24 (dinner)
Children's menu: Yes
Reservations: Yes
Payment: AE, MC, V

Well worth the 20-minute drive up Highway 154 to the San Marcos Pass in the hills above Santa Barbara, this place has so much atmosphere you can practically cut it with a knife. A century-old stagecoach stop set in an oak grove, it looks like a restaurant Tom Sawyer would love, with stone fireplaces, hidden nooks and crannies, and battered wooden walls hung with things like barbed-wire displays and hunting trophies. Outside, a cook mans a huge oak-burning barbecue, grilling marinated tri-tips, while over in front of the separate bar (a Harley riders' hangout), musicians play Grateful Dead and Crosby, Stills, & Nash songs for tips. Add a creek with a small waterfall and a kids' menu offering ribs, pasta, and giant hot dogs, and you've got a very fun family outing, especially at lunchtime, when the kids can scamper around outside and the (harmless) bikers aren't yet drinking seriously. The only problem is the service, which can drag on busy days.

ENDLESS SUMMER BAR-CAFÉ

113 Harbor Way, Santa Barbara; (805) 564-6666

Meals served: Lunch and dinner
Cuisine: Seafood/American
Entree range: $7.95–19.95
Children's menu: Yes
Reservations: Accepted
Payment: All major credit cards

Upstairs from the fancier Waterfront Grill, on the north end of the harbor with a fabulous view of the boats, the coastline, and the city, this place is a find for families who want a good meal in a great setting—a great setting, that is, with a tolerance for four-year-olds who jump on the banquettes. Kids are welcomed with a smile, crayons, and a kids' menu, and parents are rewarded with delicious clam chowder, seafood salads, simple grilled fish, and other chic, beachy fare. Before and after your meal, the kids can run around the harbor paths, looking at the boats and chasing seagulls.

LA SUPER-RICA

622 N. Milpas Street, Santa Barbara; (805) 963-4940

Meals served: Lunch and dinner
Cuisine: Mexican
Entree range: $.75–6.25 (lunch and dinner)
Children's menu: No
Reservations: Not accepted
Payment: No credit cards

This order-at-the-counter roadside joint draws people from 100 miles away. This is great Mexican soul food: beans, *queso fundido, pozole,* homemade tortillas, tamales, and cold Coronas. You eat in a tarp-covered patio on rickety plastic furniture.

PADARO STREET GRILL

3765 Santa Claus Lane, Carpinteria; (805) 566-0566

Meals served: Breakfast, lunch, and dinner
Cuisine: American
Entree range: $5–8.50 (lunch and dinner)
Children's menu: Yes
Reservations: Not accepted
Payment: All major credit cards

When the weather is fine, there is no better family restaurant in the Santa Barbara area. Order at the counter inside the restaurant, then take your food (soups, good salads, fresh fish sandwiches, burgers) to one of the picnic tables on the huge grassy lawn overlooking the ocean. After the kids wolf down their food, they can run and play (there's even a playground) while parents have a few moments of ocean-view peace, perhaps accompanied by a glass of wine. Even the family dog is welcome. Padaro Street Grill is located in the little beach town of Carpinteria, a few miles south of Santa Barbara.

Side Trip: Ojai

A haven for painters, writers, and the sort of craft-y folks who make jewelry, Ojai is also a fine family getaway for a day or two. We passed a near-perfect weekend here, staying at the serene Ojai Valley Inn and riding the inn's bikes into the dinky town for ice cream, a browse at open-air Bart's Books, a romp at Libbey Park, and a fun shopping trip at the Sunday farmers' market. The town trolley is also a hoot for kids. Try to get in a short hike in the local hills to get a view over this gorgeous valley, once a Chumash paradise, later the set for the movie *Lost Horizon*. A trail map is available at the Ojai Chamber; see How to Get Information before You Go earlier in this chapter on page 227. This is an easy, 90-minute trip from L.A., or a 20-minute trip from Santa Barbara.

FAMILY LODGING

Ojai Valley Inn and Spa

This place just keeps getting better and better. Its latest improvement is a world-class spa center, where you can experience everything from a deep-tissue massage to a facial using ancient Chumash techniques. The resort sits in the middle of a lovely golf course at the base of the Topa Topa mountains, with an adjacent 800-acre ranch that you can explore via hiking and equestrian trails; tennis courts, a beautiful swimming pool, and a lap pool are also on site. That all sounds terribly adult, but in fact children are equally catered to. For ages 3–12, Camp Ojai is one of the best (and priciest—$55 half-day, $70 full day, $50 evening) hotel children's programs we've ever experienced—our kids rode ponies, played Ping-Pong, had their faces painted, decorated hats, played in the Chumash hut, and spent a long time petting and visiting with the collection of miniature animals over in the barn area. The free bike collection even includes training-wheel models, and dinners at the Oak Cafe were some of the most pleasant family meals we've ever enjoyed (see review below). We love the beamed, tiled rooms in the old adobe wing, but the modern, upscale-motel rooms are a good value.

Country Club Road, Ojai; (805) 646-5511 or (800) 422-6524; fax (805) 646-7969. Rates $210–290, more for junior suites and suites.

FAMILY-FRIENDLY RESTAURANT

OAK CAFE AND TERRACE AT THE OJAI VALLEY INN

Country Club Road, Ojai; (805) 646-5511

Meals served: Breakfast, lunch, and dinner
Cuisine: Californian
Entree range: $10–15 (breakfast); $11.95–16 (lunch);
  $12.95–29.95 (dinner)
Children's menu: Yes
Reservations: Accepted
Payment: All major credit cards

Parents craving a civilized grown-up meal will love this idyllic terrace restaurant overlooking the golf course. Not only is there a swell kids' menu (it even offers fruit!) and a fun little goodie bag for each child, but the outdoor setting means that kids who've wolfed down their chicken fingers can safely explore the grounds while you finish your salmon in peace. The upscale, hip-American cooking is expertly prepared.

Solvang

Solvang is the town that tourism made. Its perfect placement as a stopping point on the long trip between L.A. and San Francisco—combined with the bright idea some decades ago for local businesses to emphasize the region's Danish heritage—turned it into a famously popular disembarking point for massive tour buses full mostly of seniors. The downtown, with storefronts mimicking village architecture in Scandinavia, is quite like the shopping and eating part of theme parks (areas that are, perhaps, the most senior-friendly part of theme parks). Then word got around that the Danish doo-dad shops were being replaced (as a generation of family-owned businesses died out) by outlet stores, both within the city limits and at new malls on the outskirts. Southern California families looking for a Sunday-drive destination had found the little pot of gold at the end of the rainbow.

While there are a few genuine educational sites (the **Mission Santa Ines,** the **Hans Christian Andersen Museum**), the real charm of Solvang is in its unabashed visitor-friendly services. So we recommend it as an overnight base if you plan on exploring the area's authentic attractions—which are agricultural and rural in nature. It's a great place from which to take the **Lake Cachuma** nature cruise (see Family Outdoor Adventures, page 231), or a point to set out for bike-touring the gently rolling ranchlands and apple groves of the **Santa Ynez Valley.**

Ballard School

It's fun to drive or bike past this 1883 little red schoolhouse and tell your kids that it's still in use. It's found at Cottonwood and School Streets in the village of Ballard, a few miles north of Solvang.

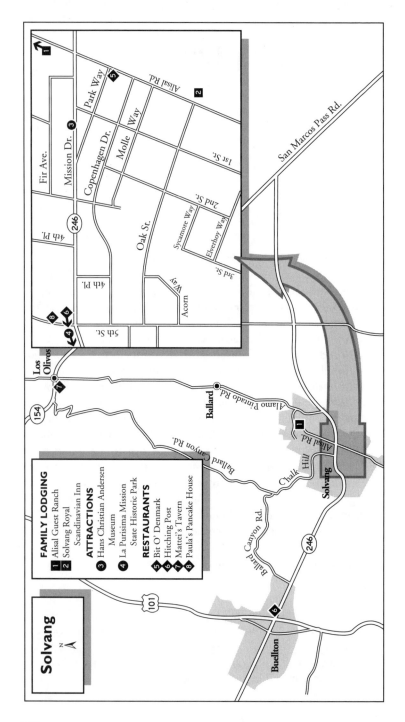

Solvang

N

FAMILY LODGING
1 Alisal Guest Ranch
2 Solvang Royal
   Scandinavian Inn

ATTRACTIONS
3 Hans Christian Andersen
   Museum
4 La Purisima Mission
   State Historic Park

RESTAURANTS
5 Bit O' Denmark
6 Hitching Post
7 Mattei's Tavern
8 Paula's Pancake House

Park Way
Alisal Rd.
Copenhagen Dr.
Molle Way
Fir Ave.
Mission Dr.
1st St.
Oak St.
2nd St.
Sycamore Way
Elverhoy Way
3rd St.
Acorn Way
4th Pl.
4th Pl.
5th St.
246
Los Olivos
154
Ballard
Alamo Pintado Rd.
Ballard Canyon Rd.
Chalk Hill
Alisal Rd.
Solvang
San Marcos Pass Rd.
Ballard Canyon Rd.
246
101
Buellton

It's especially nice for those families with several age groups. One parent can stay with little kids at the pool and not really be missing anything (it's hot, hot, hot here from late spring through fall), while older kids are let out on their own to wander the village and another parent goes to the art-gallery town of **Los Olivos** or, with grandmother, heads for the flower fields of **Lompoc.**

Family Lodging

Alisal Guest Ranch

A treasured annual retreat for many California families, Alisal is the sort of old-money, intentionally low-key family resort that you might expect to see in certain parts of New England. It's the kind of place where even though the setting is outdoorsy and active and rustic, with horseback riding, fishing, and canoeing, people are expected to dress for dinner, and children are to be on their best behavior. Golf is the central focus of the place, but that's by no means all. There are tennis courts, a swimming pool, and a private lake, but neither phones nor TVs in the 73 rooms, most of which are either two-room cottages or studios, decorated sensibly. Kids ages 6–12 are invited to join free activities, such as a pool bash, visits from professional storytellers, nature hikes, reptile nights, and a mini-rodeo; occasional teen nights are also offered. The whole family joins together for barbecues and bingo night. Although it is located just outside Solvang, about a half-hour from Santa Barbara, guests rarely leave the property.

1054 Alisal Road, Solvang; (800) 4-ALISAL or (805) 688-6411; fax (805) 688-2510. Rates $375–425 based on double occupancy, including breakfast and dinner. There is an extra charge of $70 per child ages 6–12 and $45 per child ages 3–5.

Solvang Royal Scandinavian Inn

We have vivid memories of sitting in the pool area here, looking out at the brown hills of the Santa Ynez Valley while the heat folded down on us like a sky full of blankets. Boy, were we happy to be in the pool area! In the early morning, we were just steps away from some great bakeries and fun shops, and in the evening after it cooled off, we strolled Solvang's streets as well. Rooms (there are 133 rooms and 7 suites) are a cut above many motor hotels, with country decor, VCRs, Disney Channel, and easy access to that very important pool area. Kids' menus in restaurant and room service; Ping-Pong table.

Solvang Royal Scandinavian Inn, 400 Alisal Road, Solvang; (800) 624-5572 or (805) 688-8000; fax (805) 688-0761. Rates start at $84–100 in the summer and $74–90 in the winter.

Attractions

Hans Christian Andersen Museum

1680 Mission Drive, Solvang; (805) 688-2052

Hours: Weekdays 9 a.m.–6 p.m.; Saturday and Sunday 9 a.m.–7 p.m.

Admission: Free

Appeal by Age Groups:

Pre-school	Grade School	Teens	Young Adults	Over 30	Seniors
★★	★★	★★	★★	★★	★★

Touring Time: Average 30 minutes; minimum 15 minutes

Rainy-Day Touring: Yes

Services and Facilities:

Restaurants No	Lockers No
Alcoholic beverages No	Pet kennels No
Disabled access No	Rain check No
Wheelchair rental No	Private tours No
Baby stroller rental No	

Description and Comments   A small gallery, this is actually the upstairs part of a building shared with a bookstore, The Book Loft. The feeling is like an exhibition space at a library. For fans of *The Princess and the Pea, The Little Mermaid, The Ugly Duckling,* or any other of the Danish author's classic tales, this museum offers some charming insight into the man behind the storyteller. There are little models of scenes from Andersen's life and stories, original letters by and photographs of the writer, whimsical artwork he created, and hundreds of first and early editions, as well as specially illustrated volumes of his works.

La Purisima Mission State Historic Park

2295 Purisima Road (off Highway 246), Lompoc; (805) 733-3713 or
   (805) 733-7781

Hours: Daily 9 a.m.–5 p.m.; closed Thanksgiving, Christmas, and New
   Year's Day

Admission: $5 per vehicle

Appeal by Age Groups:

Pre-school	Grade School	Teens	Young Adults	Over 30	Seniors
★★★	★★★★	★★★	★★★	★★★★	★★★★

Touring Time: Average 2 hours; minimum 1 hour, 3 hours with living
   history program

Rainy-Day Touring: Okay

Services and Facilities:

Restaurants No	Lockers No
Alcoholic beverages No	Pet kennels No; pets allowed on
Disabled access Yes	leash, even in buildings
Wheelchair rental No	Rain check No
Baby stroller rental No	Private tours Yes

Description and Comments   This tiny mission is marvelous to visit when the monthly living-history program is going on, so check ahead and see if your trip will coincide. Always held on either a Saturday or a Sunday from 11 a.m.–2 p.m., it features costumed docents going about their mission-era business, with visitors eavesdropping on them and observing as they do their tasks with period tools and techniques.

Family-Friendly Restaurants

BIT O' DENMARK

473 Alisal Road, Solvang; (805) 688-5426

Meals served: Breakfast, lunch, and dinner
Cuisine: American/Danish
Entree range: $4.95–6.50 (breakfast); $5.95–9.25 (lunch); $10.95–16.95 (dinner)
Children's menu: Yes; $5.95 complete
Reservations: Accepted
Payment: AE, D, MC, V

Many visitors feel obliged to try smorgasbord while in Solvang, and this pleasant restaurant offers a nice sampling of salads, smoked fish, and other Danish dishes, as well as American entrees. In spring and fall, the patio is a nice place to be, and there's a full bar.

HITCHING POST

Highway 246 (1 mile from 101 Fwy.), Buellton; (805) 688-0676

Meals served: Dinner
Cuisine: American/steakhouse
Entree range: $12.95–34.95 (dinner)
Children's menu: Yes; $5.95
Reservations: Necessary
Payment: AE, MC, V

A well-known steak and barbecue restaurant in a meat-eating part of the world, the Hitching Post is particularly nice in the early part of the evening while seniors are enjoying the early-bird specials and the kids are ravenous. The approach is straight out of the 1950s: Appetizers are a relish tray or shrimp cocktail, steak is cooked over an open oak fire, and the french fries are highly recommended.

MATTEI'S TAVERN

Railway Avenue at State Road 154, Los Olivos; (805) 688-4820

Meals served: Dinner nightly, lunch Saturday–Sunday
Cuisine: American
Entree range: $13–23 (dinner)
Children's menu: Yes
Reservations: Advised
Payment: MC, V

More than 100 years old, this rambling restaurant (once a stagecoach stop) has a massive stone fireplace and old photos and paintings in one room, and white wicker tablecloths under hanging plants in another. The food is Sunday-drive meets wine country, which is to say pot roast on one hand and penne pasta on the other.

PAULA'S PANCAKE HOUSE

1531 Mission Drive, Solvang; (805) 688-2867

Meals served: Breakfast and lunch
Cuisine: American/Danish
Entree range: $5.75–8.95 (breakfast and lunch)
Children's menu: No, but small/split portions available
Reservations: Not taken
Payment: All major credit cards

If the local pastry shops aren't enough fortification, head for this cheerful breakfast haven for buttermilk or thin Danish pancakes, sausages, omelets, and waffles.

San Luis Obispo

This small city is a model of workability. Its renovated downtown is lively with students from the nearby university as well as families and business-people. The mission plaza, also restored, features a running creek that's the centerpiece of the park. Although the suburbs hint at the growth that's come to the area, the city center itself is as tree-lined and friendly as ever.

There's a visitors center at 1039 Chorro Street and a trolley that runs for free along a downtown corridor of several blocks, but this is not a tourist-attraction town. It's a good base from which to visit **Hearst Castle** to the north and nearby beach towns: **Pismo, Morro Bay,** and the closest, **Avila,** just four miles from town. Take a stroll on Avila's pier, below which sea lions await scraps thrown over by fishermen, and allow time to pick seasonal fruit at the **Avila Valley Barn,** 560 Avila Beach Drive, (805) 595-2816. In the fall, the Barn is duded up with pumpkins, and a tractor-pulled hay ride and a hay maze are provided.

Mission Plaza
Found at Monterey and Chorro Streets in downtown San Luis Obispo, this former eyesore was redesigned and transformed in the 1960s into a city-center gathering place where workers eat their brown-bag lunches, children wade in the creek, and tourists head for the mission or the historic adobe.

Family Lodging

Embassy Suites Hotel

What works for business travelers works for sports teams and traveling families. We like the chance to stay up in the living room area of the suite while

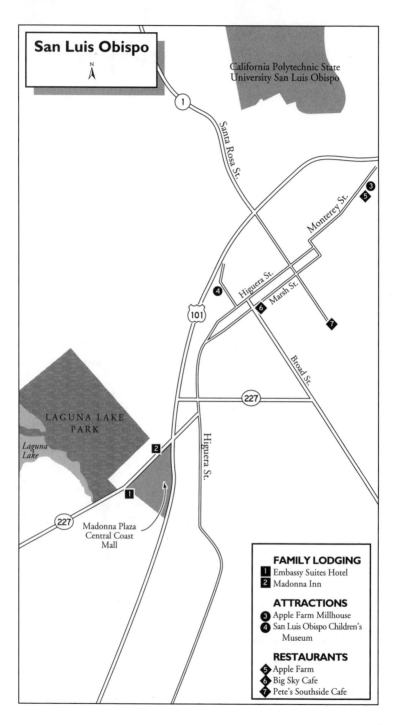

San Luis Obispo

N

California Polytechnic State
University San Luis Obispo

Santa Rosa St.

Monterey St.

Higuera St.

Marsh St.

101

Broad St.

227

LAGUNA LAKE
PARK

Laguna
Lake

Higuera St.

227

Madonna Plaza
Central Coast
Mall

FAMILY LODGING
1 Embassy Suites Hotel
2 Madonna Inn

ATTRACTIONS
3 Apple Farm Millhouse
4 San Luis Obispo Children's
Museum

RESTAURANTS
5 Apple Farm
6 Big Sky Cafe
7 Pete's Southside Cafe

the kids snooze in the bedroom, and a kitchen always makes it easier to pass on another restaurant meal if someone's too tired. This branch of the national chain has 196 suites and is connected to the Central Coast Mall, so teens can roam and younger kids can enjoy the swimming pools and spas, but downtown is too far away to walk. Breakfast included, kids' menu in restaurant and room service, Nintendo in rooms.

333 Madonna Road, San Luis Obispo; (805) 549-0800 or (800) 864-6000; fax (805) 543-5273. Rates begin at $124 winter, $134 summer.

Madonna Inn

Most people just stop here to have a bite in the restaurant and look in the elaborately overdecorated rest rooms, and to stop in the office and look at the pictures of the 109 rooms and 36 suites (no two alike) outrageously themed along the lines of Cave-Man Room (with a rock shower) and other fantasies. Ostriches, emus, and ranch animals roam the grounds. If you're willing to pay for an elaborate joke, you might like a stay here. There are kid's menus in the two restaurants.

100 Madonna Road, San Luis Obispo; (805) 543-3000 or (800) 543-9666; fax (805) 543-1800. Rates $127–230; children under age 12 stay free.

Attractions

Apple Farm Millhouse

2015 Monterey Street, San Luis Obispo; (805) 544-2040, ask for restaurant or inn

Hours: Daily 9 a.m.–6 p.m.

Admission: Free

Appeal by Age Groups:

Pre-school	Grade School	Teens	Young Adults	Over 30	Seniors
★★★	★★★	★★	★★	★★★	★★★

Touring Time: Average 30 minutes; minimum 30 minutes

Rainy-Day Touring: Better on a nice day; interior quite small

Services and Facilities:

Restaurants Next door		Lockers No	
Alcoholic beverages Yes		Pet kennels No	
Disabled access Yes		Rain check No	
Wheelchair rental No		Private tours No	
Baby stroller rental No			

Description and Comments Within the buildings of the Apple Farm Inn, behind the Apple Farm restaurant, is a replica of a nineteenth-century mill. It's a working mill, constructed with such attention to period detail (using salvaged parts from other mills) that local schoolchildren come here for field trips to see the 14-foot-high waterwheel turn the gears that turn the stones that grind the wheat or press the apples. Products made here are sold in the gift shop inside or the restaurant.

San Luis Obispo Children's Museum

1010 Nipomo, San Luis Obispo; (805) 544-5437

Hours: Daily 11 a.m.–5 p.m.; closed Wednesdays

Admission: $4.50; free for children ages 2 and under

Appeal by Age Groups:

Pre-school	Grade School	Teens	Young Adults	Over 30	Seniors
★★★★	★★★★	★	★	★	★

Touring Time: Average 3 hours; minimum 1 hour

Rainy-Day Touring: Yes

Services and Facilities:

Restaurants Nearby	Lockers No
Alcoholic beverages No	Pet kennels No
Disabled access Only to first floor	Rain check No
Wheelchair rental No	Private Tours No
Baby stroller rental No	

Description and Comments Standing exhibits at this first-rate museum include a variety of try-'em-out experiences: A Chumash cave, news desk, post office, fire station, space shuttle, restaurant, theater stocked with costumes, and Cessna 150 are among the environments kids can get into. During the school year, the museum is open only in the afternoons; in summer the hours are extended. A play area and picnic tables are outside.

Family-Friendly Restaurants

APPLE FARM

2015 Monterey Street, San Luis Obispo; (805) 544-6100

Meals served: Breakfast, lunch, and dinner daily
Cuisine: American
Entree range: $4–8 (breakfast); $5–9 (lunch); $7.25–17 (dinner)
Children's menu: Yes; $3.25–3.95
Reservations: Recommended

Payment: AE, MC, V, D

What was once a cute grandma-ish roadside cafe has become a phony theme restaurant, but the pancakes are still terrific, and kids are well catered to.

BIG SKY CAFE

1121 Broad Street, downtown San Luis Obispo; (805) 545-5401

Meals served: Breakfast, lunch, and dinner
Cuisine: Californian
Entree range: $3–8.50 (breakfast); $4.95–9.95 (lunch); $5–11.95 (dinner)
Children's menu: Yes
Reservations: Not accepted
Payment: AE, MC, V

A funky-chic cafe that's noisy, lively, colorful, and earnestly Californian, featuring local organic products. Great sandwiches, pastas, salads, Latin dishes, and homey desserts. There's even a children's menu.

PETE'S SOUTHSIDE CAFE

1815 Osos Street, San Luis Obispo; (805) 549-8133

Meals served: Lunch and dinner
Cuisine: Mexican/Caribbean
Entree range: $3–12 (lunch and dinner)
Children's menu: No, but some items as low as $2.25
Reservations: Not necessary
Payment: AE, D, MC, V

If your kids love Mexican food as much as ours, broaden their Latin-Caribbean culinary horizons with a stop here for reasonably priced Mexican staples like beef enchiladas or shrimp tacos, along with grilled fish Veracruz-style and Caribbean-style dinners with plantains on the side.

Farmers' Market

Held on Higuera Street Thursdays year-round 6:30–9 p.m., this is a popular and very worthwhile event. In addition to the usual farmers' market offerings of produce, flowers, and herbs, this festive gathering includes food booths of many kinds (don't miss the tri-tip) and street entertainment like puppet shows and jugglers.

Side Trip: Morro Bay

No one who drives this stretch of coast will forget the sight of **Morro Rock** looming 578 feet tall in this city's harbor, even if the sight lines are obstructed at some vantage points by the equally looming power plant next to the rock. The pleasures here are of a bustling harbor, a tranquil bird sanctuary, and some well-situated hotels and cafes that bring you close to the shore and its wildlife. You could also stay here and combine a visit to Hearst Castle with nature-loving time.

FAMILY LODGING

Gray's Inn

This tiny inn is located right on the waterfront in a building that also houses an art gallery. It has only three rooms, but they each have living rooms and kitchens, so this is a good value for small families who like a lively setting. No restaurant.

561 Embarcadero, Morro Bay; (805) 772-3911. Rates start at $90–130 in winter and $140–165 in summer.

The Inn at Morro Bay

Situated in Morro Bay State Park in a spot that's notable for birds, the inn has rooms furnished with brass beds and fireplaces, and two-thirds of them have ocean views. Sea otters live in the waters in front. It's a peaceful, quiet spot away from town center, with very good views. There are five "family-size" rooms, children's menus, a heated pool, and free mountain bikes, and kayak rentals are available.

60 State Park Road, Morro Bay State Park; (805) 772-5651 or (800) 321-9566; fax (805) 772-4779. Rates start at $139 in winter and $209 in summer; smaller queen rooms available at $79 in winter and $129 in summer.

The Embarcadero

This waterfront area has restaurants, fish markets, art galleries, and such, and its small-craft harbor is the embarkation point for boat cruises and fishing charters. A giant chessboard in a park along the way has hand-carved two- and three-foot-tall game pieces. The aquarium and commercial fishing docks are located here, too.

ATTRACTIONS

Morro Bay Aquarium

595 Embarcadero Street (on the waterfront), Morro Bay; (805) 772-7647

Hours: Daily 9:30 a.m.–5:30 p.m. (but may be open as late as 6 p.m.)

Admission: $2, $1 ages 5–11, free for children ages 4 and under

Appeal by Age Groups:

Pre-school	Grade School	Teens	Young Adults	Over 30	Seniors
★★★	★★	★★	★★	★★	★★

Touring Time: Average 30 minutes; minimum 10 minutes just to see the seals

Rainy-Day Touring: Bring umbrellas for outside sites

Services and Facilities:

Restaurants No	Lockers No
Alcoholic beverages No	Pet kennels No
Disabled access Yes	Rain check No
Wheelchair rental No	Private tours No
Baby stroller rental No	

Description and Comments Although this small facility doesn't hold a candle to the high-tech, super-designed glamour of the big-time aquariums, it's not crowded either, and small children won't be overwhelmed by mobs and noise. Kids can feed seals and sea lions and check on marine mammals being cared for in a rescue center, as well as look at eels, small sharks, and the like in 14 small tanks.

Morro Bay Natural History Museum

Morro Bay State Park Road, Morro Bay State Park; (805) 772-2694

Hours: Daily 10 a.m.–5 p.m.; closed Thanksgiving, Christmas, and New Year's Day

Admission: $3 adult, $1 children ages 6–12

Appeal by Age Groups:

Pre-school	Grade School	Teens	Young Adults	Over 30	Seniors
★★	★★★	★★★	★★★	★★★	★★★

Touring Time: Average 1 hour; minimum 30 minutes

Rainy-Day Touring: No problem

Services and Facilities:

Restaurants No	Lockers No
Alcoholic beverages No	Pet kennels No
Disabled access Yes	Rain check No
Wheelchair rental No	Private tours No
Baby stroller rental No	

Description and Comments   Overlooking the bay from a high, rocky bluff, the museum also overlooks a large heron rookery and has several trailheads to viewing areas. Exhibits and dioramas focus on the flora and fauna (including marine life) of the area, as well as on geology and Native American history. Check for times of nature walks and special presentations.

Family-Friendly Restaurants

BAYSIDE CAFE

10 State Park Road, Morro Bay State Park; (805) 772-1465

Meals served: Lunch daily; dinner Thursday–Sunday
Cuisine: Cal-Mexican/seafood
Entree range: $5–10 (lunch); $10–15 (dinner)
Children's menu: Yes
Reservations: Not taken
Payment: No credit cards

Located in the state park's marina area, this terrific find looks out over the waters of the back bay. It's less expensive than the waterfront restaurants, but the clam chowder and other seafood dishes are just as fresh, and the generous lunches—things like a black-bean and fish burrito or seafood taco salad—satisfy hearty appetites.

DORN'S ORIGINAL BREAKERS CAFE

801 Market Street, Morro Bay; (805) 772-4415

Meals served: Breakfast, lunch, and dinner
Cuisine: American
Entree range: $7.50–24.50 (dinner)
Children's menu: Yes
Reservations: Recommended
Payment: MC, V

This is a great place for breakfast, with a view of the Rock and specialties like seafood omelets and blueberry pancakes. Lunch and dinner dishes include seafood and meats. Located in the same white-clapboard, Cape Cod–style building since 1942, Dorn's is in great shape, with a new deck and a well-maintained decor of ship models, pictures of fishermen, and such. Parents of hungry kids take note: They begin serving dinner at 4 p.m.

MARGIE'S DINER

1698 N. Main, Morro Bay; (805) 772-2510

Meals served: Breakfast, lunch, and dinner
Cuisine: American
Entree range: $4.50–6.95 (breakfast and lunch); $7.95–12.95 (dinner)
Children's menu: No
Reservations: Not accepted
Payment: No credits cards, but personal checks okay

A proper diner, not a trendy imitation, serving chicken-fried steak, big omelets, hamburgers, shakes, and homemade pie. There's no kids' menu, but the portions are large, and they'll split plates at no extra charge.

Side Trip: Pismo Beach

This is no sissy beach—it's legal to drive on the sand here, and it's one of the few beaches in California where folks can dig up their dinner. The town itself is a time warp, with shell shops like grandma used to shop in, and lots of chowder shacks and postwar beach-town motels. Don't miss the beach, which is discussed in Best Beaches and Parks, page 230.

FAMILY LODGING

The Sandcastle Inn

Boasting an enviable beachfront location, this recently renovated place is one of the more upscale in town, with fine ocean views and a beachfront spa (but no pool). Among the 60 rooms in three stories are several family-size junior suites, one with a kitchenette. There's no restaurant, but a continental breakfast is included in the room rate.

100 Stimson Avenue, Pismo Beach; (805) 773-2422 or (800) 822-6606; fax (805) 773-0771. Rates start at $89–139 in winter, $129–239 in summer.

FAMILY-FRIENDLY RESTAURANT

GIUSEPPE'S

891 Price Street, Pismo Beach; (805) 773-2870

Meals served: Lunch and dinner
Cuisine: Italian
Entree range: $5.95–9.95 (lunch); $9.95–19.95 (dinner)
Children's menu: No
Reservations: Not accepted
Payment: AE, D, MC, V

Surely the best place in town, with or without kids, this homey, noisy, informal Italian eatery is a terrific family restaurant. Try the spaghetti and meatballs.

Side Trip: San Simeon and Cambria

The first few times we came to San Simeon, we didn't even know the place had a name. We thought of San Simeon as simply the area of motels and coffee shops near **Hearst Castle.** And that's what it is. But it is a convenient place to stay, and our kids had a great time splashing with other traveling families in a sheltered pool after a long drive. Your best bet is to arrive in the late afternoon the day before your early morning Hearst Castle tour. Swim, eat, sleep, and hit the castle the next day.

Meanwhile, Cambria is just too cute for most active families, unless you have some country-cozy-loving shop browsers. A veritable capital of bed and breakfasts, Cambria is located on the curve as the highway heads to the sea, between San Luis Obispo and San Simeon.

FAMILY LODGING

Best Western Cavalier

A utilitarian motel with 90 large rooms, many of which have stunning views of the ocean from the bluff above. Some rooms have terraces, some have fireplaces, and all have VCRs. Extras include firepits on the bluff, two swimming pools, spa, gym, children's menus in restaurant and room service, and binoculars for whale-watching.

9415 Hearst Drive, San Simeon; (805) 927-4688 or (800) 826-8168; fax (805) 927-6453. Rates $99–189.

Best Western Courtesy Inn

We don't remember much about the motel-standard rooms of this hotel, but every parking space was filled with a car that was loaded with luggage and ice chests. Kids ran up and down the outside corridors, heading for the ice machines or the indoor pool, which, in spite of its echo-ey oddness, was appreciated as the afternoon quickly cooled. Of the 115 units, 25 are efficiencies. Laundry facilities are on site, and there's a restaurant adjacent.

9450 Castillo Drive, San Simeon; (805) 927-4691 or (800) 555-5773; fax (805) 927-1473. Summer rates begin at $99; winter rates begin at $69.

San Simeon Pines

This is a hint of Big Sur before you get to Big Sur. Maybe it's the dark-shingled buildings, or the twisted cypress and pines, or the rocky beach below the motel where we spotted seals. But you know you're not in Southern California anymore, Toto. Put on a sweater, play a little shuffleboard or croquet, and enjoy the eight-acre grounds of this 125-room, 60-suite motel. There's a restaurant with kids' menu, a pool, and a playground, and breakfast is included in your stay. A much more satisfying scene than the other establishments on Moonstone Beach Drive, close to the village shops of Cambria and not far from Hearst Castle.

7200 Moonstone Beach Drive, Cambria; (805) 927-4648. Rates $76–106.

ATTRACTION
Hearst Castle/San Simeon State Historical Monument

Off Highway 1, San Simeon; (800) 444-4445

Hours: Daily 8:20 a.m.–3:20 p.m.; tours leave every 20 or 40 minutes and last for 1 hour and 45 minutes; closed Thanksgiving, Christmas, and New Year's

Admission: $14 adults, $8 children ages 6–12, free ages 5 and under

Appeal by Age Groups:

Pre-school	Grade School	Teens	Young Adults	Over 30	Seniors
★	★	★★	★★	★★★★	★★★★

Touring Time: Average 1 hour 45 minutes; minimum the same

Rainy-Day Touring: Yes

Services and Facilities:

Restaurants Concession stand

Alcoholic beverages No

Disabled access Yes

Wheelchair rental Free; call for special tours

Lockers Yes

Pet kennels No

Baby stroller rental No; not allowed on tour

Rain check No

Private tours Call (888) 438-4445

Description and Comments Face it, this isn't a great stop for young children. They just don't get it. And why should they? It's hard enough for adults to grasp the beautiful weirdness of a place that is largely made up of pieces and parts of European churches and palaces that are older than the state they are visiting (having been disassembled, shipped across the seas, and reassembled here as dining room walls and corridor embellishments). But school-age kids and teens will make it through one of the shorter tours. (We recommend the #1 introductory tour, which includes the cool swimming pools.) Everyone enjoys the bus ride up the hill, especially if some of the zoo animals that roam the grounds are out in view.

Side Trip: Big Sur

Getting there, especially from the south, can be hell with a car-sickness-prone kid, but if you have to keep pulling over, at least you'll have the awesome view as a reward. Once you get to Big Sur, you'll find a town in which the clocks seemed to have stopped back in 1971—the hippie lives here, and lives well. Oh, sure, things have gotten fancy with the recent opening of the big-bucks **Post Ranch Inn,** but you'll still see rusted-out VW vans and tie-dye. The only thing for families to do in Big Sur is soak in the natural beauty, preferably among the redwoods in **Pfeiffer State Park,** where you can easily pass a few happy days camping or staying in the lodge.

FAMILY LODGING

Deetjen's Big Sur Inn

Rich with funky, ex-hippie, Big Sur charm, Deetjen's is a ragtag collection of cottages tucked among the redwoods in a setting of great beauty. Walls may be thin, beds a little creaky, and housekeeping on the simple side, but you won't find a motel more atmospheric than this one. The restaurant serves a killer breakfast (get the pancakes), but you'll need reservations.

Highway 1 at south end of town, Big Sur; (831) 667-2377; fax (831) 667-0408. Rates range from $75 to 180.

Pfeiffer Big Sur State Park Campground/Big Sur Lodge

A beloved family campground, this park has 218 campsites nestled among the redwoods just inland from the breathtaking Big Sur coast. Each site has tables, stoves, and food lockers; some are next to Big Sur River and some are in the redwoods, while others rest in oak groves or meadows. There are no hookups, but there are showers, laundry facilities, a store, and a cafe. A more luxurious choice (in relative terms) is the park's Big Sur Lodge, where you can rent a simple motel-style cottage in the redwoods, perhaps even with a fireplace for $139 to $199 (call (831) 667-2171 for reservations—well in advance). See also the park description in Best Beaches and Parks on page 230 in this chapter.

Off Highway 1, Big Sur; (831) 667-2315; reservations through Reserve America, (800) 444-7275. Campsites $16–17.

FAMILY-FRIENDLY RESTAURANT

NEPENTHE/CAFE KEVAH

Highway 1 (south end of town), Big Sur; (831) 667-2345

Meals served: Breakfast, lunch, and dinner
Cuisine: American
Entree range: $5–15 (breakfast and lunch); $11.95–23.75 (dinner)
Children's menu: No
Reservations: Not necessary
Payment: AE, MC, V

Surely the best-view restaurant on the California coast, Nepenthe and its outdoor-cafe sibling, Cafe Kevah, can be forgiven if the food isn't memorable. We've had a decent burger and some mighty good fries, however, which tasted even better on the terrace, with the famed Big Sur coastline tumbling down below. Teenagers will like the downstairs gift shop, featuring local crafts. A fine refueling stop after the long drive from the south.

Monterey

Monterey is a beautiful city, and since its remarkable aquarium has become a top tourist attraction, it's on most must-see lists for travelers to California. And how wonderful that is, because Monterey is as much a part of how Californians feel about themselves, thanks to the novels of John Steinbeck and the recordings of the Monterey Jazz Festival, as the waterfalls of Yosemite or the star-studded sidewalks of Hollywood.

California's regions can each be symbolized by a tree that dominates the landscape. In the south, it's the palm tree; in the north, the redwood; and in the north central coast, here on the Monterey Peninsula, it's the cypress tree. The Monterey Cypress survives only on **Point Lobos,** where the dramatic trees, twisted into starkly artistic shapes by the wind, are preserved in a state reserve, but there are other varieties of cypress planted throughout the city, giving it a special dark-green canopy. Another striking characteristic of Monterey is its preserved nineteenth-century historic district, a rarity in California, but not an attraction we recommend spending much time in with young children. Instead, look to the gem in the crown of the revitalized waterfront: the **Monterey Bay Aquarium,** largest in the country.

Once a center of the commercial fishing industry, Monterey has put its resources into maintaining the city's historic buildings and beautiful setting and into creating high-quality attractions such as golf courses, the converted **Cannery area,** and the Monterey Aquarium. In many ways, it's the ideal spot for a sophisticated, luxurious adult vacation, but families will find themselves well entertained, too.

EASY MONTEREY OUTINGS

Cannery Row. Of the several self-contained mini-malls now housed in the former sardine canneries made famous by novelist John Steinbeck, we recommend Edgewater Packing Company at 640 Wave Street, (831) 649-

1899. It's more amusement park than mall, and its vintage 1905 merry-go-round will be more appealing to kids after an aquarium visit than the antiques shops, and more fun for you than the souvenir emporiums. Also look for Friends of the Sea Otter (381 Cannery Row, across from Monterey Plaza, (831) 642-9037), a store with books, gifts, and educational materials; all proceeds benefit the otters.

Fisherman's Wharf. Even kids who think seafood is yucky (seafood restaurants being the main attraction at Fisherman's Wharf) will get a kick out of the sea lions who frequent the pier area. Charter fishing boats and sight-seeing boats tie up here.

Monterey Peninsula Recreation Trail. This 18-mile trail connects parks and paths between Asilomar State Beach in Pacific Grove and the city of Castroville. It is a multi-use trail for walkers, bikers, and surrey pedalers and goes along the shore past Point Pinos Lighthouse, the Monterey Bay Aquarium, Cannery Row, the Custom House Plaza, and De Monte Beach. The trail is equipped with drinking fountains, bike racks, and benches at various points.

Old Monterey Marketplace. Tuesday afternoons year-round, this farmers' market is a great way for families to enjoy Old Monterey (as opposed to, say, a docent walking tour of the historic buildings). There are produce stalls, flowers, and arts and crafts as well as food and entertainment.

Family Lodging

Casa Munras Garden Hotel

A nice change from cookie-cutter motels, this hotel near Fisherman's Wharf fills an 1824 building on acres of landscaped grounds. The 166 rooms have some special touches, like brass beds, and there are a few family-size junior suites. Outside is a heated pool with a large shallow end for kids. A shuttle bus runs to local attractions, and you can buy aquarium tickets here.

700 Munras Avenue, Monterey; (831) 375-2411 or (800) 222-2558, (800) 222-2446 in CA; fax (408) 375-1365. Rates start at $129 in the summer and $89–99 in the winter.

Hilton Monterey

The Hilton is located a bit out of the Cannery Row fray on the south end of Monterey, convenient to Carmel. The 204 newly spiffed-up rooms include several suites and some larger executive rooms that can handle a family well. On-site fun includes a heated pool, putting green, Ping-Pong, shuffleboard, and in-room Nintendo. Kids' menus in restaurant and room service.

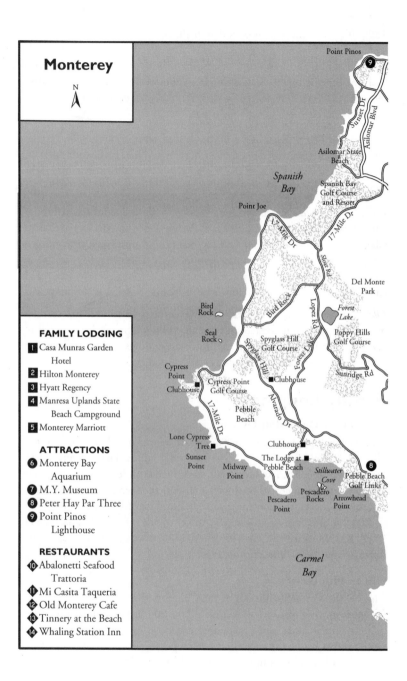

Monterey

N

FAMILY LODGING
1. Casa Munras Garden Hotel
2. Hilton Monterey
3. Hyatt Regency
4. Manresa Uplands State Beach Campground
5. Monterey Marriott

ATTRACTIONS
6. Monterey Bay Aquarium
7. M.Y. Museum
8. Peter Hay Par Three
9. Point Pinos Lighthouse

RESTAURANTS
10. Abalonetti Seafood Trattoria
11. Mi Casita Taqueria
12. Old Monterey Cafe
13. Tinnery at the Beach
14. Whaling Station Inn

Point Pinos

Sunset Dr

Asilomar Blvd

Asilomar State Beach

Spanish Bay

Spanish Bay Golf Course and Resort

Point Joe

17-Mile Dr

17-Mile Dr

Sloat Rd

Del Monte Park

Forest Lake

Bird Rock

Bird Rock

Lopez Rd

Poppy Hills Golf Course

Seal Rock

Spyglass Hill Golf Course

Forest Lake

Sunridge Rd

Cypress Point

Cypress Point Golf Course

Clubhouse

Spyglass Hill

Clubhouse

Alvarado Dr

Pebble Beach

17-Mile Dr

Lone Cypress Tree

Clubhouse

Sunset Point

Midway Point

The Lodge at Pebble Beach

Stillwater Cove

Pebble Beach Golf Links

Pescadero Point

Pescadero Rocks

Arrowhead Point

Carmel Bay

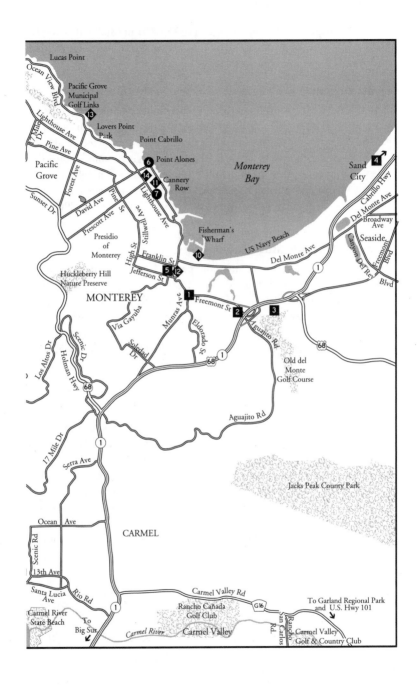

Lucas Point

Ocean View Blvd

Pacific Grove
Municipal
Golf Links

13

Lovers Point
Park

Point Cabrillo

Lighthouse Ave

Mile Dr

Pine Ave

Pacific
Grove

Forest Ave

Sunset Dr

David Ave

Pine St

Prescott Ave

Presidio
of
Monterey

6 Point Alones

14

11

7

Cannery
Row

Stillwell Ave

Lighthouse Ave

High St

Franklin St

Monterey
Bay

Sand
City

4

Cabrillo Hwy

Del Monte Ave

Broadway
Ave

Seaside

Canyon Del Rey

Blvd

Freemont Blvd

Fisherman's
Wharf

10

US Navy Beach

Del Monte Ave

1

Huckleberry Hill
Nature Preserve

Jefferson St

5 **12**

MONTEREY

Via Gayuba

Munras Ave

1 Freemont St

2

3

Aguajito Rd

68

Los Altos Dr

Scenic Dr

Holman Hwy

68

Soledad Dr

Eldorado St

68

1

Old del
Monte
Golf Course

17 Mile Dr

Serra Ave

1

Aguajito Rd

Jacks Peak County Park

Ocean Ave

CARMEL

Scenic Rd

13th Ave

Santa Lucia
Ave

Rio Rd

Carmel River
State Beach

To
Big Sur

1

Carmel River

Carmel Valley Rd

Rancho Canada
Golf Club

Carmel Valley

G16

San Carlos Rd

Rancho

To Garland Regional Park
and U.S. Hwy 101

Carmel Valley
Golf & Country Club

1000 Aguajito Road, Monterey; (831) 373-6141 or (800) HILTONS; fax (831) 655-6808. Rates start at $169 in summer, $105 in winter; children under age 18 stay free with parents.

Hyatt Regency

If you're looking for a Monterey hotel with a children's program, this is the place to be. The free Camp Hyatt program attracts 3–15-year-olds with garden-variety kids'-program amenities, mostly arts, crafts, games, and video watching. Around the large property (there are 575 guest rooms), you'll find two pools, spas, a game room, a volleyball court, tennis, a golf course, a sports bar, and a bike-rental concession. Children's menus offered.

1 Old Golf Course Road, Monterey; (831) 372-1234 or (800) 233-1234; fax (831) 375-3960. Rates start at $245.

Manresa Uplands State Beach Campground

Beach campgrounds don't get any more peaceful and lovely than this small tent-camping retreat, which forbids RVs. The location is gorgeous, on a bluff overlooking Monterey Bay, shaded by Monterey pines and eucalyptus; a trail leads down to the long sand beach. It's no wonder that every site is taken in summer, so reserve early. Fire rings, picnic tables, showers, flush toilets.

205 Manresa Beach Road (off San Andreas Road), La Selva Beach; (831) 761-1795. Campsites $16–18; reservations through Reserve America, (800) 444-7275.

Monterey Marriott

This ten-story modern hotel doesn't have much in the way of charm, but it does have views to spare, along with a relaxed family-friendly atmosphere and good family amenities. Outside, for instance, is a pool and Jacuzzi area that's protected from the chill winds. Rooms are large, with refrigerators, tables and chairs, and sometimes couches; kids get Nintendo and the Disney Channel. A children's menu is available in both the restaurant and room service, and the concierge can get you a qualified baby-sitter.

350 Calle Principal, Monterey; (831) 649-4234 or (800) 228-9290; fax (831) 372-2968. Rates start at $159.

Attractions

Monterey Bay Aquarium

886 Cannery Row, Monterey; (831) 648-4888; advance tickets (800) 756-3737; www.montereybayaquarium.org

Hours: June–August, daily 9:30 a.m.–6 p.m.; the rest of the year, 10 a.m.–6 p.m.; closed Christmas Day

Admission: $14.95 adults, $11.95 students ages 13–17 and seniors 65+, $6.95 ages 3–12 and the disabled

Appeal by Age Groups:

Pre-school	Grade School	Teens	Young Adults	Over 30	Seniors
★★★★	★★★★★	★★★★★	★★★★	★★★★★	★★★★★

Touring Time: Average 4 hours; minimum 2 hours

Rainy-Day Touring: Yes

Services and Facilities:

Restaurants Yes	Lockers Yes
Alcoholic beverages Yes	Pet kennels No
Disabled access Yes	Rain check No
Wheelchair rental Yes, free	Private tours Starts at $75 a
Baby stroller rental No	guide

Description and Comments   Don't despair. If you forget to call way, way ahead for advance tickets to the aquarium for the day of your visit, you can avoid waiting in line for too long. Ask at your hotel—many sell tickets good for the next day or two.

Is it really that crowded? Yes. Is it really worth it? Yes, especially since the recently opened Outer Bay exhibit, a million-gallon tank holding sharks, sea turtles, barracuda, and tuna, joined the spectacular three-story "kelp forest" tank, which holds hundreds of species itself. Each exhibit gives you a feeling for what you would see if you were underwater yourself, and because the tanks tower from floor to ceiling, you have the sensation of actually being on the ocean floor looking up.

But to really enjoy the aquarium, a few things should be considered. The youngest children won't find cartoon-cute animals that jump and play with balls like at Sea World, and you may discover that the beautiful, impressive tanks of jellyfish and other animals don't hold preschoolers' attention for long (although some will put nose to the glass and not move for hours). Let the little ones hang out and watch the antics of the sea otters, those charismatic mammals that swim on their backs and seem to grin at spectators. Then take them to the new Splash Zone, an experiential, interactive museum-within-a-museum designed for children from toddlers to about age nine. Young ones can climb and crawl through shore habitats, sit in a giant clam chair, handle sea critters in a touch pool, and go "inside" a penguin community. While three- to nine-year-olds stage underwater plays in the costume/puppet area, babies and toddlers can play in Coral Cove, a place just for tiny ones.

School-age kids will want to spend a lot of time at the bat-ray pool, another pet-the-fish area. There are almost 100 exhibits, including an aviary and a video feed from a submarine down in Monterey Bay. Feeding times are posted and make for a good show. There's a restaurant and a gift shop/bookstore.

M. Y. Museum

601 Wave Street, Monterey; (831) 649-6444

Hours: Monday–Sunday 10 a.m.–5 p.m., closed Wednesdays

Admission: $5, free for children ages 2 and under; Tuesday special $2 admission for all

Appeal by Age Groups:

Pre-school	Grade School	Teens	Young Adults	Over 30	Seniors
★★★★	★★★★	★	★	★	★

Touring Time: Average 2 hours; minimum 1 hour

Rainy-Day Touring: Yes

Services and Facilities:

Restaurants Yes	Lockers Yes
Alcoholic beverages Yes	Pet kennels No
Disabled access Yes	Rain check No
Wheelchair rental Yes	Private tours Photo Caravan,
Baby stroller rental Yes	ages 8+, $65–89

Description and Comments   A new interactive children's museum, this place provides hands-on, action-oriented entertainment, including life-size models that let kids fish from a boat, "buy" food and supplies, be a cook or a customer in a restaurant, and make a puppet show, among other activities. Our kids' favorites are the Magnetic Center, where they make structures out of magnetic pieces, and Build-a-House, where they don hard hats and build brick walls, fix plumbing, and hang wallpaper.

Peter Hay Par Three

17 Mile Drive, Pebble Beach; (831) 624-3811

Hours: Daily 6:30 a.m.–dark; call to make sure there are no golf clinics

Admission: $15 for as many rounds as you like

Appeal by Age Groups:

Pre-school	Grade School	Teens	Young Adults	Over 30	Seniors
★	★★★	★★★	★★★	★★	★★★

Touring Time: Average 1 hour; minimum 45 minutes

Rainy-Day Touring: No

Services and Facilities:

Restaurants Yes	Lockers No, storage available
Alcoholic beverages Yes	Pet kennels No
Disabled access Yes	Rain check No
Wheelchair rental No	Private tours Lessons
Baby stroller rental No	

Description and Comments For the budding Tiger Woodses in your family, make a stop at the Peter Hay Par Three public golf course in Pebble Beach. It's a pitch and putt that's part of the complex of famous courses that include the Pebble Beach Golf Links and the Links at Spanish Bay. No reservations needed for tee-times, but call ahead in case a golf clinic is scheduled. Nine holes; the longest is 18 yards.

Point Pinos Lighthouse

Lighthouse Avenue at Asilomar Boulevard; (831) 648-3116

Hours: Thursday–Sunday 1–4 p.m.

Admission: Free

Appeal by Age Groups:

Pre-school	Grade School	Teens	Young Adults	Over 30	Seniors
★	★★★	★★★	★★★	★★★	★★★

Touring Time: Average 45 minutes; minimum 20 minutes

Rainy-Day Touring: Not pleasant

Services and Facilities:

Restaurants No	Lockers No
Alcoholic beverages No	Pet kennels No
Disabled access No	Rain check No
Wheelchair rental No	Private tours No
Baby stroller rental No	

Description and Comments The oldest lighthouse still in operation on the West Coast, Point Pinos dates from 1855. This is a quick stop—the kids can run up the stairs to the top of the lighthouse, and there's a little museum room downstairs.

Family-Friendly Restaurants

ABALONETTI SEAFOOD TRATTORIA

57 Fisherman's Wharf, Monterey; (831) 373-1851

Meals served: Lunch and dinner
Cuisine: American/seafood
Entree range: $9–14 (lunch); $15–22 (dinner)
Children's menu: Yes
Reservations: Advised
Payment: All major credit cards

It may look like a tourist trap, but this wharf restaurant turned out to be one trap we were glad to get caught in. Famed for its calamari (squid), prepared every way imaginable, it's also a good straightforward Italian trattoria with wood-fired pizzas and decent pastas. Kids get a menu to color and choices that include pizza, pasta, or fish and chips, or they can get half portions off the regular menu. We passed a happy early evening here, eating irresistible fried calamari and sipping Chianti (or sodas) while we watched the sea lions put on a show right outside the window.

MI CASITA TAQUERIA

638 Wave Street, Monterey; (831) 655-4419

Meals served: Lunch and dinner
Cuisine: Mexican
Entree range: $4.95–7.50 (lunch and dinner)
Children's menu: Yes
Reservations: Not accepted
Payment: Cash only

This good taqueria is ideally located across the street from the M.Y. Children's Museum and two blocks from the aquarium. Order your quesadillas, soft tacos, burritos, and chips at the counter, then snag a table outside when the weather's good.

OLD MONTEREY CAFE

489 Alvarado Street, Monterey; (831) 646-1021

Meals served: Breakfast and lunch
Cuisine: American
Entree range: $3–9 (breakfast and lunch)
Children's menu: Yes, and will serve a half portion

Reservations: Not taken
Payment: MC, V, D

A good downtown choice, near Dennis the Menace Park, this popular cafe is known for its cappuccino, hefty four-egg omelets, homemade muffins, and from-scratch hash browns; breakfast is served through the lunch hour as well, but not to the exclusion of traditional lunch dishes, which include homemade soups and half-pound burgers. Children are welcomed and much in evidence.

TINNERY AT THE BEACH

631 Ocean View Boulevard, Pacific Grove; (831) 646-1040

Meals served: Breakfast, lunch, and dinner
Cuisine: American
Entree range: $4–7 (breakfast); $5–13 (lunch); $7.95–21.95 (dinner)
Children's menu: Yes
Reservations: Accepted for 6 or more
Payment: All major credit cards

After breakfast or lunch at this deservedly popular locals' spot at Lovers Point, you can walk down to a terrific little beach that's good for young children; at dinnertime, the adults can enjoy well-prepared fresh seafood (and a spectacular bay view), while the kids get their own menu.

WHALING STATION INN

763 Wave Street, Monterey; (408) 373-3778

Meals served: Dinner
Cuisine: Seafood/American
Entree range: $17.95–69.95 (dinner)
Children's menu: Yes
Reservations: Advised
Payment: All major credit cards

Located just above Cannery Row, this is a famed and elegant place, to be sure, yet the Whaling Station is exceptionally welcoming to children. When you see the rough wood beams, crisp white linens, and flickering candlelight, you'll be tempted to flee and take your five-year-old to McDonald's — but before you know it, your child will be warmly greeted and presented with a children's menu; very little ones are given goldfish crackers to keep hunger at bay. The mesquite-grilled steaks, chops, and fresh fish are excellent, and they come with a justly acclaimed artichoke appetizer.

Santa Cruz

This beautifully situated town is known for the university on a hill in the redwoods, as well as (nowadays) for its many recently arrived, well-heeled residents who supported the downtown businesses that were rebuilt after earthquake damage—so now the little town center is more picturesque (and pricey) than ever before.

Vacationing families will gravitate toward neither of these town centers, however, but instead will make for the waterfront, where the pier, boardwalk, beach, and train station come together to form a bright and cheerful summertime amusement area. Lots of motels and cafes compete for the visitor's attention, but the area is still low-key. It's a beach town, true, but not everyone who's strolling in the sun looks rich or beautiful, and fancy cars don't block the narrow streets. Rather, working-class families from inland (Salinas and east) come to the shore for much-deserved recreation to join traveling families of all income levels. In the winter, when the seaside attractions are shuttered or open only on weekends, the area assumes an off-season charm. Bargains abound in lodgings, and the beaches are still good for soulful walks, if not sunbathing. And the redwoods (there are two state parks here) know no seasons.

Family Lodging

Big Basin Redwoods State Campgrounds

One of the most beautiful state parks in California, Big Basin is home to some seriously big redwoods and some seriously fine campgrounds. If sleeping on the ground makes you grumpy, reserve one of the 35 sweet little cabins in Huckleberry Camp, each equipped with two double beds and a woodstove (bring your own sleeping bags, pillows, and wood). Huckleberry also has tent sites a short walk from the parking area, and the RV

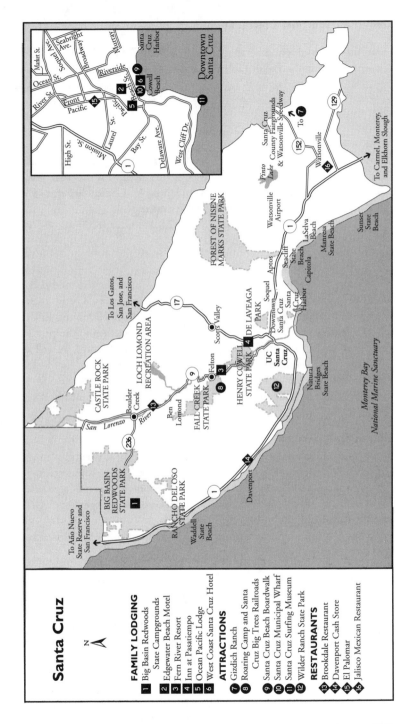

Santa Cruz

N

FAMILY LODGING
1 Big Basin Redwoods State Campgrounds
2 Edgewater Beach Motel
3 Fern River Resort
4 Inn at Pasatiempo
5 Ocean Pacific Lodge
6 West Coast Santa Cruz Hotel

ATTRACTIONS
7 Gizdich Ranch
8 Roaring Camp and Santa Cruz Big Trees Railroads
9 Santa Cruz Beach Boardwalk
10 Santa Cruz Municipal Wharf
11 Santa Cruz Surfing Museum
12 Wilder Ranch State Park

RESTAURANTS
13 Brookdale Restaurant
14 Davenport Cash Store
15 El Palomar
16 Jalisco Mexican Restaurant

campsites at Blooms and Sempervirens are among the loveliest we've seen. Lots of good hiking. Picnic tables, fireplaces, showers, flush toilets.

21600 Big Basin Highway (off Highway 1 north of Santa Cruz); (831) 338-8860; reservations through Reserve America, (800) 444-7275. Campsites $14–16, tent cabins $38.

Edgewater Beach Motel

This pleasant motel is near the beach and boardwalk, and it has a garden setting to enjoy in the summer as well as fireplaces to warm that year-round chill. There are 17 family suites, including 11 with kitchenettes. We liked the barbecue and picnic area and the heated pool.

525 Second Street, Santa Cruz; (831) 423-0440; fax (831) 423-0470. Rates: summer $169–289, winter $119–235.

Fern River Resort

This vintage resort brings you into the mountains near the redwood parks and Roaring Camp, where the popular train ride originates. The inexpensive accommodations include 13 cabins, most with fireplaces and kitchenettes; two of them sleep up to six people. Youngsters enjoy the private beach on the San Lorenzo River (the river's just wading depth), as well as the game room, volleyball, tetherball, horseshoes, and feeding the ducks. The basic rooms are equipped with Sony Play Stations and Nickelodeon.

250 Highway 9, Felton; (831) 335-4412; fax (831) 335-2418. Rates $61–100.

Inn at Pasatiempo

This nicely appointed motor inn situated near the beach has gardens, a heated outdoor pool, and an adjacent golf course. The on-site restaurant has both indoor and outdoor seating. The 52 rooms are on the large side; some have fireplaces, and all have coffeemakers and refrigerators. Kids' menus available.

555 Highway 17, Santa Cruz; (831) 423-5000 or (800) 834-2546; fax (831) 426-8775. Rates $130–165, less in winter.

Ocean Pacific Lodge

A newer motel two blocks from the wharf and boardwalk, Ocean Pacific has 57 rooms and 13 two-room suites. A continental breakfast is included in your stay; there're a pool, two spas, and a laundry room.

120 Washington Street, Santa Cruz; (831) 457-1234 or (800) 995-0289; fax (831) 457-0861. Rates: summer $105–126, winter $89–112.

West Coast Santa Cruz Hotel

This fine resort next to the boardwalk represents the high end in these parts. It's right on the sand, and all 163 rooms and 16 suites face the ocean. In addition to direct beach access, guests enjoy an outdoor pool with kids' and adult spas, two restaurants (with kids' menus), room service (also with a children's menu), and touches like in-room Play Stations and Nickelodeon.

175 West Cliff Drive, Santa Cruz; (831) 426-4330 or (800) 662-3838; fax (831) 427-2025. Rates: summer $209–239, winter $99–149.

Attractions

Gizdich Ranch

55 Peckham Road, Watsonville; (831) 722-1056

Hours: January–March, weekends 9 a.m.–5 p.m.; in April (apple blossom time), daily 9 a.m.–5 p.m.; May 1–July 31 (berry season), daily 8 a.m.–5 p.m.; August–December 31 (apple season), daily 9 a.m.–5 p.m.

Admission: Free

Appeal by Age Groups:

Pre-school	Grade School	Teens	Young Adults	Over 30	Seniors
★★★	★★★★	★★	★★★	★★★	★★★

Touring Time: Average 2 hours with picking; minimum 1 hour

Rainy-Day Touring: Not recommended

Services and Facilities:

Restaurants Yes	Baby stroller rental No
Alcoholic beverages No	Lockers No
Disabled access Access to the shops	Pet kennels No
	Rain check No
Wheelchair rental No	Private tours For groups

Description and Comments If your visit to the Santa Cruz area coincides with berry season, your kids will enjoy picking their own strawberries, boysenberries, and raspberries—and apples are on the trees for pickin' in the fall. There's a bake shop where you can watch bakers prepare pies (available for sale). You can also see apple juice pressed. Boxes of apples can be shipped.

Roaring Camp and Santa Cruz Big Trees Railroads

Graham Hill Road, Felton (6 miles north of Santa Cruz); (831) 335-4484

Hours: June 8–September 7, daily, first train leaves camp 10:30 a.m., last at 5:30 p.m.; call for schedule in spring and fall; arrive at least 30 minutes prior to departure time.

Admission: $14.50 adults, $9.50 children ages 3–12, free for ages 2 and under

Appeal by Age Groups:

Pre-school	Grade School	Teens	Young Adults	Over 30	Seniors
★★★★	★★★★	★★★	★★★	★★	★★★

Touring Time: Average 2½ hours to beach; 75 minutes to redwoods; minimum 2 hours

Rainy-Day Touring: Not recommended

Services and Facilities:

Restaurants Picnicking	Baby stroller rental No
Alcoholic beverages No	Lockers No
Disabled access Yes; no motor-ized wheelchairs	Pet kennels No, but pets allowed
	Rain check Yes
Wheelchair rental No	Private tours No

Description and Comments   America's last steam-powered passenger railroad with year-round passenger service, Roaring Camp and Big Trees operate two trains in hour-long excursions from a colorful "camp" that has a general store and outdoor barbecue. The camp re-creates a logging camp of 100 years ago, when trains hauled timber out of the mountain areas. This is one of those great tourist activities that is extremely well run. The train rides take you through beautiful forest land southbound to the beach and northbound to the redwoods. On each ride, passengers may disembark at midpoint to hike or picnic (in the redwoods) or stroll beach and boardwalk in downtown Santa Cruz and take a later train back (space permitting, so be careful during crowded months).

Santa Cruz Beach Boardwalk

400 Beach Street, Santa Cruz; (831) 423-5590; www.beachboardwalk.com

Hours: Memorial Day–Labor Day, daily 11 a.m.–10 p.m.; spring and fall, Saturday–Sunday 11 a.m.–7 p.m.

Admission: Free to boardwalk, but rides cost $1.50–3; full-day passes for unlimited rides $21.95; 60 tickets for $24.95 (good if you have more than 1 child)

Appeal by Age Groups:

Pre-school	Grade School	Teens	Young Adults	Over 30	Seniors
★★★★	★★★★★	★★★★★	★★★	★★★	★★

Touring Time: Average 3–4 hours; minimum 2 hours

Rainy-Day Touring: Not recommended

Services and Facilities:

Restaurants Yes	Lockers Yes
Alcoholic beverages Yes	Pet kennels No
Disabled access Yes	Rain check No
Wheelchair rental Free	Private tours No
Baby stroller rental Yes	

Description and Comments There's nothing quite like the screams of roller coaster riders mingling with the smell of hot dogs and salt air. Adults will be content just to stroll along the sunny beachfront boardwalk and, on one hand, admire the ocean view and, on the other, enjoy the colorful amusement-park atmosphere. The famous Big Dipper Roller Coaster dates from 1924 and the carousel from 1911, but there are also up-to-date amusements like laser tag and virtual reality. Rides tend to be traditional favorites, and there's a special little-kid area with gentle rides as well as fun booths of games, wax hand-dipping, and ice cream vendors.

Santa Cruz Municipal Wharf

Beach Street, Santa Cruz; (831) 420-6025

Hours: Daily 5 a.m.–2 a.m.

Admission: Parking $1 per hour

Appeal by Age Groups:

Pre-school	Grade School	Teens	Young Adults	Over 30	Seniors
★★★★	★★★★	★★★★	★★★★	★★★★	★★★★

Touring Time: Average 1 hour; minimum half-hour stroll

Rainy-Day Touring: Not recommended

Services and Facilities:

Restaurants Yes, many	Baby stroller rental No
Alcoholic beverages In some	Lockers No
restaurants	Pet kennels No
Disabled access Yes	Rain check No
Wheelchair rental No	Private tours No

Description and Comments This is among the best spots in the Monterey Bay Sanctuary to give the kids a glimpse of the appealing sea lions native to these waters. Just walk out on the wharf and look over the railings. There, beneath the surface, you'll see the lithe, balletic bodies of the sea lions as they swim. The bait shops on the wharf sell bags of fish to toss down to the mammals. Eight gift shops, restaurants, charter boats.

Santa Cruz Surfing Museum

Mark Abbott Lighthouse, West Cliff Drive, Santa Cruz; (831) 420-6289

Hours: Wednesday–Monday noon– 4 p.m.

Admission: Free; donation requested

Appeal by Age Groups:

Pre-school	Grade School	Teens	Young Adults	Over 30	Seniors
★★	★★★	★★★	★★★	★★★	★★★

Touring Time: Average 1 hour; minimum 30 minutes

Rainy-Day Touring: Yes

Services and Facilities:

Restaurants No	Lockers No
Alcoholic beverages No	Pet kennels No; pets allowed
Disabled access Yes	Rain check No
Wheelchair rental No	Private tours No
Baby stroller rental No	

Description and Comments   This museum actually holds some interest for non-surfers, thanks to its atmospheric location in the Mark Abbott Memorial Lighthouse on a pretty coastal stretch. Surf-history fans can check out the small but appealing collection of old photos, vintage boards, and local surf history, while others watch the sea lion colony and the surfers outside.

Wilder Ranch State Park

1401 Coast Road, Santa Cruz; (831) 426-0505

Hours: Historic complex open Wednesday–Sunday, 10 a.m.– 4 p.m.; ranch activities on weekends; park open daily sunrise to sunset

Admission: Free, but $6 for a day pass to park

Appeal by Age Groups:

Pre-school	Grade School	Teens	Young Adults	Over 30	Seniors
★★★	★★★★	★★★	★★★	★★★	★★★

Touring Time: Average 3 hours with hike; minimum 1 hour

Rainy-Day Touring: Yes, but you'll get wet

Services and Facilities:

Restaurants No	Lockers No
Alcoholic beverages No	Pet kennels No
Disabled access Yes	Rain check No
Wheelchair rental No	Private tours No
Baby stroller rental No	

Description and Comments   At this park just north of Santa Cruz, you can see what ranch life was like 100 years ago. There's a great old farmhouse, chicken coops, a working blacksmith, and a storybook barn, as well as trails and natural wonders like a beachside fern grotto. Call to ask about the schedule of living-history weekends, when docents dress in costume and go about daily ranch life circa 1890.

Family-Friendly Restaurants

BROOKDALE RESTAURANT

Brookdale Lodge, 11570 Highway 9, Brookdale; (831) 338-2699

Meals served: Dinner Wednesday–Saturday; Sunday brunch and dinner
Cuisine: Continental
Entree range: $14–34 (dinner)
Children's menu: Yes; $9.95
Reservations: Recommended
Payment: All major credit cards

This upscale public restaurant is part of a country club/condo complex. The appeal for kids is the natural brook flowing right through the middle of the restaurant. Two tiers of tables line the sides of the brook, which is rock-strewn and babbling.

DAVENPORT CASH STORE

31 Davenport Avenue (9 miles north of Santa Cruz on Highway 1);
(800) 870-1817 or (831) 426-4122

Meals served: Breakfast, lunch, and dinner
Cuisine: Californian
Entree range: $4.50–9.95 (breakfast); $7–12 (lunch); $8.95–24.95 (dinner)
Children's menu: No
Reservations: Not accepted
Payment: AE, MC, V, D

Perfectly sited for travelers who decide to head north to San Francisco without having a big lunch in Santa Cruz, this is a very popular stop. Sometimes there's a long wait, but the cinnamon buns are worth it. We enjoyed the woodsy, airy room and the beautifully prepared pastas, salads, and homemade breads. Vegetarian dishes are a specialty.

EL PALOMAR

1336 Pacific Avenue, Santa Cruz; (831) 425-7575

Meals served: Lunch, dinner, and Sunday brunch
Cuisine: Mexican
Entree range: $7–20 (lunch and dinner)
Children's menu: Yes
Reservations: Yes
Payment: All major credit cards

This noisy, lively restaurant and bar has several high-ceilinged, beamed dining rooms and some striking murals, thanks to its location in a historic landmark hotel. It's everybody's favorite restaurant, busy even on week-nights, so it's overwhelming for the youngest ones but fun for older kids. You'll enjoy excellent Mexican regional dishes like mole, fabulous fish tacos, and some specialties like funnel-shaped tacos—a cut above your average Cal-Mex establishment, but still casual and reasonably priced.

JALISCO MEXICAN RESTAURANT

610 Main Street, Watsonville; (831) 728-9080

Meals served: Lunch and dinner
Cuisine: Mexican
Entree range: $6.95–13.95 (lunch and dinner); combination dinners
   $9.95–10.95
Children's menu: No
Reservations: Necessary on Friday night
Payment: All major credit cards

Locals come here on Friday nights to hear the real mariachis perform, and their music typically captivates kids. The food is straightforward, authentic Mexican, everything from the kid-quesadilla basics to saucy entrees.

Part Five

The Sierra Nevada

Literary giants and legendary explorers have put their pens to use in describing the sights found in the regions in and around the Sierra Nevada mountain range of eastern California. From Lake Tahoe's blue, blue water to Half Dome's moonlit granite curve to the awe-inspiring sequoias, the wonders contained in these landscapes are so extraordinary that Americans have enshrined all or parts of them as national parks, forests, and preserves. From south to north, we will consider the following destinations in this Sierra Nevada chapter: **Death Valley, Sequoia/Kings Canyon, Mammoth Lakes** (with side trips to **Bodie** and **Mono Lake**), **Yosemite,** and **Lake Tahoe** (the California section of South Lake Tahoe as well as North Lake Tahoe). The regions we are discussing are for the most part mountainous, except for Death Valley, which is, of course, the lowest point on the continent, and they stretch in length along more than half the state.

Although our enthusiasm for California's national parks is unbounded, our children have had occasion to groan about driving another four hours "to see some more big rocks," so we caution families about being overly ambitious in planning visits to too many of the state's remarkable landscapes. Unless you are literally going to be traveling for several weeks, don't try to see all the parks or destinations mentioned in this chapter; instead, do as Californians do, and concentrate on one or two at a time. Then make plans to stay in the park you select or its vicinity and consider a few activities or excursions to bring variety to your days: a guided tour, a horseback ride, a rope-climbing session, a river swim, or even an outlet-shopping day.

Let the season be your first guide in planning your visit to this region. Both winter and summer vacations can be terrific at some of these sites, but your children's ages and your family's interests should be taken into consideration. Again, from south to north: Death Valley is most pleasant and popular between October and April, with high season being in March

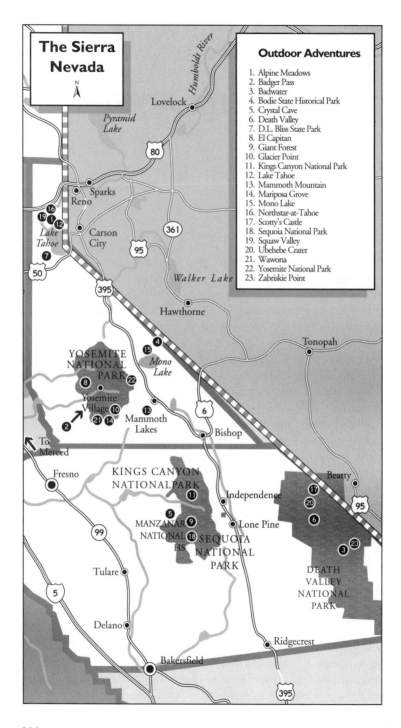

The Sierra Nevada

N

Outdoor Adventures

1. Alpine Meadows
2. Badger Pass
3. Badwater
4. Bodie State Historical Park
5. Crystal Cave
6. Death Valley
7. D.L. Bliss State Park
8. El Capitan
9. Giant Forest
10. Glacier Point
11. Kings Canyon National Park
12. Lake Tahoe
13. Mammoth Mountain
14. Mariposa Grove
15. Mono Lake
16. Northstar-at-Tahoe
17. Scotty's Castle
18. Sequoia National Park
19. Squaw Valley
20. Ubehebe Crater
21. Wawona
22. Yosemite National Park
23. Zabriskie Point

(although European visitors often prefer the extreme heat of summer, we don't advise it with kids—they'll be fabulously uncomfortable). **Mammoth Mountain** and the town of Mammoth Lakes have two peak seasons—winter for skiing and other snow sports, summer for hiking and mountain biking. Sequoia/Kings Canyon has traditionally been a spring-summer-fall destination, but family snow play is burgeoning there, and rangers now lead snowshoe walks and other activities in the winter months. Yosemite is popular year-round, its beauty chronicled by photographers and writers in every season, although summer is its busiest. And Tahoe has distinctly different pleasures in summer (boating, swimming, hiking) and winter (skiing).

You don't have to be a camper to enjoy these national parks and Big Wonders, but camping is a wonderful option at all of these sites. It is necessary to plan ahead and make reservations whenever possible. There are also lodges and motels in every area, but a limited number of rooms, so advance planning (several months before summer) is necessary to secure the most desirable accommodations. Camping reservations may (and should) typically be made three months in advance. Mammoth and Lake Tahoe have full-fledged towns, with shopping and movie theaters (and, in the case of the Nevada side of South Lake Tahoe, casinos) in addition to lodging and restaurants.

FOR SKIERS ONLY

We couldn't possibly do justice to the many, many ski mountains in the Sierra. Instead, we'll give you the short list of our five favorite Sierra family ski resorts. For more comprehensive information on skiing, see *The Unofficial Guide to Skiing in the West.*

Alpine Meadows. This large North Tahoe mountain has excellent snow, less of a scene than glitzier Squaw, and what may be the best children's ski school in the state, staffed by first-rate instructors. There are more snowboarders than there used to be, which may please your 12-year-old (if not you), but skiers have hardly been forced out. 2600 Alpine Meadows Road, Tahoe City, (530) 583-4232 or (800) 441-4423.

Badger Pass. The conditions aren't always ideal, and the quality of skiing is on the lower end, but that didn't stop us from falling in love with this place. It's the ski mountain that time forgot, with a small beamed lodge, the cheapest ski-mountain cafeteria in the West, friendly people, good Nordic trails, and a very good learn-to-ski program for children and adults. The beginner-intermediate runs are great for learning and cruising, and the lift tickets and packages are the least expensive we've seen. Good skiers and cool teens, however, might get bored. The mountain is easily reached from accommodations on the valley floor. Yosemite National Park, (209) 372-1446.

Mammoth Mountain. We learned to ski at Mammoth as teenagers, and it remains a teen haven to this day—in fact, it's a haven for every sort of skier, because its vastness can accommodate everyone. It'd take you a week to ski every run. Very good children's programs and lessons are run out of both the main lodge and Canyon Lodge, and nearby condos are plentiful. The downside is the crowding on weekends when Southern California locals pour in, but the addition of more high-speed lifts has dramatically improved the situation. For details, see Mammoth Mountain profile under Attractions, page 319.

Northstar-at-Tahoe. A large, upscale snow resort with well-designed and maintained areas for downhill skiers, snowboarders, and Nordic skiers. The children's programs and ski schools are impressive. For details, see Northstar listing, page 336.

Squaw Valley. Like Mammoth, this mountain (actually mountains) is so huge that it takes days to ski it all. Unlike at Mammoth, lift lines are short, if encountered at all. Lots of beginner runs, lots of expert runs, even more groomed intermediate runs, and a separate children's ski area. For details, see Squaw listing in Lake Tahoe Attractions, page 341.

GETTING THERE

Because the territory covered is so huge, we will devote a section of each destination's coverage to getting there.

HOW TO GET INFORMATION BEFORE YOU GO

Caltrans Highway Conditions (for winter driving in mountains); (800) 427-7623. (This number cannot be reached from all calling areas.)

Death Valley National Park, Death Valley 92328; (760) 786-2331; www.nps.gov/deva.

Sequoia and Kings Canyon National Parks, Three Rivers 93271; (209) 565-3134.

Sequoia and Kings Canyon National Parks, Guest Services (authorized concessionaire handling lodging except for camping and other services in the two parks), P.O. Box 789, Three Rivers 93271; (559) 565-3341; fax (559) 565-3730.

Lake Tahoe Visitor Information; (800) AT-TAHOE.

National Parks Camping Reservations: (800) 365-2267 for Sequoia/ Kings Canyon and Death Valley; for Yosemite, (800) 436-7275.

Mammoth Lakes Visitors Bureau, P.O. Box 48, Mammoth Lakes 93546; (888) 466-2666; www.visitmammoth.com.

Mammoth Visitor Center and Ranger Station; (760) 924-5500. Has up-to-date information on opening dates of campgrounds (700 sites at elevations above 7,500 feet) in Inyo National Forest.

North Lake Tahoe Central Reservations Service; (800) 824-6348 or (530) 583-3494; www.tahoefun.com.

The Best Parks

This entire chapter is nothing but the best parks, so they're not listed under this heading—they're described in detail throughout the chapter, as "town" descriptions and sometimes under Attractions. Look for specifics under the particular area that interests you.

Family Outdoor Adventures

Again, this chapter is nothing but. They're not listed up front, because they're plentiful at every spot in these wilderness areas. Check for details in individual geographic areas.

Calendar of Festivals and Events

January

Cross-Country Ski Fest, Mammoth; (760) 934-2442.

South Lake Tahoe Annual Winter Celebration. Includes Celebrity Ski Classic at Heavenly as well as other ski and snowboard races, concerts, and ice-sculpting contest; (530) 544-5050.

February

Sierra Sweepstakes Sled Dog Races, Truckee. Thousands gather to watch the dogsleds race at the Truckee-Tahoe airport; (530) 587-2757.

National Women's Snowboard and Ski Festival, Mammoth; (760) 934-0745.

March

Snowfest, Lake Tahoe. Tahoe's ten-day Snowfest celebration includes more than 100 events, ranging from a penny carnival, parades, and snow-sculpture contests to a polar swim and a "wild thing" costume party; (530) 583-7625.

April

Easter Egg Hunt and Playday, Mammoth Lakes; (760) 934-8989.

May

Mammoth Lakes Basin Spring Trout Derby; (760) 934-7566.

June

Lake Tahoe Summer Music Festival. Extends throughout June and July at various locations around the lake; (530) 583-3101.

High Sierra Shootout. Powerboat regatta from Tahoe City to Tahoe Vista; (530) 581-4700.

America's Most Beautiful Bike Ride. Hundreds of cyclists ride the 72-mile shoreline road around Lake Tahoe; (702) 588-9658.

July

Fourth of July Celebration, Mammoth Lakes. Includes Lions Club pancake breakfast, horseshoe tournament, a very popular parade, Fire Department open house, U.S. Forest Service Fire Department open house, and fireworks at Crowley Lake; (760) 934-1699.

Fourth of July Celebration, Lake Tahoe. Includes fireworks at the beach in Tahoe City, craft fair and music festival at Truckee High School, and parade and party in Truckee; (530) 587-2757.

Children's Fishing Festival, Mammoth, Snowcreek Ponds. For ages 1–15; kids learn to fish, free tackle provided; (760) 934-7566.

Celtic Festival, Mammoth Lakes. Music, dancing, pub grub, and more; (760) 934-2156

August

Mammoth Concerts in the Pines. Free music presentations and a variety of music festivals throughout the month, including folk, chamber, and country-western; (760) 934-2409.

Mono Lake Restoration Days. Biking and the symbolic bringing of water to the beleaguered lake; (760) 647-6596.

Tahoe Wooden Boat Week. Show of antique and vintage wooden boats and other maritime events; (530) 525-5225.

September

Labor Day Arts and Crafts Festival, Mammoth. A village arts celebration of the end of summer; (760) 934-2125.

October

Annual Native American Snow Dance Festival, Lake Tahoe. Washo, Paiute, Shoshone, and Miwok tribes dance for plentiful snow (it started during a long drought); arts and crafts fairs, foods; (800) GO-TAHOE.

Kokanee Salmon Festival, Lake Tahoe Visitors Center. Two-day festival celebrating the spawning of local salmon. With family activities such as art displays, nature walks, a children's fishing booth, and interpretive talks at the fish windows of the Lake Tahoe Visitors Center (see listing page 339); (530) 573-2600.

December

Mammoth Lakes Town Christmas Tree Lighting Ceremony; (760) 934-8989.

Sleigh Ride and Breakfast with Santa, Mammoth; (760) 934-6161.

Alpenlight Festival, Lake Tahoe. Events at various North Shore locations, including parties, sleigh rides, and window-decorating contests; (530) 581-6900.

LITTLE MOMENTS IN BIG PLACES

Sometimes the vastness of these remarkable Western landscapes—big skies, big mountains, big lakes—is just too much for kids to absorb, and they respond with indifference or ennui. We looked for ways to bring the wonders of the region down to their scale and offer some activities and strategies that have worked for us.

1. While a sports-loving middle-schooler and Mom went for a challenging hike in Yosemite (up many, many steps to Vernal Falls), Dad and a younger sister rented bikes and took a leisurely ride along the flat, paved bike path of Yosemite Valley that winds through meadows and campgrounds. Deer, squirrels, and other kids were out in view, and those easy two hours live on in her memory.

2. After panning for gold in Gold Country, we began our time in Yosemite by stopping for a picnic at a spot where the Yosemite

River makes a sweeping curve and Half Dome can be seen rising majestically above the treetops. The kids didn't even look up at the mighty landmark, though, because while wading in the icy stream, they realized that the water was flecked with gold. So they began to gather and scrutinize every pebble just in case one was a real nugget.

3. At Family Camp Montecito Sequoia, the youngest children are taken on a "fishing trip," in which they lie on their stomachs on a dock over the little lake and reach down with nets to try to scoop up the tadpoles and guppies they can see below. Our daughter now indignantly says the nets had holes big enough to allow every fish to swim through, but at the time she was, at age four, an enthralled and determined sportswoman.

4. Because of the unique sudden coolness of the desert night, the Furnace Creek Inn in Death Valley has a huge fireplace in the pool area. My daughter floated in the 85° pool water (heated by natural hot springs), gazing at the early-rising "children's moon" as the sky started to glow pink with a dramatic desert sunset. After getting out, she wrapped herself in a big towel and warmed herself happily by the fireplace. The juxtaposition charmed her.

5. In an inspired moment while enjoying a condo vacation in Mammoth, we agreed to stop (after hiking and before hitting the pool) at the town's bead shop and let the kids each browse among the bins with a muffin tin. They picked out a variety of beads and something to string them on, and left with little bags and triumphant airs. That night, the usual plea for a movie on video was replaced by the quiet sound of kids creating.

6. At Mono Lake, the adults read interpretive plaques and shook their heads over water-use controversies, but the kids didn't come alive until we joined a ranger walk at lake's edge and the story of those teeny tiny brine shrimp (specimens scrutinized) and the funny little fly larvae was revealed.

Death Valley

Often, city or suburb dwellers find that gazing on open vistas refreshes the mind and broadens mental horizons. In contrast to the close-up visual density of our daily lives (from nearby computer screen to a horizon cluttered with singe), there are places where emptiness is neither a sign of failure nor simply an affront to commercial enterprise. This vast area is one.

Arriving in Death Valley, we found the spaces to be affirmingly vast and the views cleansing—barren mountains, untrafficked roads stretching empty for miles in both directions, sky as a presence. The children felt it, too, though they didn't articulate the sensation, but fell silent and gazed about them when we stopped for cold drinks and directions.

As we explored, the vastness was broken up into little sections, each with a history, a personality, and a name. Such places as **Scotty's Castle, Zabriskie Point, Ubehebe Crater,** and **Badwater** became real to us. Where there had seemed to be a great nothingness we found a little bit of everything.

GETTING THERE

By Car. Death Valley is about 300 miles northeast of L.A. and 525 miles southeast of San Francisco. It's a long drive no matter which way you come, and you can't cross those mountains just anywhere. From L.A., take State Highway 14 north to US 395 north to a fork in the road called Olancha, where you pick up Highway 190 (scenic route) east to Death Valley. From San Francisco, your best bet is to pick one or two other parks to include in your trip and to access Death Valley after visiting Yosemite or Sequoia, both directly between S.F. and your goal.

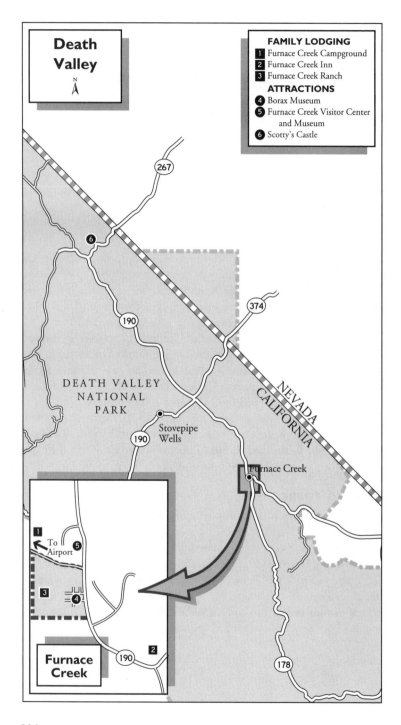

Death Valley

N

FAMILY LODGING
1 Furnace Creek Campground
2 Furnace Creek Inn
3 Furnace Creek Ranch

ATTRACTIONS
4 Borax Museum
5 Furnace Creek Visitor Center and Museum
6 Scotty's Castle

267

6

374

190

NEVADA
CALIFORNIA

DEATH VALLEY
NATIONAL
PARK

190
Stovepipe Wells

Furnace Creek

1
To Airport
5

3
4

190
2

Furnace Creek

178

Family Lodging

Furnace Creek Campground

Part of the Furnace Creek complex described next. A good bet for families. There are 20 tent spaces and 180 tent or RV spaces with fireplaces, tables, water, and flush toilets. Not all campsites have shade.

Highway 190, Death Valley; (760) 786-2345.

Furnace Creek Inn

This 66-room luxury hotel is truly something special, offering real comfort in an incredibly isolated location. You might be hot and dusty from a hike, but after a shower and a swim in the warm spring-fed pool and a cool drink on your room's balcony, you'll feel lucky indeed. The rooms, remodeled in the late 1990s, are true to a mid-century feeling in decor that fits nicely with the desert setting. The dining room was too formal for us to enjoy with the kids except at breakfast (although there is a kids' menu). We went down the hill to the Ranch part of the resort (see separate listing below). The hotel is on a hill above the valley, so views are spectacular, especially at sunrise.

Highway 190, Death Valley; (760) 786-2361. Rates $230–325 in winter, $155–210 in summer.

Furnace Creek Ranch

At the bottom of the hill is the other part of the Furnace Creek Resort, the more boisterous, motel- and camping-focused area, where restaurants, laundry services, tennis courts, and spring-fed swimming pools serve visitors in a grassy, shady oasis. The 255 units range in quality from okay to very good, depending on whether they've been upgraded. There are three restaurants on the grounds, and plenty of kids running around playing basketball, tennis, Nintendo, and (desert) sand volleyball.

Highway 190, Death Valley; (760) 786-2345. Rates $90–130; kids under age 18 stay free.

Attractions

Borax Museum

Furnace Creek Ranch, Death Valley; (760) 786-2345

Hours: Daily 8:30 a.m.–4 p.m., closed noon–1 p.m. for lunch

Admission: Free

Appeal by Age Groups:

Pre-school	Grade School	Teens	Young Adults	Over 30	Seniors
★★	★★	★★	★★★	★★★	★★★

Touring Time: Average 40 minutes; minimum 20 minutes

Rainy-Day Touring: Yes (it doesn't rain anyway)

Services and Facilities:

Restaurants At resort	Lockers No
Alcoholic beverages At restaurants	Pet kennels No
Disabled access Yes	Rain check No
Wheelchair rental At registration	Private tours No
Baby stroller rental No	

Description and Comments Whether or not you stay at Furnace Creek Inn or Furnace Creek Ranch, you'll end up spending some time at the ranch because of the amenities, including horseback riding. (Don't bother with the horseback trail ride, though—it's a dull walk.) You can while away some time by strolling through the old mining equipment graveyard behind this museum, or if the hour is right, through the museum itself. Twenty-mule-team borax doesn't mean much to those too young to have seen the Ronald Reagan commercials in the early 1960s, but if you think about it and talk about it a bit, the idea of actually handling a team of 20 mules will begin to sink in.

Furnace Creek Visitor Center and Museum

Death Valley National Park, Death Valley; (760) 786-2331

Hours: Daily 8 a.m.–6 p.m.

Admission: $10

Appeal by Age Groups:

Pre-school	Grade School	Teens	Young Adults	Over 30	Seniors
★★	★★	★★	★★	★★★	★★

Touring Time: Average 1 hour for exhibits, slide show, and questions; minimum 30 minutes

Rainy-Day Touring: Yes

Services and Facilities:

Restaurants At ranch	Lockers No
Alcoholic beverages At restaurants	Pet kennels No
Disabled access Yes	Rain check No
Wheelchair rental No	Private tours No
Baby stroller rental No	

Description and Comments The central source for visitor information while in Death Valley, the center has an hourly slide show orientation, a small museum, and schedules of programs offered at campsites around the valley. The bookstore operated by Death Valley History Association has a number of children's publications.

Scotty's Castle

Death Valley Ranch, Death Valley National Park, Death Valley; (760) 786-2392

Hours: Tours daily 9 a.m.–5 p.m.

Admission: $8 adults, $6 disabled adults and seniors, $4 children ages 6–11, free for children age 5 and under

Appeal by Age Groups:

Pre-school	Grade School	Teens	Young Adults	Over 30	Seniors
★★	★★★★	★★★★★	★★★★★	★★★★★	★★★★★

Touring Time: Average 50 minutes; minimum 50 minutes

Rainy-Day Touring: Yes, for inside

Services and Facilities:

Restaurants Yes, snackbar	**Lockers** No
Alcoholic beverages No	**Pet kennels** No
Disabled access Good	**Rain check** No
Wheelchair rental Yes, free	**Private tours** No
Baby stroller rental No	

Description and Comments   Together with Hearst Castle and the Will Rogers House, Scotty's Castle forms a picture of a grand period in California in the late 1920s and early 1930s, when personalities and the houses they occupied were larger than life. This remarkable mansion museum is shown today by docents who offer living-history tours, pretending as if you are arriving guests of the owner, Chicago millionaire Albert Johnson, and they're showing you around. In its way, it rivals the stately homes and castles of Europe, with its carpets from Majorca, ceramics from Italy, custom wrought-iron fixtures in fantasy shapes, and huge redwood beams. The kids listened intently to the story of the trickster Scotty the caretaker, who persuaded many that this was his house. At the end, it was extraordinary in a goofy way to stand in the resonating vibration of the player organ as it played "Pomp and Circumstance" and we wended our way down the circular steps of a turret.

Sequoia and Kings Canyon

These twin parks are administered jointly but were established separately, Sequoia in 1890 and Kings Canyon in 1940. Today's visitors might not know, as they drive from place to place in the pine forests, whether they are entering Kings Canyon or leaving Sequoia. Overall, most of the park acreage is given over to wilderness areas, but 90 miles of paved roads allow for access to the groves of sequoias and some other natural wonders. A special experience is a stay at **Montecito-Sequoia Family Vacation Camp,** a family camp open year-round (see listing on page 310). Sequoia is home to the world's largest tree, the **General Sherman,** found in the **Giant Forest.**

GETTING THERE

By Car. Highway 198 leads into Sequoia National Park from the southwest; Route 180, the General's Highway, connects the parks. The Foothill Visitors Center (phone (559) 565-3134) is at the entrance to the park. It's the park headquarters, and rangers here will collect an entrance fee.

Family Lodging

Buckeye Tree Lodge

There are several motels in Three Rivers, a short distance from the entrance to Kings Canyon National Park, and this is one of the more comfortable. It has 12 rooms, and it's in a woodsy setting next to a river; some rooms have balconies overlooking the river. There's also one room with a kitchenette and one two-bedroom cottage with a fireplace and a kitchen. Pool and a playground, refrigerators in the rooms, and a restaurant nearby.

40105 Sierra Drive, Three Rivers; (559) 561-5900. Rates $79–95.

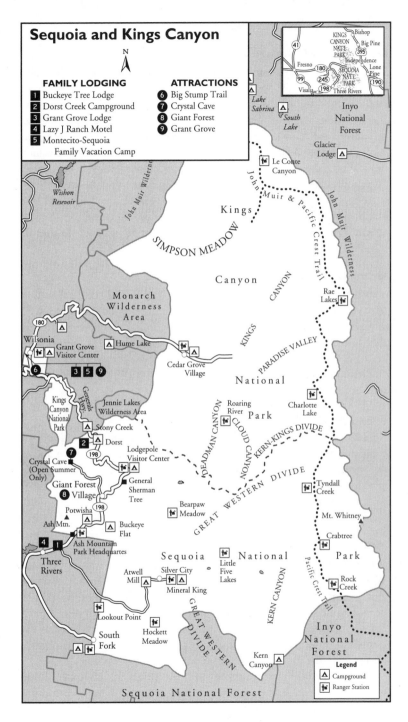

Sequoia and Kings Canyon

N

FAMILY LODGING
1 Buckeye Tree Lodge
2 Dorst Creek Campground
3 Grant Grove Lodge
4 Lazy J Ranch Motel
5 Montecito-Sequoia
   Family Vacation Camp

ATTRACTIONS
6 Big Stump Trail
7 Crystal Cave
8 Giant Forest
9 Grant Grove

Bishop
KINGS CANYON NAT'L PARK
Big Pine
Fresno
Independence
Lone Pine
SEQUOIA NAT'L PARK
Visalia
Three Rivers

Lake Sabrina
South Lake
Inyo National Forest
Glacier Lodge

Wishon Reservoir

John Muir Wilderness

Le Conte Canyon

John Muir & Pacific Crest Trail

John Muir Wilderness

Kings

SIMPSON MEADOW

Canyon

Monarch Wilderness Area

Rae Lakes

KINGS CANYON

PARADISE VALLEY

Wilsonia
Grant Grove Visitor Center
Hume Lake

Cedar Grove Village

National

Kings Canyon National Park

Generals Hwy.

Jennie Lakes Wilderness Area

Roaring River

DEADMAN CANYON

CLOUD CANYON

Park

Charlotte Lake

KERN-KINGS DIVIDE

Stony Creek
Dorst

Crystal Cave (Open Summer Only)

Lodgepole Visitor Center

GREAT WESTERN DIVIDE

Tyndall Creek

Giant Forest Village
General Sherman Tree

Bearpaw Meadow

Mt. Whitney

Crabtree

Potwisha
Ash Mtn.
Buckeye Flat

Ash Mountain Park Headquartes

Sequoia

National

Park

Three Rivers

Atwell Mill
Silver City
Mineral King

Little Five Lakes

KERN CANYON

Rock Creek

Lookout Point

GREAT WESTERN DIVIDE

Hockett Meadow

South Fork

Kern Canyon

Inyo National Forest

Pacific Crest Trail

Legend
▲ Campground
Ⓧ Ranger Station

Sequoia National Forest

309

Dorst Creek Campground

The best family campground in Sequoia/Kings Canyon is Dorst, which also happens to be one of the many national-park campgrounds that accept reservations—so make them very, very early. Kids run wild here, making friends at other tent sites, jumping in gentle Dorst Creek, and running in the meadowy areas. This is a great base for exploring the redwood forests and hiking to little peaks and creeks. Hume Lake, a great swimming and fishing destination, is close by, and you can pick up supplies easily at Lodgepole. Flush toilets, fireplaces, picnic tables, food lockers.

(Note that there are 12 other campgrounds in the parks; call the National Park Reservation Service, (800) 365-2267, for details.)

Off General's Highway, a few miles north of the Lodgepole Visitors Center; (559) 565-3341; reservations (800) 365-2267. Campsites $16.

Grant Grove Lodge

This is not a lodge but more accurately a collection of 52 small cabins that look far more picturesque on the outside than they feel on the inside. We'd advise taking a picture here rather than staying, but if you must, you'll find that only nine have electricity and indoor plumbing. The others have kerosene lanterns, outdoor wood stoves, and shared bathhouses.

Grant Grove, Three Rivers; (559) 335-2314; fax (559) 335-2364. Rates start at $38 in summer.

Lazy J Ranch Motel

An 18-room motel with a real ranch feel—cottages are scattered around meadows, and there's a path down to the river. Several units have one or two bedrooms, and five cottages have kitchens. There's a pool, a playground, and laundry facilities.

39625 Sierra Drive, Three Rivers; (559) 561-4449 or (800) 341-8000. Rates $58–76.

Montecito-Sequoia Family Vacation Camp

When we stayed here it seemed like some California version of Lake Wobegon: All the men were good-looking, and all the women were above average. Something about the mountain-air atmosphere and the choice to be with your kids at summer camp made for a lot of conviviality among the adults. Parents never had to cook a meal, but plenty gathered at the camp "bar" for a glass of wine in the early evening hours. And plenty gathered early in the morning at the daily songfest before activities.

Kids are divided into age groups with counselors, and they can, if you wish, spend specified hours in the counselors' care while you pursue your own camp activities (archery, anyone?) or leave the premises to hike or sight-see. Meals are taken together, and evening activities like games and costume parties are designed for the whole family. This is truly the best of both worlds for those who'd rather join their kids at camp than send them (especially the too-young ones). This former girls' camp is within the national park itself, within easy distance of Crystal Cave and some of the most famous big trees. Open all year, it offers cross-country skiing and ice skating on the lake in the winter, and water skiing, horseback riding, pool swimming, and many other activities in the summer. There are 36 rustic motel-type rooms with private baths, and 13 family camping cabins (beds, but bring your own linens; they have electricity and wood-burning stoves but no running water—bathhouses are nearby). You can sign up for the whole camp, or stay for a day or two between camp sessions in the summer.

8000 General's Highway, Grant Grove, Kings Canyon National Park; (559) 565-3388 or (800) 227-9900; fax (559) 565-3223. Six-night stay in cabin $585 per child ages 2–12, $645 per adult; in lodge rooms $680 per child, $730 per adult, all meals included.

Attractions

Big Stump Trail

Near the entrance to Kings Canyon National Park; (559) 335-2856

Hours: Daily 24 hours, weather permitting

Admission: Free

Appeal by Age Groups:

Pre-school	Grade School	Teens	Young Adults	Over 30	Seniors
★★	★★	★★	★★★	★★★	★★★

Touring Time: Average 3 hours; minimum 30 minutes

Rainy-Day Touring: No, and hard to tour in snow

Services and Facilities:

Restaurants In Grant Grove	Lockers No
Alcoholic beverages Yes	Pet kennels No
Disabled access No	Rain check No
Wheelchair rental No	Private Tours No
Baby stroller rental No	

Description and Comments This one-and-a-half mile nature loop has a wonderful disaster theme that appeals to school-aged kids. It shows, in its short distance, all sorts of natural and human-caused damage that the sequoias have endured. There's one tree that was hit by lightning, another that was shattered by loggers, and a huge stump that was created, ironically, when one of the largest sequoias was felled for display in New York.

Crystal Cave

9 miles from Lodgepole Visitor Center; (559) 565-3341

Hours: Mid-May–October 11 a.m.–4 p.m., 1-hour daily tours; early spring and fall tours Friday–Sunday 11 a.m.–4 p.m. on the hour

Admission: $5 adults, $2.50 ages 6–12, free for ages 5 and under (tickets at Lodgepole or Foothill Visitors Centers only)

Appeal by Age Groups:

Pre-school	Grade School	Teens	Young Adults	Over 30	Seniors
★★★	★★★★	★★★	★★★	★★★	★★

Touring Time: Average 2 hours; minimum 1-hour tour plus time to hike steep half-mile trail from parking area to cave entrance

Rainy-Day Touring: Okay

Services and Facilities:

Restaurants No	Lockers No
Alcoholic beverages No	Pet kennels No
Disabled access No	Rain check No
Wheelchair rental No	Private tours Group tours only
Baby stroller rental No	

Description and Comments Not far from the Giant Forest (see profile below) is the Crystal Cave. We like cave tours when there are plenty of people and the caves aren't too dark and spooky but, rather, full of stalactites and stalagmites. So we like the one-hour tour of Crystal Cave with the Organ Room and the Marble Room. And it's nice in the summer to spend some time in the cool underground. Note that this tour is neither stroller- nor wheelchair-accessible, and backpacks are not allowed.

Giant Forest

Highway 198, Sequoia National Forest; (559) 565-3782

Admission: Free (park has vehicle entrance fee)

Appeal by Age Groups:

Pre-school	Grade School	Teens	Young Adults	Over 30	Seniors
★★★★	★★★★	★★★★	★★★★	★★★★	★★★★

Touring Time: Average 2–3 hours; minimum 30 minutes without the walk

Rainy-Day Touring: Come prepared and you won't be miserable

Services and Facilities:

Restaurants Yes	Disabled access Limited
Alcoholic beverages No	Wheelchair rental No

Baby stroller rental No	Rain check No	
Lockers No	Private tours No	
Pet kennels No		

Description and Comments In the Giant Forest, you'll find the General Sherman Tree and the Congress Trail. The 2,500-year-old tree is one of those superlatives every visitor to the region must pay homage to. It's the biggest measured tree in the world, as tall as a 27-story building. Near this giant specimen in Sequoia National Park is the Congress Trail, a two-mile, self-guided loop that makes a nice outing for walking families, because it winds through several magnificent groves of sequoias. Stop at Lodgepole Visitor Center for trail and other information.

Grant Grove

Kings Canyon; (559) 335-2856

Hours: Daily 8 a.m.–5 p.m.

Admission: Free (park has $10 vehicle entrance fee)

Appeal by Age Groups:

Pre-school	Grade School	Teens	Young Adults	Over 30	Seniors
★★★★	★★★★	★★★★	★★★★	★★★★	★★★★

Touring Time: Average 2 hours with visitors center, refreshments, and self-guided nature walk; minimum 1 hour

Rainy-Day Touring: No, and hard to tour in the snows

Services and Facilities:

Restaurants Yes	Lockers No
Alcoholic beverages Yes	Pet kennels No
Disabled access Yes	Rain check No
Wheelchair rental No	Private tours No; interpretive
Baby stroller rental No	hikes available

Description and Comments This mountain village is a kind of headquarters for Kings Canyon. It's a few miles from the park entrance and adjacent to the General Grant Grove stand of giant sequoias. In the village are a lodge, a little market, and a visitors center. The grove itself is an impressive stand of sequoias that was not too much for us to enjoy in an hour's part-drive, part-stroll from tree to tree. There's a twin sisters tree, with two trees growing from a single trunk; a fallen 120-foot-diameter tree that forms a tunnel; and the General Grant, the third-largest known tree in the world, at 267 feet high, with a circumference of almost 108 feet.

Mammoth Lakes

This is the easiest mountain resort in California to recommend to visitors, because you don't have to be a certain kind of traveler to enjoy it. It's the kind of place that has such a wide range of options that two very different families might spend time there and never cross paths. Ski season used to be the main season, but we had one of the most fun summer family vacations ever by basing ourselves here for a week in a condo (very reasonably priced because they're so plentiful) and scheduling one special activity a day. Summer or winter, Mammoth Mountain is the scene of many sports competitions, from mountain biking to snowboarding, and there are running marathons scheduled here weekly throughout the non-snow season. If you happen upon one of these special events, let the kids hang out for awhile and watch—they may see a young sports hero followed around by a TV crew.

GETTING THERE

By Plane. A small regional airline, Mountain Air Express, offers scheduled service between Mammoth and some of the area's smaller but convenient airports. You could depart from Long Beach or Burbank near L.A., or from San Jose near San Francisco, or from San Diego. Call (562) 595-1011, or log onto www.MountainAirExpress.com. A larger airport is in the planning stages.

By Car. This is one of the easiest mountain communities to take kids to in the world—the approaches via US 395 from Bishop in the south and Yosemite out of Lee Vining in the northeast are on a multi-lane, modern highway, whose broad pavement curves slowly and gradually up into the higher elevations. There's none of the hours of switchbacks that so often unnerve (and make ill) the little ones. Summer driving times are approximately 5½ hours each from L.A. or San Francisco. It's about 100 miles from Yosemite Valley.

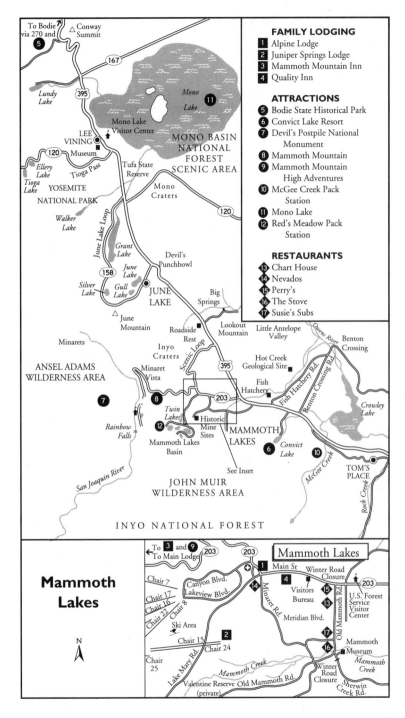

Family Lodging

Alpine Lodge

On the shuttle-bus line to the ski mountain (not to be scoffed at in the winter), this functional 126-room motel has an indoor pool with Jacuzzi and a community lounge with a fireplace on the second floor. For families, it also has also four two-bedroom cottages with kitchens.

6209 Minaret Road, Mammoth Lakes; (760) 934-8576 or (800) 367-2250. Rates are $83–103 winter and summer; kids under age 17 stay free.

Juniper Springs Lodge

This woodsy new lodge/condo is Phase One of Mammoth's plan to become a ski resort with the swank of, say, Park City or Copper Mountain. Located at the base of Chair 15, Juniper Springs Lodge combines the services of a hotel—daily maid service, bellmen, coffee shop, concierge, ski check—with the convenience of condo living—each of the 174 units, even the studios, has a full kitchen. It's more expensive than renting a condo in one of the many nearby complexes, but because of the ski-in/ski-out location and the full-service aspect, many families consider it money well spent. Extras include a pool, spa, and laundry room. Be forewarned that in spring, the snow melts first on the Juniper Springs side of the moutnain, so you may have to take a shuttle or drive over to the main lodge.

4000 Meridian Way, Mammoth Lakes; (760) 924-1102 or (888) 311-1102. Rates are $145–545 for studio to three-bedroom condo.

Mammoth Mountain Inn

This ski resort hotel isn't as spectacular as the various resorts in Lake Tahoe, but it's not as pricey either, and it is terribly convenient. A lot of families will be pleasantly surprised to find that they can afford one of the 213 rooms, 43 two-bedroom units, or 14 three-bedroom units in this hotel at the foot of the main lodge and many of the ski lifts. The best time to stay here is winter; although there are summer activities, the many sports events make for a sometimes-congested area, and other hotels and condos are more central to town pleasures. There's a child-care center with storytellers and magicians performing at different times, a game room, free ski check, and kids' menus in the restaurants and in-room service.

Highway 203 next to ski area, Mammoth; (760) 934-2581; fax (760) 934-0701. Rates start at $99 in the summer, $115 in the winter.

Quality Inn

The second-floor lounge of this otherwise routine motel makes for a less claustrophobic feel for guests in the winter. There are 61 rooms (with

Go Rent a Condo

The lodging of choice for visitors to Mammoth is a rental condo—it gives you room for the fishing poles and mountain bikes. Most are privately owned by passionate skiers or fishing enthusiasts who use the apartments or townhouses themselves and rent them out through agencies when they're not in residence. They're furnished according to the owners' taste, but we've found them to be typically pleasant and homey, with well-equipped kitchens and usually VCRs and other amenities. Many complexes have pools, game rooms, and the like. Any of the agencies listed below will send you listings of condos available by size and price. Some visitors opt for condo areas with good views high up near the ski area, but we prefer the complexes in the village itself, so we can walk to get a sandwich or pizza. On one stay, we were within walking distance of a stable, where we signed up for trail rides.

Prices begin at $54 per night for four people based on a seven-night stay and go up to $350 per night, with most in the $100–150 a night range.

- Mammoth Country Reservations, (800) 255-6266, www.4mammoth.com

- Mammoth Lakes Accommodation Service, (800) 843-6285 or (760) 934-3931

- Mammoth Premier Reservations, (800) 336-6543 or (760) 934-6543

- Mammoth Properties Reservations, (888) MAMMOTH, www.mammoth-lodging.com

- Mammoth Reservation Bureau, (800) 462-5571

- Mammoth Sierra Reservations, (800) 325-8415

coffeemakers, microwaves, refrigerators, and free movies), an indoor Jacuzzi, and a free continental breakfast.

3537 Main Street, Mammoth Lakes; (760) 934-5114 or (800) 626-1900; fax (760) 934-5165. Rates are $79–99 in summer, $89–109 in winter; kids under age 12 stay free.

Attractions

Devil's Postpile National Monument

Mammoth Visitor Center and Ranger Station; board shuttle in front of Mammoth Mountain Inn at the ski area; (760) 872-4881

Hours: Last bus leaves Mammoth Mountain at 5:25 p.m. and Red's Meadow at 6:15 p.m.

Admission: Shuttle $7 adults, $4 children ages 5–12, free for children ages 4 and under

Appeal by Age Groups:

Pre-school	Grade School	Teens	Young Adults	Over 30	Seniors
★★★★	★★★★★	★★★★★	★★★★★	★★★★★	★★★★★

Touring Time: Average half to full day; minimum 2 hours

Rainy-Day Touring: Not recommended

Services and Facilities:

Restaurants Cafe at Red's Meadow Resort	Wheelchair rental No
	Baby stroller rental No
Alcoholic beverages At cafe and store	Lockers No
	Pet kennels No
Disabled access No; private cars admitted	Rain check No
	Private tours No

Description and Comments   Don't leave the Mammoth area without spending a day in the Devil's Postpile National Monument. We set aside about two-thirds of a day and boarded the shuttle, getting off at the Devil's Postpile trailhead. Before we'd walked five minutes we found a lovely picnic spot next to a roaring river. We continued to the Postpile (half-mile easy walk from the bus stop), and then on to Rainbow Falls, where scores of people, including families with grandmothers whose shoes were not made for walking, either looked at the 100-foot falls from a viewpoint or continued down stairs and a steep path to the bottom of the falls to fully enjoy the thundering waters of the San Joaquin River. Rainbow Falls is a one-and-a-half-mile walk from the bus stop through mostly dusty flatlands. Other shuttle bus stops include lakes, falls, and Red's Meadow Resort, a pack station for trail rides with a cafe and store for campers.

To reach Devil's Postpile, day-use visitors entering the area after 7: 30 a.m. must use the shuttle bus (except for vehicles carrying 11 or more people or non-ambulatory people). The trip takes 45 minutes to the last stop, and riders get on and off at several points; the round-trip is about two hours.

Mammoth Mountain

Mammoth Lakes; (888) 4-MAMMOTH or (760) 934-0745; bike park
  (760) 934-0706; gondola (760) 934-2571; www.mammoth-mtn.com

Hours: Vary by activity

Admission: Varies by activity

Appeal by Age Groups:

Pre-school	Grade School	Teens	Young Adults	Over 30	Seniors
★★★	★★★★★	★★★★★	★★★★★	★★★★★	★★★★★

Touring Time: Average depends on your sign-up choices; minimum at
  least 1 hour to get the lay of the land

Rainy-Day Touring: Yes, depends

Services and Facilities:

Restaurants Yes, several	Lockers Yes
Alcoholic beverages Yes	Pet kennels No
Disabled access Limited	Rain check No
Wheelchair rental No	Private tours Ski, snowboard,
Baby stroller rental No	and mountain bike

Description and Comments   The official ski area and the hotel and restaurants adjacent to it are known as Mammoth Mountain. To visitors, it simply feels like a little complex at the top of a winding road above the town of Mammoth Lakes. Head here and review the offerings, no matter what season you're arriving.

In winter, this is one of the best ski mountains in the West, serviced by seemingly endless high-speed lifts; in the summer, the gondola continues to run as a scenic ride to the top of the mountain. Winter skiing and snowboarding options for families include group and individual lessons as well as an excellent children's half-day and all-day ski and snowboard school (all-day includes lunch and supervision), as well as a three-day snowboard camp for groups of five or more compatible kids.

In the summer, a mountain-bike trail area, the Mammoth Mountain Bike Park, is created in the ski-run areas, and it includes a "little riders fun zone" for four-and-up riders just learning. Some lifts carry bikes and riders up the mountain, but you should start on the most modest hills—it can be a lot scarier than you might think, pointing a bike down these steep trails. The fantastic ropes-course outfitters (see next listing) have their sign-up area here, and they also set up one of those big faux mountains with hooks and nooks on it, so everyone can try rock climbing, complete with ropes and harnesses. This is also the place to catch the shuttle to Devil's Postpile (see previous listing). In the summer, an outdoor barbecue cafe is set up in the middle of the whole scene.

Mammoth Mountain High Adventures: Rock Climbing, Ropes Courses, and Orienteering Courses

1 Minaret Road, Mammoth Mountain Ski Area; (760) 924-5683

Hours: Late June–late August, daily 10 a.m.–6 p.m.

Admission: Single zip junior ropes course $6; overall junior course with 2 zips $13; climbing wall: $6 single climb, $13 1 hour, $22 all day; ropes course: $40 per person for family package

Appeal by Age Groups:

Pre-school	Grade School	Teens	Young Adults	Over 30	Seniors
★	★★★★★	★★★★★	★★★★★	★★★★	★★★
	(10 and up)				

Touring Time: Average up to 5 hours; minimum 15–20 minutes

Rainy-Day Touring: No problem

Services and Facilities:

Restaurants Cafe at rock-climbing area	Baby stroller rental No
	Lockers No
Alcoholic beverages Yes	Pet kennels No, pets allowed to be
Disabled access Limited, but	tied up
programs available	Rain check Yes
Wheelchair rental No	Private tours Yes, and classes

Description and Comments We signed up our older child for the ropes course (open to ages ten and up), but the whole family followed the group into the forest setting where the course is laid out, and we had a great afternoon watching participants of several age groups master climbing and other challenges on platforms, trapezes, rope ladders, and other equipment high in the treetops. Bring water and other drinks and snacks, and maybe a blanket to sit on. We highly recommend these courses. The same outfitter offers orienteering (ages ten and up), in which you learn to use compass, map, and other techniques to find your way at a running speed over a cross-country course. They've also set up a 32-foot climbing rock at the Mammoth Mountain ski area (see page 319) where even the youngest (children under age 14 need a partner to belay them) can get hoisted in a harness several feet in the air. At that site, there's a junior ropes course that allows the younger ones (ages 4–9) to move through three challenges and end with a long pulley ride down from a medium-high platform.

Happy Trails

For a memorable way to take your children into the Sierras, head out on horseback. Several outfitters offer everything from half-hour, hand-led rides for six-year-olds and younger to week-long pack trips into the John Muir Wilderness. Here are three favorite outfitters:

- Convict Lake Resort, (760) 934-3800. This cabin-campground resort offers 75-minute rides around lovely Convict Lake every day, for children ages 7 and older (grown-ups, too). It's a mellow, beautiful ride at a reasonable price ($27).

- McGee Creek Pack Station, (800) 854-7407. The possibilities are vast here, from a one-hour ride along McGee Creek, to a day trip into historic McGee Canyon, to week-long riding or pack-mule trips into the John Muir Wilderness. A popular family option is a ride-in camping trip to McGee's wilderness base camp; the horses return home, leaving you to hike, fish, and sing around the campfire until they return to collect you a few days later.

- Red's Meadow Pack Station, (760) 934-2345. Near Devil's Postpile and Rainbow Falls, this is a tidy mountain resort complete with cabins, a general store, and a cafe. The Tanner family leads all sorts of outings, from one-hour rides to a five-day parent-child summertime pack trip up into either the Ansel Adams or John Muir Wilderness areas, in which families with children as young as five years old sleep at two well-equipped base camps.

Family-Friendly Restaurants

CHART HOUSE

106 Old Mammoth Road, Mammoth Lakes; (760) 934-4526

Meals served: Dinner
Cuisine: American/steakhouse
Entrée range: $12.95–39.95
Children's menu: Yes
Reservations: Advised
Payment: All major credit cards

It's a chain, so we resisted coming at first, but after several discouraging meals at overpriced, bad-quality restaurants around town, we came here and were pleased. We got what we paid for—well-prepared, high-quality steak, fresh fish, and the famed salad bar, served in a relaxing environment. Share a piece of mud pie for the whole table.

NEVADOS

Main Street and Minaret Road, Mammoth Lakes; (760) 934-4466

Meals served: Dinner
Cuisine: American/Californian
Entrée range: $13–22
Children's menu: Yes
Reservations: Advised
Payment: All major credit cards

We were surprised at the quality of the cooking at this stylish, upscale restaurant—it could pretty much hold its own in L.A., which is not true of most Mammoth restaurants. And despite the niceness of the place, children are welcome, with a fixed-price $9.95 menu (steak, pasta, or shrimp, including salad and dessert). We particularly liked the creative pasta dishes, and there's a pretty good wine list.

PERRY'S

3399 Main Street, Factory Outlet Mall, Mammoth Lakes; (760) 934-6521

Meals served: Breakfast, lunch, and dinner
Cuisine: American
Entrée range: $3–8 (lunch); $8–16 (dinner)
Children's menu: Yes
Reservations: Not accepted
Payment: All major credit cards

A welcome discovery in a town where many restaurants are run-down, Perry's is popular, bright, and lively—maybe too much so for some when it gets crowded. The food is simple and satisfying: a good salad bar, pizzas, burgers, pastas. Patio dining, sports on TV.

THE STOVE

644 Old Mammoth Road, Mammoth Lakes; (760) 934-2821

Meals served: Breakfast (until 2 p.m.), lunch, and dinner

Cuisine: American
Entrée range: $2.95–7 (breakfast); $6–7 (lunch); $7.95–11.95 (dinner)
Children's menu: No
Reservations: No
Payment: AE, MC, V

This little restaurant in a small converted house sometimes seems to be bursting at the seams with muscular young men in ski or mountain-bike clothing, wolfing down enormous portions of what they must consider to be fuel as opposed to food. Our kids liked the booths, the charming memorabilia decor (it's been around for nearly 30 years), and the homey dinner specials complete with side dishes.

SUSIE'S SUBS

588 Old Mammoth Road, Mammoth Lakes; (760) 934-7033

Meals served: Lunch and dinner
Cuisine: Sandwiches
Entrée range: $2.99–5.50 (lunch and dinner)
Children's menu: Yes
Reservations: No
Payment: No credit cards

We went back again and again to this made-to-order sandwich counter for provolone and avocado subs (among other choices) to take with us on hikes and excursions. Fresh ingredients, best bread, terrific combinations.

Side Trips

ATTRACTIONS

Bodie State Historic Park

20 miles from Bridgeport; (760) 647-6445

Hours: Often closed because of inaccessible roads in winter, so call ahead; otherwise, open Memorial Day–Labor Day, daily 9 a.m.–7 p.m.; the rest of the year, 9 a.m.–4 p.m.

Admission: $2 adults, $1 children under 6

Appeal by Age Groups:

Pre-school	Grade School	Teens	Young Adults	Over 30	Seniors
★	★★★★	★★★★	★★★★	★★★★	★★★★

Touring Time: Average 2–3 hours; minimum 1 hour (not counting drive time)

Rainy-Day Touring: Not recommended

Services and Facilities:

Restaurants No	Lockers No
Alcoholic beverages No	Pet kennels No; leash required, $1
Disabled access No	fee
Wheelchair rental No	Rain check No
Baby stroller rental No	Private tours No

Description and Comments   This remarkable ghost town is all alone in its remote valley, so it's the fullest experience of the *real* Old West available today. It's located north of the turnout to Yosemite from US 395; from the highway, you take another road 13 miles east—the last three miles of which are hard-packed unpaved—and arrive at the state historical park. The only services in Bodie are rest rooms near the parking lot and a small museum/bookstore that is sometimes manned by volunteers. There is no snack bar, and the temperatures can be very hot in summer and cold in winter, so bring at least the appropriate rations.

The ghost town is preserved by the park service in a state of "arrested decay," which means that the rangers and volunteers keep the buildings from falling down (by strengthening foundations, shoring up walls, replacing broken glass or loose bricks), while allowing them to look as if they might fall down at any moment. In its golden years, Bodie had 10,000 residents, and people lived here until the 1940s. Artifacts inside and outside the buildings—furniture, wagons, trucks, mining equipment, beauty-shop fixtures, curtains—are left from all periods of the town's occupation. Visitors walk around the dirt streets on a self-guided tour, peeking into the windows of houses and churches, the schoolhouse (with a map showing the world as it was just before World War I), and the gas station. A detailed brochure tells about the inhabitants of each address and what is known of their fates.

Our school-age kids enjoyed the chance to inhabit the past, but the heat and strong sunshine cut into their patience and endurance, so we stayed for a shorter time than we might have with history-buff adults. Younger children would do better with a less authentic link to the past.

Mono Lake

Highway 395 near Lee Vining; (760) 647-3044 or (760) 647-3000; www.rs.fsfed.us/inyo

Hours: In summer, daily 9 a.m.–4:30 p.m.; limited hours in winter

Admission: $2 in visitors center

Appeal by Age Groups:
(Add ★★ to each if ranger walk included)

Pre-school	Grade School	Teens	Young Adults	Over 30	Seniors
★	★★	★★	★★	★★★	★★★

Touring Time: Average 1 hour visitors center and nature walk, ranger walk 1½ hours; minimum 30 minutes

Rainy-Day Touring: Not recommended

Services and Facilities:

Restaurants In Lee Vining	Baby stroller rental No
Alcoholic beverages In Lee Vining	Lockers No
	Pet kennels No
Disabled access Visitors center and to viewing veranda	Rain check No
	Private tours No
Wheelchair rental No	

Description and Comments   Families spending time in the Mammoth area may want to take an excursion to Mono Lake to experience a strange and beautiful landscape of a large flat lake in a desert-like setting with shoreline formations of "tufa" columns rising like stalagmites above the surface of the water. We simply stopped at the Mono Basin Scenic Area Visitors Center to enjoy the view and walk the nature trail, then we learned that a ranger walk was scheduled soon, so we joined it and had a wonderful experience. The walk included touching, tasting, smelling, and looking through binoculars and magnifying glasses and was conducted right along the lake's shore. The center also offers a stargazing and storytelling program, a "sounds of the creek" walk, and other hikes and talks at campgrounds and other sites around the Inyo National Forest. It's also possible to go on guided canoe and kayak tours of the lake.

Yosemite

National parks sometimes seem as if they have never changed and never will because of the timeless beauty of their monumental landscapes. But of course, the parks have man-made roads, visitors centers, campgrounds, and other facilities, and not only have these changed through the years, but the public's and the National Park Service's ideas about the best way to make the parks accessible have changed through the years. Yosemite is one of several national parks that are in the middle of a transition period.

The 1997 flood destroyed or damaged much of the Yosemite infrastructure, including roads, motel rooms, campsites, and staff dormitories. The National Park Service responded to the cataclysm by putting into immediate effect a long-term plan designed to update, upgrade, and improve Yosemite's infrastructure and make visitor facilities more environmentally friendly. According to the Park Service, the flood "underscored the wisdom of long-term plans for the park which call for removal of campgrounds and other facilities from the Merced River flood plain." So not all structures were rebuilt; those that had been scheduled to be moved to less environmentally sensitive areas are or will be rebuilt at new sites. The campground closures reduced the total number of campsites in Yosemite to 441.

Reservations for campsites at Yosemite may be made beginning at the 15th of each month for up to three months in advance by calling (800) 436-7275. Reservations for hotels, motels, and tent cabins within Yosemite may be made for up to a year in advance. Call (559) 252-4848 for Yosemite reservations.

The camp entrance fee is $20 per car. Once you've arrived and settled into your camp or cabin, please try to use your car as little as possible and use the park's convenient free shuttle service to get to trailheads and other areas.

There are several Yosemite web pages to explore. The National Park Service site is at **www.nps.gov/yose/** and has park information and "Yosemite

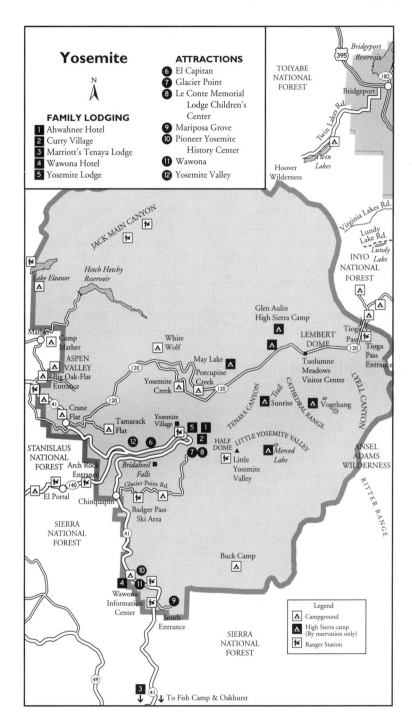

Yosemite

N

FAMILY LODGING
1. Ahwahnee Hotel
2. Curry Village
3. Marriott's Tenaya Lodge
4. Wawona Hotel
5. Yosemite Lodge

ATTRACTIONS
6. El Capitan
7. Glacier Point
8. Le Conte Memorial Lodge Children's Center
9. Mariposa Grove
10. Pioneer Yosemite History Center
11. Wawona
12. Yosemite Valley

Bridgeport Reservoir

TOIYABE NATIONAL FOREST

Bridgeport

Twin Lakes Rd.

Hoover Wilderness

Twin Lakes

Virginia Lakes Rd.

Lundy Lake Rd.

INYO NATIONAL FOREST

Lundy Lake

JACK MAIN CANYON

Lake Eleanor

Hetch Hetchy Reservoir

Mather

Camp Mather

ASPEN VALLEY

Big Oak-Flat Entrance

Crane Flat

Tamarack Flat

White Wolf

Yosemite Creek

May Lake

Porcupine Creek

Glen Aulin High Sierra Camp

LEMBERT DOME

Tuolumne Meadows Visitor Center

Tioga Pass

Tioga Pass Entrance

LYELL CANYON

Sunrise

Trail

CATHEDRAL RANGE

Vogelsang

TENAYA CANYON

ANSEL ADAMS WILDERNESS

RITTER RANGE

STANISLAUS NATIONAL FOREST

Arch Rock Entrance

El Portal

Chinquapin

Yosemite Village

Bridalveil Falls

Glacier Point Rd.

Badger Pass Ski Area

HALF DOME

Little Yosemite Valley

LITTLE YOSEMITE VALLEY

Merced Lake

Buck Camp

SIERRA NATIONAL FOREST

Wawona Information Center

South Entrance

SIERRA NATIONAL FOREST

To Fish Camp & Oakhurst

Legend
- Campground
- High Sierra camp (By reservation only)
- Ranger Station

Notebooks" with visuals. The Yosemite Association's site, **www.yosemite. org,** has visitor information, a bookstore, class listings, and a live camera view of Glacier Point. The Yosemite Concessions Services page at **www. yosemitepark.com** has lodging and park activity information, links to other Yosemite sites, and an online gift shop.

GETTING THERE

By Car. The most common approach to the park is from the west, via the town of Merced, which is reached by taking Interstate 5 south from San Francisco or north from L.A. and then transitioning to State Highway 140 east. Visitors who are also seeing Mammoth, Death Valley, or Lake Tahoe might approach from the east, via the town of Lee Vining, by taking US Highway 395 north or south, then State Highway 120 west into the park.

By Bus. Be really respectful and leave your smelly car behind, traveling via the Yosemite Connection/Grayline, (209) 384-1315 or, in California, (800) 369-PARK. There's service from the Merced Amtrak Station and Transportation Center to Yosemite Valley Visitors Center several times a day.

Family Lodging

Ahwahnee Hotel

This National Historic Landmark hotel is a favorite for outdoorspeople and city-slicker visitors alike, and it's often sold out. Its stone and wood architecture sets a great mood, and its Native American artifacts and decor are authentic and museum-quality. In addition to 97 lodge rooms, there are 26 cottages, a good choice for families. It's not the most kid-friendly lodging in the park—lots of wealthy retirees visit here, and they like to sit quietly in the awesome public areas, reading or doing elaborate jigsaw puzzles; when we visited, we felt like we had to constantly hush our children and keep them away from those jigsaw puzzles. On the other hand, it does have a pool and a children's play area, and the restaurant is polite to children and has a children's menu. And, of course, you can always take them outdoors into the vastness of the valley, just outside the door.

Yosemite National Park; (559) 252-4848; fax (559) 456-0524. Peak-season rates start at $216.

Curry Village

After the flood, this area was restored with fewer but better accommodations. The offerings are mostly rustic wooden cabins, with or without private baths, and tent cabins (the least expensive lodging in the park). There are now about 300 units altogether, about 120 with private baths. When we stayed here, we were quite pleased with the location for the kids, because of the bustling village atmosphere with pool, cafeteria, snack bar, mini-market, etc. The cabins were mostly family-occupied, and over several days, the youngsters made friends with neighbors and pool playmates. It's also a center of activities and services, including tour departures, raft rentals, cross-country ski rentals, bike rentals, etc. From mid-November to March there's an outdoor ice-skating rink (rare in California!), open day and night and with rentals. Overall, Curry Village is lively and active; don't look for quiet, secluded moments.

Yosemite National Park; (559) 252-4848. Rates start at $40.75 for canvas-top tent cabin; summer-only housekeeping camp rates are $43.75 for one to four people.

Marriott's Tenaya Lodge

Two miles from Yosemite's south entrance in the town of Fish Camp, this newer full-service resort makes an excellent vacation base, even if it does imprint a sense of chain-corporate America on a previously funky little mountain village. Spread among the trees are 244 rooms, two restaurants, a playground, and two pools, one indoor and one out. Some suites have soaking tubs. The popular room for families is the double deluxe, a larger room with a sitting area, a sofa bed, and a balcony with a forest view. At the activities desk, you can sign up for a flashlight hike for the kids, a narrated bus tour of the valley, and a guided ten-mile hike to a 30-foot waterfall; other fun stuff to do includes mountain-bike rentals, volleyball, croquet, and fishing at nearby Bass Lake. Camp Tenaya, the program for children ages 5–12, operates all summer with day or evening activities and includes meals. Each summer has a different theme; cost ranges from $25 to $35, depending on time.

1122 Highway 41, Fish Camp; (559) 683-6555 or (800) 635-5807; fax (559) 683-8684; www.tenayalodge.com. Rates $209–259; children stay free when sharing room with parents.

Wawona Hotel

Located in the Mariposa Grove area of the park, nearly 30 miles from the Valley, the Wawona, too, is a National Historic Landmark. This is a less crowded area, and there's an almost secluded feeling to the hotel, a favorite with Yosemite lovers who want to avoid the hustle and bustle of the valley. Come here in the off season and you're likely to see deer, coyote, foxes, and other wildlife right in front of the hotel. The homey, rustic rooms are spread among whitewashed turn-of-the-last-century buildings with great front porches; ask for spacious or connecting rooms as there are a variety of options among the 105 rooms (50 with private baths). There's a big lawn with a pool, tennis courts, and a nine-hole golf course. Restaurant on site, store nearby.

Highway 41, Wawona, 27 miles south of Yosemite Valley, Yosemite National Park; (559) 252-4848; fax (559) 456-0542. Rates without a bath, $70.75; with bath, $97.50.

Yosemite Lodge

Conveniently located and neither as grand as the Ahwahnee nor as down-home as Curry Village, Yosemite Lodge provides the middle-ground non-camping accommodations in the park. Activities right around the lodge are plentiful. The short walk to Yosemite Falls begins just across the street; the lodge has a bike-rental shop, many paved trails adjacent, and a terrific pool. There are three restaurants, one with a children's menu. Learn-to-ski packages are offered during the middle of the week in the winter.

Yosemite National Park; (559) 252-4848; fax (559) 456-0542. Rates: cabin with no bath $56.25, cabin with bath $72.50, standard hotel room $86.75.

Attractions

Wawona

Highway 41 south of Yosemite Valley; (209) 375-9501; in off-season, call (209) 372-0200

Hours: Spring and summer, Wawona Information Station open daily 9 a.m.–5 p.m.; off-season hours may be limited

Admission: $20 per vehicle at park entrance

Appeal by Age Groups:

Pre-school	Grade School	Teens	Young Adults	Over 30	Seniors
★★★	★★★★	★★★★★	★★★★★	★★★★★	★★★★★

Touring Time: Average several days; minimum 1 day, 1 night

Rainy-Day Touring: Possible

Services and Facilities:

Restaurants Yes		Lockers No	
Alcoholic beverages Yes		Pet kennels No	
Disabled access Some		Rain check No	
Wheelchair rental No		Private tours No	
Baby stroller rental No			

Description and Comments This south entrance area of Yosemite is loved by some visitors as a base because of its relative peace and quiet. There's no lack of things to do, however; here's where the Mariposa Grove of redwoods and the Pioneer Yosemite History Center are found. You can stay in the charming, rustic (and inexpensive) old white-sided Wawona Hotel (see profile, page 329).

The Wawona Information Station, at the park's south entrance, has maps, wilderness permits, trail guides, and books. A free shuttle bus from the information station takes visitors to the Mariposa Grove of giant sequoias; it operates daily in the summer beginning mid-May, 9 a.m.–6 p.m.

Yosemite Valley

Yosemite Village west of the main post office; (209) 372-0264

Hours: Visitors center open daily 8 a.m.–5 p.m.

Admission: $20 per vehicle at park entrance

Appeal by Age Groups:

Pre-school	Grade School	Teens	Young Adults	Over 30	Seniors
★★★	★★★★★	★★★★★	★★★★★	★★★★★	★★★★★

Touring Time: Average several days; minimum a half-day

Rainy-Day Touring: Possible; can be pretty and quiet

Services and Facilities:

Restaurants Yes	Lockers Food lockers to prevent
Alcoholic beverages Yes	bear problems
Disabled access Yes, ask at visitors	Pet kennels No
center	Rain check No
Wheelchair rental No	Private tours No
Baby stroller rental No	

Description and Comments Much is written in travel literature about Yosemite being more than the Yosemite Valley area, and it's true, the famous park has miles of wilderness for hiking and camping, and plenty of room in which to spread out if you get off the beaten path. But visitors don't need to apologize for actually liking the valley, with its ranger talks, its world-famous waterfalls and much-photographed views, and its abundant wildlife and scenic bike rides. We know many Californians who return (often with kids in tow) year after year to the valley to settle in for a week of hiking, biking, and campfire-going. These repeaters tell us that Yosemite is a large park with a varied topography and that they do go on excursions, such as the easy walk to Mirror Lake or on one of a zillion incredible hiking trails. But they still love the valley.

Along with the Yosemite Valley Visitors Center, in Yosemite Village west of the main post office, you'll find a museum, gallery, wilderness supply shop, and trailheads to two nature trails.

YOSEMITE'S LITTLE JOYS

Bike Riding. Bikes can be rented at Yosemite Lodge or Curry Village, and there are level trails crisscrossing the entire valley floor.

Early-Morning Photography Walks. These leave at around 8:30 a.m. and last for one hour from either the Ahwahnee or Yosemite Lodge.

El Capitan. Take some moments while you're in Yosemite to look at this granite wall at different times of the day. There are often climbers working their way up the face, and if you go to the meadow across from it with binoculars, you can watch their progress. At night, you can see the climbers' lights, or on a full-moon night, simply admire the dazzling rock itself. See Rock-Climbing Classes below for your own adventurous climbing kids.

Family Walks. These begin at the Valley Visitors Center, led by a ranger-naturalist.

Glacier Point. Most families stop here for just a half-hour on their way into or out of the valley, but don't neglect to make the stop. It's the picture-postcard view of your dreams, and even the kids will be awestruck. The scenic overlook is 30 miles (1 hour) from the valley, and the road is open from late spring through early fall. There's a snack stand open 9 a.m.–sundown.

Horseback Riding. Weather permitting, two-hour and half-day rides depart spring through fall from stables in the valley and at Wawona. Call (209) 372-8348 for more information.

Le Conte Memorial Lodge Children's Center. In the summer months, there are programs for kids ages 5–10. (209) 372-4542.

Mariposa Grove. The largest of three sequoia groves in Yosemite has been a magnet for visitors since the mid-nineteenth century. The grove's Grizzly Giant tree, 2,700 years old, is believed to be the oldest living sequoia. There's a small log cabin museum at the grove (May 22–fall, open 10 a.m.–5 p.m.). To reach the grove, take the free shuttle bus from Wawona, then follow the interpretive trail signs for a self-guided walking tour. Weather permitting in the summer, a guided tram tour ($8 adults, $4 for kids ages 4–12, children under age 4 free) leaves every 20 minutes for a one-hour tour through the upper and lower groves.

Pioneer Yosemite History Center. This cluster of historic buildings at Wawona is the center of living-history programs and other activities for children. A jailhouse, miner's cabin, and covered bridge can be explored in a 30-minute self-guided tour; there's a stagecoach ride, and there are sometimes demonstrations and crafts depending on the season, such as soapmaking, yarn-spinning, and Christmas crafts. The bookstore is open 9 a.m.–5 p.m. in the summer.

Rock-Climbing Classes. Yosemite Mountaineering School and Guide Service, (209) 372-1406. Beginning rock-climbing classes are offered from

Easter through mid-October; kids must be at least 10 years old. Mike Corbett's one-hour talk/walk about the history of climbing in Yosemite leaves from either the Ahwahnee or the Yosemite Lodge twice a week at 8:30 a.m.

Tours of the Valley. Two-hour, half-day, and all-day summer tours of the major landmarks of Yosemite Valley are given daily, in part to reduce the flow of auto traffic on the few roads on the valley floor. The summer tour vehicle is completely open-air and allows riders to see in all directions; winter tours are in heated buses. There's also a two-hour moonlight tour in the summer. We thought the tour was an easy, helpful way to get the lay of the land, and we found the guide's comments on wildlife particularly interesting. Call the Yosemite Lodge tour desk at (209) 372-1240 for fees and times.

Waterfalls. Waterfalls from below and waterfalls from above are one of the attractions at Yosemite, but depending on the time of year and the amount of snowmelt the area is receiving, some of the falls may or may not be filled with water. One of the most popular hikes in Yosemite is up to the top of Vernal Falls, and for purists it's probably a discouraging experience—literally hundreds of people at a time are working their way up and down the waterside trail that goes from the base of the falls to a pool (where people swim) at the top (from which some hikers continue on up to other pools). But families with active preteens and teens may find this a great way to participate in the democratic appreciation of a great national park. The other hikers are from all over the country and the world, and it makes for a fine outdoor social occasion, if not a wilderness experience. Lower Yosemite Falls and Bridalveil Falls can be enjoyed with just short, easy walks from shuttle stops. Yosemite Falls, with its 2,425-foot drop, can be seen from Glacier Point.

Wildlife. Please, please review safety information about sharing the park with bears and mountain lions, and watch your children closely at all times. You will also see deer, coyote, squirrels, and other smaller animals. Do not feed or disturb wildlife—doing so is a violation subject to fine.

Lake Tahoe

This is a big lake, to be sure—it's 22 miles long and 12 miles wide, with 72 miles of shoreline—but the special characteristic remembered by most visitors here is not the size but the beautiful deep, dark blue of the water. Surrounded by pine forests, and able to be seen from above on some scenic roads and hikes, Lake Tahoe presents an indelible impression. That inky blue water will turn swimmers blue, too—it seldom gets warmer than 60°, even in the middle of summer. We found it ideal for instantly soothing aching muscles or swelling feet after a hike in the hot sun, but parents of little ones will want to pull them out of the water for a towel rubdown every now and then.

Two-thirds of the lake is in California, and one-third in Nevada. The several communities on the lake's shore are quite different and are concentrated either north or south. The North Shore California towns of **Tahoe City** and **Tahoe Vista** are summer sports centers, where the best Jet Ski rentals are located and where water-skiers rule. The South Shore includes some Nevada territory, so there are casinos, but the town of **South Lake Tahoe** also offers family-friendly swim beaches, hikes, and sight-seeing excursions. There is skiing on both sides of the lake. The west side of the lake offers access to the hiking trails of the **Desolation Wilderness** and **El Dorado Village;** the east side offers highway junctions to Nevada's gambling centers and historic silver-mining towns.

Getting There

By Car. Lake Tahoe is most easily reached by car from San Francisco; it's 200 miles northeast of the Bay Area. Your route in will depend on whether you're headed for the North or South Shore areas. For North Shore, take Interstate 80 east to Truckee; for South Lake Tahoe, take US Highway 50 east.

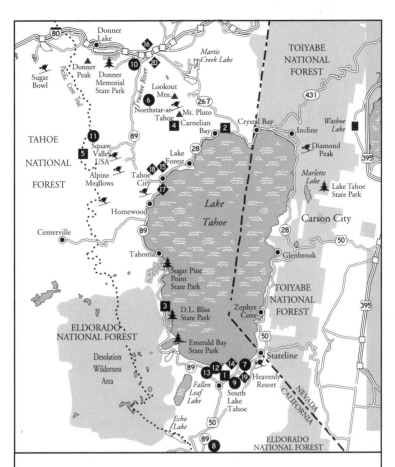

Lake Tahoe

N

FAMILY LODGING

1. Camp Richardson Resort
2. Cedar Glen Lodge
3. D.L. Bliss State Park
   Campground
4. Northstar-at-Tahoe Resort
5. Resort at Squaw Creek

ATTRACTIONS

6. Adventure Park
7. Heavenly Aerial Tram/
   Monument Peak Restaurant

8. Lake Tahoe Visitors Center
9. Saw Mill Pond
10. Sierra Nevada Children's Museum
11. Squaw Valley USA
12. Tahoe Amusement Park
13. Tallac Historic Site

RESTAURANTS

14. Beacon Restaurant
15. The Bridge Tender
16. Ernie's Coffee Shop
17. Fire Sign Cafe
18. Lakehouse Pizza
19. Monument Peak Restaurant
20. Squeeze Inn

By Air. Among the airlines serving Reno/Tahoe International Airport (60 miles east of the lake area) are Alaska Air, America West, American, Continental, Delta, Northwest, Reno Air, Southwest, Skywest, TWA, and United.

Family Lodging

Camp Richardson Resort

This unique, rustic resort has been home to vacationing families for more than 70 years—it's no grand ski complex, but rather a jumble of lodges, cabins, and campsites in a pine woods at the shore of the lake. The lodge has a pleasant public space with a big stone fireplace and the wonderful Beacon restaurant. The beach is the big draw for many; it's one of the best for swimming, and the full-service marina is a bustling center of water sports, renting kayaks, windsurfing gear, and more. The 36 lodge rooms and 39 cottages vary in decor and layout; some have terraces, fireplaces, and/or kitchens, but the cabins don't have TVs or phones. Also on premises are an ice cream shop and cafe/bakery, children's playground, bike-rental shop, and stable. There's a seven-night minimum for efficiency units in July and August.

1900 Jameson Beach Road, South Lake Tahoe; (530) 541-1801 or (800) 544-1801; fax (530) 541-2793; resort accommodations and boathouse, (530) 541-1801. Rates in lodge $85–130 in summer, $75–85 in winter.

Cedar Glen Lodge

A very good value for families, this small motel is located across the highway from a nice beach in Tahoe Vista on the North Shore. It's tucked in the pine woods, with a playground, pool, hot tub, and barbecues. Two two-bedroom units with kitchens are found among the rooms and cabins. There's no restaurant, but a basic continental breakfast is free.

6589 N. Lake Boulevard, Tahoe Vista; (800) 500-TAHOE or (530) 546-4281; fax (530) 546-2250. Rates $50–150.

D. L. Bliss State Park Campground

It's blissful here, all right, especially for children, who never tire of scrambling over the boulders, playing hide-and-seek behind the pines, and exploring the gorgeous white-sand Lester Beach, or close-by Emerald Bay. Bliss has three clumps of campsites; if you want to be closest to Lester Beach, reserve a site between 141 and 168. Hot showers, flush toilets, picnic tables, firepits, wood for sale.

Rte. 89, Tahoma; (530) 765-3023; reserve through Reserve America, (800) 444-7275. Campsites $16, $22 for beach sites.

Northstar-at-Tahoe Resort

This Squaw Valley rival resort has everything an active family could dream of spread over its 600 acres. You and/or your kids can mountain bike, pony ride, join guided hikes, ski, tackle a climbing wall, learn orienteering, take a ropes course, swim in heated pools, play tennis—it's exhausting just considering the options. The Minor's Camp program handles kids ages 3–12, with skiing lessons and snow play in winter and all sorts of amusements year-round. The accommodations range from upscale motel rooms to suites to fully equipped condos, found one mile from the main complex. There are five restaurants, most of which have kids' menus.

Highway 267 north of Lake Tahoe, 6 miles south of Truckee; (530) 562-1010 or (800) 466-6784; fax (530) 562-2215; www.skinorthstar.com. Rates $99–303 in summer and $149–450 in winter.

Resort at Squaw Creek

Modern mountain architecture makes this a distinctly Tahoe resort, with contemporary buildings at the center of 632 acres designed so every room has a view of the Sierra. The resort is a little town, actually, and in the winter especially, families can find all they need for a vacation right within the complex: shopping, skiing (direct access to Squaw Creek mountain lifts), world-class golf, junior tennis programs, even lawn games. In the summer, the wonderful, landscaped pool complex boasts a water slide; in the winter there's an ice rink. Of the 403 rooms and suites, the best bet for families is a suite, some of which have fireplaces. The Mountain Buddies Club offers half- and full-day programs (swimming, hiking, crafts, and games) for kids ages 4–13, as well as separate teen programs. One drawback: The lodging is not connected to the lobby area except by outdoor walkways, so in the winter, guests must go outside to get to restaurants.

400 Squaw Creek Road, Squaw Valley; (530) 583-6300 or (800) 327-3353; fax (530) 581-6632. Rates start at $300; packages and specials are less.

Little People's Adventures

This day camp accepts children ages 5–12 for one or more days with reservations a day in advance. Camp space is limited to 15 kids a day, though, so inquire about availability during the time you plan to visit. Kids are supervised by first-aid– and CPR–certified counselors who take them on adventures ranging from bowling to bouldering. They must bring proof of medical coverage, lunch, water, and equipment. P.O. Box 2914, Olympic Valley, CA 96146, (530) 581-4LPA. The camp operates daily from June to Labor Day, and on weekends through September.

TAHOE TREASURES

D. L. Bliss State Park. This park contains some great camping, terrific beach and boating areas, and several wonderful trails for day hikers, including the dreamy 4.5-mile Rubicon Trail, which snakes along the shore through the woods to the beach, where you can swim and picnic. Another hike, less than a mile long, takes you to an old lighthouse, and another, just one mile round-trip, takes you to the remarkable Balancing Rock. 168 campsites (see page 336). Nine miles north of South Lake Tahoe on Highway 89; (530) 525-7277 or (530) 525-7982.

Truckee Historic Town Center. Almost 100 nineteenth-century buildings remain in this town, and visitors can get an Old West feel on Commercial Row, where wooden sidewalks remain. The historic area is largely cafes and shops, as well as the Southern Pacific Railroad Depot Gallery; the Bar of America, with its photos of famous outlaws; and the Old Truckee Jailhouse Museum (10142 Jibboom Street, behind Commercial Row; (530) 582-0893; free admission, open weekends), which features real cells, historic photos, and Chinese-American historical items. Truckee is located on Interstate 80, 20 minutes north of Lake Tahoe.

Attractions

Adventure Park

1030 Merced Street, Berkeley; (530) 562-2285 or (510) 525-9391

Hours: Wall, summer, Wednesday–Sunday 10 a.m.–6 p.m.; junior ropes
   course, Wednesday–Sunday 10 a.m.–5 p.m.; senior ropes course,
   Thursday–Saturday 12:30–5 p.m., Sunday 10 a.m.–1: 30 p.m.

Admission: Ropes course $43 for each participant; climbing wall
   $13/hour or $22 day pass; orienteering $10 kids, $15 adults

Appeal by Age Groups:

Pre-school	Grade School	Teens	Young Adults	Over 30	Seniors
★	★★★★	★★★★★	★★★	★★	★

Touring Time: Average depends on activity; minimum 1 hour on climbing wall

Rainy-Day Touring: No

Services and Facilities:

Restaurants In resort		Lockers No
Alcoholic beverages In resort		Pet kennels No
Disabled access Possible		Rain check No
Wheelchair rental No		Private tours Yes, private courses
Baby stroller rental No		

Description and Comments   This ropes-course, orienteering-course, and climbing-wall complex is similar to the one described in the Mammoth section of this chapter. Participants meet at the Mountain Adventure Shop in Northstar Village in Truckee and go to either the ropes-course area (in the woods, with ladders, cables, and games), the start-off point for an orienteering course (hiking exploration, maps, compass), or the climbing-wall.

Heavenly Aerial Tram/Monument Peak Restaurant

Heavenly Ski Resort, Ski Run Boulevard, South Lake Tahoe; (775) 586-7000; www.skiheavenly.com

Hours: Summer, daily 10 a.m.–4 p.m.; winter, Monday–Friday 9 a.m.–4 p.m.; Saturday, Sunday, holidays, 8:30 a.m.–4 p.m.

Admission: Summer tram adults $15, children ages 6–12 $10, under age 6 ride free; winter ski-lift ticket $52

Appeal by Age Groups:

Pre-school	Grade School	Teens	Young Adults	Over 30	Seniors
★	★★★★	★★★★★	★★★★★	★★★★★	★★★★

Touring Time: Average 2 hours; minimum 15 minutes

Rainy-Day Touring: Not good for hiking

Services and Facilities:

Restaurants Yes	Lockers In winter
Alcoholic beverages Yes	Pet kennels No
Disabled access Tram only	Rain check No
Wheelchair rental No	Private tours No
Baby stroller rental No	

Description and Comments   Theme parks sometimes try to duplicate the thrill of a ski gondola or tram ride, but there's nothing like the real thing. The ride itself is a spectacular mile-long ascent to a point 2,000 feet above Lake Tahoe. At the top is a cafe with a large deck and a self-guided nature trail. For a memorable supper, come just before sunset and eat enjoying the view—the lake reflects the gorgeous light.

Lake Tahoe Visitors Center

Highway 89, 4 miles south of US 50 and Highway 90, South Lake Tahoe; (530) 573-2600

Hours: Summer, daily 8 a.m.–4:30 p.m.; closed in winter

Admission: Free

Appeal by Age Groups:

Pre-school	Grade School	Teens	Young Adults	Over 30	Seniors
★★★	★★★	★★★	★★★	★★★	★★★

Touring Time: Average depends on trail chosen; minimum 30 minutes

Rainy-Day Touring: Okay on paved path

Services and Facilities:

Restaurants Nearby	Lockers No
Alcoholic beverages Yes	Pet kennels No; pets allowed on
Disabled access Yes	leash
Wheelchair rental Yes, free	Rain check No
Baby stroller rental No	Private tours No

Description and Comments While one parent peruses the maps and brochures, another can take the kids along one of the six self-guided nature trails here. Among the trail attractions is an underground fish-viewing chamber that provides a window on the lake's aquatic life. Interpretive programs are offered on site June–Labor Day, 10 a.m.–8 p.m.

Saw Mill Pond

Past the Y at Lake Tahoe Boulevard and Saw Mill Road, Lake Tahoe Basin
Mgt., 870 Emerald Bay Road, South Lake Tahoe; (530) 573-2600

Hours: 24 hours daily year-round

Admission: Free

Appeal by Age Groups:

Pre-school	Grade School	Teens	Young Adults	Over 30	Seniors
★★★★	★★★★	★★★	★	★	★

Touring Time: Average 2 hours; minimum 1 hour

Rainy-Day Touring: Yes, but you'll get wet

Services and Facilities:

Restaurants 2 miles from civilization	Baby stroller rental No
	Lockers No
Alcoholic beverages Yes	Pet kennels No; pets allowed on
Disabled access Not yet, in the works	leash
	Rain check No
Wheelchair rental No	Private tours No

Description and Comments Serious fishing families will scoff, but for non-fishing adults, this is a pleasant little pond for introducing your kids to the activity. Kids under age 13 fish free in this pretty little pond stocked with trout by the California Department of Fish and Game, but you must supply your own bait and equipment. It's not open to anyone over age 14, so parents can teach but not fish. The pond is popular for ice skating and hockey in winter.

Sierra Nevada Children's Museum

1140 Donner Pass Road, Truckee; (530) 587-5437

Hours: April–November, Wednesday–Saturday 10 a.m.– 4 p.m.

Admission: $3, free for children under age 2

Appeal by Age Groups:

Pre-school	Grade School	Teens	Young Adults	Over 30	Seniors
★★★★	★★★★	★★	★	★	★

Touring Time: Average 2 hours; minimum 1 hour

Rainy-Day Touring: Yes

Services and Facilities:

Restaurants Next door

Alcoholic beverages Next door

Disabled access Yes

Wheelchair rental No

Baby stroller rental No

Lockers Cubbyholes

Pet kennels No

Rain check No

Private tours No

Description and Comments A modest example of its kind, but, for very little ones, a welcome respite from the macho world of skiing or waterskiing. A variety of educational hands-on exhibits are here, as well as some imaginative temporary special exhibits and arts and crafts projects.

Squaw Valley USA

1960 Squaw Valley Road, Squaw Valley; (800) 545-4350 or (530) 583-5585; www.squaw.com

Hours: Daily year-round

Admission: Varies by activity

Appeal by Age Groups:

Pre-school	Grade School	Teens	Young Adults	Over 30	Seniors
★★★	★★★★★	★★★★★	★★★★★	★★★★	★★★

Touring Time: Average 1 day; minimum 1½ hours

Rainy-Day Touring: Not great

Services and Facilities:

Restaurants Yes

Alcoholic beverages In some restaurants

Disabled access Yes

Wheelchair rental Yes

Baby stroller rental No

Lockers Yes

Pet kennels No; dogs on leash allowed in summer

Rain check No

Private tours No

Description and Comments   There's little to remind visitors of the 1960 Winter Olympics that were held here, but there's plenty to do year-round. Summer activities include an aerial tram ride to the High Camp Bath and Tennis Club, where you can swim, mountain bike, play tennis, and bungee jump—all at an altitude of 8,200 feet. In winter, don't miss the chance to ice skate in the beautiful outdoor Olympic Ice Pavilion (it's even open in summer). The Headwall Climbing Wall (adults $7 hour, children ages 12 and under $10 per hour; (530) 583-7673) is an indoor climbing wall at the cable-car building with both easy and difficult routes; harness and ropes are supplied, and climbing shoes can be rented. And, of course, there's the skiing, some of the best in the West, on groomed runs with spectacular views of the lake. Kids get their own ski area, Children's World, with a playground, ski school, day-care center, and complete facilities.

Tahoe Amusement Park

2401 Lake Tahoe Boulevard, South Lake Tahoe; (530) 541-1300

Hours: Off-season, daily 11 a.m.–6 p.m.; summer, daily 10 a.m.–10 p.m.

Admission: Varies by ride

Appeal by Age Groups:

Pre-school	Grade School	Teens	Young Adults	Over 30	Seniors
★★★★	★★★★	★★★	★	★	★

Touring Time: Average 2 hours; minimum 1 hour

Rainy-Day Touring: Very poor

Services and Facilities:

Restaurants Snack bar and picnic area	Baby stroller rental No	
Alcoholic beverages No	Lockers No	
Disabled access Yes	Pet kennels No	
Wheelchair rental No	Rain check Yes	
	Private tours No	

Description and Comments   It's just a small facility (11 rides), but the mini–Ferris wheel, slide, merry-go-round, electric golf, and miniature golf make for a nice afternoon. It's a reminder of how far a few small rides can carry vacationing kids.

Tallac Historic Site

Highway 89, 3.5 miles north of South Lake Tahoe, next to Camp Richardson; (530) 541-5227

Hours: Late May–early September, daily 10 a.m.–4 p.m.; closed Tuesdays

Admission: Free

Appeal by Age Groups:

Pre-school	Grade School	Teens	Young Adults	Over 30	Seniors
★★	★★★	★★★	★★★	★★★	★★★

Touring Time: Average 2 hours; minimum 45 minutes

Rainy-Day Touring: Yes, places to escape from rain

Services and Facilities:

Restaurants Adjacent

Alcoholic beverages At restaurant

Disabled access About 50% of buildings

Wheelchair rental No

Baby stroller rental No

Lockers No

Pet kennels No; pets allowed on leashes

Rain check No

Private tours Yes

Description and Comments   There are several mansion museums in the Tahoe area, but the most interesting with children is a three-building complex in South Lake Tahoe called Tallac Historic Site. It's accessible by paved bike paths from the town and is adjacent to white-sand beaches and a couple of easy hiking trails, so it makes for a nice destination for a bike ride or combination sight-seeing/swimming/hiking afternoon. The buildings are composed of a 1921 "log cabin" estate that is now a museum, with exhibits on Washoe Indians and the history of the estate owners; an 1894 mansion retreat still in the process of being restored; and a 1923 estate used for music and arts events, where you'll find several cabins turned over to crafts and arts exhibits and workshops for children.

Family-Friendly Restaurants

BEACON RESTAURANT

Richardson's Resort, 1900 Jameson Beach Road, South Lake Tahoe; (530) 541-0630

Meals served: Lunch, dinner, and weekend brunch

Cuisine: American

Entrée range: $6–25 (lunch and dinner)

Children's menu: Yes

Reservations: Recommended

Payment: MC, V, D

Sitting on the deck here, eye-level with that blue, blue lake, watching kids in their bathing suits pad barefoot and dripping up to the takeout window for a snow cone, made us want to be a kids again. Then again, watching the gang of 20-somethings laughing over margaritas made us want to be footloose and single again. But then, as we looked around our own table at the contented smiles as we scarfed down our just-fine summer-vacation food in a carefree, boat-and-beachy setting, we were, of course, happy to be who we are and where we were.

THE BRIDGE TENDER

30 N. Lake Boulevard, Tahoe City; (530) 583-3342

Meals served: Lunch and dinner
Cuisine: American
Entrée range: $4.95–7.95 (lunch and dinner)
Children's menu: No
Reservations: Not accepted
Payment: D, MC, V

A noisy, casual locals hangout in the heart of Tahoe City, the Bridge Tender is known for its delicious, messy burgers, its ribs, its onion rings, its mountain-folk bar scene, and its location right next to Fanny Bridge—so named for the dozens of fannies sticking up in the air on summer days as people lean over the bridge to see (and feed) the huge spawning trout. Older kids will like the food and scene at this place, and little ones will love tossing bread crumbs down to the fish.

ERNIE'S COFFEE SHOP

1146 Emerald Bay Road, South Lake Tahoe; (530) 541-2161

Meals served: Breakfast and lunch
Cuisine: American/coffee shop
Entrée range: $3.95–7 (breakfast and lunch)
Children's menu: Yes
Reservations: Not necessary
Payment: No credit cards

Just a place where neighbors gather to drink coffee and chew the fat before the day gets too far along. You and the kids will be comfortable here.

FIRE SIGN CAFE

1785 W. Lake Boulevard, Tahoe City; (530) 583-0871

Meals served: Breakfast and lunch
Cuisine: American

Entrée range: $5–6.95 (breakfast and lunch)
Children's menu: Yes
Reservations: Not taken
Payment: MC, V

A good stop between hikes, this modern coffee shop has a nice woodsy atmosphere and an outside deck for summertime. Choices include teriyaki steak, a turkey club sandwich, veggie baked potatoes, and awesome breakfasts, especially the buckwheat pancakes and lattes. The staff brings out a basket of toys and crayons for kids. Expect a wait on Sunday morning.

LAKEHOUSE PIZZA

120 Grove Street, Tahoe City; (530) 583-2222

Meals served: Breakfast, lunch, and dinner
Cuisine: American
Entrée range: $6–9 (lunch and dinner); pizzas $8–22
Children's menu: No
Reservations: Not taken
Payment: AE, MC, V

Only in Lake Tahoe can you find a modest pizza parlor with terrific outdoor deck dining right at the water's edge. Straightforward pizza, pastas, and Chinese chicken salads. Sometimes they'll give the kids some pizza dough to play with, which was a huge hit with the four-year-old at the next table the last time we were there.

MONUMENT PEAK RESTAURANT

Heavenly Ski Resort, Ski Run Boulevard, South Lake Tahoe; (530) 544-6263

Meals served: Lunch and dinner
Cuisine: Californian/American
Entrée range: $7.95–9.95 (lunch); $19.95–34.95 (dinner)
Children's menu: Yes
Reservations: Required for dinner
Payment: All major credit cards

Although the fun is in the getting here on the aerial tram, it's not a bad restaurant considering how far the staff has to come to cook. And you can't beat the view. It's a special-event-feeling place at dinner, when the steak and seafood dishes get pricey; for families with younger kids, it's best at lunch.

SQUEEZE INN

10060 Commercial Row, Truckee; (530) 587-9814

Meals served: Breakfast and lunch
Cuisine: American
Entrée range: $3–8.50 (breakfast and lunch)
Children's menu: No
Reservations: Not accepted
Payment: No credit cards

This old favorite is nice in the morning, when bright light streams through the stained glass. There are all sorts of hanging treasures to distract you while you choose one of 57 kinds of omelets, or opt for one of the interesting, tasty sandwiches. Lively atmosphere, lots of locals, and generally a wait for a table.

Part Six

San Francisco Bay Area

Simply put, we can't get enough of the Bay Area. We've both visited with our kids several times and still feel there's more to explore, as well as many favorites to revisit. The city of **San Francisco** appeals to every age group, though since it is intensely urban, it's easiest with the five-and-up set, who are old enough to walk the steep streets and jump on cable cars. Compact and easily navigable, it has something for every kid: great parks, museums (of science, art, even blue jeans), fun ferries, buses, subways, and cable cars, cool shops, street music, and so much more. Theme-park junkies can venture out to **Vallejo** to **Marine World Africa USA,** or south to **Paramount's Great America in Santa Clara.** East in **Berkeley** are the **University of California** and the wonderful **Charles Lee Tilden Regional Park;** north in **Marin** are redwoods, beaches, and charming small towns. Everywhere there is great food—many of the country's best restaurants live in the Bay Area, and some are even welcoming to children.

If you only have two or three days and your kids haven't experienced San Francisco, stick to the city and you won't be sorry. The city center is compact and easy to negotiate, so in just a few days you can easily hit the hot spots, from cable car and ferry rides to the **Exploratorium, Zeum,** and **Golden Gate Park.** If you have more time, you'll be able to add some wonderful adventures to the itinerary: kayaking **Tomales Bay in Marin,** for instance, or BARTing over to Berkeley, or even tackling one of the suburban theme parks.

GETTING THERE

By Plane. Most major airlines serve one or both of the region's airports: San Francisco International Airport, (650) 876-7809, a 20-minute drive south of downtown, and Oakland International Airport, (510) 577-4000,

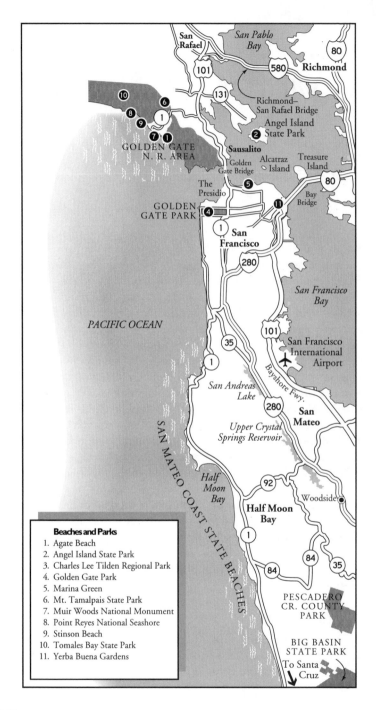

Beaches and Parks

1. Agate Beach
2. Angel Island State Park
3. Charles Lee Tilden Regional Park
4. Golden Gate Park
5. Marina Green
6. Mt. Tamalpais State Park
7. Muir Woods National Monument
8. Point Reyes National Seashore
9. Stinson Beach
10. Tomales Bay State Park
11. Yerba Buena Gardens

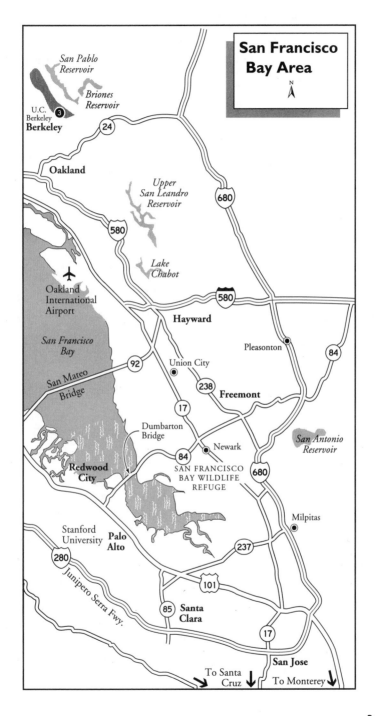

San Francisco
Bay Area

San Pablo
Reservoir

Briones
Reservoir

U.C.
Berkeley
Berkeley

Oakland

Upper
San Leandro
Reservoir

Lake
Chabot

Oakland
International
Airport

San Francisco
Bay

San Mateo
Bridge

Dumbarton
Bridge

**Redwood
City**

Stanford
University **Palo
Alto**

Junipero Serra Fwy.

Hayward

Pleasonton

Union City

Freemont

Newark

SAN FRANCISCO
BAY WILDLIFE
REFUGE

San Antonio
Reservoir

Milpitas

**Santa
Clara**

San Jose

To Santa
Cruz

To Monterey

24

680

580

580

92

238

17

84

680

237

280

101

85

17

84

3

which is more convenient for the East Bay and departures to Northern California. BART connects Oakland Airport to downtown San Francisco.

By Train. Amtrak delivers visitors from Southern California, the Pacific Northwest, and the Midwest. Call (800) USA-RAIL.

By Car. The major highways heading into San Francisco are Highway 101, which heads south to L.A. and north to the Oregon border, and Highway 80, which leads to Oakland, Sacramento, Lake Tahoe, and Nevada. Parking is a challenge in the city; expect to pay dearly for hotel parking.

How to Get Information before You Go

> *Berkeley Convention and Visitors Bureau, 2015 Center Street, Berkeley 94704; (510) 549-7040 or (800) 847-4823.*

> *Marin County Convention and Visitors Bureau, Avenue of the Flags, San Rafael 94093; (415) 499-5000; www.visitmarin.org/.*

> *San Francisco Convention and Visitors Bureau, P.O. Box 429097, San Francisco 94142-9097. Visitor Information Center, Lower Level, Hallidie Plaza, 900 Market Street; (415) 391-2000; www.sfvisitor.org.*

> *Sausalito Visitors Center, 780 Bay Street, Sausalito 94965; (415) 332-0505.*

Child Care/Baby-Sitting

American Childcare Services. 353 Sacramento Street, Suite 600; (415) 285-2300. Activity programs and in-room care.

Starr Belly Child Care Services. 3505 Sonoma Boulevard, #200, Vallejo; (707) 557-9268. Licensed, bonded, in-room child care throughout the greater Bay Area even up into the wine country.

The Best Beaches and Parks

Agate Beach. It's a bit of a challenge to reach this 6.6-acre beach park, found at the end of a 300-yard, sometimes steep gravel path that is neither stroller- nor wheelchair-friendly. The reward, however, is considerable: an excellent tidepooling beach teeming with sea life. (Remember, no collecting allowed.) Ranger tours are limited but certainly possible; call the County of Marin Parks Service to arrange one, (415) 499-6405. Highway 1 to Elm Road, Bolinas, (415) 499-6387.

Angel Island State Park. Between the congested urbanity of San Francisco and the pampered suburbanity of Tiburon lies this wonderfully unspoiled island, a terrific day or half-day trip for families. Once a Civil War garrison, then an immigration center ("Ellis Island of the West"), Angel Island is now devoted to hiking, mountain biking, kayaking, and beach fun. Ferries from San Francisco and Tiburon pull into Ayala Cove, where you can rent bikes or kayaks, take a tram tour, or pick up a hiking map. The paved, five-mile Perimeter Road is the favorite hiking/biking destination, thanks to its incredible bay/city views; some of the unpaved hiking trails may be too challenging for little kids. See also the Kayaking listing under Family Outdoor Adventures. Call (415) 435-1915 for information.

Charles Lee Tilden Regional Park. If you visit the Berkeley area by car (BART won't get you this far), set aside a few hours to explore this storybook-perfect park in the hills. Within the more than 2,000 acres are amusements for all ages, from the pony rides (call (510) 527-0421) and the petting farm in the Nature Area to the beach at Lake Anza and the many hiking trails. You'll also find an old hand-carved merry-go-round (call (510) 524-6773), a miniature steam train (call (510) 548-6100), playgrounds, and naturalist programs. Off Grizzly Peak Boulevard, Berkeley, (510) 525-2233. Open on weekends.

Golden Gate Park. One of the country's great urban parks, Golden Gate is 1,000 acres of family fun, worthy of a full day or more. Its various activities are sometimes driving-distance apart, separated by rolling acres of parkland. In Attractions, you'll find descriptions of its museums (the California Academy of Sciences and the M. H. De Young); in Family Outdoor Adventures, you'll find advice on biking, horseback riding, and skating the park. But that's just the beginning. Very young children will spend several happy hours at Stow Lake, (415) 752-0347, for example. We've circumnavigated the island of this tiny lake with a succession of three-year-olds in paddleboats who, at rental time's end, hop onto the shore, beg us to buy popcorn, and feed the ducks for another hour. There's also a children's playground with great slides and equipment accessible to those with disabilities; a 1912 carousel ($1) with a veritable Noah's ark of animals to ride (including frogs, cats, and zebras!); and fields and facilities for playing soccer, tennis, baseball, golf, or croquet. The Japanese tea garden is a lovely interlude for grandparents and grandchildren. It's open daily 9 a.m.–6:30 p.m.; tea and cookies are served in the tea house ($2 adults, $1 seniors and children). Of course, families picnic in the many meadows. There's a buffalo paddock, an arboretum, a Victorian glass conservatory, a windmill, and access to the beach. Pick up a map to the park at McLaren Lodge (Stanyan and Fell Streets) and consider taking the free guided walking tour conducted by park docents, (415) 263-0991. Bordered by Fulton, Stanyan, Lincoln, and Great Highway.

Muir Woods National Monument. One of the Bay Area's last uncut stands of old-growth redwoods lives in this small national forest. The largest trees—250 tall, 14 feet across, and 1,000 years old—are found in Bohemian Grove and Cathedral Grove, both of which are accessed via stroller-friendly, less-than-a-mile trails that head out from the main parking lot. In the spring, kids can try to spot baby salmon in Redwood Creek. Come early to avoid the afternoon crowds, and stop at the visitors center to pick up the free, very cool Junior Ranger pack, complete with bug box and activity guide. This is a forest of awe, mystery, and beauty, appreciated by everyone from toddlers to teens. Open daily; admission $2 for adults, free for children. Located on Highway 1 near Mill Valley, 12 miles north of the Golden Gate Bridge, (415) 388-2595.

Point Reyes National Seashore. Remote and gloriously wild, this national park preserves 65,000 acres of coastal property on the north end of Marin County. It is a paradise for bird-watchers—more than 45% of the bird species in North America have been sighted here—for hikers, and for lovers of romantically windswept, rocky, foggy beaches.

The beach hikes are fairly challenging, but for families with younger kids, there are several easy walks that begin at the Bear Valley Visitors Center (Bear Valley Road off Highway 1 near Olema, (415) 663-1092). Walk the quarter-mile trail to Kule Loklo, a replica of a Coast Miwok Indian village. Another short walk takes you across fern-filled gullies and scrambling over fallen logs to Morgan Horse Ranch, where you can watch cowboys train horses for the park rangers to use and walk through historic stables. School-age kids like the half-mile Earthquake Trail, which follows a fracture zone of the famed San Andreas Fault; an exhibit displays a seismograph and photos of the 1906 quake in San Francisco. Point Reyes Station, (415) 663-1092. For a longer but still easy hike, take the three-mile Bear Valley Trail.

Farther afield are more treasures, most notably Point Reyes Lighthouse, built in 1870 and found at the bottom of a 300-step walkway (warning for parents of whiny preschoolers) on Point Reyes Headlands (Sir Francis Drake Boulevard, (415) 669-1534). The visitors center has exhibits on whales and lighthouses, and from January to April the lighthouse is a superb place to look for the migrating gray whales. Elsewhere you'll find great beaches to comb (Drakes is a good one), but the water's too cold and rough for swimming.

Stinson Beach. A grand, sweeping beach some three and a half miles long, Stinson changes from a cold, rough, riptide-laden place in the winter and spring to a peaceful, delightful, small-surf beach in the summer. It's ideal for a family beach day in July and August, though the water is frosty by Southern California standards. The little town of Stinson Beach, with a couple of restaurants and shops, is just a half-block away. Picnic area, rest rooms, snack bar, outdoor (cold) showers, lifeguards (in summer). Highway 1 at Panoramic Highway, north of San Francisco, (415) 868-0942.

Tomales Bay State Park. The former home of the Miwok Indians, this is a beautiful retreat with lots for families. Its several beaches include Heart's Desire, a sheltered cove with wading lagoon, picnicking, and easy hiking trails through groves of pines. Kayaking is also popular here; see the Kayaking listing in Family Outdoor Adventures. Pierce Point Road, near Inverness, (415) 669-1140.

Yerba Buena Gardens. The construction dust has finally settled, and $56 million later, San Francisco has a swell new hub for children. Atop the roof of Moscone Center South, in between the Museum of Modern Art and the new temple of high-tech consumerism, the Metreon entertainment mall, Yerba Buena Gardens has something for every kid. There's a state-of-the-art ice-skating rink, a cheerful bowling alley, a hand-carved 1906 carousel, a fabulous hands-on, high-tech arts museum (Zeum), a hip urban playground bordered by a child-size botanical maze . . . and a Starbucks for Frapuccino-swilling 12-year-olds. For free fun, bring a picnic lunch to the open, grassy knolls in the center of the gardens, where kids can run behind the huge waterfall-fountain, then head over to the pit-style playground. Kids slide down giant tubes, bounce giant balls on the springy recycled-sneaker playground surface, and lose themselves in sand-and-water play. To learn more about Zeum, see its listing in Attractions; for details on the other admission-charging venues, see the Yerba Buena Gardens listing in Attractions.

Family Outdoor Adventures

Bicycling. At the north end of Golden Gate Park, you can rent bikes at Golden Gate Park Bike and Skate (3038 Fulton, at 6th, (415) 668-1117), then set off and explore the park's 1,017 acres, which are crisscrossed with paths; if you follow Kennedy Drive west, you'll hit the oceanfront bike path at Ocean Beach, which goes for three level miles. Stash a picnic in a backpack, and you've got a great family day. (Note that Kennedy is a functioning street, but it's closed to cars on Sundays.)

Also within the city limits is a wonderful adventure: riding across the Golden Gate Bridge. Pick up rental bikes and a route map at Blazing Saddles Bike Rentals (1095 Columbus Avenue, Fisherman's Wharf, or at Pier 41, (415) 202-8888), ride across the bridge, refuel with lunch in Sausalito, then catch the ferry back—there's a bike-return spot at the ferry terminal. Your kids need to be confident riders, because you share the road with cars.

If you have older children who are avid mountain bikers, you'll want to go to Mt. Tamalpais State Park (Panoramic Highway off Highway 1, Marin County, (415) 388-2070), where the mountain bike was invented in 1974 by a few broke gearheads. The trails, views, and thrills are first-rate. You can rent gear on the way there at Start to Finish Bicycles, 1820 4th Street, San Rafael, (415) 459-3990.

Fishing. Fishing can be a great family bonding activity, and the deep-sea fishing is good in the Bay, even better when the boats venture under the Golden Gate into the Pacific, in search of striped bass, salmon, and giant sturgeon. It's not cheap, though—a full day costs about $55, with kids charged roughly half-price. A number of companies run boats out of the Fisherman's Wharf area. For salmon fishing, reserve a trip with Wacky Jacky (473 Bella Vista Way, San Francisco, (415) 586-9800), whose boats are modern, fast, and cool.

Hill Walking. Looking for an outdoor family challenge offering exercise, adventure, and great views? Try climbing the urban mountains of San Francisco—in other words, stair climbing. What can be so tedious in a gym is a joy in this city, and kids feel a tremendous sense of accomplishment at cresting one of the famed peaks. Our favorites are the stairs up to Coit Tower on the edge of North Beach, off Greenwich Street, which pays off in an extraordinary view and a look at the evocative WPA murals inside the tower; the stairs up Vallejo Street in Russian Hill to Ina Coolbrith Park, a terraced city park with killer views and great hide-and-seek possibilities; and, of course, a climb up Lombard Street, the famous winding road.

Horseback Riding. Within the city, the only place to ride is at Golden Gate Park. The one-hour guided rides will give you your park bearings in the most enjoyable way imaginable. Children must be at least eight years old to ride, but younger kids aren't neglected—they get a pony ride. Call (415) 668-7360. To ride in the redwoods, head up to Sunset Corral in the Marin County town of Novato (2901 Vineyard Road, (415) 897-8212). This high-quality stable leads hourly, brunch, and sunset rides up into the oak- and redwood-covered Novato hills, following the ancient trails of the Miwok Indians. Children over age six are welcome on rides.

Kayaking. The hot outdoor activity of the moment is kayaking in Marin County's Tomales Bay, a spectacular coastal wilderness refuge. A full-service kayak company, Blue Waters Kayaking in Inverness (phone (415) 669-2600, web site www.bwkayak.com), can teach your family how to kayak, rent you the boats, or take you on a naturalist-led tour of the coves and sealife in the bay. The best bet for families (with kids ages eight and up) is the guided three-hour morning paddle on weekends ($49 per person), which pairs one adult with one child in each kayak; you'll paddle to hidden beaches and look for seals, bat rays, and birds. Over in Sausalito is Sea Trek (Schoonmaker Point Arena, (415) 488-1000), which will take you paddling to see a bird refuge, sea lions, and Angel Island; it also has a three-hour guided, kid-oriented paddling adventure ($50 adults, $40 children).

Skating. Two spots are perfect for family skating: Marina Green, the easy 1.5-mile waterfront park with great bay views (rent gear at Marina Skate and Snowboard, 2271 Chestnut Street at Scott Street, (415) 567-8400), and Golden Gate Park, especially on Sunday when the main street is closed (rent at Golden Gate Park Skates and Bikes, 3038 Fulton Street at 6th Avenue, (415) 668-1117).

Whale-Watching. Oceanic Society Expeditions heads out in search of the gray whale from Fort Mason Center in the Marina District (call (415) 441-1106; reservations required weeks in advance). The all-day outings are held on weekends and some Fridays in winter and spring; the cost is $50 for adults, $48 for children ages 10–15 (under age 10 aren't welcome); Friday trips are a bit cheaper. After the gray whale season, the tours become nature cruises to the Farallon Islands, in pursuit of humpback and blue whales and other marine life. These are rustic, nature-focused trips, and you'll need to bring your own food and drink. No handicapped access.

Calendar of Festivals and Events

January

Sea Lion Arrival, Pier 39, San Francisco. A celebration of the annual return of the sea lions to the bay for breeding; (415) 705-5500.

Chinese New Year Celebration, San Francisco. The city's largest festival, featuring a lavish parade from Market and 2nd to Columbus Avenue, with a festival and street fair in Chinatown; (415) 982-3000.

March

St. Patrick's Day Parade, San Francisco; (415) 661-2700.

April

Cherry Blossom Festival, Japantown and Japan Center, San Francisco. Japanese food, music, *taiko* drumming, martial arts, and more; (415) 563-2313.

Native American Strawberry Festival, Point Reyes National Seashore; (415) 663-1092.

San Francisco International Film Festival. Worthwhile for teens; (415) 931-FILM.

Berkeley Bay Festival, Berkeley Marina area. Held on a Saturday in late April or early May. Offers food, music, entertainment, boat tours, and free sailing; (510) 644-8623.

May

Cinco de Mayo Celebration, Mission District, San Francisco. Arts, crafts, food, music, and parade in the city's vibrant Latino community; (415) 826-1401.

San Francisco Youth Arts Festival, Golden Gate Park; (415) 759-2916.

Bay to Breakers Footrace, San Francisco. The world's largest footrace is also the most colorful—most of the 70,000-plus participants dress in costume; (415) 777-7770.

Berkeley Free Folk Festival, Berkeley. Acoustic folk festival in mid-May, including a children's concert and workshops; (510) 843-3810.

June

ZooFest for Kids, San Francisco Zoo. Festival, live entertainment, up-close encounters with animals; (415) 753-7165.

North Beach Festival, Grant and Green, San Francisco. The city's oldest street fair is refreshingly low-key and funky, with great food, live music, and good crafts; (415) 403-0666.

Street Performers Festival, Pier 39. Jugglers, magicians, unicyclists, slack-rope walkers, and more; (415) 705-5500.

Make a Circus, Golden Gate Park and other city parks. Mid-June to early August. Kids take part in circus workshops as well as watch professional circus performers; (415) 242-1414; www.makeacircus.org.

Stern Grove Midsummer Music Festival, Stern Grove, San Francisco. Free classical music performances by top artists in a lovely outdoor setting; (415) 252-6252.

July

San Francisco Chronicle Fourth of July Waterfront Festival, Fisherman's Wharf. Food, amusements, arts, and a fabulous fireworks show; (415) 777-7120.

San Francisco Cable Car Bell-Ringing Competition, Union Square. The much-esteemed cable car conductors put on a show; (415) 6SF-MUNI.

Books by the Bay, Ferry Building area, San Francisco. Books, author readings, music, children's activities; (415) 927-3937.

Marin County Fair and Exposition. A classic county fair; (415) 449-6400.

Berkeley Kite Festival, Chavez North Waterfront Park, Berkeley. Last weekend in July; (510) 235-5483.

September

Renaissance Pleasure Faire, Blackpoint Forest, San Francisco. An in-costume celebration of sixteenth-century England, with performers, theater, food, dance, music, and more; (800) 523-2473.

San Francisco Shakespeare Festival, Golden Gate Park. Free plays in the park; (415) 383-9378.

Farmers' Market Harvest Fair, San Rafael; (415) 456-FARM.

El Grito Celebration (call (415) 585-2043) and Festival de las Americas (call (415) 826-1401), Mission District, San Francisco. Celebrations of Mexican Independence Day and the Latin American Food Festival, with lots of great music, traditional dance, and food.

October

Italian Heritage Day Celebration, North Beach and Fisherman's Wharf, San Francisco. Parade, Queen Isabella coronation, and celebration of Italian culture and Columbus's discovery; (415) 434-1492.

The Cannery's Halloween Festival, San Francisco. For more than 20 years, kids have come to the Cannery for a costume contest, games, cookie decorating, and trick-or-treating in the shops; (415) 771-3112.

Indigenous People's Day, Berkeley. Held the Saturday closest to October 12. Berkeley's answer to the traditional Columbus Day parade, featuring a Pow Wow and Indian Market; (510) 525-3048.

November

Great San Francisco Snow Party, Pier 39. Learn-to-ski park and snow play for kids; (415) 705-5500.

December

Christmas at Sea, Hyde Street Pier, Fisherman's Wharf. Santa, caroling, storytelling, cookies, and more on the historic ship *Balclutha;* (415) 929-0202.

Telegraph Avenue Holiday Street Fair, Berkeley. A vibrant street market and festival held the two weekends before Christmas; (510) 287-9377.

San Francisco

Even though this polished, chic waterfront city was home of the original yuppie, it's still a wonderful place to visit with children, especially school-age kids, who can appreciate the big-city energy, not to mention hop on cable cars and safely hold on all by themselves. San Francisco doesn't have theme parks, but who needs 'em when the city itself is one big theme park? Rounding a corner on a cable car, driving down **Lombard Street,** cutting through the fog on a ferry boat, paddling a kayak around **Angel Island,** cycling over the **Golden Gate Bridge**—these are thrills that a kid remembers.

When Erin was seven years old (Colleen speaking), we went on a special one-on-one mother-daughter trip to San Francisco. We did the hokey tourist stuff I'd usually avoid, and we had a ball. Here were her highlights, and any child under the age of ten would adore the same things:

- An afternoon at the **Exploratorium,** the hands-down highlight of the trip, and a winner for any child, teenager, or adult.
- Riding up and down **Nob Hill** on a cable car, hanging off the side.
- Strolling past the sidewalk vendors at **Fisherman's Wharf,** and splurging on her most cherished memento, the $1.50 caricature of herself.
- Picking out a chocolate bar at **Ghirardelli.**
- Riding the ferry to **Tiburon,** then spending an hour climbing the waterfront rocks.
- Racing from toy to toy at **FAO Schwartz.**
- Studying with amazement the 1906 post-fire photos of the city at the **Cable Car Museum.**

Older kids and teens might find Fisherman's Wharf and Ghirardelli a bit predictable, but they'll love the video arcade at **Pier 39,** the spiffy shops of **Union Street,** the claymation studio at **Zeum**, the now-upscale tie-dye wares of **Haight-Ashbury,** and a roller-blading session along **Marina Green.** And since San Francisco has become a sort of sophisticated Disneyland for grown-ups, parents enjoy a family trip there as much as the kids. For starters, they're going to eat way, way better than in Anaheim.

WORDS OF WISDOM

Mark Twain's quip, "The coldest winter I ever spent was a summer in San Francisco," may be the most overquoted line in guidebook history, but it's for a very good reason: When a fog bank moves in, you'll be chilled to the bone, even if it's July. Be prepared with warm clothing. And note that San Franciscans are a dressy lot by laid-back California standards, so bring something nice to wear if you'll be eating in better restaurants or going out on the town.

If you're bringing a car into the city, be aware that parking is costly, and street spots are as rare as sunny days in June. If you do find a spot, and it's on a hill, make sure to curb the wheels, or you'll face a nasty ticket (and risk a smashed car).

GETTING THERE IS ALL THE FUN

Not only is San Francisco happily navigable without a car, but its various forms of public transportation—cable car, subway, ferries, taxis—are as fun for kids as the city's best amusements. Here are the basics on each:

Cable Cars. Part of the city's vast Muni service (San Francisco Municipal Railway), the cable cars are the city's Pied Pipers, an irresistible lure to children. They run on three routes in the heart of the city, connecting Market Street/Union Square to Fisherman's Wharf, and Union Square to Ghirardelli Square, and running from the downtown financial district near the Ferry Building over Nob Hill to Van Ness. In peak tourist times (which, thanks to conventions, is almost always), expect long lines at the end stations near Union Square and the wharf; we've had better luck catching a ride several blocks up the hill from either of these stops (the cars are sometimes not fully loaded to allow for passengers to get on at later stops). If the city's really crowded, avoid the Powell Line completely and climb up Nob Hill to catch the California Line, which is typically half-empty.

The best way to enjoy cable cars the old-fashioned way (as actual transportation) is to designate one day as cable-car day. Leave your hotel very early in the morning before breakfast the way my daughter Irene and I did recently (Susan speaking). The cars start running at 6:30 a.m., so there we were, virtually alone, stepping onto the Powell line car, buying an all-day pass from the conductor, transferring at the top of the hill, then riding

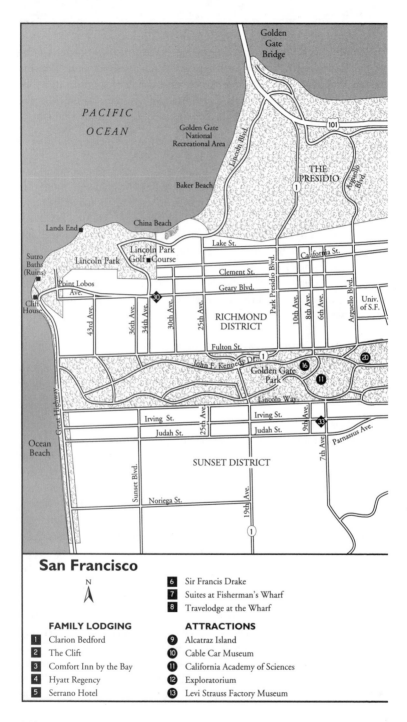

San Francisco

N

A

FAMILY LODGING

1 Clarion Bedford

2 The Clift

3 Comfort Inn by the Bay

4 Hyatt Regency

5 Serrano Hotel

6 Sir Francis Drake

7 Suites at Fisherman's Wharf

8 Travelodge at the Wharf

ATTRACTIONS

9 Alcatraz Island

10 Cable Car Museum

11 California Academy of Sciences

12 Exploratorium

13 Levi Strauss Factory Museum

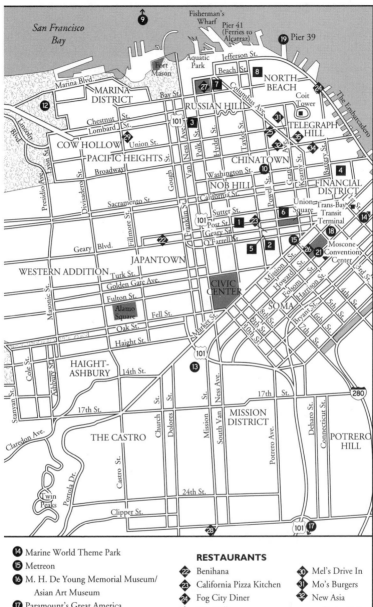

San Francisco Bay

Fisherman's Wharf

Pier 41 (Ferries to Alcatraz)

Pier 39

9

Aquatic Park

Jefferson St.

Beach St.

8

NORTH BEACH

27 **7**

Marina Blvd.

MARINA DISTRICT

Fort Mason

Bay St.

24

Coit Tower

The Embarcadero

12

Chestnut St.

Lombard St.

RUSSIAN HILL

101

3

31

TELEGRAPH HILL

35

COW HOLLOW

Union St.

Lincoln Blvd.

PACIFIC HEIGHTS

Broadway

CHINATOWN

32

34

Presidio Ave.

Divisadero St.

Sacramento St.

Washington St.

10

FINANCIAL DISTRICT

4

NOB HILL

California St.

Union Square

Trans-Bay Transit Terminal

14

Sutter St.

6

Fillmore St.

Geary Blvd.

Post St.

1 **23**

18

Geary St.

O'Farrell St.

22

JAPANTOWN

5 **2** **15**

26 **21**

Moscone Convention Center

WESTERN ADDITION

Turk St.

Golden Gate Ave.

Masonic St.

Fulton St.

CIVIC CENTER

Mission St.

Howard St.

Folsom St.

Harrison St.

SOMA

Alamo Square

Fell St.

Oak St.

Haight St.

HAIGHT-ASHBURY

14th St.

13

17th St.

280

Cole St.

Ashbury St.

Stanyan St.

Claredon Ave.

Church St.

Dolores St.

Mission St.

South Van Ness Ave.

MISSION DISTRICT

Potrero Ave.

Deharo St.

Connecticut St.

POTRERO HILL

THE CASTRO

Castro St.

Portola Dr.

Twin Peaks

24th St.

Clipper St.

28

101 **17**

14 Marine World Theme Park

15 Metreon

16 M. H. De Young Memorial Museum/ Asian Art Museum

17 Paramount's Great America

18 San Francisco Museum of Modern Art

19 Pier 39

20 San Francisco Zoo

21 Yerba Buena Gardens and Zeum

RESTAURANTS

22 Benihana

23 California Pizza Kitchen

24 Fog City Diner

25 Gira Polli

26 In the Night Kitchen

27 La Pasta

28 La Taqueria

29 Mel's Diner

30 Mel's Drive In

31 Mo's Burgers

32 New Asia Restaurant

33 PJ's Oyster Bed

34 Tommaso's Restaurant

35 Viva

along with the office workers down the steep and dramatic California line to the end. We hopped off, enjoyed breakfast, and then hopped on again and headed for Chinatown. We reboarded later in Chinatown and continued on to our next stop. Later we visited friends, but that same evening after dinner we arrived back downtown via BART and used our passes to board the once-again nearly vacant cable cars at the foot of Powell, riding back up the hill a few blocks to our hotel. At the end of the day we'd had a half-dozen cable car rides, hadn't waited in line for any of them, and had gotten where we were going, too. The fare is $2 (kids under age five free) for a one-way ride; Muni Passes (available throughout town) allow unlimited rides on the cable cars, trolleys, and light-rail buses for $6 a day or $10 for three days. For more information, call (415) 673-MUNI.

Ferries. The view of San Francisco from the water surrounding it is one of the most memorable sights in the world, and you can thrill to it (without having your kids even realize you're wasting time looking at scenery) by hopping onto one of the commuter ferries used to bring office workers from the suburbs into downtown's financial district. The fun for them, of course (and for adults, too), is in the boat ride, and nobody in your family will argue against a ferry to wherever and back—an hour on the bay, standing at the rail with the gulls sporting behind you and the wind in your face, will knock the airplane and hotel-room blahs right out of everyone's system.

From Pier 43½, within easy distance of a number of tourist attractions, is the disembarkation point for the Red-and-White Fleet, which will take you (famously) to Sausalito, but also to Tiburon, Muir Woods, and Angel Island, (415) 447-0597. But we've had a great trip on a high-speed commuter ferry, buying sodas at the snack bar and then heading out to the benches on deck to shiver with the sensation of passing under the majestic Bay Bridge on the way to Alameda, where the ferry docks at a decidedly less picturesque point than in Sausalito (an abandoned military base). We had fun because we found ourselves near the end of Market Street where Golden Gate Ferries leave from the Ferry Building, so we simply asked about the next ferry and got on for a round trip. We might just as easily have gone to Sausalito, where you can while away a few hours in shops and cafes, or to Larkspur, (415) 389-8899. Ask your hotel concierge to call for updated departure times to give yourselves an idea of the season's schedule (typically the commuter ferries run for a few hours in the morning and afternoon-evening, but not in the midday), then be ready to take a ride.

Trolleys. The newest addition to San Francisco's already-great public transportation system combines retro charm for parents, with novelty for kids. Running along the refurbished Embarcadero, ending at Fisherman's Wharf, the new F Line is made up of brightly colored trolley buses salvaged from several American cities, inluding LA's long-lamented Red Cars. Regular MUNI rates apply.

Subway. The Bay Area Rapid Transit (BART) system whisks riders under the bay from downtown San Francisco to Berkeley and Oakland. The trains are clean, quiet, and modern, and kids love the ride—not to mention the cool automated ticket dispensers and sucker-uppers at the high-tech stations. Fares are modest; children under age four ride free, and those ages 5–12 can get a huge discount from outside vendors, which are listed in brochures at every BART station. You can even board at one of the Market Street stops and go just one or two stops in either direction—it's more fun to ride an escalator underground and board a train than it is to drag a dead-tired toddler along the sidewalks of those long city blocks. For information on stations and maps, call (510) 464-6000.

Taxis. To children who live in the suburbs, nothing is more cosmopolitan than hopping in a cab and being whisked off someplace. My seven-year-old's first ride in a taxi was as thrilling as her first ride on Dumbo at age four. Stay away from the unlicensed gypsy cabs (generally black sedans), but otherwise feel safe in any of the city's licensed cabs. And the short distances within San Francisco mean that taxi rides are a real bargain, especially with three or four people; fares are typically in the $4–8 range. Cabs are easy to find at hotels and in downtown; otherwise, call or ask your restaurant host to order one. Our favorite companies are Luxor (415) 282-4141) and Veteran's (415) 552-3181).

SPENDING IT

Compact, stylish, and relentlessly prosperous, San Francisco draws shoppers from the entire West, including children. Here are our kids' favorite S.F. shops.

Borders Books and Music, 400 Post Street, Union Square, (415) 399-1633. A swell kids' area, along with magazines, an espresso bar, CDs, and more. Watch for story times.

FAO Schwartz, 48 Stockton Street, Union Square, (415) 394-8700. Overwhelming, noisy, and mobbed, this is three stories of toy nirvana, with plenty set out for testing and playing.

Ghirardelli Chocolate Manufactory, Ghirardelli Square, Northpoint and Larkin, (415) 775-5500. Chocolate bars, chocolate cable cars, chocolate coins—you get the picture. In the rear is a Willy Wonka fantasy: a picture window overlooking a giant vat of chocolate being stirred by mechanical paddles. Next door is an ice cream parlor that serves great hot fudge sundaes. Irresistible.

Niketown, 278 Post Street, Union Square, (415) 392-NIKE. There's something creepy about this futuristic, Big Brotherish shrine to athletic consumerism, but there isn't a preteen or teen out there who won't insist on a visit.

Puppets on the Pier, Pier 39, Fisherman's Wharf, (415) 781-4435. From finger puppets to marionettes, they're all here, often in performance out in the front of the shop.

Quantity Postcards, 1441 Grant Avenue, North Beach, (415) 986-8866. Our older kids are as enthralled with this collection of thousands of postcards as we are. The coolest browse in town, with cheap, quirky souvenirs.

Sanrio, 39 Stockton Street, Union Square, (415) 981-5568. Hello Kitty heaven or hell, depending on where you stand on the issue.

Tower Records, 2525 Jones Street, Fisherman's Wharf, (415) 885-0500. The very first Tower, and a good one, with everything a Walkman-eared kid could want.

Two Special Fountains

Two fountains in two well-traveled parts of San Francisco—Ghirardelli Square and Union Square—were a gift to children from San Francisco–based sculptor Ruth Asawa. One, at the grand Hyatt at Union Square (345 Stockton Street), is a drum-shaped fountain that straddles some steps and can be viewed from below (as you climb the steps), from the sides, and from above. You can touch it and get as close as you want, because the drum is covered with bronze relief panels cast from sculpted figures, as well as landscape features that were fashioned by Asawa and scores of kid and adult helpers out of a dough mixture called "baker's clay." (Asawa, mother of six children, first used the medium to keep small hands busy, then came to use it in her professional life.) The panoramic scenes are of San Francisco itself, with some fantasy folks (Raggedy Ann, Superman) thrown in. One could easily pass it by, but if you take a moment with kids after a day or two in the city, they'll see all the places they've visited, represented in whimsical, whirling relief: Golden Gate Bridge, Lombard Street, the Ferry Building, the parks, some schools and neighborhoods. Chinatown has a dragon; there are kite flyers and clowns, City Hall, trains, and taxis.

Over at Ghirardelli Square, toddlers and their parents spend happy times dipping fingers and toes into the Mermaid Fountain, a more traditional shape with a pool and some central figures—but especially fun for kids because some of the sculpted features, like frogs, extend out to the sides, where visitors sit and splash.

Family Lodging

Clarion Bedford

A good value a few blocks west of Union Square (on the fringe of seediness but not quite), this modest high-rise is extremely popular, so reserve early if you hope to get one of the parlor or family suites, most of which can comfortably house a group. Also request a higher-up room, which adds both views and quiet to the mix. Rooms have small refrigerators, baby-sitting can be arranged, and though the cafe doesn't have a children's menu, it has kid-friendly food, like little pizzas.

761 Post Street, Union Square; (415) 673-6040; fax (415) 563-6739. Rates start at $159; children under age 12 stay free with a parent.

The Clift

If you want to give your kids (or yourself) a taste of early San Francisco elegance, splurge on this grand old hotel located in the theater district, a short walk to Union Square. Despite the high ceilings, burnished woodwork, and chandeliers, children are warmly welcomed. Childproofed rooms are equipped with protected sockets and faucets, as well as kid-size tables and chairs, baby shampoo, kid-size robes, board games, and milk and cookies at turndown. Complete baby supplies are available, along with baby-sitting and children's menus. For a real thrill, take the kids for a ride in the complimentary limo. Grown-up amenities include a fitness center and one of the city's handsomest bars, the Redwood Room. Service is superb, and rooms are extremely comfortable.

495 Geary, near Union Square; (415) 775-4700 or (800) 652-5438; fax (415) 776-9238. Rates start at $255; children under age 18 stay free; packages and discounts often available.

Comfort Inn by the Bay

The value is good at this 135-room motel, located six blocks from Ghirardelli Square on busy Van Ness Avenue. Some rooms have bay views, a generous continental breakfast is free, and seasonal specials can bring the room rates as low as $70. Expect a clean, no-frills motel, and you won't be disappointed.

2775 Van Ness Avenue, near Fisherman's Wharf; (415) 928-5000 or (800) 228-5150; fax (415) 441-3990. Rates start at $129; children under age 12 stay free in parents' room; special discounts sometimes offered.

Hyatt Regency

This 17-story atrium hotel impresses kids with its gee-whiz slickness—they love the indoor glass elevators, the fountain, and the vastness of the lobby. The Embarcadero location affords good access to ferries, cable cars, shopping, and lots of restaurants. Rooms are generously sized, typically boasting coffeemakers and refrigerators; views are plentiful.

5 Embarcadero Center, Embarcadero; (415) 788-1234 or (800) 233-1234; fax (415) 398-2567. Rates $199–360; children under age 18 stay free in parents' room, or adjoining rooms available at half price; ask about special packages.

Serrano Hotel

The newest member of the stylish Kimpton Hotel family, this carefully renovated charmer boasts games as its theme, so our kids love it. The lobby has several seating areas built around chess, checkers, backgammon, and tic-tac-toe tables; rooms are equipped with playing cards, puzzles, and Nintendo; and a call to the front desk will have your room supplied with any of dozens of board games, from Twister to Trivial Pursuit. The rooms are lovely but small, so families might need a suite or adjoining rooms. The Serrano is located in the theater district, three blocks west of Union Square, and has all the upscale modern essentials: fitness room, in-room high-speed Internet access, free newspapers, morning Starbucks, evening wine tastings, and good sound-proofing.

405 Taylor Street, Union Square; (415) 885-2500 or (877) 294-9709; fax (415) 474-4879. Rates $125–369 for rooms, $399 for suites.

Sir Francis Drake

I have a sentimental attachment to this Union Square hotel (Colleen speaking)—my family stayed here on my first trip to San Francisco when I was ten years old, and my sister and I were enthralled with the doormen in Beefeater costumes, not to mention the cable cars right out front. The Beefeaters and cable cars are still captivating children, only now the rooms have been tastefully modernized, with rustic furniture and floral fabrics; the studio-style executive rooms have sleeper sofas and are a good family choice. Some rooms have refrigerators, there's free Nintendo on the TV, and the touristy but perfectly fine Cal-Italian restaurant has a kids' menu. Let the concierge book you a baby-sitter, and head upstairs for a memorable grown-up night at Harry Denton's Starlight Room on the roof, a Sinatraesque 1950s throwback that's one of the city's most happening nightclubs.

450 Powell Street, Union Square; (415) 392-7755 or (800) 227-5480; fax (415) 395-8599. Rates start at $165; packages and free upgrades often available.

Suites at Fisherman's Wharf

An excellent base for families who want to be near the wharf, this 24-room all-suite hotel was thoroughly renovated in 1997. Each unit is about 550 square feet, containing a bedroom with queen bed, a living room with queen sleeper sofa, and a full compact kitchen complete with dishwasher and cookware. It's located two blocks up from the wharf, right on the cable-car line, which means the front-facing view rooms can get noisy; if you want quiet, pick a viewless room in back. Rates include an adequate continental breakfast and wine, tea, and cookies in the afternoon.

2655 Hyde, Fisherman's Wharf; (415) 771-0200 or (800) 227-3608; fax (415) 346-8058. Rates start at $279; children under age 11 stay free, over age 11 $10 charge.

Travelodge at the Wharf

The only bayfront hotel on Fisherman's Wharf, this Travelodge is a family favorite for three reasons: its outdoor heated pool, protected from the wind by the courtyard; its location, an easy walk to lots of attractions; and its partnership with the 1950s diner Johnny Rockets, which connects to the pool area, so kids can have shakes and fries poolside. Prices are moderate given the location; rooms are motel-basic but well maintained. There are three family suites with pull-out sofas.

250 Beach; (415) 392-6700 or (800) 333-3333; fax (415) 986-7853. Rates $145–225; kids under age 18 free with parent.

Attractions

Alcatraz Island

Blue and Gold Fleet

Pier 41, Fisherman's Wharf; (415) 705-5555

Hours: Tours leave daily at 30-minute intervals, 9:30 a.m.–4:15 p.m.; the Evenings on Alcatraz tours leave Thursday–Sunday 4:15 p.m. and 5:10 p.m., later departure times in summer

Admission: $12.25 adults with recorded tour, $8.75 without; $10.50 for seniors age 62+ with recording, $7 without; $7 ages 5–11 with recording, $5.50 without; Evenings on Alcatraz are $19.75 ages 18–61, $17 age 62+ and ages 12–17, $10.50 ages 5–11

Appeal by Age Groups:

Pre-school	Grade School	Teens	Young Adults	Over 30	Seniors
★	★★★	★★★★★	★★★★★	★★★★	★★★★

Touring Time: Average 2 hours; minimum 2 hours

Rainy-Day Touring: Tours run unless the captain feels it's dangerous

Services and Facilities:

Restaurants Snack bars on boats only	Baby stroller rental No
	Lockers No
Alcoholic beverages No	Pet kennels No
Disabled access Yes	Rain check Yes
Wheelchair rental No, but ask about SEAT	Private tours No

Description and Comments   Definitely too eerie for preschoolers, Alcatraz is significant and memorable for teenagers. This fabled maximum-security prison, isolated as it is on an island with the city so tantalizingly visible, is both a powerful reality and a striking metaphor. Its thoughtful adaptation as an "attraction" has made it an important historic site. The bleak corridors, now thronged with tourists, are nevertheless strangely quiet as visitors, each with his or her audio tour set, listen to the tales of individual prisoners trying to escape, hear the sounds of the occupied prison re-created, and stand before the unimaginably small and dark isolation cells. Don't go without the audio tour—the dimension of sound is what brings the ghosts back to these sad halls.

Cable Car Museum

1201 Mason Street, Nob Hill; (415) 474-1887

Hours: Winter, 10 a.m.–5 p.m.; April–September, 10 a.m.–6 p.m.

Admission: Free; donations welcome

Appeal by Age Groups:

Pre-school	Grade School	Teens	Young Adults	Over 30	Seniors
★★★	★★★★	★★★	★★	★★★	★★★

Touring Time: Average 1 hour; minimum 30 minutes

Rainy-Day Touring: Yes

Services and Facilities:

Restaurants No	Lockers No
Alcoholic beverages No	Pet kennels No
Disabled access Limited	Rain check No
Wheelchair rental No	Private tours No
Baby stroller rental No	

Description and Comments   School-age kids are fascinated by the cable car, not just because it is open-air but because it is propelled by some mysterious force that requires a strong man to yank on big metal handles. A fairly brief visit to this extremely noisy museum will dispel the mystery in a most enjoyable way. The functioning hub of the cable-car system, this 1907 red brick building sits atop the vast pulley/cable system that hauls the cars up Nob Hill, and enough of that system is visible to make it understandable to kids. What my daughter found even more fascinating than the cables and the prototype cars, however, were the ancient 25-cent photo-viewfinders that show before and after pictures from the great 1906 quake and fire—she was astounded by the devastation and amazed at how the city rebuilt itself.

California Academy of Sciences

Music Concourse, Golden Gate Park; (415) 750-7145

Hours: Summer (Memorial Day–Labor Day), 9 a.m.–6 p.m.; winter, 10 a.m.–5 p.m. daily

Admission: $8.50 adults, $5.50 seniors, students, and youths ages 12–17, $2 children ages 4–11, free for children under age 4

Appeal by Age Groups:

Pre-school	Grade School	Teens	Young Adults	Over 30	Seniors
★★★	★★★★★	★★★★	★★★★	★★★★	★★★★★

Touring Time: Average 2 hours in each; minimum 1 hour in each

Rainy-Day Touring: Yes

Services and Facilities:

Restaurants Yes	Lockers No
Alcoholic beverages Yes	Pet kennels No
Disabled access Yes	Rain check No
Wheelchair rental Yes, free	Private tours Docent tours
Baby stroller rental No	

Description and Comments "Earth, Ocean, Space, All in One Place" is the motto of this extraordinary museum triplex in the heart of Golden Gate Park, and indeed it delivers the universe. Under one umbrella operation, there are really three separate museums—the Steinhart Aquarium, the Morrison Planetarium, and the Natural History Museum—and each is worth a trip.

The Natural History Museum is one of the world's largest, and the exhibits are unusually creative. Young kids get to touch shark jaws and dinosaur bones, try on ethnic costumes, and dig through boxes of shells in the Discovery Room; elementary-school kids get to survive an earthquake in the SafeQuake Ride; and everyone gets to immerse themselves in California's natural world via Wild California.

The wild ocean world is showcased in the aquarium, which can be entered with an admission ticket to the Natural History Museum. If you can't get down to the biggie in Monterey, you should spend a couple of hours checking out the plentiful sea life here. Highlights include the Touch

Tidepool, where kids can hold a sea star or anemone; the living tropical reef, home to sharks and dazzlingly colorful fish; the somber alligators; and the huge fish roundabout.

Through the Natural History Museum is Morrison Planetarium, a cool spot for 10–18-year-olds, where the stargazing is awesome and the Laserium light show is loud and dazzling (but inappropriate for little ones).

For a sneak peak in advance, have your web-savvy kids check out www.calacademy.org.

Exploratorium

Palace of Fine Arts, 3601 Lyon Street; (415) 563-7337; www.exploratorium.com

Hours: Memorial Day–Labor Day, Tuesday–Sunday 10 a.m.–6 p.m. (Wednesday to 9 p.m.); in winter, Tuesday–Sunday 10 a.m.–5 p.m. (Wednesday to 9 p.m.)

Admission: $9 adults, $7 seniors and students, $5 children ages 6–17 and people with disabilities, $2.50 ages 3–5, free for children under age 3

Appeal by Age Groups:

Pre-school	Grade School	Teens	Young Adults	Over 30	Seniors
★★★★	★★★★★	★★★★★	★★★★★	★★★★★	★★★★★

Touring Time: Average 4 hours; minimum 2 hours

Rainy-Day Touring: Fine

Services and Facilities:

Restaurants	Yes	Lockers	Yes
Alcoholic beverages	No	Pet kennels	No
Disabled access	Yes	Rain check	No
Wheelchair rental	Yes, free	Private tours	No
Baby stroller rental	No		

Description and Comments Even childless adults find themselves drawn back to the Exploratorium, so seductive are its science-geek charms. More than 500 hands-on exhibits fill a sprawling warehouse-style space within the grand Palace of Fine Arts on the west end of the Marina district; there's so much to experience that you may want to visit twice to do the place justice. Kids and grown-ups get to feel, touch, see, and wonder, in the Distortion Room, the Shadow Box, the two-way mirrors, the interactive video discs, the computer finger painting, the optical illusions—it goes on and on. Kids over age seven (and their parents) who aren't claustrophobic or skittish can brave the Tactile Dome, where you squeeze through in total darkness, experiencing only touch sensations. Each "exhibit" is really an activity: a machine, a device, or a Rube Goldberg concoction designed to illustrate a scientific principle. These principles range from the swimming habits of fish to optical illusions to the physics of tornadoes.

On our first visit, the first floor alone (which begins with biology-related exhibits) exhausted us, so we had to return to discover the ultra-cool area upstairs, with its sight- and sound-perception exhibits. From this mezzanine area, we looked down on the work area where the exhibits are created and were amused and entertained to watch graduate-student types hard at work on these most appreciated of science projects.

Scattered throughout the vast space are guides (mostly college students) who love to explain the gizmos to the kids, so don't be shy to flag them down. The grounds alone—rolling lawns, meandering pond, ducks, gorgeous trees—are worth a visit, so pack a picnic lunch to enjoy before or after your exploration.

Levi Strauss Factory Museum

250 Valencia, San Francisco; (415) 565-9159

Hours: Guided tours only, Tuesday–Wednesday at 9 a.m., 11 a.m., 1:30 p.m.

Admission: Free; reservations required

Appeal by Age Groups:

Pre-school	Grade School	Teens	Young Adults	Over 30	Seniors
★	★★	★★★★	★★★	★★	★★

Touring Time: Average 1½ hours; minimum 1-hour guided tour

Rainy-Day Touring: Yes

Services and Facilities:

Restaurants No	Lockers No
Alcoholic beverages No	Pet kennels No
Disabled access Limited	Rain check No
Wheelchair rental No	Private tours No
Baby stroller rental No	

Description and Comments A teenager without jeans is as inconceivable as a baby without diapers. That's what makes this museum an essential stop for older kids (but dull for four-year-olds). At this first Levi's factory, they'll learn about the social history of blue jeans from their invention in the nineteenth century to today. A cool video showcases the highlights in blue-jean history, and the factory shop sells way hip reproductions of vintage jeans and denim jackets. This free museum and the factory store are accessible by guided tours only, just two days a week, and reservations are required.

Metreon

4th & Mission, south of Market; (415) 369-6000; www.metreon.com

Hours: Daily 10 a.m.–10 p.m.; hours vary for some attractions

Admission: $6 per person; for The Way Things Work, $4 per person; for movie theaters, ticket prices vary; Attraction Access $20 per person (uses a point system to allow event-entrance and use of games in the Airtight Garage); unlimited gaming for $10 Sunday, Tuesday, and Thursday.

Appeal by Age Groups:

Pre-school	Grade School	Teens	Young Adults	Over 30	Seniors
★★★★	★★★★	★★★★★	★★★★★	★★★★	★★★

Note: Pre-school appeal-rating is for Where the Wild Things Are only

Touring Time: Average 3 hours, including shopping but excluding movies; minimum 1 hour

Rainy-Day Touring: Excellent

Services and Facilities:

Restaurants Yes	Lockers No
Alcoholic beverages Yes	Pet kennels No
Disabled access Yes	Rain check No
Wheelchair rental Yes	Private tours No
Baby stroller rental Yes	

Description and Comments If you recoil at shameless consumerism, steer clear of this gleaming new high-tech mall—it's guaranteed that your kids will adore it and will immediately beg mercilessly for piles of $20 bills to spend on playing, watching, eating, and buying. On the edge of Yerba Buena Gardens, this Sony-owned complex is part state-of-the-art movie house (with both stadium-style theaters and IMAX); part theme park (with attractions based on books, *Where the Wild Things Are, The Way Things Work,* and *The Airtight Garage);* part unbelievably cool video arcade; and part shopping mall (anchored by the Sony Style and Playstation stores and augmented by a huge Discovery Channel store, a Starbucks kiosk, and several restaurants).

What you do will depend on the ages of your children and your willingness to part with money. Toddlers up through about age eight (although our ten-year-old loved it) should be taken straight to Where the Wild Things Are. The bad news is that you have to walk through the gift shop and restaurant to get there, which will send four-year-olds into an "I want, I want" attack. The good news is that it's worth the trouble and cost. The children start in Max's room at night and are then turned loose into a self-directed exploration of Maurice Sendak's land of the Wild Things. Seven-year-old Emily adored the hidey-holes, the goblin-basher mallet game, the huge monsters that move when a child stands in just the right spots, the rope swings, giant featherweight blocks, and interactive sound effects.

Even though they'll be itching to get at the video games, elementary-school-age kids should be lured into The Way Things Work, a fascinating 3-D film-and-exhibit experience that celebrates inventions and inventors. Again, there's a themed shop to negotiate; it's hard to resist toys like Chinese yo-yos and make-your-own clocks.

Older kids won't rest till they get inside the Airtight Garage. Inspired by Jean "Moebius" Giraud's graphic novel of the same name, this is like no video arcade you've ever seen (and it's more expensive than any video arcade, too). It's built around three games Moebius designed for Metreon. Our favorite is Hyperbowl, a virtual bowling alley in which you bowl through the streets of San Francisco or ancient Rome; game-crazy teens will go for Quaternia, a complex capture-the-flag game that can be played by up to 31 people at once at the numerous stations. The best value is on Sunday, Monday, Tuesday, and Thursday evenings, when unlimited gaming is $10; otherwise a game-lover could blow through plenty more. There is, of course, a Moebius shop as well, aimed at teens, along with several other cutting-edge video games.

M. H. De Young Memorial Museum/Asian Art Museum

Golden Gate Park, in Central Concourse by 8th Avenue; (415) 750-3600

Hours: Tuesday–Sunday 9:30 a.m.–5:30 p.m.; open until 8:45 p.m. on first Wednesday of each month

Admission: $7 ages 18–64, $5 age 65+, $4 ages 12–17, free for children ages 11 and under; first Wednesday of each month is free all day

Appeal by Age Groups:

Pre-school	Grade School	Teens	Young Adults	Over 30	Seniors
★★	★★★	★★★	★★★★	★★★★	★★★★

Touring Time: Average 1 hour; minimum 1 hour

Rainy-Day Touring: Yes

Services and Facilities:

Restaurants Yes	Lockers No
Alcoholic beverages Yes	Pet kennels No
Disabled access Yes	Rain check No
Wheelchair rental No	Private tours Yes
Baby stroller rental No	

Description and Comments A classic big-city art museum, this is actually two in one: the De Young houses primarily American art, while the Asian, of course, showcases work from about 40 Asian countries. Most kids handle art museums in small doses, growing numb after an hour or so, and that's certainly true here, where the collection is vast. They'll probably respond best to the American classics—works by James Whistler, John Singer Sargent, Mary Cassatt, and Grant Wood—and the more fanciful Asian sculptures and ceramics.

San Francisco Museum of Modern Art

151 Third Street at Mission; (415) 357-4000

Hours: Friday–Tuesday, 11 a.m.–6 p.m.; Thursday 11 a.m.–8:45 p.m.; closed major holidays and Wednesdays

Admission: $9 adults, $6 seniors, $5 students, free for children ages 11 and under; first Tuesday of each month free

Appeal by Age Groups:

Pre-school	Grade School	Teens	Young Adults	Over 30	Seniors
★★	★★★	★★★	★★★	★★★	★★★

Touring Time: Average 3 hours; minimum 1½ hours

Rainy-Day Touring: Yes

Services and Facilities:

Restaurants Yes	Lockers No
Alcoholic beverages Yes	Pet kennels No
Disabled access Yes	Rain check No
Wheelchair rental Yes, free	Private tours Free docent-led
Baby stroller rental No	

Description and Comments   This heavily patronized museum is in a beautifully designed (by Mario Botta) building, nice and compact, so museum fatigue never gets a chance to set in. My 11-year-old daughter had learned about Frida Kahlo and Jackson Pollock in school and so was pleased to find their works represented here. The small permanent collection of twentieth-century masters is a mini-tour of modern art, and the changing exhibits often include photography, which can be highly accessible to kids in a museum setting. A very low-key interactive area of four computers with headsets attached allowed us to click on a painting we'd seen to learn more—and the five-minute "Making Sense of Modern Art" explained what parents couldn't in an hour.

Pier 39

Beach Street and the Embarcadero; (415) 981-PIER; pier39.com

Hours: Open daily; hours vary by activity, shop, or restaurant

Admission: Free overall, but rides charge fees

Appeal by Age Groups:

Pre-school	Grade School	Teens	Young Adults	Over 30	Seniors
★★	★★★	★★★★	★★	★	★★

Touring Time: Average 3 hours; minimum 1 hour

Rainy-Day Touring: Yes, for inside activities

Services and Facilities:

Restaurants Yes	Lockers No
Alcoholic beverages In restaurants	Pet kennels No; leashed pets
Disabled access Yes	allowed on pier
Wheelchair rental No	Rain check No
Baby stroller rental No	Private tours No

Description and Comments This is really a kitschy, crowded mall, not an attraction, but it's a mighty seductive mall for kids, and it borders on being a theme park. It can be an expensive place if you fall prey to the rides and shops, but one of its greatest charms is free: the thriving sea lion community at the end of the 1,000-foot K pier, which fascinates toddlers and teens alike. On weekends, docents offer free programs about the sea lion, (415) 705-5500. The view is also free, and it's a doozy, taking in everything from Coit Tower to the Golden Gate Bridge.

After you've enjoyed the simple pleasures, the kids will be on you to start spending. A good start is the intense, surround-screen movie, *The Great San Francisco Adventure* (shown at the Citibank Cinemax Theater, (415) 956-3456; admission is $7.50 adults, $6 seniors age 55+, and $4.50 for children ages 6–12), which tells the history of San Francisco in 30 minutes. The free earthquake exhibit at the theater entrance is also well worth a look.

Next, head for Underwater World (phone (415) 623-5300; admission $12.95 adults, $6.50 ages 3–11, $9.95 seniors, family rate $29.95 for 2 adults and 2 children), where you walk through 300 feet of acrylic tunnels through a huge aquarium, surrounded by thousands of Bay Area fish. The Blue and Gold Fleet also runs its bay tours from Pier 39, (415) 705-5444.

Older kids will want a turn on TurboRide (phone (415) 392-8872; admission $8 adults, $5 seniors and children), a simulated high-tech, special-effects roller coaster that gives a pretty impressive thrill but is too scary for many young children. While the big kids are on TurboRide, you can take littler ones to the low-key, double-decker carousel.

Other kid fun includes a large, well-maintained video arcade, cookie vendors, and lots of shops (Cartoon Junction, Wound About, The Marine Mammal Store, Magnetz Max, and the Warner Bros. Studio Store are big hits). If you have teens who need time away from parents, Pier 39 is a great self-contained place to drop them for a few hours.

San Francisco Zoo

1 Zoo Road, 45th Avenue at Sloat Boulevard, Golden Gate Park; (415) 753-7080

Hours: Daily 10 a.m.–5 p.m.

Admission: Non–San Francisco residents pay $9 adults, $6 seniors 65+ and kids ages 12–17, $3 ages 3–11, free for children age 2 and under; San Francisco residents pay $7 adults, $3.50 youths and seniors, $1.50 ages 3–11; first Wednesday of each month free admission

Appeal by Age Groups:

Pre-school	Grade School	Teens	Young Adults	Over 30	Seniors
★★★★★	★★★★	★★★	★★★	★★★	★★★

Touring Time: Average 3 hours; minimum 1½ hours

Rainy-Day Touring: Limited

Services and Facilities:

Restaurants Yes	Lockers No
Alcoholic beverages Yes	Pet kennels Yes
Disabled access Limited	Rain check No
Wheelchair rental Yes	Private tours No
Baby stroller rental Yes	

Description and Comments After years of gradual improvements, this old zoo has become a pretty wonderful place to spend an afternoon, and it's a must-visit for families with children under age seven or so, thanks to the exceptional Children's Zoo. Located right near the entrance, and charging an extra buck, it goes far beyond the typical mangy petting area. There's the Barnyard, with plenty of animals to pet, but also a chick hatchery, a nature trail, a deer park, families of mice, and an enthralling indoor Insect Zoo. Just outside its entrance is a good playground and carousel ($1 a ride). Young kids could spend an hour or two here and happily skip the larger zoo. But that's not to say it deserves skipping—there's plenty to see, in improved, more naturalistic settings. Our two favorites are the huge Gorilla World and the Primate Discovery Center, home to many species of rare and endangered monkeys. Our kids also loved seeing the penguins get their dinner, usually about 3 p.m. every day.

Yerba Buena Gardens

Rooftop of Moscone Center South, between Mission, 3rd, Folsom, and 4th Streets; general information, (415) 541-0312; skating or bowling, (415) 777-3727

Hours: Gardens open 24 hours daily; hours vary for attractions

Admission: Free to gardens and playground; carousel ride, $1; skating center $6 adults, $4.50 children; bowling fees vary

Appeal by Age Groups:

Pre-school	Grade School	Teens	Young Adults	Over 30	Seniors
★★★★	★★★★	★★★★	★★★	★★★	★★★

Touring Time: Average 1½ hours; minimum 30 minutes

Rainy-Day Touring: Yes for indoor attractions, no for park

Services and Facilities:

Restaurants Yes	Lockers No
Alcoholic beverages No	Pet kennels No
Disabled access Yes	Rain check No
Wheelchair rental No	Private tours No
Baby stroller rental No	

Description and Comments   Spread over the vast squatness of the Moscone Center, this new rooftop children's center has something for every kid, from sand play for toddlers to the ultra-cool Zeum for tech-crazy teens. For a description of the park, see page 353 under Best Beaches and Parks at the beginning of this chapter; for details on Zeum, see its listing under Attractions on page 378.

Aside from the park space and Zeum, Yerba Buena Gardens has several kid-pleasing opportunities. First is the ornate, hand-carved, 1906 carousel, which is unfortunately housed in a glass structure; protection from the elements gives it more operating days and helps its preservation. Inside or out, it's a fine carousel that's well worth a ride; next to it is a food cart serving hot dogs and snacks.

Past Zeum, over near the playground, are the other two indoor amusements: the Ice Skating Center and the Bowling Center. Both are brand-spanking-new and state-of-the-art; the huge window in the skating rink offers a great view of downtown San Francisco, so you almost feel like you're skating outside, and the bowling alley is spotless and cheerful, unlike most urban bowling alleys, which tend toward the grim.

An entire day could easily be passed here. Gather for a picnic in the park, then send older kids into Zeum to make a video or do an art project, while you sip a latté (yes, there's a Starbucks) and watch the little ones ride the carousel and play in the playground, before treating the whole gang to a session of skating or bowling. You could end the day by walking next door to the Metreon to catch a movie and have dinner.

Zeum

Yerba Buena Gardens, 221 4th Street, South of Market, (415) 777-2800; www.zeum.org

Hours: During school year, Saturday and Sunday, school vacations, and Monday holidays 11 a.m.–5 p.m., and specified weekday afternoons for special workshops; summer, Wednesday–Friday noon–6 p.m., Saturday and Sunday 11 a.m.–5 p.m.

Admission: $7 adults, $6 students, $5 children ages 5–18; free for members

Appeal by Age Groups:

Preschool	Grade School	Teens	Young Adults	Over 30	Seniors
★	★★★★★	★★★★★	★★★★	★★★	★★★

Touring Time: Average 3 hours; minimum 2 hours

Rainy-Day Touring: Yes, excellent

Services and Facilities:

Restaurants No		Lockers No	
Alcoholic beverages No		Pet kennels No	
Disabled access No		Rain check No	
Wheelchair rental No		Private tours No	
Baby stroller rental No			

Description and Comments   If there was ever a place that will make you wish to be 12 years old again, Zeum is it. A nonprofit, wildly creative, hands-on art and technology center, this is more a big-kid arts play place than a museum. In the Animators Studio, kids sketch characters of their own making, storyboard a story, then bring it to life in a claymation film. They get to do every step of the process (with help from plenty of staff members if needed). It was a dream come true for my ten-year-old, Erin, who could have spent days here. In the Learning Lab, kids try digital photography and digital animation, and if that's not fun enough, they can design their own web pages. In the Production Lab, kids work together (bring friends!) to make a multimedia video—they're the actors, directors, special-effects technicians, sound-effects technicians, and camera operators. In the Main Gallery, artists-in-residence help kids do everything from build architectural models to publish their own books.

Zeum is heaven for kids from about the second or third grade through high school, but it's boring for younger ones, who won't have the patience or physical skills to tackle these projects. And be forewarned that this is not a quick-drop-in place—come prepared to spend the afternoon, so your children have time to become fully absorbed. Last time we were here, the city was mobbed, but Zeum was half-empty, with plenty of staff members and easy access to the labs and studios.

Family-Friendly Restaurants

BENIHANA

1737 Post Street, Union Square; (415) 563-4844

Meals served: Lunch and dinner
Cuisine: Japanese
Entree range: $15–44.75
Children's menu: Yes, $6.95–7.95
Reservations: Recommended
Payment: All major cards

Sure, it's touristy and gimmicky, but it's great fun for kids, and the mainstream Japanese food is fine and not threatening to picky eaters. You sit around a grill while a showman chef cooks your meal, tossing knives around, cutting food in mid-air, flipping shrimp, and making jokes. It's so entertaining that they're more likely to try some new, scary food.

CALIFORNIA PIZZA KITCHEN

438 Geary Boulevard, Union Square; (415) 563-8911

Meals served: Lunch and dinner
Cuisine: Californian
Entree range: $4.99–6.99 (lunch); $7.99–12.99 (dinner)
Children's menu: Yes, $3.50
Reservations: Not accepted
Payment: AE, DC, MC, V

Despite San Francisco's immense popularity as a family vacation spot, it's hard to find a good parent-child restaurant in Union Square. This import from L.A. is your best bet, and it's sure to make you all happy. Kids get a coloring menu, crayons, cups with lids, and tasty little pizzas and pastas; parents get chic designer pizzas and pastas (try the shrimp-pesto pizza), fresh salads, and wine by the glass.

FOG CITY DINER

1300 Battery Street, Financial District; (415) 982-2000

Meals served: Lunch and dinner
Cuisine: Modern American
Entree range: $10–15 (lunch); $15–25 (dinner)
Children's menu: No

Reservations: Recommended
Payment: All major credit cards

A great place for parents to get a taste of modern American cooking, San Francisco–style, in a lively setting that's kid-friendly. Located on the North Beach/Battery waterfront (but lacking a view), Fog City is a cross between a train-car diner and old San Francisco bar and grill, with roomy booths, an open kitchen, and lots of hustle and bustle. Prices are modest, given the hipness of the place, and food is delicious: crab cakes, skinny fries, chicken on a biscuit with Virginia ham and morels, Cobb salad sandwich, outstanding meat loaf, grilled-cheese sandwiches, homey desserts. We go in the 3–5 p.m. range to avoid the constant crowds.

GIRA POLLI

659 Union Street, North Beach; (415) 434-4472

Meals served: Dinner
Cuisine: Italian
Entree range: $9.95–14.65 (dinner)
Children's menu: No
Reservations: Advised
Payment: AE, MC, V

The Italian take on the roast chicken craze, serving wonderful wood-fired roast chicken with Italian herbs, along with Sicilian potatoes, Swiss chard, carrots, and rolls. The roast lamb and pastas are tasty as well.

IN THE NIGHT KITCHEN

Metreon, 4th & Mission, south of Market; (415) 369-6080

Meals served: Lunch and dinner
Cuisine: American
Entree range: $6–9
Children's menu: Yes, $2.50–5
Reservations: Not accepted
Payment: All major credit cards

In between the Where the Wild Things Are gift shop and Where the Wild Things Are play place is this Sendak-themed diner, a bright, noisy, open place in which no one will bat an eye if your three-year-old dumps ketchup on the floor. The cafe touts its often-organic ingredients, although we'd hardly call this health food, given the number of people eating burgers and fries. Still, the food is fresher and tastier than the usual kid fare, and the menu goes well beyond chicken fingers: noodle soup, fresh fruit with yogurt dip, make-your-own PB & J's, decorate-your-own cupcakes, and for grown-ups, a tasty turkey-avocado club or albacore tuna salad. A good spot before or after a Metreon or IMAX movie or an outing to adjacent Yerba Buena Gardens.

LA PASTA

Ghirardelli Square, 900 North Point Street, Fisherman's Wharf; (415) 749-5288

Meals served: Lunch and dinner
Cuisine: Italian
Entree range: $9–13 (lunch); $13–17 (dinner)
Children's menu: Yes
Reservations: Accepted
Payment: All major credit cards

This strategically located restaurant is a when-worlds-collide sort of place—it has a fairly sophisticated Italian seafood menu (cioppino, mussels, etc.) alongside a children's menu (chicken fingers, bland pasta). The staff consults with adults about wines and plays with kids, offering markers for the paper-covered tables. It begins serving dinner quite early, which is when we arrived for our last visit; we were joined by a man offering his girlfriend and her two kids a special birthday dinner, a large tourist family ("Yes!" said the little girl, "By the window, woo-hoo!"), and other families. There's a great view of the piers and bay.

LA TAQUERIA

2889 Mission Street, Mission District; (415) 285-7117

Meals served: Lunch and dinner
Cuisine: Mexican
Entree range: $1.60–4.50 (lunch and dinner)
Children's menu: No
Reservations: Not accepted
Payment: No credit cards

The largely Latino Mission District, south of downtown's Market Street, is blessed with many fine taco joints, and this is one of the finest. Timid eaters will be pleased with a cheese quesadilla and a fresh strawberry liquado (shake); braver kids will adore the huge burritos and savory soft tacos filled with pollo (chicken), carnitas (pork), or carne asada (grilled beef).

MEL'S DINER

2165 Lombard Street, Marina; (415) 921-3039

Meals served: Breakfast, lunch, and dinner
Cuisine: American
Entree range: $4–7 (lunch); $7–12 (dinner)
Children's menu: Yes
Reservations: Not accepted
Payment: No credit cards (ATM inside)

A copy of the parent restaurant near Golden Gate Park, this Mel's is well located for a lively diner meal after a visit to the Exploratorium or a skate along the Marina Green.

MEL'S DRIVE IN

3355 Geary Boulevard, near Golden Gate Park; (415) 921-3039

Meals served: Breakfast, lunch, and dinner
Cuisine: American
Entree range: $4–7 (lunch); $7–12 (dinner)
Children's menu: Yes
Reservations: Not accepted
Payment: No credit cards

This is the original Mel's, lionized in *American Graffiti* and beloved by many a San Francisco kid. Oldies blare, waitresses talk smart, and milk shakes are thick and good. Our kids adore the kids' menu, the crayons, the music, the floats, and the grilled-cheese sandwiches served in a toy Corvette.

MO'S BURGERS

1322 Grant Street, North Beach; (415) 788-3779

Meals served: Breakfast, lunch, and dinner; no dinner Saturday–Sunday
Cuisine: American
Entree range: $3.25–6.50 (breakfast); $5–9 (lunch); $7.50–12.50 (dinner)
Children's menu: Yes
Reservations: Not accepted
Payment: V, MC

This is likely the best burger in San Francisco, a town that takes the burger pretty seriously. A simple, friendly spot not far from the Wharf, serving fresh, perfectly cooked burgers.

NEW ASIA RESTAURANT

772 Pacific Avenue, Chinatown; (415) 391-6666

Meals served: Breakfast, lunch, and dinner
Cuisine: Chinese
Entree range: $1.80–3.20 (per dim sum order)
Children's menu: No
Reservations: Not accepted
Payment: AE, MC, V

The best family-oriented restaurant in Chinatown, New Asia makes a mean dumpling for breakfast or lunch and fine Chinese seafood dishes for dinner. If your kids have never experienced dim sum, when waitresses wheel around carts laden with dumplings, noodles, meats, and strange sweets, bring them here. They'll recoil in horror at the chicken feet, but they'll love the fluffy white bao buns stuffed with pork, and the savory little sui mai. At dinnertime, kids are always happy with a big plate of Chinese noodles or fried rice. Come early to beat the lunchtime line.

PJ'S OYSTER BED

737 Irving Street, Richmond District; (415) 566-7775

Meals served: Lunch and dinner
Cuisine: Seafood
Entree range: $7–11 (lunch); $20–25 (dinner)
Children's menu: Yes
Reservations: Accepted
Payment: AE, DC, MC, V

For great San Francisco–style seafood and a casual, noisy, child-friendly setting, skip the Fisherman's Wharf tourist traps and stop here instead. It's ideally located for a lunch or dinner before or after a day in nearby Golden Gate Park. The clam chowder will ward off the worst fog attack, and the gumbo, oysters, and all-you-can-eat crawfish will make parents happy. The kids' menu includes fried shrimp, a change from the usual chicken fingers.

TOMMASO'S RESTAURANT

1042 Kearny, North Beach; (415) 398-9696

Meals served: Dinner
Cuisine: Italian

Entree range: $9–20
Children's menu: No
Reservations: Not accepted
Payment: AE, DC, MC, V

Almost a cliche of what an old North Beach pizza joint should look like, Tommaso's is the real thing, from its rickety white wooden table nooks, to its old brick pizza oven, to its chipped walls hung with photos of the restaurant's patron saint, Francis Ford Coppola. En route here, you may have to distract the kids' attention from the nearby triple-X theater, but once inside, you'll be rewarded with superb, inexpensive food that's a far cry from Domino's. Calzones are hearty and cheesy, thin-crust pizzas are saucy and delicious, and vegetables hail from local organic farms (if they have a fresh tomato-mozzarella salad on special, get it).

VIVA

1224 Grant Avenue, North Beach; (415) 989-8482

Meals served: Lunch and dinner
Cuisine: Italian
Entree range: $8–13 (lunch and dinner)
Children's menu: No
Reservations: For large parties only
Payment: All major credit cards

When our taxi hit a traffic snarl at this dense intersection, we despaired of being able to withstand hunger pains any longer. So we hopped out and stepped into the first bright Italian restaurant we saw. We felt sure Viva would be a cynical establishment, since it is located right on the main drag and seems to cater to tourists who, like us, can't walk another step but don't know where they are. Instead, we were joined by large family parties of San Franciscans, who ordered plate after plate of pasta and pizzas for the table. We were thrilled with an appetizer "spread feast" of tapenade, eggplant, sun-dried tomatoes, and artichoke spreads, followed by rich pastas.

Side Trips

ATTRACTIONS

Paramount's Great America

2401 Agnew Road (Great America Parkway exit off 101), Santa Clara; (408) 988-1776

Hours: 10 a.m.–various closing times depending on month. Closed November–February; open Saturday–Sunday only in March–May and September–October; open daily end of May–end of August

Admission: $36.99, $26.99 seniors and disabled guests, $19.99 ages 3–6, free for children ages 2 and under

Appeal by Age Groups:

Pre- school	Grade School	Teens	Young Adults	Over 30	Seniors
★★★★	★★★★★	★★★★★	★★★★	★★★★	★★★

Touring Time: Average 6–8 hours; minimum 4 hours

Rainy-Day Touring: Rides still function, and the lines are shorter

Services and Facilities:

Restaurants Yes	Lockers Yes
Alcoholic beverages Yes	Pet kennels No
Disabled access Yes	Rain check No
Wheelchair rental Yes	Private tours No
Baby stroller rental Yes	

Description and Comments An amusement park taken to the highest level, Great America has an American-heritage theme, with six zones devoted to different epochs in our history. But the themes are merely window dressing—this place is really about thrills. Some of its rides are so intense they leave parents a quivering mess, but 12–19-year-olds can't get enough—like the Drop Zone, the world's tallest free-fall ride, and Top Gun, where you'll experience a zero-gravity barrel roll and 360° vertical loop, among other psychological and physiological challenges. Those seeking slightly less terrifying thrills have lots more to choose from, including the IMAX theater shows (which can be too intense for little ones), a few fun water-rapids rides (expect to get wet), and the famed Grizzly, Northern California's largest wooden roller coaster.

Although ultimately this place is really best for kids ages ten and up, young ones are hardly neglected. They get their own area, Forest of Fun (part of Carousel Plaza), with a double-decker carousel, a mini–roller coaster, several other younger-kid rides, and wandering Hanna-Barbera characters, like Scooby Doo; the live music and ice shows are good for all ages as well. And our second-grader went wild for Nickelodeon's Splat City, where she got slimed.

Don't expect cool San Francisco weather here—it's an entirely different climate, demanding plenty of sunscreen, drinking water, and hats in summertime. If you don't want to succumb to the pricey, junky food in the park, make use of the pleasant picnic area outside the front gates.

Marine World Theme Park

2001 Marine World Parkway (off I-80), Vallejo; (707) 644-4000

Hours: Spring and fall 10 a.m.–8 p.m., summer 10 a.m.–10 p.m.; closed November–late March

Admission: $35.99 adults, $26.99 seniors 60+, $17.99 less than 48" tall

Appeal by Age Groups:

Pre-school	Grade School	Teens	Young Adults	Over 30	Seniors
★★★★	★★★★	★★★★	★★★★	★★★★	★★★★

Touring Time: Average 6 hours; minimum 3–4 hours

Rainy-Day Touring: Yes, but you'll get wet

Services and Facilities:

Restaurants Yes	Lockers Yes
Alcoholic beverages Yes	Pet kennels No
Disabled access Yes	Rain check No
Wheelchair rental Yes	Private tours No
Baby stroller rental Yes	

Description and Comments   Formerly known as Marine World Africa USA, this animal-oriented theme park has recently spiffed itself up, renovating existing shows and adding new ones; the new name is more streamlined, emphasizing the more dominant marine-life side of the park. Animal shows are the park's strong suit, each running 20 minutes or so, and many get quite crowded. As at Sea World, the killer whale and dolphin shows are lots of fun (and wet—if you sit in front, you'll get splashed). Traveling on the moving ramp through the Shark Experience, where sharks swim around you on three sides, is a very cool experience, and the sea lion show is charming.

Out of water, you'll find lots of animals from around the world in different park zones, from kangaroos to camels, and the experiences are interactive whenever possible, whether it's riding an elephant or feeding a giraffe. (Butterfly World is particularly enchanting for young ones.) In the process, kids learn quite a bit about animals, their habitats, their diets, and their fragility in a people-dominated world.

When your six-year-old has had enough of sitting through shows and needs to blow off steam, he'll have fun in the Gentle Jungle play area, or in the Whale of a Time World, where a life-size blue whale makes for a great play structure.

Its lack of scary rides and interactive nature makes this a very appealing theme-park day for families with different ages to please—a four-year-old and a 14-year-old will both be happy.

Note that for families staying in San Francisco, you can reach Marine World via the Blue and Gold Ferry, with a combination ticket that includes both the scenic one-hour ferry ride and park admission.

Berkeley

Nationally known as the home of U.C. Berkeley and one of the seminal birthplaces of the hippie movement, Berkeley is a dynamic little city that is particularly wonderful for teenagers. The campus is inspirational to wander, and the still-funky downtown is colorful and great fun to shop, thick with coffeehouses, bookstores, theaters, handmade jewelry, and street musicians. Most 16-year-olds could spend a week here and not be bored. Kids of all ages will like the cool, hands-on **Lawrence Hall of Science** on campus, as well as the sprawling **Charles Lee Tilden Park** on the outskirts of town (see Best Beaches and Parks, page 351). This college town is found east of San Francisco across the bay and can be easily reached on a BART subway or by car across the Bay Bridge; taxi rides are costly.

Family Lodging

Claremont Resort and Spa

This grand Victorian rambler in the Berkeley hills (on the Oakland border) is the place for society locals to have weddings and parties, and now that it's been polished to a sheen in a recent renovation, it's a pretty good family retreat as well. While children are not exactly catered to—there's neither a children's program nor Nintendo on the TV—there are two beautiful pools, children's tennis lessons, baby-sitter referrals, and lots of grounds to run around; new management is considering playing up the family angle, so ask if kid-oriented programs have been added when you call.

41 Tunnel Road, Oakland; (510) 843-3000 or (800) 551-7266; fax (510) 843-6239. Rates start at $204–875 for a high-end suite.

Gramma's Rose Garden Inn

As sweet a place as its name suggests, this longtime favorite of visiting professors occupies two old mansions in the middle of the good shopping/

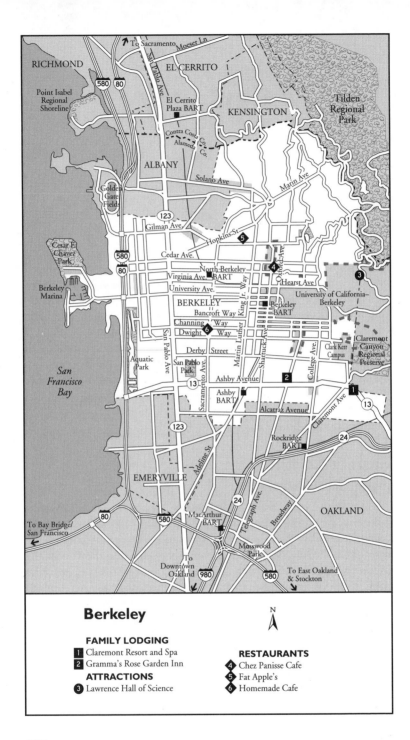

Berkeley

N

FAMILY LODGING
1 Claremont Resort and Spa
2 Gramma's Rose Garden Inn

ATTRACTIONS
3 Lawrence Hall of Science

RESTAURANTS
4 Chez Panisse Cafe
5 Fat Apple's
6 Homemade Cafe

walking area near the U.C. campus. It has the charms of a bed-and-breakfast (fireplaces, quirky rooms, evening wine and cheese), but unlike at most bed-and-breakfasts, families are welcome—some rooms are big enough for several, and they'll bring in a futon for $10 more. There's a lawn to play on outside, and kids can opt for cookies and milk instead of wine and cheese.

2740 Telegraph Avenue, Berkeley; (510) 549-2145; fax (510) 549-1085. Rates $99–165.

Attraction

Lawrence Hall of Science

Centennial Drive below Grizzly Peak Boulevard, U.C. Berkeley; (510) 642-5133

Hours: Daily 10 a.m.–5 p.m.

Admission: $6 adults, $4 students and seniors, $2 ages 3–6

Appeal by Age Groups:

Pre-school	Grade School	Teens	Young Adults	Over 30	Seniors
★★★	★★★★	★★★★	★★★	★★★	★★★

Touring Time: Average 3 hours; minimum 2 hours

Rainy-Day Touring: Yes

Services and Facilities:

Restaurants	Yes	Lockers	No
Alcoholic beverages	No	Pet kennels	No
Disabled access	Yes	Rain check	No
Wheelchair rental	No	Private tours	No
Baby stroller rental	No		

Description and Comments A smaller version of San Francisco's Exploratorium, this university science museum encourages kids to touch and experience, starting with the 60-foot-long DNA model outside, which doubles as a climbing structure. A particular favorite of our kids is the Biology Discovery Lab, which on weekends and summer days allows them to examine frogs, pet snakes, and hold a tarantula. Elsewhere they can play math puzzle games, try to get magnets through a maze, look through telescopes, create their own laser-light show, and get inside the human brain. Prepare for some serious begging for a souvenir from the exceptional gift shop, stocked with gee-whiz toys, science experiments, puzzles, books, and all sorts of fun and educational kids' stuff.

Family-Friendly Restaurants

CHEZ PANISSE CAFE

1517 Shattuck Avenue, Berkeley; (510) 548-5049

Meals served: Lunch and dinner
Cuisine: Modern American
Entree range: $12–18 (lunch); $15–25 (dinner)
Children's menu: Yes, during the week only
Reservations: Not accepted
Payment: All major credit cards

If your kids are the least bit interested in food—or if you are—bring them to the casual cafe above Alice Waters's more serious restaurant, the birthplace of California cuisine. It's lively, friendly to kids (they even get crayons), and moderately priced, considering the exceptional quality of the food. (The midweek children's menu gives three courses for $8.) Thanks to Waters's slavish devotion to farm-fresh produce (most grown just for this restaurant), even the simplest cheese pizza sings with flavor. Great salads, sophisticated pizzas, grilled fish, and homey desserts. To beat the crowds, we like to come for a very early lunch.

FAT APPLE'S

1346 Martin Luther King Boulevard, Berkeley; (510) 526-2260

Meals served: Breakfast, lunch, and dinner
Cuisine: American
Entree range: $5–9 (lunch); $10–15 (dinner)
Children's menu: No
Reservations: Not accepted
Payment: MC, V

Fans drive across the Bay Bridge to sit in this plain coffee shop and eat some terrific diner cooking: oatmeal-apple pancakes, homemade soups, dreamy cheese puffs, perfect burgers, fresh berry pies. There's no need to have a kid's menu when you have a grown-up menu that speaks so profoundly to kids.

HOMEMADE CAFE

2454 Dwight Way, Berkeley; (510) 845-1940

Meals served: Breakfast (available all day) and lunch
Cuisine: American
Entree range: $5–8 (breakfast and lunch)
Children's menu: No
Reservations: Not accepted
Payment: No credit cards

Breakfast nirvana, known for its pancakes, French toast, and egg scrambles. As is usually the case at great breakfast cafes, however, there's always a crowd, so be prepared to wait. Lunch runs to clever, tasty sandwiches.

Marin County

With its redwood forests, creeks, rolling hills, and proximity to San Francisco just across the **Golden Gate Bridge,** it's no surprise that Marin County is home to some of the priciest real estate in the nation. Fortunately, you don't have to take on a million-dollar mortgage to enjoy its spectacular parks, beaches, and atmospheric small towns. Under the Best Beaches and Parks and Family Outdoor Adventures sections starting on page 350, you'll find details on Marin's great outdoors, from **Muir Woods** walks to **Tomales Bay** kayaking to **Mt. Tam** mountain biking. En route to these adventures, you'll find spiffy towns worth a stop, stroll, and nosh, especially **Mill Valley, Larkspur, Olema,** and **San Rafael.** From San Francisco, you can reach two of the county's most popular and charming towns, **Sausalito** and **Tiburon,** by ferry; both are fun to explore.

Family Lodging

Manka's Inverness Lodge

Ideally located in a forest at the edge of Point Reyes National Seashore, this former hunting and fishing lodge pretty much defines Northern California funky. It's eclectic, eccentric, and utterly charming, a hodgepodge of lodge rooms, motel rooms, a cabin, even an odd old house called the Chicken Ranch. The whole place is ruled by Louie, a lumbering golden lab who's kind to children. A few of the accommodations can house a family—like the one-bedroom, $185 cabin with a king bed and a queen sleeper sofa—and the good restaurant will make special orders or half portions for kids.

30 Callendar Way, Inverness; (415) 669-1034 or (800) 585-6343. Rates start at $135.

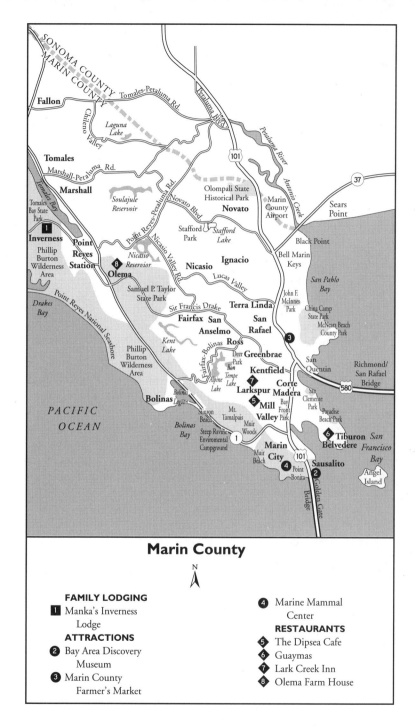

Marin County

N

FAMILY LODGING

1 Manka's Inverness Lodge

ATTRACTIONS

2 Bay Area Discovery Museum

3 Marin County Farmer's Market

4 Marine Mammal Center

RESTAURANTS

5 The Dipsea Cafe

6 Guaymas

7 Lark Creek Inn

8 Olema Farm House

Attractions

Bay Area Discovery Museum

Fort Baker, 557 McReynolds Road, Sausalito; (415) 487-4398

Hours: Tuesday–Thursday 9 a.m.–4 p.m., Friday–Sunday 10 a.m.–5 p.m.

Admission: $7 adults, $6 children over age 1

Appeal by Age Groups:

Pre-school	Grade School	Teens	Young Adults	Over 30	Seniors
★★★★	★★★★	★★★	★★	★★	★★

Touring Time: Average 2 hours; minimum 1 hour

Rainy-Day Touring: Yes

Services and Facilities:

Restaurants	Lunch cafe	Lockers	No
Alcoholic beverages	No	Pet kennels	No
Disabled access	Yes	Rain check	No
Wheelchair rental	No	Private tours	No
Baby stroller rental	No		

Description and Comments Tucked under the Marin side of the Golden Gate Bridge, this is one of the better children's museums in California, especially for kids under age 11. It's hands-on, interactive, and fun, emphasizing the bayside location instead of generic kid stuff. Kids love the Underwater Sea Tunnel, which lets them crawl "under" the bay, and the full-size Discovery Boat, where they can be fishermen. Other cool exhibits include the Maze of Illusions and computer lab. There's a separate, equally fun play area for toddlers, a decent cafe, and a cool gift shop. There's even a carousel for kids who insist on a theme-park ride.

If you don't have a car, you can reach the museum from the Sausalito ferry terminal via a shuttle, which runs daily 11 a.m.–5:30 p.m. and costs $2 round-trip.

Marin County Farmer's Market

3501 Civic Center Drive, San Rafael; (415) 456-FARM

Hours: Thursday and Sunday 8 a.m.–1 p.m.; some summer evenings

Admission: Free

Appeal by Age Groups:

Pre-school	Grade School	Teens	Young Adults	Over 30	Seniors
★★★★	★★★★	★★★★	★★★★	★★★★	★★★★

Touring Time: Average 1 hour; minimum 30 minutes

Rainy-Day Touring: Yes, but you'll get wet

Services and Facilities:

Restaurants In town	Lockers No
Alcoholic beverages In town	Pet kennels No
Disabled access Yes	Rain check No
Wheelchair rental No	Private tours No
Baby stroller rental No	

Description and Comments One of the nation's best farmers' markets is held every Thursday and Sunday morning at the Marin County Civic Center, and it's worth a detour. The center alone is worth a look, as one of the last and most significant of Frank Lloyd Wright's buildings. And the market is as much fun for kids as for food-loving baby boomers. There's usually a balloon artist and storyteller, a man on roller skates selling eggs, street musicians, and a small-town party atmosphere. Along with superb organic produce, you can buy boutique cheeses, condiments, oils, and fresh breads and graze on tamales, pancakes, and sausage sandwiches. In summer, the market is sometimes held in the evening; call for details.

Marine Mammal Center

Marin Headlands, near Sausalito; (415) 289-7325

Hours: Daily 10 a.m.– 4 p.m.; closed Thanksgiving, Christmas, and New Year's Day

Admission: Free

Appeal by Age Groups:

Pre-school	Grade School	Teens	Young Adults	Over 30	Seniors
★★	★★★	★★★	★★★	★★★	★★★

Touring Time: Average 1½ hours; minimum 45 minutes

Rainy-Day Touring: Yes

Services and Facilities:

Restaurants No	Lockers No
Alcoholic beverages No	Pet kennels No
Disabled access Yes	Rain check No
Wheelchair rental No	Private tours No, docents avail-
Baby stroller rental No	able on weekends

Description and Comments Part of the Golden Gate National Recreation Area, this nonprofit group rescues, rehabilitates, and releases ocean mammals that have been injured or orphaned or that become ill. It's one of the largest wild-animal hospitals in the world, and it welcomes animal-loving children, who can observe the volunteers and vets tending to the sea lions, dolphins, seals, and otters. Exhibits teach kids about the mammals and about marine ecology and conservation.

Family-Friendly Restaurants

See also Marin County Farmer's Market under Attractions, page 394

THE DIPSEA CAFE

200 Shoreline Highway, Mill Valley; (415) 381-0298

Meals served: Breakfast and lunch
Cuisine: American
Entree range: $5–8 (breakfast and lunch)
Children's menu: Yes
Reservations: Not accepted
Payment: AE, DC, MC, V

A fantasy family restaurant done up like a nineteenth-century farmhouse, Dipsea is idyllically located creekside, and picture windows bring in views of the footbridge and ducks outside. This is a fine spot to fuel up for a hike along one of the terrific, not-too-challenging local trails. Although the cooking can suffer from a slapdash approach, it's generally quite satisfying: pancakes, eggs, biscuits, and smoothies for breakfast, and burgers, Caesar salad, grilled ahi salads for lunch.

GUAYMAS

5 Main Street, Tiburon; (415) 435-6300

Meals served: Lunch and dinner
Cuisine: Mexican
Entree range: $11–19
Children's menu: No
Reservations: Accepted
Payment: AE, DC, MC, V

If the sun is shining, take advantage of it and treat the kids to a 30-minute ferry ride to the impossibly bucolic town of Tiburon (the ferry passes right by Alcatraz, which is a thrill). This slick waterfront restaurant, just a few steps from the ferry landing, is most notable for its huge patio with a fabulous view of the bay and San Francisco. The yuppie-ized Mexican food is perfectly fine, especially when accompanied by a margarita and the dreamy view. There's no kids' menu, but the kitchen is happy to make plain quesadillas. If you score the right patio table, you can let the kids scramble over adjacent waterfront rocks while you linger a while and watch them from your seat.

LARK CREEK INN

234 Magnolia Avenue, Larkspur; (415) 924-7766

Meals served: Lunch, dinner, and Sunday brunch
Cuisine: Modern American
Entree range: $8.50–14.50 (brunch); $9–15 (lunch); $14–25 (dinner)
Children's menu: Yes
Reservations: Essential
Payment: AE, DC, MC, V

A very special special-occasion restaurant, Lark Creek is a wonderful place to experience California cuisine. Located in a turn-of-the-century mansion at the edge of a redwood canyon a short drive north of the Golden Gate Bridge, this is one of the best restaurants in the Bay Area, with or without kids. Unlike at the region's other top restaurants, however, children are warmly welcomed and catered to with their own menu (field-green salads, great chicken fingers, pasta). The kitchen takes American classics — crab Cobb salad, grilled quail salad, oak-roasted chicken — to lofty levels, and the desserts alone (butterscotch pudding, devil's food cake with espresso ice cream) are worth the trip. In summer, request a garden table outside.

OLEMA FARM HOUSE

10005 Highway 1, Olema; (415) 663-1264

Meals served: Lunch and dinner; breakfast on weekends only
Cuisine: American
Entree range: $4.75–8 (breakfast and lunch); $8–16 (dinner)
Children's menu: No
Reservations: Advised
Payment: AE, MC, V, D

Both convenient and charming, this is a good place to eat before or after a day at Point Reyes, thanks to its location near the lighthouse, beaches, and visitors center. On your way into the 1856 farmhouse building, take a peek at the cowhide-upholstered saloon — it will wow any cowboy-loving kid. In the boarding house–style dining room, people put away large portions of clam chowder, oyster stew, barbecued oysters, and prime rib, as well as hearty, good-quality breakfasts. There's no children's menu, but kids will have no trouble finding something good (without slimy oysters) to eat.

Part Seven

Gold Country

California's Gold Country might sound to the uninitiated like a vaguely educational collection of musty historic sites. And indeed, parents intent on reading every paragraph of every historic marker could probably bore their kids in this region. But the rest of us can have a grand, old-fashioned time in the villages and towns along Highway 49, panning for gold, riding horses, exploring caves, scrambling around ruins, walking Native American trails, and even white-water rafting.

Gold Country consists of a string of picturesque small towns and cities strung along the grassy foothills of the Sierra Nevada east of Sacramento. It's the area called the Mother Lode by the '49ers, the thousands of gold-seekers who rushed here from all over the world after John Marshall's 1848 discovery of gold at John Sutter's mill.

The area is particularly rich in Chinese-American history, because the Sacramento Delta was originally reclaimed by Chinese laborers, and many of these Chinese railroad workers went on to become miners. The Delta town of Locke was founded by Chinese immigrants, and Gold Country landmarks include 100-year-old buildings that housed stores owned by Chinese pioneers.

We'll concentrate here on the former mining boomtowns along Highway 49 between Nevada City and Columbia. **Sacramento** is our gateway city and could be used as an airport/rental car starting point, but families might also consider touring the southern part of Gold Country before or after some time in Yosemite. (Yosemite is covered in the Sierra Nevada part.)

The nineteenth-century historic districts of the towns are usually surrounded by twentieth-century American small towns, commercial districts, and residential areas, so travelers won't lack access to motels, minimarts, fast food, and, in some cases, fine dining.

The region is anchored by four fascinating state parks, each worthy of a half-day stop. In **Grass Valley,** in the northern part of Gold Country, you'll find **Empire Mine State Historic Park,** the site of one of the oldest and richest gold mines in California. In the middle part of the region is **Chaw'Se Indian Grinding Rock State Historic Park,** once the seasonal meeting place of the Miwoks, and the only California state park that focuses primarily on Native American culture. A short easterly side trip from Highway 49 brings you to **Calaveras Big Trees State Park,** where you will see the majestic giant sequoias. In the southern section of the Mother Lode is **Columbia State Historic Park,** the most fully preserved of the gold rush towns, whose old brick buildings now house museums, shops, cafes, hotels, and a theater.

Between these main attractions, various tiny gold rush towns each offer one or two interesting sites to explore, as well as enjoyable activities like cave tours, hiking, and berry-picking.

Kids of at least elementary-school age will enjoy Gold Country the most. They should be old enough to want to pan for gold or ride a mule. Allow plenty of time, at least a few days, depending on the number of sites you want to explore. Distances aren't great between towns, but much of the fun comes in stopping for an hour here or there. We steer you to our favorite places in Gold Country; expect serendipity to lead you to some surprises along the way.

For first-time visitors, a Gold Country introduction allows for travels either in the northern part (via Sacramento) or the southern part (via Yosemite). Allow three days and two overnights in either case. For the northern part, begin with a day and a night in Sacramento, then drive on to Grass Valley and Nevada City for another day and a night. Add a day for such activities as river rafting, if you can. In the south, choose any of the Gold Rush towns as a base depending on your desired activities (historic sights, cave exploration, river rafting) for a one-day add-on (Columbia State Park only) to a Yosemite trip or a two- or three-day exploration of several different towns.

GETTING THERE

By Plane. Sacramento International Airport is 15 minutes from downtown Sacramento. Various airlines offer service, including Alaska, America West, American, Delta, Northwest, Southwest, TWA, United, and US Airways. Rent a car, and proceed by car, or join a sight-seeing tour such as one from Frontier Tours/Sacramento Gray Lines, 2600 North Avenue, Sacramento, (800) 356-9838.

By Train. Amtrak offers direct service on the California Zephyr east from the Bay Area and west from Chicago, and on the Coast Starlight south

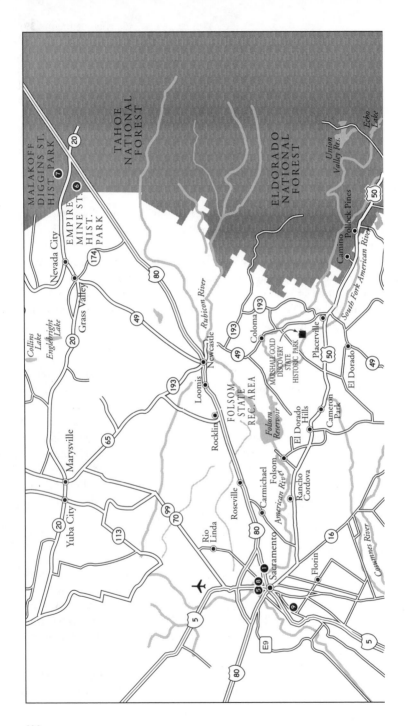

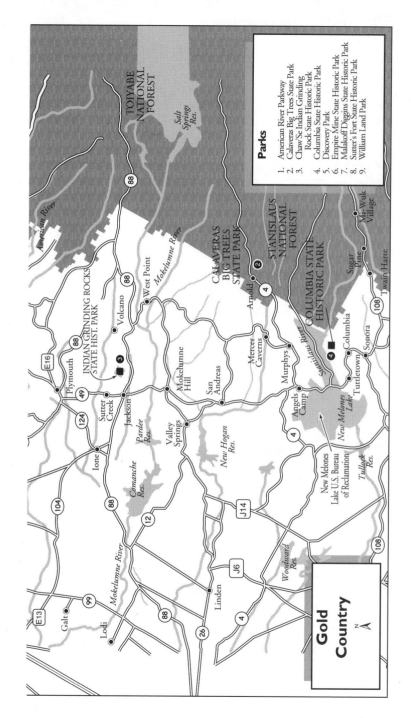

Parks

1. American River Parkway
2. Calaveras Big Trees State Park
3. Chaw'Se Indian Grinding Rock State Historic Park
4. Columbia State Historic Park
5. Discovery Park
6. Empire Mine State Historic Park
7. Malakoff Diggins State Historic Park
8. Sutter's Fort State Historic Park
9. William Land Park

TOIYABE NATIONAL FOREST

Salt Springs Res.

American River

West Point

Mokelumne River

Volcano

INDIAN GRINDING ROCKS STATE HIST. PARK

CALAVERAS BIG TREES STATE PARK

STANISLAUS NATIONAL FOREST

Mi-Wuk Village

Sugar Pine

Twain Harte

Arnold

COLUMBIA STATE HISTORIC PARK

Plymouth

Mercer Caverns

Murphys

Columbia

Sonora

Mokelumne Hill

San Andreas

Angels Camp

Tuttletown

Sutter Creek

Jackson

Pardee Res.

Valley Springs

New Hogan Res.

New Melones Lake

New Melones Lake U.S. Bureau of Reclamation

Tulloch Res.

Ione

Comanche Res.

Mokelumne River

Woodward Res.

Galt

Lodi

Linden

Gold Country

N

401

from Vancouver/Seattle and north from San Diego/Los Angeles. There are also commuter trains several times daily from the Bay Area and San Jose.

By Car. From the San Francisco Bay Area, take I-80 west to I-5 north. From the L.A. area, take I-5 north. From Reno/North Lake Tahoe, take I-80 west; from Reno via South Lake Tahoe, take I-50 west. From Yosemite, take Highway 99 north.

How to Get Information before You Go

> *Amador County Chamber of Commerce, 125 Peek Street, Suite B, Jackson 94562; (209) 223-0350.*

> *Calaveras Lodging and Visitors Association, 1211 S. Main Street, Angels Camp 95222; (209) 736-0049.*

> *Grass Valley and Nevada County Chamber of Commerce, 248 Mill Street, Grass Valley 95945; (530) 273-4667.*

> *Nevada City Chamber of Commerce, 153 Main Street, Nevada City 95959; (530) 265-2692.*

> *Old Sacramento Visitor Information Center, Front Street at K Street, Sacramento 95814; (916) 442-7644.*

> *Sacramento Convention and Visitors Bureau, 1421 K Street, Sacramento 95814; (916) 264-7777.*

The Best Parks

American River Parkway. This meandering park runs through Sacramento and its suburbs along the banks of the American River for more than 30 miles. The Jedediah Smith Memorial Bicycle trail here winds for 23 miles from Old Sacramento to Beals Point in the town of Folsom. It's also great for jogging, horseback riding, picnics, river rafting, fishing, and birding. For maps and information, call (916) 875-6961 or (916) 875-6672; to rent bikes, try American River Bike Centers, 9203 Folsom Boulevard, Sacramento, (916) 363-6271.

Discovery Park. This Sacramento County park situated at the confluence of the Sacramento and American Rivers is near Old Sacramento and is another starting point for bike trails. Boat launching, picnic area, horseshoes, archery, rest rooms, barbecues. (916) 875-6672.

William Land Park. The 15-acre Sacramento Zoo (admission $5 adults, $3.75 ages 3–12; (916) 264-5885) is located here, as well as a public golf course, picnic area, and amusement area. The best thing about Land Park is Fairytale Town, a wonderful amusement park for the 1–5-year-old set (admission $3.75 adults, $3.50 ages 3–12; (916) 264-5233). Spread over several flat acres, everything is preschool-sized. They can walk through storybooks, from Humpty Dumpty to Robin Hood; there's a barn house, pirate ship, Cinderella's carriage, and King Arthur's castle, along with puppet shows and a pony ride. Bring a picnic and hang out for a few hours. Sutterville and 17th Avenue, Sacramento; (916) 455-5014.

State Historic Parks. Because many state parks in Gold Country are also the region's primary historical attractions, we've placed their individual descriptions under Attractions in each section. We covered Sutter's Fort State Historic Park, Empire Mine State Historic Park, Chaw'Se Indian Grinding Rock State Historic Park, Calaveras Big Trees State Park, and Columbia State Historic Park. In addition, Malakoff Diggins State Historical Park is discussed under the listing for Chute Hill Campground on page 417.

Family Outdoor Adventures

Bicycling. See American River Parkway, under The Best Parks on page 402.

Caving. Several cave systems first explored by miners in the 1850s are open to the public today. The world down under can be creepy or awesome, depending on your child's perspective. For an introduction to caves, check out Mercer Caverns near Murphys, (209) 728-2101, which is open daily from the end of May through the end of September; admission for an hour's guided tour is $8 for adults and kids over age 11 and $4 for ages 5–11.

An exhilarating experience for teens is to descend into Moaning Cavern on a 180-foot rappel. Moaning Cavern is open year-round and also offers guided 45-minute walking tours (includes steep spiral staircase) and a three-hour Adventure Tour (reservations required) that involves climbing and narrow passages. General admission is $6.75 adults, $3.50 ages 6–12. Located near Vallecito; phone is (209) 736-2708.

Houseboating. The Sacramento River Delta area offers about a thousand square miles of calm-water waterways, and even the least water-savvy family can enjoy an afternoon on a flat-bottomed patio boat or a few days on a meandering houseboat. You can drive one of these boats more or less as you would, say, a 1958 Buick, while the kids fish, sunbathe, and watch for heron and other water birds. Tie up at a small-town marina on one of the many islands or to a tree stump and swim or picnic on shore.

Houseboats are usually offered for three to seven nights and can sleep one or two families; patio or fishing boats can be rented for a day's water play. Among the houseboat companies renting in the Delta: Forever Resorts, (800) 255-5561 or (480) 998-1981; www.foreverresorts.com; and Seven

Crown Resorts, (800) 752-9669; www.sevencrown.com. For one-day boat rentals, contact Paradise Point Marina, 8095 Rio Blanco Road, Stockton, (209) 952-1000 (houseboats, ski, patio, and fishing); or Sacramento Boat Rentals, (916) 321-0007 or (916) 455-8614 (power boats).

River Rafting. With older, water-safe kids, you can up the excitement and take a white-water rafting trip, which range in thrill level from mild to wild. There are several popular rafting areas on the American, Stanislaus, and Tuolumne Rivers in Gold Country, heading out of such rendezvous points as Columa, Angels Camp, Sacramento, and Stockton. Typically ranging from two days to a week, trips are offered from April through October; the wildest rapids are found in early spring, when runoff is greatest. Some outfitters offer quickie half-day rides. In many overnight trips, you camp out in style en route, with cooking and camp chores provided by staff members; at the journey's end, a van will take you back to the starting point. Some companies have overnight packages with nearby bed-and-breakfast inns or motels.

It is generally recommended that children under age 12 go on a raft that's powered by a guide; minimum ages vary by the excursion, with age six being about the youngest. Fares range from $70 to 200 per person for half- or all-day excursions and include meals and transportation back to the rendezvous point.

We know many families who have had excellent white-water adventures with an outfitter called A Whitewater Connection, (530) 622-6446 or (800) 336-7238; www.whitewaterconnection.com. Its home base is a beautiful 40-acre private campground (complete with horseshoes, fishing, and gold panning) alongside the south fork of the American River in the heart of Gold Country, next to Marshall Gold Discovery State Park. Kids over age six can participate in the Class III trips, which range from a half-day to two days, and there's a great discounted two-day trip for families with little kids. Mom gets to go rafting one day, Dad the other, while a parent plays at camp with the little ones. Other rafting companies include Whitewater Excitement, (800) 750-2386; All-Outdoors Whitewater Rafting Trips, (925) 932-8993 or (800) 247-2387; Arta River Trips, (209) 962-7873; and O.A.R.S. River Trips, (209) 736-2902 or (800) 346-6277, www.oars.com

THE SCHOOLHOUSES OF GOLD COUNTRY

Nothing will bring the Gold Rush era alive for your kids more than the sight of the wonderful one-room schoolhouses of the region. Almost every historic town has one, some fully restored and open for pretending, some shuttered and awaiting renovation, and a few turned into private homes. Each is named for its town.

- Old Sacramento Schoolhouse (phone (916) 383-2636) is a yellow, wood-frame building, beautifully restored and dramatically situated at the waterfront with Tower Bridge rising behind it. Kids can swing in the schoolyard (note the outhouse), and the classroom's open for exploring Monday–Saturday, 9:30 a.m.–4:30 p.m. and Sunday afternoons noon–4:30 p.m. Admission is free.

- Columa Schoolhouse is part of Marshall Gold Discovery State Historic Park (phone (916) 622-3470) and can be found, like other historic buildings, by referring to the guide map available at the Gold Discovery Museum.

- Fiddletown Schoolhouse (circa 1850) is a beautiful shell of a building, waiting to be restored. It has the classic schoolhouse shape with the little bell tower.

- Sutter Creek School (1871), an imposing two-story stone building on a hill east of the town center, is fun to drive past.

- Volcano School, impeccably restored, is now a private residence and can't be toured, but it has a marker.

- Altaville School (1858) is red brick with dainty white trim; it was used until 1950.

- Murphys Grammar School (1860) was, until it closed in 1973, California's oldest public school. It's on a hill near the corner of Main and Jones Streets and awaits restoration.

- Columbia School House (phone (209) 532-0150) is at the north end of Columbia and makes for a nice walk through the residential blocks (imagine living in a state historic park!) up the hill to the building that housed the state's first public school. Built in 1860, it's a two-story brick building; the old town cemetery is located in back.

Calendar of Festivals and Events

January
Martin Luther King Community Celebrations, Sacramento. Parades, activitities; (916) 452-5052.

February
Chinese New Year Celebration, Isleton, Sacramento. Parades, music, street fair; (916) 777-5880.

March

Mariposa Storytelling Festival, Mariposa; (209) 966-2456.

April

Pioneer Traders' and Crafts Fair, Sutter's Fort, Sacramento. Modern-day craftspeople offer 1840s-era goods for sale; (916) 445-4422.

Festival de la Familia, Old Sacramento and Downtown Plaza. Held the last Sunday of each April, this is a hugely popular festival celebrating the heritage of more than two dozen Latin American countries. Puppet shows, games, storytelling, music, dancing, and food; (916) 264-7777 or (916) 446-6223.

Opening Day, Sacramento Rivercats Minor League Baseball. Season goes through September at brand-new Raley Field, an old-fashioned ballpark complete with children's play area; 1001 Second Street; (916) 447-HITS; www.rivercats.com.

May

Sacramento County Fair; (916) 263-2975.

Fireman's Muster, Columbia. Vintage hand-pumped fire engines; (209) 532-0150.

Jumping Frog Jubilee, Angels Camp. Continuing the tradition begun by Mark Twain's story, this famed frog-jumping contest is held the third week in May as part of the Calaveras County Fair, which also boasts pig races, carnival rides, and a kid's play area; (800) 225-3764 or (209) 736-0049.

June

Crawdad Festival, Sacramento; (916) 717-5880.

WNBA Basketball. Women's professional basketball team, The Monarchs, is popular with families—through September; (916) 928-6900.

July

Placer County Fair, Highway 65, Roseville; (916) 786-2023.

August

California State Fair, Cal Expo, Capital City Freeway and Exposition Boulevard, Sacramento. One of the nation's largest state fairs, complete with rodeo riding, fireworks, and Kid's Park; (916) 263-3247; www.bigfun.org.

September

Black Bart Day, San Andreas. Kids love this tribute to the most fiendish stagecoach robber in Gold Rush days. Parade, tug-of-war, barbecue, visit to the jail Black Bart occupied; (209) 754-3361.

Native American Festival, Chaw'Se Indian Grinding Rock State Park. On the weekend following the fourth Friday in September, Native American tribes gather to celebrate with food, dances, and games; (209) 296-7488.

Gold Rush Festival, Old Sacramento. Old Sacramento is closed to cars and its streets are covered with dirt during this four-day annual event. Period-appropriate tents and booths include blacksmith's tent, jail, and apothecary; (916) 264-7777.

Gold Country Fair, Auburn; (916) 885-5616.

October

Harvest Hunt and Goosebump Express, Old Sacramento. Halloween season is celebrated with a pumpkin patch at the railroad museum and a train ride with ghouls and goblins on board; (916) 552-5252.

December

Cornish Christmas Street Celebration, Grass Valley. Held one evening a week in December, this honors the Cornish heritage of many in this former mining center and includes performances by the Grass Valley Cornish Choir and street stalls with traditional foods and crafts; (916) 272-8315.

Lamplight Tour, Columbia. The town re-creates a different year in its history each December, and docents lead visitors through town by lamplight to "eavesdrop" on nineteenth-century goings-on; (209) 532-0150.

Kid-Coveted Souvenirs

Minerals Everywhere, you'll find gold (and fake gold, of course). Little vials of water with microscopic gold flecks fascinate kids and are inexpensive or come from their own gold-panning efforts (for which they'll be charged a fee by a whiskered miner).

Hats Bonnets for the girls can be expensive but may be cherished; miner's felt floppy hats or various historically inaccurate but fun versions of coonskin and cowboy hats are popular with boys.

Old Bottles Gold Country is dotted with antiques shops to lure the tourist, and if parents can't resist browsing, kids might have fun picking out an old glass bottle of curious shape and color (but not of great age if you want it to be affordable).

Sacramento

Although Sacramento seems off the beaten track because of its inland location, it was once a major hub thanks to its busy riverfront (now a vital outdoor recreation area) and its position as a gateway to Gold Country, the Sierra, and the agricultural valley areas of the state. As the state capital, it's often filled with California schoolkids visiting the buildings where legislators make the laws, and its **Old Sacramento** and **Sutter's Fort** historic areas allow kids to visit environments that bring history to life.

For vacationing families, Sacramento can be a convenient base for several days of varied activities in the region, but we don't recommend an extended stay in the city unless you're visiting friends. Accommodations, although often very competitive in price, tend to be geared to the capital's many business visitors, and only a few hotels (see below) are located in family-friendly areas (most of the chains are in desolate, freeway-adjacent locations). Bed-and-breakfast inns are isolated in quiet residential areas throughout the city.

Instead, plan a convenient overnight at the beginning or end of a few days devoted to houseboating on the Delta or exploring Gold Country, especially if you're arriving in the area by plane.

Family Lodging

Holiday Inn, Capitol Plaza

Located at Capitol Plaza, this 364-room motel is in a mixed-use area that includes an upscale shopping plaza with movie theaters and restaurants, a pedestrian walkway (under the freeway) to Old Sacramento, and pedestrian access to the city's business district. From here your teens can walk to the movies while you and the toddlers play in the pool, and then you can all stroll out to one of the lively restaurants nearby. There is a coffee shop with a kids' menu; room service has its own menu that includes kids' items.

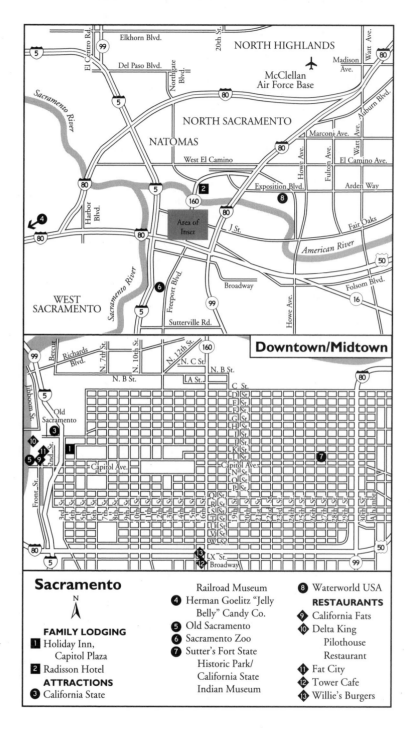

Sacramento

N
↑

FAMILY LODGING
1. Holiday Inn, Capitol Plaza
2. Radisson Hotel

ATTRACTIONS
3. California State Railroad Museum
4. Herman Goelitz "Jelly Belly" Candy Co.
5. Old Sacramento
6. Sacramento Zoo
7. Sutter's Fort State Historic Park/ California State Indian Museum
8. Waterworld USA

RESTAURANTS
9. California Fats
10. Delta King Pilothouse Restaurant
11. Fat City
12. Tower Cafe
13. Willie's Burgers

Five rooms are suites with refrigerators. Baby-sitting is available. There are no special kids' programs.

300 J Street, Sacramento; (916) 446-0100. Rates $80–122 for rooms, $175–350 suites; children under age 18 stay free.

Radisson Hotel

One of the few resort-like lodgings in the area, this 309-room motor inn is situated on 18 acres with a small lake; some rooms have patios or decks. Kids are welcomed, and they stay free in their parents' room, with an extra charge for rollaways. Some suites. Family-oriented extras include baby-sitting, a swimming pool, bike rentals for hitting the American River trail, paddleboats, and, for older teens, dancing nightly to a deejay.

500 Leisure Lane, Sacramento; (916) 922-2020 or (800) 333-3333. Rates $98–159.

Attractions

California State Railroad Museum

125 I Street, Old Sacramento; (916) 445-7387 or (916) 448-4466

Hours: Daily 10 a.m.–5 p.m.; closed Thanksgiving, Christmas, New Year's Day

Admission: $6 age 13+, $3 ages 6–12, free for age 5 and under

Appeal by Age Groups:

Pre-school	Grade School	Teens	Young Adults	Over 30	Seniors
★★	★★★	★★	★★	★★★	★★★★

Touring Time: Average 3 hours; minimum 2 hours

Rainy-Day Touring: Yes

Services and Facilities:

Restaurants No	Lockers No
Alcoholic beverages No	Pet kennels No
Disabled access Yes	Rain check No
Wheelchair rental Yes	Private tours No, docents
Baby stroller rental No	available

Description and Comments An impressive museum that grabs visitors in several ways, with movies, miniatures, and hands-on experiences. Displays include 21 restored locomotives and train cars, some of which you can walk through. Ticket allows for admission to the restored Central Pacific Passenger Station, and in the summer there are hourly steam train rides from the Central Pacific Freight Depot.

Herman Goelitz ("Jelly Belly") Candy Co.

About one hour from Sacramento off Chadbourne Road, exit from 180 on Jelly Bean Lane, Fairfield; (707) 428-2838

Hours: Drop-in tours daily 9 a.m.–5 p.m.; closed New Year's Day, Easter Sunday, Thanksgiving Day, and Christmas Day

Admission: Free

Appeal by Age Groups:

Pre-school	Grade School	Teens	Young Adults	Over 30	Seniors
★★★	★★★	★★	★★	★★	★★

Touring Time: Average half-hour to 1 hour; minimum half-hour

Rainy-Day Touring: Yes

Services and Facilities:

Restaurants Yes	Lockers No
Alcoholic beverages No	Pet kennels No
Disabled access Yes	Rain check No
Wheelchair rental No	Private tours No
Baby stroller rental No	

Description and Comments This candy factory offers youngsters a vivid picture of where jelly beans come from. Small groups take a guided walk along elevated walkways through candymaking areas. Video monitors provide over-the-shoulder veiws of the candy makers at work. Free samples are given to tour participants. There's also a cafe, picnic area, and extensive retail store, where the coveted item is a bag of "Belly Flops," or irregular jelly beans.

Old Sacramento

Four blocks bounded by Capitol Mall, I Street, 2nd Street, and the Sacramento River; (916) 264-7777

Hours: Varied

Admission: Free to area; some attractions charge

Appeal by Age Groups:

Pre-school	Grade School	Teens	Young Adults	Over 30	Seniors
★★	★★★	★★	★	★★	★★★

Touring Time: Average 4 hours; minimum 2 hours

Rainy-Day Touring: Not great for enjoying the walk around district

Services and Facilities:

Restaurants Yes, many	Baby stroller rental No
Alcoholic beverages In some cafes and clubs	Lockers No
	Pet kennels No
Disabled access Yes	Rain check No
Wheelchair rental No	

Description and Comments   This restored historic district has an especially pleasurable area at the waterfront, where wooden walkways face the river. Here you'll find Tower Bridge, a unique Delta King paddlewheel boat hotel, and boat docks where visiting cruise ships and yachts tie up for an hour or a day. The area is home to several museums, including the California Railroad Museum (see page 410), the California Military Museum, and the Discovery Museum (where kids can see a million dollars in real gold at the Mother Lode exhibit). But overall, there are more souvenir shops and cafes than historic points of interest, so the effect can sometimes be of a completely commercial, tourist-tacky area. We recommend a morning visit with a stroll around the waterfront, followed by a museum visit, lunch, and a bit of shop-crawling.

Between May and October, the River Otter Water Taxi (ticket booth near Rio City Café) departs several times a day on an hour-long loop of the river ($5 adults, $2 kids).

Sacramento Zoo

3930 West Land Park Drive; (916) 264-5885; www.saczoo.com

Hours: Daily 9 a.m.–4 p.m. June 1–Labor Day, 10 a.m.–4 p.m. rest of the year; closed Thanksgiving Day and Christmas Day

Admission: Adults: $6 weekends and holidays, $5.50 weekdays; children ages 3–12: $4.25 weekends, $3.75 weekdays; free for ages 2 and under

Appeal by Age Groups:

Pre-school	Grade School	Teens	Young Adults	Over 30	Seniors
★★★★	★★★★	★★	★★	★★	★★

Touring Time: Average 3–4 hours; minimum 1 hour

Rainy-Day Touring: Yes

Services and Facilities:

Restaurants Snack bars	Lockers No
Alcoholic beverages No	Pet kennels No
Disabled access Yes	Rain check No
Wheelchair rental Yes, free	Private tours No
Baby stroller rental Yes	

Description and Comments Zoo camps and overnight safaris are among the special kids activities at this friendly, mid-size (400 animals) zoo. There are weekend hippo, giraffe, and chimpanzee talks. Key to Adventure is a new, easy audio tour: a key activates "talking boxes" at certain exhibits, so you can hear fun facts, stories, and songs about the animals.

Sutter's Fort State Historic Park/
California State Indian Museum

Sutter's Fort: 2701 L Street at 27th; Indian Museum: 2618 K Street; (916) 445-4422 (fort); (916) 324-0539 (general information line) or (916) 324-0971 (Indian Museum)

Hours: 10 a.m.–5 p.m. daily; closed holidays

Admission: (separate admissions) $3 adults and $1.50 children ages 6–12 in the fort and Indian Museum

Appeal by Age Groups:

Pre-school	Grade School	Teens	Young Adults	Over 30	Seniors
★★	★★★	★★	★★	★★	★★★

Touring Time: Average 2 hours each; minimum 1 hour each

Rainy-Day Touring: Not pleasant

Services and Facilities:

Restaurants No	Lockers No
Alcoholic beverages No	Pet kennels No
Disabled access Somewhat limited	Rain check Yes
Wheelchair rental No	Private tours No
Baby stroller rental No	

Description and Comments If you visit at a time when you can see a living-history program, kids get an especially three-dimensional view of the past. Costumed docents demonstrate spinning, weaving, and cooking in this reconstructed fort with buildings that include a candle-making room, cooperage, trading post, and blacksmith shop. The audio wands for a self-guided tour are free and fun.

The California State Indian Museum is part of the complex and has exhibits that connect well with youngsters—exhibits featuring artifacts that include games, toys, feather baskets, and jewelry. Some hands-on exhibits.

Sutter's Fort Trade Store sells period toys, games, and clothing.

Waterworld USA

1600 Exposition Boulevard; (916) 924-0556 or (916) 924-3747

Hours: Mid-June–Labor Day, daily 10:30 a.m.–6 p.m.; open some weekends and shorter hours at other times

Admission: $17.99, $9.99 seniors, $12.99 for children under 48" tall, free for children ages 2 and under; additional fees for lockers, tubes; parking $5

Appeal by Age Groups:

Pre- school	Grade School	Teens	Young Adults	Over 30	Seniors
★★★★★	★★★★★	★★★★★	★★★★	★★★★	★★

Touring Time: Average 5 hours; minimum 3 hours

Rainy-Day Touring: No

Services and Facilities:

Restaurants Yes	Lockers Yes, fee
Alcoholic beverages Yes	Pet kennels No
Disabled access Yes	Rain check Yes
Wheelchair rental No	Private tours No
Baby stroller rental No	

Description and Comments   The summer heat in this part of the state can be startling to many—it's unrelieved by ocean breezes. We love water parks for a great change from sight-seeing, a chance for adults to read and talk, a safe environment for kids to splash, and a cool, summery time for all. Waterworld has all the features a family looks for in a water park: wave pool, toddler wading area, a moving-water river tubing area, and, of course, slides—five of 'em.

Family-Friendly Restaurants

CALIFORNIA FATS

1015 Front Street, Old Sacramento; (916) 441-7966

Meals served: Lunch and dinner
Cuisine: Pacific Rim
Entree range: $8–13 (lunch); $13–23 (dinner)
Children's menu: Yes
Reservations: Accepted
Payment: AE, DC, MC, V

A chic spin-off of the legendary Frank Fat's, the Chinese restaurant that's fed legislators and lobbyists for years, this Old Town hot spot is more Pacific Rim than Chinese, serving things like Asian pizzas, seared ahi, and venison in cashew crust. The kids' menu includes the grilled-cheese basics, but it also offers a terrific chow mein. The restaurant is lively and handsome, decorated with photos of Sacramento's Chinese immigrants.

DELTA KING PILOTHOUSE RESTAURANT

1000 Front Street, Old Sacramento; (916) 441-4440

Meals served: Lunch Monday–Saturday, dinner nightly, Sunday buffet
  brunch
Cuisine: American
Entree range: $9.95 children, $19.95 adults (brunch); $7.95–9.95 (lunch);
  $16.95–29.95 (dinner)
Children's menu: Yes, $5.95
Reservations: Recommended, especially on weekends
Payment: AE, MC, V

When you see the historic landmark paddlewheeler at the dock in Old Town,
your kids will clamor to go on board, but be forewarned: This is the kind of
restaurant seniors select for a picturesque lunch or dinner, and noisy
preschoolers will disrupt the atmosphere. With elementary age or older kids,
go ahead and give it a try, but know that the food doesn't live up to its slightly
pretentious presentation—and besides, the views of the river can be had from
the dock itself. On the other hand, it's a good bet for a one-grandparent, one-
child brunch, lunch, or dinner that's to be a bit special.

FAT CITY

1001 Front Street, Old Sacramento; (916) 446-6768

Meals served: Lunch, dinner, and Sunday brunch
Cuisine: American
Entree range: $8–15 (lunch and brunch); $12–18 (dinner)
Children's menu: Yes
Reservations: Accepted for large parties only
Payment: AE, MC, V

Run by the Fat family, descendants of Chinese immigrant railroad workers and now the city's leading restaurateurs, Fat City is the best family-
oriented restaurant in Old Town. It's a pretty place, with a fine view of the
river and passing carriages. The straightforward California fare—salads,
sandwiches, fresh fish, burgers—is quite good.

TOWER CAFE

1518 Broadway, William Land Park; (916) 441-0222

Meals served: Breakfast, lunch, and dinner
Cuisine: California

Entree range: $3–6.95 (breakfast); $3–7.95 (lunch); $7.95–15.95 (dinner)
Children's menu: Yes, $4.95
Reservations: Not necessary
Payment: AE, MC, V

One of those fun restaurants that is discovered by a new generation of hipsters every few years, the Tower Cafe is located in a landmark building that also houses a revival movie house. It serves creative, reasonably priced fusion cuisine of the Asian-burrito variety, as well as burgers, pastas, and good wine by the glass. The outdoor tables are wonderful in spring and early summer, and at Sunday brunch there's a mean French toast. The location is perfection, at the entrance to William Land Park.

WILLIE'S BURGERS

2415 16th Street, William Land Park; (916) 444-2006

Meals served: Lunch and dinner
Cuisine: American
Entree range: $1.65–2.90
Children's menu: No
Reservations: Not accepted
Payment: Cash only

Located across from Land Park, this plain but clean joint makes the best (and messiest) burger in town. The fries and chocolate shakes are also outstanding.

Northern Gold Country: Grass Valley and Nevada City

Northern Gold Country extends into the mountains above Sacramento, but distances are greater and the driving harder between attractions, so we recommend a beginning or end at Nevada City. Grass Valley and Nevada City are small cities so close that they alternate Fourth of July celebrations between them. Both have beautiful, hilly settings with historic town centers of nineteenth-century buildings given over, for the most part, to such contemporary uses as shops and galleries. Grass Valley is the busier of the two, but Nevada City is best for overnighting and is great for antiquing and strolling to admire Victorian houses. We recommend a half-day visit to **Empire Mine State Historic Park.**

Family Lodging

Chute Hill Campground

The best family campground in Gold Country, Chute Hill is part of Malakoff Diggins State Historical Park, comprising the old mining town of North Bloomfield and the old Diggins hydraulic mining operation, which in its heyday was an environmental nightmare. Today, there are excellent tent and camper sites as well as a few old prospectors' cabins under huge ponderosa pines overlooking the town and Diggins. Kids will love walking to the museum town, with its general store and blacksmith; swimming in Blair Lake, which has a wooden raft in its center; and taking flashlights on a hike to Hiller Tunnel, a cool remnant from mining days. Water, flush toilets, wood for sale, picnic tables, fire rings.

23579 N. Bloomfield Road, Nevada City; (530) 265-2740. Reservations advised. Tent sites $7, cabins $15.

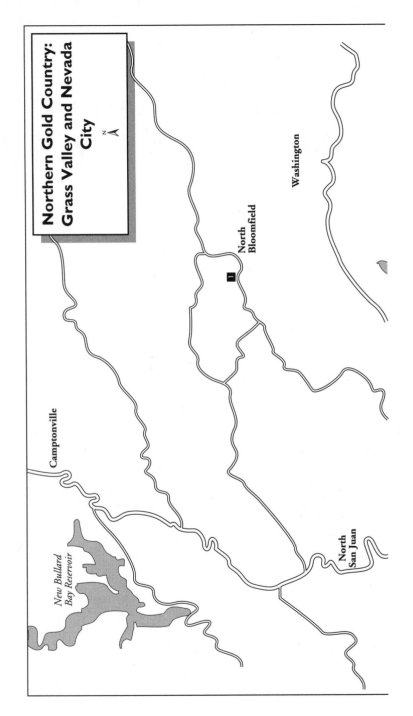

Northern Gold Country:
Grass Valley and Nevada
City

N

Camptonville

New Bullard
Bay Reservoir

North
Bloomfield

Washington

North
San Juan

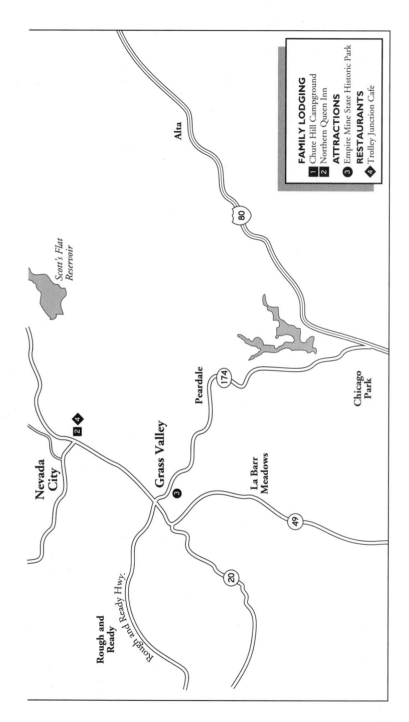

FAMILY LODGING
1 Chute Hill Campground
2 Northern Queen Inn
ATTRACTIONS
3 Empire Mine State Historic Park
RESTAURANTS
4 Trolley Junction Cafe

Northern Queen Inn

This pleasant facility is an affordable haven. Its 70 rooms, suites, and efficiency units are adjacent to easy parking but built along a woodsy creek. Some are individual cottages with lofts, decks or terraces, kitchens, and wood-burning stoves or fireplaces; even the basic rooms have little refrigerators and coffeemakers. Our kids found blackberry vines on the hillside behind the deck. There's a picnic area, a good restaurant (see page 421) that overlooks the creek's huge waterwheel, and restored train cars next door. Children under age six stay free.

400 Railroad Avenue, Nevada City; (530) 265-5824. Rates $79–99.

Attraction

Empire Mine State Historic Park

10791 E. Empire Street, Grass Valley; (530) 273-8522

Hours: Daily 9 a.m.–6 p.m.

Admission: $3 adults, $1 kids ages 6–12

Appeal by Age Groups:

Pre-school	Grade School	Teens	Young Adults	Over 30	Seniors
★	★★★	★★★	★★★	★★★★	★★★★

Touring Time: Average 3 hours; minimum 1 hour

Rainy-Day Touring: Not recommended

Services and Facilities:

Restaurants No	Lockers No
Alcoholic beverages No	Pet kennels No; dogs must be
Disabled access Limited	leashed
Wheelchair rental No	Rain check No
Baby stroller rental No	Private tours No

Description and Comments   This state park is quite undervisited, but if you take the time, it takes you beyond the legends and stories. Kids who spend a few hours here will get a real sense of mining, from the individual miner's point of view (witness the Cornish dinner pails on exhibit) to an overview of how gold is extracted from rock. The Empire Mine was one of the oldest and richest mines in California. Cornish miners dug 367 miles of tunnels here, going more than 10,000 feet deep underground.

Call ahead for tour times (March–November) and bring a picnic lunch; there's no food for sale at the park, and the brisk mountain air made us ravenous in minutes. Begin in a little screening room at the visitors center with a viewing of movies with vintage footage of miners at work and then, by all means, join a ranger walk for a guided tour of the site's owner's mansion, mining offices (with period office fixtures), clubhouse, and mineshaft entrance. Then get out your camera for a stroll around a graveyard of rusty mining equipment. If you hike, there are ten miles of trails here, too. Restoration and interpretive exhibit work is ongoing, and there is a fundraising drive under way to develop an underground tour.

Family-Friendly Restaurant

TROLLEY JUNCTION CAFE

Northern Queen Inn, 400 Railroad Avenue, Nevada City; (530) 265-5259

Meals served: Breakfast and lunch Monday–Wednesday; breakfast, lunch, and dinner Thursday–Sunday
Cuisine: American
Entree range: $3.25–6.95 (breakfast); $5.95–7 (lunch); $6.75–14.95 (dinner)
Children's menu: Yes
Reservations: Recommended
Payment: All major credit cards

There's a lot of charm and good food at this fun place overlooking the woods, creek, and waterwheel, but for kids, the biggest appeal is the train ride across the parking lot. The train runs in summer (tickets are $3 for kids and $6 for adults). From the French toast to the omelets to the ribs, the food is generous and carefully prepared, and the children's menu is extensive.

Central Gold Country: Jackson, Volcano, and Murphys

This is the road-trip part of Gold Country. Highway 49 leaves the more developed areas along the Sacramento-to-Tahoe thoroughfare and becomes more countrified. The highway goes through the business or historic center of some Gold Rush towns; others are a few miles off the main drag. There are too many small towns, each with a historic landmark or two, to mention here; one of the most attractive is **Sutter Creek,** a Victorian/New Englandy–looking town that's home to many artisans. **Volcano,** a town that was a highlight for our kids, is listed below as an attraction in and of itself. This is also the region for cave touring (see Family Outdoor Adventures, page 403) and the site of **Indian Grinding Rock** and **Cala-veras Big Trees State Parks.**

Family Lodging

El Campo Casa Resort Motel

An older motel, not quite dating back to the Gold Rush days (its bathrooms have circa 1950s tile) but with some good features for families. Its 15 rooms are comfortable if not spacious, and there's a playground, swimming pool with an extra-shallow section, and barbecue for guest use.

12548 Kennedy Flat Road, Jackson; (209) 223-0100. Rates $63–72.

Jackson Holiday Lodge

A kitchen away from home is sometimes a blessing, and this place has eight duplex housekeeping cottages, some with their own patios. The pool's open in the summer. It's right on Highway 49, but not too noisy.

850 N. Highway 49, P.O. Box 1147, Jackson; (209) 223-0486; fax (209) 223-2905. Rates $50–80; children under age 16 stay free.

Murphys Historic Hotel and Lodge

For families who will be spending time in the caves near Murphys, this well-maintained hostelry (part 1855 landmark, part new rooms) is quite serviceable, and the tree-shaded town center offers restaurants and shops. The restaurant and old saloon are popular stops for weary modern '49ers. If you're visiting in summer, be warned that the historic rooms are not air-conditioned.

457 Main Street, Murphys; (209) 728-3444; fax (209) 728-1590. Rates $70–80; children ages 12 and under stay free.

Attractions

Amador County Museum

225 Church Street, Jackson; (209) 223-6386

Hours: Wednesday–Sunday 10 a.m.–4 p.m.

Admission: Free

Appeal by Age Groups:

Pre-school	Grade School	Teens	Young Adults	Over 30	Seniors
★★	★★	★★	★★	★★	★★★

Touring Time: Average 1½ hours; minimum 30 minutes

Rainy-Day Touring: Yes

Services and Facilities:

Restaurants No	Lockers No
Alcoholic beverages No	Pet kennels No
Disabled access Limited	Rain check No
Wheelchair rental No	Private tours No
Baby stroller rental No	

Description and Comments A small-scale museum that offers an overview of Gold Rush history, at a point in the drive when kids have seen enough to be able to attach facts to sights and when they'll still be seeing more that will apply. You'll see models of mines, a gold room, and a child's period bedroom.

Calaveras Big Trees State Park

In Arnold, 20 miles northeast of Murphys; (209) 795-2334

Hours: Daily sunrise to sundown

Admission: $5 per car, $1 per dog

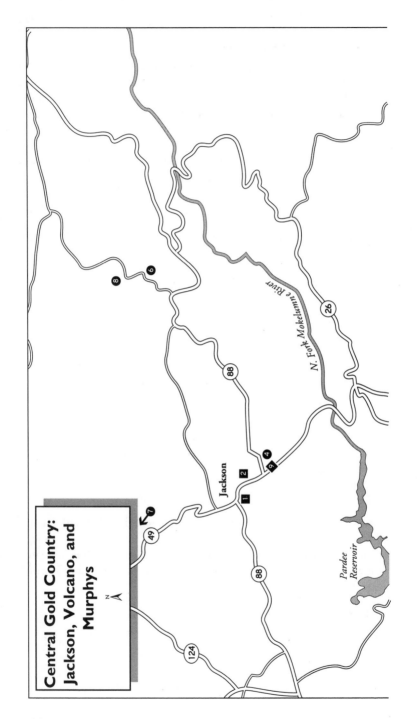

Central Gold Country: Jackson, Volcano, and Murphys

N

Jackson

N. Fork Mokelumne River

Pardee Reservoir

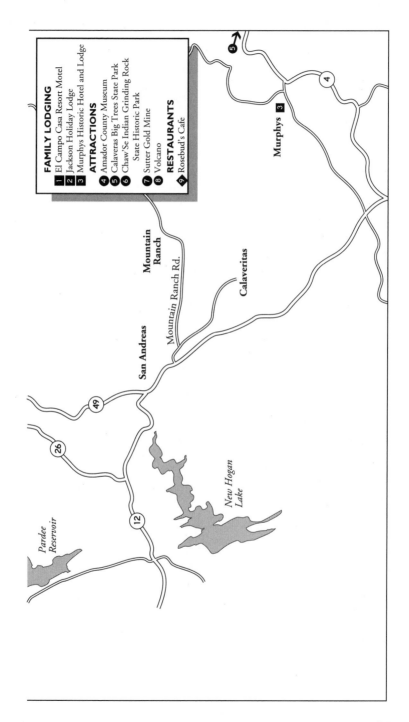

FAMILY LODGING
1 El Campo Casa Resort Motel
2 Jackson Holiday Lodge
3 Murphys Historic Hotel and Lodge

ATTRACTIONS
4 Amador County Museum
5 Calaveras Big Trees State Park
6 Chaw'Se Indian Grinding Rock State Historic Park
7 Sutter Gold Mine
8 Volcano

RESTAURANTS
9 Rosebud's Cafe

Murphys 3

Mountain Ranch

Calaveritas

Mountain Ranch Rd.

San Andreas

New Hogan Lake

Pardee Reservoir

Appeal by Age Groups:

Pre-school	Grade School	Teens	Young Adults	Over 30	Seniors
★★★	★★★★	★★★★	★★★★	★★★★	★★★★

Touring Time: Average 2 hours; minimum 1 hour

Rainy-Day Touring: Not recommended

Services and Facilities:

Restaurants No	Lockers No
Alcoholic beverages No	Pet kennels No
Disabled access Yes, except trails	Rain check No
Wheelchair rental No	Private tours No
Baby stroller rental No	

Description and Comments   Native Americans had known about and held sacred the giant sequoias of this grove for eons when it was discovered by outsiders during the Gold Rush. For the next 20 years, although the big tree groves of Yosemite and Sequoia were discovered, the Calaveras site was the most visited and best known. Its tourist hotels continued as popular and stylish destinations until the turn of the century. Today, the park is less well known, and its South Grove remains secluded and primeval. The North Grove's self-guided, one-mile trail and the "Three Senses" trails are the best for non-hiking families. Creek swimming, developed campgrounds with 129 campsites, and a rustic recreation hall make it one of the most attractive Gold Country camping areas.

Chaw'Se Indian Grinding Rock State Historic Park

14881 Pine Grove–Volcano Road; (209) 296-7488

Hours: Dawn to dusk daily

Admission: $5 per private vehicle

Appeal by Age Groups:

Pre-school	Grade School	Teens	Young Adults	Over 30	Seniors
★★★	★★★	★★★	★★★	★★★	★★★

Touring Time: Average 2 hours; minimum 1 hour

Rainy-Day Touring: Not recommended

Services and Facilities:

Restaurants No	Lockers No
Alcoholic beverages No	Pet kennels No
Disabled access Yes	Rain check No
Wheelchair rental No	Private tours No
Baby stroller rental No	

Description and Comments You get the idea that there are rocks here, but few visitors are prepared for the sight of hundreds of feet of flat limestone outcropping spread out over the rolling countryside. A closer look reveals more than a thousand mortar cups (or *chaw'ses*) chiseled into the largest rock, which also displays 363 petroglyphs. The mortar cups were used for grinding acorns and seeds, staples in the Miwok people's diet. The Regional Indian Museum exhibits and slide show illuminate the hunting and gathering way of life of ten Sierra Nevada tribes, and a full-scale model roundhouse, bark conical dwelling, and football field provide further insight into daily life a hundred years ago. Twenty-one campsites with tables and stoves; piped water, rest rooms, but no showers.

Sutter Gold Mine

Highway 49 between Sutter Creek and Amador City; (209) 223-0350.

Description and Comments As we went to press construction was underway of a restored gold mine and visitors center offering tours and gold-panning. Call for current information before your trip.

Volcano

Choose a loop trip from Highway 49. We took Gopher Flat Road from Sutter Creek, which turns into Shake Ridge Road and winds 13 miles to Daffodil Hill, first planted in the 1800s and bursting with 400,000 flowers in the spring. The exciting Ram's Horn Grade was a dramatic 3-mile descent to Volcano. We took the Pine Grove–Volcano Road out to Indian Grinding Rock. No phone.

Admission: None

Appeal by Age Groups:

Pre-school	Grade School	Teens	Young Adults	Over 30	Seniors
★	★★★	★★★	★★★	★★★	★★★

Touring Time: Average, allow an hour's stop to buy a soda or coffee and take a walk; minimum 30 minutes

Rainy-Day Touring: Not recommended

Services and Facilities:

Restaurants Volcano General Store	Baby stroller rental No
	Lockers No
Alcoholic beverages Bar in town	Pet kennels No
Disabled access Limited	Rain check No
Wheelchair rental No	Private tours No

Description and Comments Traveling south, you'll see Plymouth, Amador City, and Sutter Creek before you come to the turnoff for Volcano. Sutter Creek appeals to many adults because its historic buildings mix so pleasantly with its tasteful modern development. But we recommend a side trip combined with a visit to Indian Grinding Rock. There are four different scenic routes that converge in Volcano, where you'll find a park with grassy mounds and ruins, a few places to get refreshments, and some charming residential blocks. Volcano General Store has a wonderfully atmospheric old soda-shop counter that serves kid chow like burgers and hot dogs.

Family-Friendly Restaurant

ROSEBUD'S CAFE

26 Main Street, Jackson; (209) 223-1035

Meals served: Breakfast and lunch
Cuisine: American
Entree range: $3.25–9 (lunch)
Children's menu: Yes
Reservations: Not accepted
Payment: MC, V

A sweet little cafe with an art deco look and a wonderful children's menu, offering waffles, junior cheese omelets, even a small turkey hot plate with homemade mashed potatoes. Parents can get a proper latte and a good meal, too. Breakfast is served all day.

Southern Gold Country: Columbia and Sonora

If it's living history you want, this part of the Mother Lode is the place to get it, before heading on to the scenic wonders of Yosemite, or back north or south to big-city civilization. Enjoy the oak- and pine-dotted hills and the river vistas, but be prepared for hot, hot weather in the summer.

Family Lodging

Best Western Sonora Oaks

This 101-room motel may be a chain, but it nevertheless has a rural feel, with an oak grove in its backyard and a pool that's a necessity in the summer. Ask for a deluxe king room, which has both a king bed and a queen sleeper sofa. There's an adjacent coffee shop with a children's menu, and children under age 12 stay free.

19551 Hess Avenue, Sonora; (209) 533-4400 or (800) 532-1944. Rates start at $79.

Attraction

Columbia State Historic Park

4 miles north of Sonora on Highway 49, Columbia; (209) 532-4301 (museum), (209) 532-0150 (park administrative offices), (209) 532-4644 for play info, (209) 532-0663 for horseback info, (209) 532-9693 for info about gold panning or mine tours

Hours: Daily 9 a.m.–5 p.m.; tours at 11 a.m. and 1:30 p.m.

Admission: Free to park, various charges at concessions

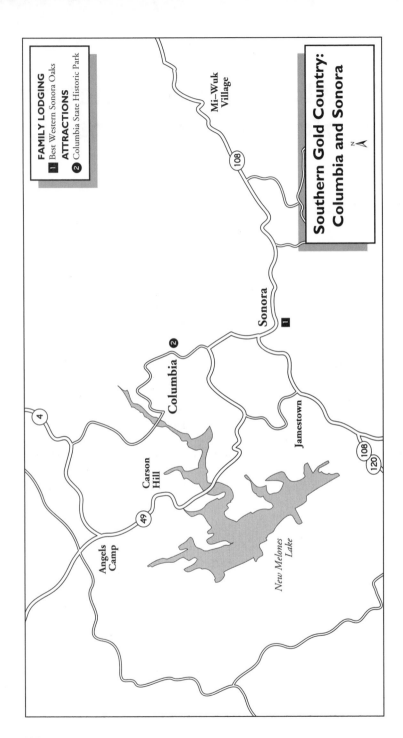

FAMILY LODGING
1 Best Western Sonora Oaks
ATTRACTIONS
2 Columbia State Historic Park

Southern Gold Country:
Columbia and Sonora

N

Mi–Wuk
Village

108

Sonora
1

Columbia 2

Jamestown

108
120

Carson
Hill

4

49

Angels
Camp

New Melones
Lake

Appeal by Age Groups:

Pre-school	Grade School	Teens	Young Adults	Over 30	Seniors
★★	★★★★	★★★	★★★	★★★	★★★

Touring Time: Average 4 hours; minimum 2 hours

Rainy-Day Touring: Not recommended

Services and Facilities:

Restaurants City Hotel; ice cream parlor

Alcoholic beverages Yes

Disabled access No

Wheelchair rental No

Baby stroller rental No

Lockers No

Pet kennels No; dogs allowed on leash

Rain check No

Private tours No

Description and Comments   More modest (by far) than a theme park, more honky-tonk than you'd expect in something called a historic park, Columbia is actually a perfect stop for school-age kids. It's a historic landmark, a four-block area of intact 1850s and 1860s buildings (which survived because after a fire the town was rebuilt almost entirely in brick), but it's also a tourist town. There are concessions operating within the park that allow you to pan for gold, go on a mine tour, and go on a horseback or stagecoach ride throughout the town. You can brave the ghosts and stay in a restored historic hotel right in the park (phone (209) 532-1479; operated by hotel students at a nearby community college), attend a play at the town playhouse (though it will likely be a modern show), sip a sarsaparilla and listen to bluegrass music at the saloon, watch the blacksmith work, and browse for souvenirs and knickknacks or head for the ice cream parlor.

Part Eight

Northern California

Sparsely populated, rich in dramatic landscapes, Northern California is given over in large part to national forest land. The coastal area (roughly Sonoma, Mendocino, and Humboldt Counties) begins in the south as rugged, beautiful beach country and leads to the Redwood Empire, home of the big trees. It's bounded on the east by the north-south chain of mountains known as the Coast Range. Immediately to the east of the mountains is a huge swath of forest. From south to north, **Mendocino National Forest** merges into **Trinity National Forest** and Trinity into **Klamath National Forest.** In northern mid-state is **Lake Shasta,** a man-made lake of immense proportions and a major recreation site, and **Mount Shasta.** East of Shasta is **Lassen National Park,** with its volcanic wonders and many more acres of national forest. Directly north of San Francisco is the famous wine-producing region of Napa Valley, not covered in any detail here, as its primary pleasures are adults-only.

Many of the small towns and cities of Northern California have neighborhoods catering to tourists and travelers, but these are sometimes simply a few motels and chain restaurants near the freeways. In this region, the fact that a town has a larger population may mean that it has more industry and jobs, not more vacation options, so we've organized this chapter around counties instead of cities. We feature only selected Northern California counties with significant family-vacation options.

These are, on the coast, the counties of **Sonoma,** for its agricultural producers and historic sites; **Mendocino,** for whale-watching, the Skunk Train, tide pools, and picturesque shop-filled towns; and **Humboldt,** with three state parks of giant redwoods and the huge, primeval oasis of **Redwood National Park.** Inland we'll focus on **Trinity, Shasta,** and **Siskyou Counties** for the **Shasta-Trinity National Recreation Area,** with Lake Shasta as its centerpiece (allow a few days for houseboating or Jet Skiing here) and Mount Shasta farther north.

A significant number of city, state, and county parks in this region have summer swimming options, so when you load up the car in the morning, keep bathing suits and inflatable rafts within easy reach. Your midday stop can be a festive highlight at a beautiful redwood-forest recreation area, where you can swim, play a little catch, and picnic.

Because children are famously indifferent to scenery, the spectacular but challenging winding roads of the Northern California coast should be carefully reviewed before setting out on road trips. Parents of children who get motion sickness should also plan carefully.

The same is true for inland scenic routes. Although the Trinity National Forest is a beautiful region of pine-covered slopes and rocky chasms plunging to rivers far below, it took us much longer to cover the miles than we had anticipated. On one vacation, we had to change our itinerary mid-trip to allow enough time in one place to actually get out into the outdoors we'd spent so much time driving through. We had to take one national park off our list of stops, because we didn't want to just look at this wonderful region through the car window. We wanted to enjoy the great outdoors by having enough time to boat, horseback ride, hike, and swim when we arrived at our destinations. If you hope to do the same, allow plenty of travel time.

GETTING THERE

By Plane. If you're flying into the western United States, you can investigate connecting regional air service into one of Northern California's small-city airports and rent a car on arrival. For example, Alaska Airlines serves Eureka/Arcata and Redding airports from Portland, Oregon; United Express offers service to Eureka/Arcata or Redding from San Francisco.

By Train. Amtrak's Coast Starlight goes from Sacramento through Chico, Redding (access Lake Shasta), and Dunsmuir (access Mount Shasta) before continuing on to Seattle. Call (800) USA-RAIL.

By Car. California Highway 1 north of San Francisco takes you to the Mendocino coast. Continue on US 101 from San Francisco to get to Sonoma and the Redwood Empire area. For a direct drive to the Shasta-Trinity area, take Interstate 5 north from Sacramento.

HOW TO GET INFORMATION BEFORE YOU GO

California State Parks information, P.O. Box 942896, Sacramento 94296-0001; (916) 653-6995; ceres.ca.gov/parks/.

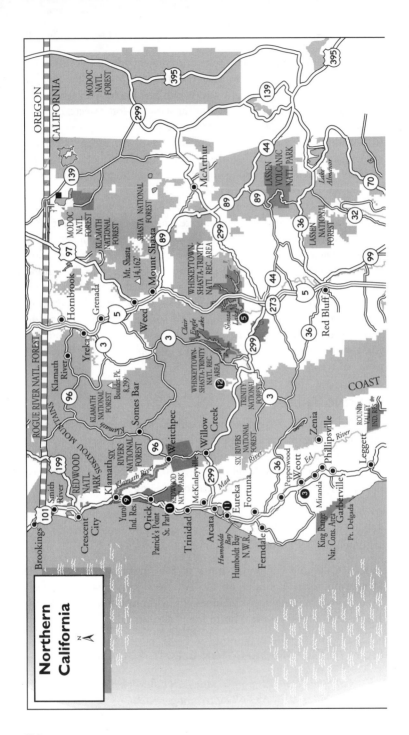

Northern California

N

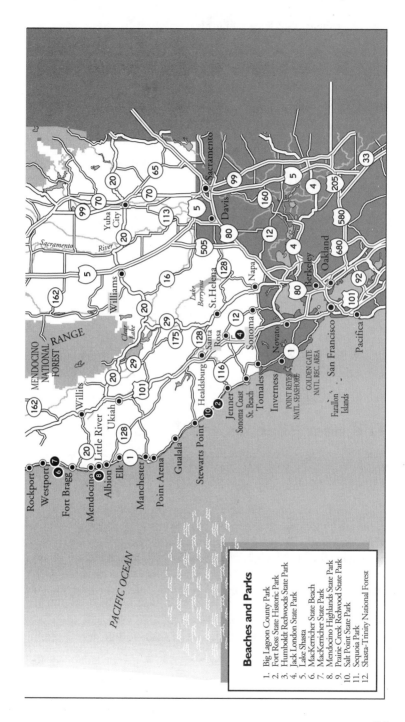

Beaches and Parks

1. Big Lagoon County Park
2. Fort Ross State Historic Park
3. Humboldt Redwoods State Park
4. Jack London State Park
5. Lake Shasta
6. MacKerricher State Beach
7. MacKerricher State Park
8. Mendocino Highlands State Park
9. Prairie Creek Redwood State Park
10. Salt Point State Park
11. Sequoia Park
12. Shasta-Trinity National Forest

Eureka/Humboldt County Convention and Visitors Bureau, 1034 Second Street, Eureka 95501; (707) 443-5097 or (800) 346-3482; www.redwoodvisitor.org.

Fort Bragg–Mendocino Coast Chamber of Commerce, P.O. Box 1141, Fort Bragg 95437; (800) 726-2780 or (707) 961-6300; www.mendocinocoast.com.

Greater Santa Rosa Conference and Visitors Bureau, 9 Fourth Street, Santa Rosa 95401; (707) 577-8674 or (800) 404-7673.

Mount Shasta Chamber of Commerce, 300 Pine Street, Mount Shasta 96067; (916) 926-4865 or (800) 926-4865.

National Parks Camping Reservations (for Whiskeytown National Recreation Area, including Mt. Shasta); (800) 365-2267; reservations.nps.org.

Sonoma County Convention and Visitors Bureau, 5000 Roberts Lake Drive, Rohnert Park 94928; (707) 565-2146.

Sonoma Valley Visitors Bureau, 453 First Street East, Sonoma 95476; (707) 996-1090.

Trinidad Chamber of Commerce, P.O. Box 356, Trinidad 95570; (707) 677-0591.

The Best Beaches and Parks

Note: Swimming is not permitted at some of Northern California's rugged beaches because of dangerous water conditions. Never leave children unattended near the ocean anywhere in this region.

Big Lagoon County Park. Although it's a popular park, the setting here is one of splendid isolation, and although it's adjacent to the highway and thus easily accessed, the huge expanses of beach, water, and sky make it seem remote. It's a county (read low-budget) campground, so it's more rustic than amenity-laden. The site makes a nice break between the northern redwoods and Eureka. Fee for day use and camping. Boat launching, picnicking, camping, fishing, swimming, sanitary facilities, and cold running water. Reservations are not accepted; campsites are on a first-come, first-served basis. Seven miles north of Trinidad, exit Highway 101 at Big Lagoon Park Road.

Humboldt Redwoods State Park. The most famous part of Humboldt Redwoods State Park is the dramatic Avenue of the Giants, a winding bypass road, with turnouts and parking areas, that curves along the south fork of the Eel River through a magnificent forest of redwoods. You feel as if you're moving through a green undersea world as you drive for miles under the forest canopy, only occasionally coming into a sunny meadow. Slanting beams of sunlight impart that sense of sanctuary and awe so often remarked upon in connection with the big trees. You'll find picnicking, swimming, and other recreation along the drive, as well as towns about every six miles.

Also, the chance to camp in the redwoods is not to be missed—hours spent in those awe-inspiring groves are unlike any other camping experience. See the Family Lodging section on page 461 for details. The park has remarkable scenic picnic areas, and the campgrounds are near trails into the most important redwood groves. Gentle, easy self-guiding nature trails may be found at several locations; don't miss the half-mile Founders Tree Trail, which leads to the massive Founders Tree and the Dyerville Giant, a 500-ton redwood that crashed to the ground several years ago. There are bike trails, and a park auto tour is available. Humboldt Redwood State Park, 45 miles south of Eureka on Highway 101, (707) 946-2409. Visitors center next to Burlington Campground, 2 miles south of Weott.

MacKerricher State Beach. You won't find sunbathers and bikini-clad Rollerbladers on this stretch of rugged, often foggy coastline, but rather hikers, bikers, and anglers, along with horseback riders and whale- and seal-watchers. Look for the Seal Point Trail, a short walk leading out to Seal Rocks, where you'll find loads of sunbathing seals. North of Seal Rocks is a popular spot for ocean fishing, and the whole area has great tidepooling at low tide. For a great adventure, contact Ricochet Ridge Ranch, (707) 964-7669, about its guided horseback rides on the beach or in the redwoods. There are many wheelchair-accessible areas, as well as superb tent and RV campsites (call (800) 444-7275 for reservations). Three miles north of Fort Bragg on Highway 1 near Cleone, (707) 937-5804.

Salt Point State Park. A 6,000-acre park encompassing six miles of rugged coastline, Salt Point is a well-loved tidepooling spot. There are trails for hiking and horseback riding, but it's the hidden coves, with their secret spots and strange sandstone formations, that appeal to little ones. Twenty miles north of Jenner on Highway 1, (707) 847-3221 or (707) 865-2391.

Sequoia Park. This lovely city park in Eureka offers a free zoo where you can see animals native to the area, such as bears, elk, and deer, as well as exotic species. There are also picnic areas, a playground, a duck pond, and more than 50 acres of North Coast redwoods. In the summer months a petting zoo is open Tuesday–Sunday, 11 a.m.–3 p.m. The zoo is closed Mondays, but the park itself is open every day. W and Glatt Streets, Eureka, (707) 442-6552.

Other outstanding parks are listed throughout this part as Attractions.

Family Outdoor Adventures

Boating on Lake Shasta. One of the most memorable days of our Northern California vacation was spent on a patio boat on Lake Shasta. We donned bathing suits and sunscreen in our motel room, packed rented fishing poles and hot dogs for barbecuing, grabbed the two-person inflatable rowboat and some rope, and headed for the rental dock. Over the next idyllic hours, we took turns driving the flat-bottomed boat over calm lake waters, marveling at how close the forested mountains looked in the clear, high-elevation air. We cooked on the grill and took turns swimming off the side or floating in the inflatable rowboat tied behind the bigger boat. We tied up on shore from time to time, fished over the side, and waved to other patio boaters as they passed. Motel reservations the night before and the night after at Bridge Bay Lodging at Lake Shasta allowed us to fully enjoy the long day on the lake. (Call Seven Crowns Resorts, (800) 752-9669, for information on lodging and renting houseboats or patio boats.)

Hiking. Whether it's poking along a half-mile, stroller-friendly trail in a redwood forest or negotiating a beach trail for an entire morning, you are guaranteed to spend time hiking in Northern California. So integral is the experience that we won't even get into details here, because this chapter is loaded with descriptions of state, national, and regional parks and their trails.

Horseback Riding in the Redwood Empire. Although horseback riding for casual visitors is available throughout the state, in the Northern California area the trail rides lead you along routes that are really the stuff of fantasy. Picture yourself cantering along the beach? The one-and-a-half-hour ride at Richochet Ridge Ranch takes you to MacKerricher State Park for a good portion of the saddle time, and you'll ride right along the tideline and be able to see seals on the offshore rocks, and, in season, whales. (Richochet Ridge Ranch, 24201 N. Highway 1, Fort Bragg, (707) 964-7669, both group and private rides available.)

Thinking of a few days or a full vacation at a family-oriented ranch resort? See the listing for Coffee Creek Ranch on page 466. Do you have preteen and teen riders ready for the adventure of an overnight pack trip into the wilderness, or at least a day-long trip along the Klamath River? Combine a wilderness pack ride with a ranch stay, or try a "saddle and paddle" package that combines trail rides with rafting or mountain biking at Marble Mountain Ranch (see page 462).

How about a moonlight trail ride with your older kids? Try the guided trail rides (children must be eight or older) through Jack London State

Park with the Sonoma Cattle Company in Glen Ellen, (707) 996-8566. $45 per person for a two-hour ride.

River Rafting. The ocean may be wilder way up north, but the rivers tend to be milder, making for excellent, not-too-scary rafting trips suitable for kids as young as four years old. One of the best rivers for families is Trinity, which wanders along the Trinity Alps Wilderness. Companies to try include Bigfoot Rafting (Willow Creek, (530) 629-2263 or (800) 722-2223) or Aurora River Adventures (Willow Creek, (800) 562-8475), which have half- to two-day trips on Class I and II stretches for families; ask about the one that goes to ancient Hupa Indian sites, or the one with a professional storyteller on board. Over Shasta way, the Klamath River is another gentle one that can be great for family rafting; Turtle River Rafting (Mt. Shasta, (530) 926-3223 or (800) 726-3223) has trips geared to kids ages 4–11.

Whale-Watching on the Mendocino Coast. If you're a winter or spring visitor to Northern California, be sure to join locals for the annual whale-watching rites. Gray whales pass this coast on their way south to Baja California between December and February and on their return home to the Bering Sea from mid-March through April. The high bluffs along the shoreline in the Mendocino area offer ideal viewing from land; there are programs and docent-led walks at MacKerricher State Park near Fort Bragg, Mendocino Highlands State Park in Mendocino, and Point Cabrillo Lightstation near Mendocino, (707) 937-0816. Watchers look for spouts (up to ten feet high) at a quarter-mile to two miles from shore and for the magnificent sight of a whale breaching—jumping clear of the water and falling back with a huge splash.

Once found in the eastern Pacific, Korea, and the Atlantic Ocean, gray whales in the latter two regions were wiped out by whaling in the nineteenth century. Eastern Pacific gray whales, whose population shrank to numbers as low as 1,000, are now, thanks to their protected status since 1937, thought to number between 13,000 and 20,000. They migrate at speeds of about four to five miles an hour.

When looking from shore, it's hard to fully appreciate the size of these mammals, so many wildlife enthusiasts take a whale-watching boat trip. Noyo Harbor in Fort Bragg is an embarkation point for several such charters, which cost about $20 per person for a two-hour trip. For information, contact Anchor Charters (call (707) 964-4550), Patty-C (call (707) 964-0669), Rumblefish (call (707) 964-3000), or Telstar Charters (call (707) 964-8770).

Calendar of Festivals and Events

February

World Championship Crab Races, Del Norte County Fairgrounds, Highway 101, Crescent City. People bet scrip from local stores on little rock crabs, who race down ramps; afterward, festival-goers feast on Dungeness crabs or hot dogs. Children's games and contests; (707) 464-3174.

March

Mendocino Coast Whale Festival in Mendocino and Fort Bragg. First weekend (Mendocino) and third weekend (Fort Bragg) in March. Many events, including wine tasting, seafood chowder tasting, carriage rides, food booths, street entertainment, 10K/5K run, craft fair, and doll show; (707) 961-6300.

April

Sebastapol Apple Blossom Festival. Parades, flower show, and self-guided 35-mile driving tour of apple-blossom country; (707) 823-3032.

May

World Championship Great Arcata to Ferndale Cross-Country Kinetic Sculpture Race, Ferndale. Memorial Day weekend. A wild three-day race between fantastic sculpture-mobiles made from old lawnmower, bicycle, and motorcycle parts; many kids enter the race; (707) 725-3851.

June

Russian River Rodeo Parade and BBQ, Guerneville. Bronco busting, barrel races, and Stumptown Days parade; (707) 869-1959.

July

Mendocino Fourth of July Parade; (707) 961-6300.

Fourth of July Parade and Old-fashioned Celebration, July Fourth, Sonoma Plaza; (707) 966-1090.

Windsor Founder's Day, July Fourth, Windsor. Fireworks, children's games, music; (707) 838-1260.

Living History Day, Fort Ross. Bring a picnic lunch to this in-costume reenactment of the fort's history; (707) 847-3286.

Sonoma County Fair, Sonoma County Fairgrounds. Late July–early August. Classic county fair; (707) 528-3247.

August

Klamath Salmon Festival, downtown Klamath. Sponsored by the local Yurok tribe, with a traditional salmon barbecue, parade, logging show, face painting, dugout canoe races, and brush-dance demonstrations; (707) 482-2921.

September

Bigfoot Days, Willow Creek. A three-day festival in honor of the oft-sighted but never-verified beast of the north. Parade, barbecue, horseshoe tournament, games, and, on Labor Day, a kids' day with sack races and other fun games; (916) 629-2693.

Paul Bunyon Days, Fort Bragg. Also on Labor Day weekend, this fair shows off the legendary strength of the loggers in various competitions. The kids love the Paul Bunyan Parade, the Fire Department Water Fight, and the Kiddie Games; (707) 961-6300.

December

Truckers Lighted Christmas Parade, Humboldt; (707) 443-5097.

California State Parks Mail-Order Catalog

Prepare for your trip with an advance look at some of the California State Parks you'll visit. You can order videos, books, recreation guides, and other reference materials, as well as gift items—all by phone or mail order. All purchases directly benefit the state park system, and many items are sold exclusively through the parks. And when you order your wildlife viewing guide or your hiking maps or your book on camping written by an eight-year-old, you might also order a Walking Bears tote bag for your kid and fill it with a child-size, take-apart fishing pole, a California poppy T-shirt, a red-cedar bookmark, baby California quail finger puppets, an acorn flip toy, a twig whistle, a bear mask, a pine needle basket kit, and a Bear Republic pillow (all available from the state parks catalog). Then, the first time you go to a state park, get your child his or her junior ranger logbook. Each time an activity is finished, a ranger will stamp the book. Buttons, certificates, and patches are awarded. You'll have a happy camper in the back seat for sure. Call the California State Parks Store between 8 a.m. and 5 p.m. PST, (800) 777-0369.

Sonoma County: Sonoma, Santa Rosa, Windsor, Forestville, and Glen Ellen

Almost as famous a wine country now as Napa, Sonoma County is actually a mixed agricultural area with a variety of outstanding products, including cheese, apples, wine, and carnivorous plants. Families traveling on Highway 101 will find such rest-stop recreations as skating rinks, bumper cars, and a steam railway in the city of **Santa Rosa,** which also has one of the area's airports. The historic town center of **Sonoma** is a nice lunch stop—a stroll through the fort where the Bear Flag Revolt took place can be combined with a meal and a look at the cheese-making process. But although some of the wineries serve juice or soda, we don't recommend tasting-room stops for families.

Much is made of the Jack London State Park, but we don't think kids get it, even if they've read *White Fang* (how to explain the connection between the stories and the ruins of a dream house?); however, the outdoor activities at this park can be fun.

Family Lodging

Best Western Sonoma Valley Inn

A pleasant 75-room motel just a block away from Sonoma Plaza, with a pool and garden setting. Courtyard rooms have private balconies and fireplaces, all rooms have coffeemakers and refrigerators, and a continental breakfast is delivered to your room. Children under age 12 stay free; activity packages; baby-sitting available.

550 2nd Street, W. Sonoma; (707) 938-9200 or (800) 334-5784. Rates are $119–249, depending on season.

Flamingo Resort Hotel

A family-run resort with 136 rooms spread over 10 acres of grounds and spa facilities, this Santa Rosa hotel boasts a playground, lawn games, pool,

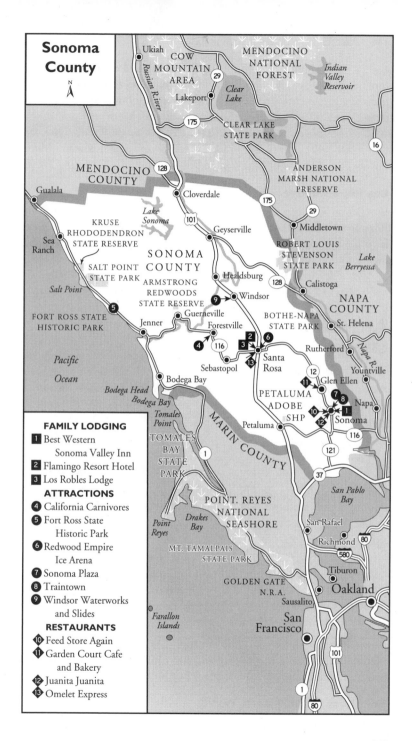

Sonoma County

N

Ukiah
COW
MOUNTAIN
AREA
Lakeport
Clear
Lake
MENDOCINO
NATIONAL
FOREST
Indian
Valley
Reservoir
CLEAR LAKE
STATE PARK
16
Russian R.
128
MENDOCINO
COUNTY
Gualala
Cloverdale
Lake
Sonoma
101
Geyserville
175
29
Middletown
ANDERSON
MARSH NATIONAL
PRESERVE
ROBERT LOUIS
STEVENSON
STATE PARK
Lake
Berryessa
KRUSE
RHODODENDRON
STATE RESERVE
SONOMA
COUNTY
Sea
Ranch
SALT POINT
STATE PARK
ARMSTRONG
REDWOODS
STATE RESERVE
Healdsburg
128
Calistoga
Salt Point
Windsor
BOTHE-NAPA
STATE PARK
NAPA
COUNTY
St. Helena
FORT ROSS STATE
HISTORIC PARK
Guerneville
Forestville
Jenner
116
Sebastopol
Santa
Rosa
Rutherford
Napa R.
Yountville
Pacific
Ocean
Bodega Bay
12
Glen Ellen
Napa
Sonoma
Bodega Head
Bodega Bay
PETALUMA
ADOBE
SHP
116
Tomales
Point
TOMALES
BAY
STATE
PARK
Petaluma
121
37
San Pablo
Bay
1
POINT REYES
NATIONAL
SEASHORE
Point
Reyes
Drakes
Bay
MARIN COUNTY
San Rafael
Richmond
80
MT. TAMALPAIS
STATE PARK
Tiburon
580
GOLDEN GATE
N.R.A.
Sausalito
Oakland
Farallon
Islands
San
Francisco
101
1
80

FAMILY LODGING

1 Best Western
   Sonoma Valley Inn
2 Flamingo Resort Hotel
3 Los Robles Lodge

ATTRACTIONS

4 California Carnivores
5 Fort Ross State
   Historic Park
6 Redwood Empire
   Ice Arena
7 Sonoma Plaza
8 Traintown
9 Windsor Waterworks
   and Slides

RESTAURANTS

10 Feed Store Again
11 Garden Court Cafe
   and Bakery
12 Juanita Juanita
13 Omelet Express

wading pool, tennis courts, and horseback riding. All the public areas are completely smoke-free. The hotel offers a daytime child-care program, including games, arts, and crafts, for kids from 4 months to 12 years old, for the modest fee of $1.25 an hour; reservations are essential.

2777 4th Street, Santa Rosa; (707) 545-8530 or (800) 848-8300; fax (707) 528-1404. Rates $119–199 at height of tourist season (May–October); children under age 12 stay free.

Los Robles Lodge

Families on a budget should check out this good, midsize motel in Santa Rosa. In addition to the pool, there's also a hot tub, a coffee shop, and a good lawn for running around; inside your room, you'll get a coffeemaker and fridge. Your pet can stay with you, too.

1985 Cleveland Avenue, Santa Rosa; (707) 545-6330 or (800) 255-6330. Rates $99–140 depending on season; children under age 16 stay free.

Attractions

California Carnivores

7020 Tranton-Healdsburg Road, Forestville; (707) 838-1630

Hours: Daily 10 a.m.– 4 p.m., closed Thanksgiving, December 24 and 25, New Year's Day

Admission: Free

Appeal by Age Groups:

Pre-school	Grade School	Teens	Young Adults	Over 30	Seniors
★★★	★★★	★★	★★	★★	★★

Touring Time: Average 1 hour; minimum 30 minutes

Rainy-Day Touring: Yes; no problem in greenhouses

Services and Facilities:

Restaurants No	Lockers No
Alcoholic beverages No	Pet kennels No pets allowed
Disabled access Yes	Rain check No
Wheelchair rental No	Private tours No
Baby stroller rental No	

Description and Comments   This is a farm that specializes in insect-eating plants; 350 varieties are on display, and many are for sale. Picnic areas. Kids must be accompanied by adults, but there's no age limit.

Fort Ross State Historic Park

19005 Coast Highway 1, Jenner; (707) 847-3286

Hours: Park open daily dawn–dusk; fort open daily 10 a.m.– 4:30 p.m., closed Thanksgiving and Christmas Day

Admission: $6 per private vehicle

Appeal by Age Groups:

Pre-school	Grade School	Teens	Young Adults	Over 30	Seniors
★★★	★★★★	★★★★	★★★★	★★★★	★★★

Touring Time: Average 2 hours; minimum 1 hour

Rainy-Day Touring: Not recommended

Services and Facilities:

Restaurants Nearby	Lockers No
Alcoholic beverages No	Pet kennels No
Disabled access For some areas	Rain check No
Wheelchair rental No	Private tours Yes
Baby stroller rental No	

Description and Comments   Its spectacular location on a high bluff above the roiling ocean would be reason enough to stop here, but Fort Ross is also a great reconstruction of the Russian-American Company's 1812 outpost. Here's one of the few places to learn about a foreign power's one-time foothold on continental America. You'll see reconstructed 12-foot-high stockades, soldiers' barracks, and an octagonal Orthodox chapel, as well as museum displays on Native American, Russian, and Yankee culture. Russian Orthodox services are held Memorial Day and Fourth of July.

Redwood Empire Ice Arena

1667 W. Steele Lane, Santa Rosa; (707) 546-7147, gallery/gift shop (707) 546-3385

Hours: Complicated because of many ice shows, but call for skate times; consider reserving for an ice show; public skate times vary, but there are some public hours daily

Admission: $7.50 adults, $6.50 ages 11 and under; skate rental $2 per person

Appeal by Age Groups:

Pre-school	Grade School	Teens	Young Adults	Over 30	Seniors
★★★★	★★★★	★★★	★★	★★	★★

Touring Time: Average 3 hours to skate and shop; minimum 1 hour to see gallery and gift shop

Rainy-Day Touring: Just dandy

Services and Facilities:

Restaurants Full service	Lockers Yes
Alcoholic beverages No	Pet kennels No
Disabled access Yes	Rain check No
Wheelchair rental No	Private tours No; limited private
Baby stroller rental No	rentals possible

Description and Comments   Built by *Peanuts* creator Charles Schulz for his own kids, this rink offers rentals and has ice shows, but some visitors come just to enjoy Snoopy's Gallery and Gift Shop. The gift shop carries the largest collection of Snoopy merchandise in the world, and the gallery is a second-floor museum of Schulz awards, original drawings, and memorabilia.

Sonoma Plaza

Spain and First Streets, Sonoma; Sonoma Valley Visitors Center, (707) 996-1090

Hours: State Historic Park, daily 10 a.m.–5 p.m., closed New Year's Day, Thanksgiving, and Christmas Day; shops and cafe hours vary

Admission: Mission and Vallejo home: $2, $1 ages 6–12

Appeal by Age Groups:

Pre-school	Grade School	Teens	Young Adults	Over 30	Seniors
★★	★★	★★★	★★★	★★★★	★★★★
		(shops)	(shops)		

Touring Time: Average 2 hours; minimum 1 hour

Rainy-Day Touring: Not recommended

Services and Facilities:

Restaurants Yes	Baby stroller rental No
Alcoholic beverages At some	Lockers No
restaurants	Pet kennels No
Disabled access Yes	Rain check No
Wheelchair rental No	Private tours No

Description and Comments   California was proclaimed a republic when the Bear Flag was raised here in 1846; a few weeks later it became a state. The plaza itself, created in 1835, is now a national historic landmark. Sonoma State Historic Park is also here, and it includes a hotel and barracks, the mission, and, at another location, a historic residence. The mission has exhibits of religious and ranching life, and on weekends children can help bake bread in the garden workshop area (call (707) 938-1519). Historic buildings are interspersed with contemporary shops and restaurants; all surround a pleasant park square. Mallards on the pond are endlessly fascinating to toddlers—save some bread crumbs for the waddlers.

Sonoma Cheese Factory (on the plaza at 2 Spain Street, (707) 996-1000) is a gourmet deli with some exhibits, videos, and demonstrations relating to the manufacture of Sonoma Jack Cheese. If you're in town on Tuesday, don't miss the evening farmers' market, 5:30–8:30 p.m.

Traintown

20264 Broadway, Sonoma; (707) 938-3912

Hours: Memorial Day–end of September, daily, train leaves every half-hour, 10 a.m.–5 p.m.; Friday–Sunday rest of year

Admission: $3.75 adults, $2.75 kids and seniors; carousel and Ferris wheel $1 per ride

Appeal by Age Groups:

Pre-school	Grade School	Teens	Young Adults	Over 30	Seniors
★★★★★	★★★★	★	★	★	★

Touring Time: Average 1½ hours; minimum 45 minutes

Rainy-Day Touring: Not recommended

Services and Facilities:

Restaurants Snack bar	Lockers No
Alcoholic beverages No	Pet kennels No
Disabled access Yes	Rain check Unused tickets can be
Wheelchair rental No	used another time
Baby stroller rental No	Private tours No

Description and Comments Take a ride on a one-fourth-scale railroad that replicates a steam train of the 1890s used in the mountains. The 20-minute trip winds through ten acres of forest, past lakes and through tunnels to a miniature town. There's also a merry-go-round and petting zoo.

Windsor Waterworks and Slides

8225 Conde Lane, Windsor; (707) 838-7760

Hours: Mid-June–early September, daily 11 a.m.–7 p.m.; May 1–mid-June and early September–late September, Saturday–Sunday 11 a.m.–7 p.m.

Admission: $13.25 for slides, pool, and picnic area; $7.25 to pool and picnic area only; free for children under age 4

Appeal by Age Groups:

Pre-school	Grade School	Teens	Young Adults	Over 30	Seniors
★★★	★★★★	★★★	★★★	★★	★★

Touring Time: Average 5 hours; minimum 3 hours

Rainy-Day Touring: No problem

Services and Facilities:

Restaurants Yes, snack bar

Alcoholic beverages No

Disabled access Yes

Wheelchair rental No

Baby stroller rental No

Lockers Yes

Pet kennels No

Rain check Yes; for lightning only

Private tours No

Description and Comments Convenient to Santa Rosa and Highway 101 is this water park—more modest than the Raging Waters type of chain, but still a nice respite during a summer vacation. It has four slides, a pool, a splash fountain, a Ping-Pong table, and an arcade, as well as barbecue and picnic areas.

Family-Friendly Restaurants

FEED STORE AGAIN

529 First Street West, Sonoma; (707) 939-7147

Meals served: Breakfast, lunch, and dinner
Cuisine: American
Entree range: $3.75–8.50 (breakfast); $2.95–8.75 (lunch); $5–12 (dinner)
Children's menu: Yes, $3.95
Reservations: Not necessary
Payment: AE, D, MC, V

Although the ducks seem to have moved to the plaza nearby, there's still a pond in the shady garden patio here. It's part of an overall farmhouse atmosphere in this old-feed-store cafe that specializes in homemade pastries and breads and sandwiches, very good burgers and onion rings.

GARDEN COURT CAFE AND BAKERY

13875 Sonoma Highway 12, Glen Ellen; (707) 935-1565

Meals served: Breakfast and lunch; dinner first and second Wednesday of month by reservation only
Cuisine: American
Entree range: $3.25–10 (breakfast and lunch)
Children's menu: Yes
Reservations: Not taken on weekends
Payment: MC, V

The bright, peaceful interior of this countryish cafe is perhaps the best place to sit, because sometimes the body shop next door makes the patio a bit noisy. The children's menu is cheerful, with choices ranging from Goldilocks porridge (an oatmeal that's not too hot, not too cold, but just right) to turkey sandwiches and small salads. Regular menu items are sometimes imaginative (banana pancakes, grilled artichoke sandwich), sometimes traditional (chicken salad, Cobb salad). A different soup and fresh pastries (cookies, brownies, coffee cake) are offered daily.

JUANITA JUANITA

19114 Arnold Drive, Sonoma; (707) 935-3981

Meals served: Lunch and dinner
Cuisine: Mexican
Entree range: $2.50–9.95 (lunch and dinner)
Children's menu: No
Reservations: Not taken
Payment: No credit cards

A friendly, locals restaurant, this place puts a healthful spin on the Mexican standards. So aside from the usual tacos and burritos, you can get a veggie tamale and grilled mushroom quesadilla. Kids love the homemade chips; parents like sampling from the roster of beers, including some locally brewed.

OMELET EXPRESS

112 Fourth Street, Railroad Square, Santa Rosa; (707) 525-1690

Meals served: Breakfast and lunch
Cuisine: American
Entree range: $6–8
Children's menu: Yes
Reservations: Not taken
Payment: MC, V

This bright, cheerful diner is a good spot for breakfast or lunch en route north or south: bagels, omelets, sandwiches, burgers, and such.

Mendocino County: Mendocino, Fort Bragg, Willits, and Leggett

The Mendocino Coast is considered one of the most beautiful and romantic places in the world, but it loses some of its charm if you have a four-year-old throwing up in the back seat. Travel time along the scenic 80-mile "Dramamine Drive" (**Highway 1**) between **Bodega Bay** and **Fort Bragg** can take twice as long as you might think looking at a mileage chart. The pace is slow due to hairpin turns—but you're grateful it is slow when you encounter the careening log trucks. It all makes for a much longer time between bathroom stops than the map might suggest.

Traveling at a leisurely pace, and with plenty of picnic supplies for tailgate lunches (and with kids capable of scrambling down a fern-covered gully for a desperation rest stop), we have had a wonderful and memorable family drive along Coast Highway 1. But if your children are under six years of age or prone to car sickness, or if you want to cover a lot of miles (say, to get to the redwoods near Eureka or the Oregon border), we suggest the drive along 101, with its rolling agricultural landscape, instead of dramatic ocean cliffs. You can access the major Mendocino attractions using connecting roads from 101.

Of course, whale-watchers (see page 439) should base themselves on the coast, and for families who like to stroll historic districts and visit shops, the little Mendocino towns have fine restaurants, elegant inns, and beautiful shops.

The towns of **Mendocino** and **Fort Bragg** make the best overnight bases for families. Fort Bragg is less picturesque, but it's the best point to board the area's major family attraction, the **Skunk Train.**

Family Lodging

Emandal

A laid-back family camp with few structured activities, this is a working ranch and farm complete with pigs, cows, and pickle-making. Don't expect

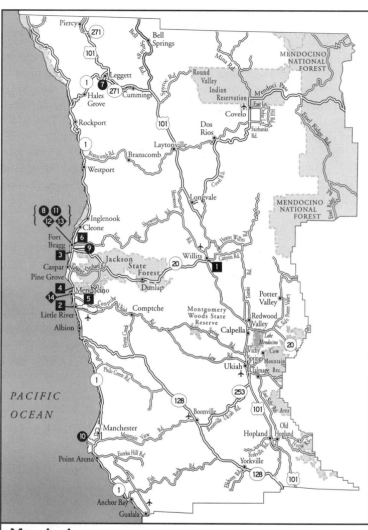

Mendocino County

N
ʌ

FAMILY LODGING

1 Emandal
2 Little River Inn
3 Pine Beach Inn
4 Russian Gulch State
   Park Campground

5 Stanford Inn by the
   Sea/Big River Lodge
6 Surf Motel

ATTRACTIONS

7 Drive-Thru Tree Park
   (a.k.a. Chandelier Tree)
8 Fort Bragg Footlighters
9 Mendocino Coast
   Botanical Gardens
10 Point Arena Lighthouse
   and Museum

11 The Skunk Railroad/
   California Western
   Railroad

RESTAURANTS

12 Cliff House
13 Egghead Omelettes
   of Oz
14 Mendocino Cafe

luxury—the charming little redwood cabins lack hot water, and you'll have to walk a bit to the bathrooms and showers—but do expect reasonable comfort and old-fashioned farm charms, from hearty (and organic) home-cooked meals to swimming holes (in the Eel River), hiking trails, campfire songs, berry-picking, even helping with such farm chores as feeding the chickens. It's located inland from Mendocino near Willits, which is the end of the line for the Skunk Train.

16500 Hearst Post Office Road, Willits; (707) 459-5439 or (800) 262-9597; fax (707) 459-1808; www.emandel.com. Rates for one-week summer sessions $684 adults, $115–450 per child, depending on age; limited two- to four-night weekend stays available.

Little River Inn

Ideally located above the ocean and next to Van Damme State Park (which has an excellent beach and an easy trail through a pygmy forest of dwarf pines), this is a terrific small resort that's more welcoming than most here in the land of romantic bed-and-breakfasts. The best bet for families is the Farmhouse, one mile from the inn, an old house converted to a duplex; the downstairs (which starts at $125) has two bedrooms, a living room with wood-burning stove, and a full kitchen. There's also a good family suite in the main complex, as well as comfortable rooms, most with superb views. Extras include a nine-hole golf course, tennis, gardens, and a highly regarded restaurant with a children's menu.

7751 N. Highway 1, Little River; (707) 937-5942 or (888) 466-5683; fax (707) 937-3944; www.littleriverinn.com. Rates $100–275.

Pine Beach Inn

There's room to run at this moderately priced, family-friendly coastal inn four miles south of Fort Bragg. The 50 rooms (including nine suites) sit on an 11-acre site that spills onto a little sandy beach cove fed by a small creek. Elsewhere on the grounds are two tennis courts, lawns, and a restaurant (closed Mondays), which has a children's menu and a Sunday brunch.

16801 N. Highway 1, south of Fort Bragg; (707) 964-5603; fax (707) 964-4237. Rates start at $115 for one to four people and a view, or $85–95 with no view.

Russian Gulch State Park Campground

Tucked under a picturesque bridge just north of Mendocino, this is a beautiful little campground that's perfect for family tent or RV camping. There are only 30 sites, each with picnic table and fireplace, and what it lacks in isolation it makes up for in beauty and convenience. The campground itself is tucked into a little canyon; just across a stream is the white-sand beach, which is warmer and more protected than most in these parts.

The town of Mendocino, with shops, food, and charm galore, is an easy hike of less than a mile, and there are other family-friendly walks among the giant ferns and redwoods, and along the dramatic coastal headland. You can fish, swim, explore, and cycle, as well as rent a canoe from Catch-a-Canoe and Bicycles, Too! ($18 per hour, $54 per day; (707) 937-0273) and paddle on the Big River estuary to look for seals and osprey. Showers, flush toilets, wood for sale.

Off Highway 1 just north of Mendocino; (707) 937-5804; reserve through Reserve America, (800) 444-7275. Campsites $16 per night.

Stanford Inn by the Sea/Big River Lodge

This four-diamond hotel describes itself as a "self-sustaining ecosystem." Its ten acres of landscaped grounds include a certified organic garden, nursery, and working farm, and guests can take classes in organic gardening and medicinal herbs—it's all so Mendocino here. The farm animals include a dozen llamas and nearly as many cats, as well as bunches of horses, dogs, and black swans. You'll also enjoy the indoor swimming pool, complimentary full breakfast, complimentary video library, and mountain bikes. There are 33 wood-paneled rooms and suites, many with four-poster beds and wood-burning stoves or fireplaces, found in an ivy-covered lodge and four cottages. Baby-sitting, VCRs, mini-refrigerators, coffeemakers, vegetarian restaurant (breakfast and dinner only).

44850 Comptche-Ukiah Road, Mendocino; (800) 331-8884; fax (707) 937-0305. Rates start at $215; children ages 3–18 are charged an additional $25.

Surf Motel

A good choice for families on a budget, this motel is well located in Fort Bragg, not far from the Skunk Train. The two apartment units sleep up to six and are a particularly good value. Outside there's a barbecue and picnic area, landscaped grounds, and fish-cleaning facilities. Refrigerators can be put in rooms for $6 extra. There's no restaurant, but the kids will be happy to spot the McDonald's right across the street.

1220 S. Main Street, Fort Bragg; (707) 964-5361; fax (707) 964-3187. Rates start at $59; $6 extra for children over age 9; apartment units $125.

Attractions

Drive-Thru Tree Park (a.k.a. Chandelier Tree)

Highway 101 in Legget; (707) 925-6464
Hours: Daily 8:30 a.m.–7 p.m.
Admission: $3 per vehicle

Appeal by Age Groups:

Pre-school	Grade School	Teens	Young Adults	Over 30	Seniors
★★★	★★★	★★★	★★★	★★	★★

Touring Time: Average 15 minutes; minimum 5 minutes

Rainy-Day Touring: Okay

Services and Facilities:

Restaurants No	Lockers No
Alcoholic beverages No	Pet kennels No
Disabled access Yes	Rain check No
Wheelchair rental No	Private tours No
Baby stroller rental No	

Description and Comments On US 101 in Leggett, a town situated where Coast Highway veers in and meets up with US 101, you'll find the famed drive-through tree: a privately owned, 315-foot-tall redwood, 21 feet in diameter, that had a car-sized tunnel carved into it in the mid-1930s. It's weird, but it's memorable. Picnic facilities are on site.

Fort Bragg Footlighters

248 E. Laurel, Fort Bragg; (707) 964-3806

Hours: Memorial Day–Labor Day; show starts 8 p.m., Wednesdays and Saturdays and the Sunday before Labor Day

Admission: $10 adults, $8 children and seniors

Appeal by Age Groups:

Pre-school	Grade School	Teens	Young Adults	Over 30	Seniors
★	★★★★	★★★	★★★	★★★	★★★★

Touring Time: Average 2 hours; minimum 1½ hours

Rainy-Day Touring: Yes

Services and Facilities:

Restaurants No	Lockers No
Alcoholic beverages No	Pet kennels No
Disabled access Yes	Rain check No
Wheelchair rental No	Private tours No
Baby stroller rental No	

Description and Comments What to do for a special outing at night? This 1890s-style musical comedy and melodrama is something they won't see on MTV, but it fits in nicely with the historical era they'll see in the architecture of Mendocino. This 50-year-old company has its own theater, and it performs the same show year in and year out: "The Play Must Go On, Or: We Still Got It."

Mendocino Coast Botanical Gardens

18220 N. Highway 1 (2 miles south of Fort Bragg); (707) 964-4352

Hours: March–October, daily 9 a.m.–5 p.m.; November–February, daily 9 a.m.–4 p.m.

Admission: $6 adults, $5 seniors over 60, $2 teens 13–16, $1 children ages 6–12, free for children 5 and under

Appeal by Age Groups:

Pre-school	Grade School	Teens	Young Adults	Over 30	Seniors
★★	★★★	★★★	★★★	★★★	★★★★

Touring Time: Average 3 hours; minimum 1 hour

Rainy-Day Touring: Not recommended

Services and Facilities:

Restaurants Yes; garden setting	Baby stroller rental No
Alcoholic beverages No	Lockers No
Disabled access About 1 mile of paved trails	Pet kennels No
	Rain check Yes
Wheelchair rental Electric carts	Private tours Yes

Description and Comments Botanical gardens, with their smooth paths and landscaped environments, can make a pleasant park-like stop for families with strollers and young children who need some safe, easy running time. This 47-acre facility is known for its rhododendrons and fuchsia gardens. Families will enjoy the easy one-mile loop trail to the ocean, and youngsters who liked the movie *Fern Gully* will find the fantasy come to life in the Fern Canyon section, with its six small wooden bridges over the creek. Deer, squirrels, and other wildlife can sometimes be seen. Food, gift shop, retail nursery.

Point Arena Lighthouse and Museum

Off Highway 1 just north of Point Arena; (707) 882-2777

Hours: Daily 11 a.m.–3:30 p.m.

Admission: $3 adults, $1 children ages 12 and under

Appeal by Age Groups:

Pre-school	Grade School	Teens	Young Adults	Over 30	Seniors
★★★	★★★★	★★★★	★★★★	★★★★	★★★★

Touring Time: Average 1 hour; minimum 30 minutes

Rainy-Day Touring: Yes

Services and Facilities:

Restaurants No	Lockers No
Alcoholic beverages No	Pet kennels No
Disabled access No	Rain check No
Wheelchair rental No	Private tours No
Baby stroller rental No	

Description and Comments The first lighthouse at this location was destroyed in the 1906 San Francisco earthquake; the current historic building, now restored, dates from 1907. It towers 115 feet over the sea, which makes for a swell view. A small museum is located next to the lighthouse in the 1869 Fog Signal Building.

The Skunk Railroad/California Western Railroad

Highway 1 and Laurel Street, Fort Bragg; (707) 964-6371

Hours: Half- and full-day trips from Fort Bragg or Willits available early June–early September, from Fort Bragg only during rest of year

Admission: Round-trip Fort Bragg–Northspur fares are $27 adults, $14 kids ages 5–10

Appeal by Age Groups:

Pre-school	Grade School	Teens	Young Adults	Over 30	Seniors
★★★★★	★★★★★	★★★	★★★★	★★★★★	★★★★★

Touring Time: Average 4–5 hours for half-day trip, including boarding time, etc.; minimum half-day ride is 3½ hours

Rainy-Day Touring: Not recommended

Services and Facilities:

Restaurants Snack bar at North-spur	Baby stroller rental No
	Lockers No
Alcoholic beverages Yes	Pet kennels In the area
Disabled access Yes	Rain check Yes
Wheelchair rental No	Private tours Yes

Description and Comments It's a family joke that Mom liked this train ride even more than the kids did, but part of my pleasure in the excursion was of the happy-surprise variety. So many tourist attractions are somewhat cynically run, with little in the way of extras, that I was especially pleased with the go-the-extra-mile attitude of this recreational railroad company.

We boarded the 1920s-era passenger cars of the diesel train at the Skunk Depot in Fort Bragg and settled in to enjoy the 40-mile trip through forest and meadowland, over bridges and trestles, through tunnels and around curves. I was happy enough, and then a friendly, strolling, guitar player began walking through the cars, adding a festive touch with railroad-themed folk songs. At Northspur, the round-trip mid-point railroad camp, we disembarked and enjoyed a cool interlude in a shady grove where picnic tables, refreshment stands, and souvenir stands offer a country-fair feeling. From the camp, you can continue on to Willits or return to Fort Bragg, and passengers beginning in Willits (a town near Highway 101) can do the same. The round trip from Fort Bragg to Northspur is about 3½ hours long, and reservations are advised during high season.

Family-Friendly Restaurants

CLIFF HOUSE

1011 S. Main Street, Fort Bragg; (707) 961-0255

Meals served: Dinner
Cuisine: American/seafood
Entree range: $12.95–19.95
Children's menu: Yes
Reservations: Necessary
Payment: All major credit cards

Although its seafood specialties and floor-to-ceiling windows with a lovely view of Noyo Harbor and its boats and gulls (from all tables) mean that many touring seniors gravitate here, it's not a stiff, formal place. You'll have to make reservations and be ready for a real, sit-down meal, but casual dress is okay; beer and wine are available.

EGGHEAD OMELETTES OF OZ

326 N. Main Street, Fort Bragg; (707) 964-5005

Meals served: Breakfast and lunch
Cuisine: American
Entree range: $5–13 (breakfast and lunch)
Children's menu: No
Reservations: Not accepted
Payment: MC, V

A fanciful place devoted to the land of Dorothy and Toto, Egghead is a great place to know about, if only for its location one block from the Skunk Train depot. Fortunately, the food is as appealing as the location: every sort of omelet imaginable, carefully prepared and happily split in two for kids, along with great pancakes and, at lunch, soups, salads, and burgers.

MENDOCINO CAFE

10451 Lansing Street, Mendocino; (707) 937-2422

Meals served: Lunch and dinner
Cuisine: Pacific Rim
Entree range: $6–9.99 (lunch); $9.95–14.95 (dinner)
Children's menu: No
Reservations: Not accepted
Payment: MC, V

Tell the kids it's Chinese or Mexican food, but know that you're settling in for some Pacific Rim contemporary cuisine, with bistro favorites enlivened by Asian and Latin influences. There's no children's menu, but the wait staff will recommend the simple pasta with marinara or the quesadilla. Chicken, steak, and fresh fish entrees come with a choice of garlic mashed potatoes or rice, and there are some ramen noodle bowl offerings at dinner and a steamed veggie bowl at lunch. Just don't look for sandwiches or burgers.

Humboldt and Del Norte Counties: Eureka, Trinidad, and Klamath

The most northerly coast of California is big country—big trees, big rivers, big mountains, and long distances. There are both state and national redwood parks, quaint seaport villages, and plenty of opportunities for outdoor adventures, from river rafting to rock climbing. The city of **Eureka** is the best base for exploring the area, and it's where you'll connect to the highway east to **Lake Shasta.**

Whatever you do up here, make sure to visit **Humboldt Redwoods State Park,** especially **Avenue of the Giants,** the road winding through an astounding primeval redwood forest. See page 436 for details. If at all possible, you should camp out in the state park, one of the most beautiful family campgrounds in the country. See the next page for information.

OLD TOWN EUREKA

The renovated Victorian-era neighborhood brings the days of the free-spending lumber barons to mind, but Old Town Eureka also makes for a fun afternoon of dining and shopping. We don't recommend taking the kids on the historic walking tours, but look for the crafts shop at the **Northern Indian Development Council** on F Street.

TRINIDAD

A picturesque village perched on a promontory above a tiny harbor with a pier, a lighthouse (replica of the 1871 original), and a dozen pretty shops and cafes, Trinidad is home to some motels and bed-and-breakfasts, and it makes a restful overnight on the way to or from the redwoods. We hiked the **Trinidad Head Trail** to look down on the beach, had supper in the harbor, and had a fine time shopping in the crafts stores.

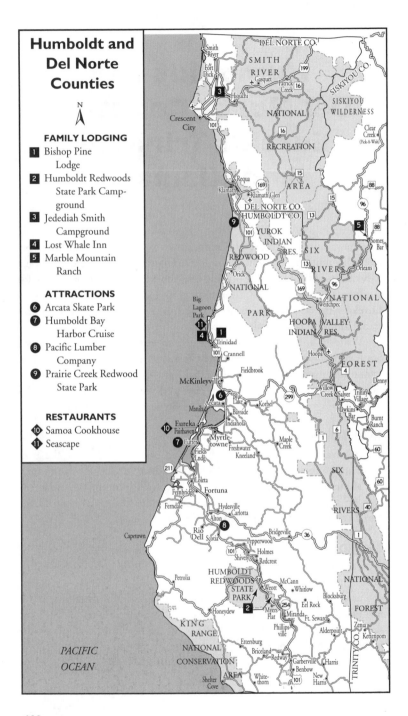

Humboldt and Del Norte Counties

N

FAMILY LODGING
1. Bishop Pine Lodge
2. Humboldt Redwoods State Park Campground
3. Jedediah Smith Campground
4. Lost Whale Inn
5. Marble Mountain Ranch

ATTRACTIONS
6. Arcata Skate Park
7. Humboldt Bay Harbor Cruise
8. Pacific Lumber Company
9. Prairie Creek Redwood State Park

RESTAURANTS
10. Samoa Cookhouse
11. Seascape

Family Lodging

Bishop Pine Lodge

A funky little cabin resort in the pines behind the village of Trinidad. We loved the old-fashioned playground and the chance to sit on the porch and look at those bright, bright stars in the rural sky. Twelve wooden cottages and two two-bedrooms; some have kitchens. Outside is a barbecue area.

1481 Patricks Point Drive, Trinidad; (707) 677-3314; fax (707) 677-3444. Rates are $96 for four people, and $104 with a kitchen; add $8 per extra person or pet.

Humboldt Redwoods State Park Campground

Try to spend more time in this remarkable state park than just driving through to see the trees. The best way to help your family absorb the majesty of the giant redwoods is to live with them for a day or two, at one of the park's two campgrounds: Burlington, near the park headquarters, or Hidden Springs. Each area has rest rooms, hot showers, and laundry tubs, as well as evening campfire programs and interpretive programs in the summer.

45 miles south of Eureka off Highway 101, Humboldt; (707) 946-2409; reservations through Reserve America, (800) 444-7275. Campsites $12–16 per night, $22–25 with hookups.

Jedediah Smith Campground

The happiest stay of my family's see-the-redwoods trip when I was a kid, Jedediah Smith continues to be a superb family campground in a setting of God-fearing beauty. The Smith River runs right through the redwood-studded campground, and kids love to splash, fish, and paddle rafts in it. This park is warmer than some of the coastal camps, because it's inland enough to avoid much fog. A footbridge over the river leads to the marvelous Simpson-Reed Discovery Trail, an educational loop that's easy even for toddlers. Flush toilets, showers, picnic tables, fireplaces.

4241 Kings Valley Road, Crescent City; (707) 464-6101; reservations through Reserve America, (800) 444-7275. $16 per campsite, plus reservation fee of $7.50.

Lost Whale Inn

Usually a bed-and-breakfast on a prime piece of coastal land like this is aimed at romancing couples, and children are as welcome as Scud missiles. Not so here. Some of the rooms and suites are great for families (ask for one with a sleeping loft), and while they're certainly charming, with wood floors and ocean views, they're not full of delicate antiques. The kids won't mind the lack of TV when they can pick berries, play in the playhouse and playground, feed ducks, and look for whales or sea lions. The rough beach is fun for (supervised) rock climbing, but not swimming or sand play.

3452 Patrick's Point Drive, Trinidad; (707) 677-3425 or (800) 677-7859; www.lostwhaleinn.com. Rates $140–170 May–October, $110–140 October–April.

Marble Mountain Ranch

For the ambitious, this budget dude ranch at the edge of the Marble Mountain wilderness offers pack trips into the wilds. For the rest of us, it's possible to enjoy a night or a week in the company of the ranch's 18 horses and various dogs, goats, and chickens. Self-guided activities include horseback riding and, in fall, drift-boat fishing; guided excursions include rafting, mountain biking, and horseback riding (one-hour to custom multiday adventures). The lodge serves family-style meals nightly ($16 per adult) and a weekend Western barbecue, and the deli packs lunches to take along on hikes. Accommodations vary from RV hookups and tent sites to no-frills housekeeping cabins (sleep up to six) and better-equipped "deluxe cabin homes."

92520 Highway 96, Somes Bar; (800) KLAMATH or (530) 469-3322; fax (530) 469-3357. Housekeeping cabins $60 for two people, plus $20 per extra person, depending on age (kids under age 6 stay free); deluxe cabin homes $100 double occupancy, plus $30 per extra person (kids under age 6 stay free); tent sites and RV hookups $15; all-inclusive family vacations offered; package includes accommodations, meals, and one activity per day.

Attractions

Arcata Skate Park

1062 G Street, Arcata; (707) 822-3619

Hours: Open daily in daylight hours

Admission: Free

Appeal by Age Groups:

Pre-school	Grade School	Teens	Young Adults	Over 30	Seniors
★	★★★	★★★	★★	★	★

Touring Time: Average 2 hours; minimum 1 hour

Rainy-Day Touring: No

Services and Facilities:

Restaurants No	Lockers No
Alcoholic beverages No	Pet kennels No
Disabled access No	Rain check No
Wheelchair rental No	Private tours No
Baby stroller rental No	

Description and Comments A recently opened public park just for skaters sounds like a good bet for those whose boarders have brought helmets and other safety equipment on the trip (it's required here). In-line skaters and skateboarders alike can try their skills on three bowls with rails—one measuring 7 x 20 feet, a 4-foot-tall fun box, and a snake run with "lots of vertical edges."

Humboldt Bay Harbor Cruise

Foot of C Street, Eureka; (707) 444-9440

Hours: March–October, cruises depart Monday–Saturday at 1 p.m., 2:30 p.m., and 4 p.m., Sunday 1 p.m. and 2:30 p.m.

Admission: $9.50 adults, $8.50 ages 12–17, $6.50 ages 4–11

Appeal by Age Groups:

Pre-school	Grade School	Teens	Young Adults	Over 30	Seniors
★★★★	★★★★	★★★	★★★	★★★★	★★★★

Touring Time: Average 3 hours; minimum 2 hours (allow for boarding, etc.)

Rainy-Day Touring: Not recommended

Services and Facilities:

Restaurants Cocktail, brunch, dinner cruises
Alcoholic beverages Yes
Disabled access Yes
Wheelchair rental With notice
Baby stroller rental No

Lockers No
Pet kennels No; pets allowed on cruise
Rain check Yes
Private tours No

Description and Comments A 1910 ferry takes visitors on a 1-hour, 15-minute tour of the Humboldt Bay area, past sawmills, a former Indian village, and bird habitats. Kids can watch for fishing boats and special birds.

Pacific Lumber Company

Main Street, Scotia; (707) 764-2222

Hours: Open in summer only; plant tours Monday–Friday 8 a.m.–10:30 a.m. and 11:30 a.m.–2 p.m.; museum open Monday–Friday 7 a.m.–2 p.m.; closed holidays

Admission: Free

Appeal by Age Groups:

Pre-school	Grade School	Teens	Young Adults	Over 30	Seniors
★	★★★★	★★★★	★★★★	★★★	★★★

Touring Time: Average 1½ hours; minimum 1 hour

Rainy-Day Touring: Not recommended

Services and Facilities:

Restaurants Nearby	Lockers No
Alcoholic beverages Nearby	Pet kennels No
Disabled access No	Rain check No
Wheelchair rental No	Private tours Special arrangements
Baby stroller rental No	

Description and Comments   Located 27 miles south of Eureka, this redwood processing plant offers summertime self-guided tours of current operations, as well as a logging museum of former and current products, equipment, company coins, and artifacts. The company was established in 1869, and the town, one of the last remaining company towns in the United States, in 1910. Visitors get a pass for the tour at the museum, then proceed along a catwalk past various stages of processing, including the thrilling high-water-pressure debarker. Too noisy for very young children.

Prairie Creek Redwood State Park

Highway 101 6 miles north of Orick; (707) 464-6101, ext. 5301

Hours: Daily 24 hours

Admission: Day-use fee $5, $1 per dog (must be leashed); limited number of day-use permits issued

Appeal by Age Groups:

Pre-school	Grade School	Teens	Young Adults	Over 30	Seniors
★★★★	★★★★	★★★	★★★★	★★★★	★★★★

Touring Time: Average a half-day; minimum 2 hours

Rainy-Day Touring: Not great

Services and Facilities:

Restaurants No	Lockers No
Alcoholic beverages No	Pet kennels No
Disabled access On some trails	Rain check No
Wheelchair rental No	Private tours No
Baby stroller rental No	

Description and Comments   This state park is also a UNESCO-designated World Heritage Site. It's particularly worth a family visit because of its daily (in summer) one-hour junior ranger programs for children ages 7–12. The other great reason, aside from the usual amazing forests of redwoods, is the herd of protected native Roosevelt elk roaming the 40,000 acres, often in the meadow near the highway. The 75 miles of trails include wheelchair-accessible routes. Interpretive exhibits on the elk and other flora and fauna of the region are offered. A nature walk near the visitors center takes you to Chimney Tree, where a family lived in the 1930s; little kids love the half-mile loop trail into Fern Canyon. Beach camping; 100 family campsites.

Family-Friendly Restaurants

SAMOA COOKHOUSE

445 W. Washington, Samoa Road, Eureka; (707) 442-1659

Meals served: Breakfast, lunch, and dinner
Cuisine: Lumberjack American
Entree range: $2.95–4.85 for children, $6.95 adults (breakfast); $3.50–4.95 children, $7.95 adults (lunch); $3.95–5.95 children, $11.45 adults (dinner); children under age 5 eat free
Children's menu: No
Reservations: First-come, first-served
Payment: AE, D, MC, V

If you have an overeater in the family, don't stop here. It's an old lumber-camp cookhouse, and it serves meals as if we were all lumberjacks. Diners seat themselves at long tables, and family groups are brought platters heaped with chicken, ham, or fish (depending on what the cook's up to that night), vegetables, breads, and dessert—it's an all-you-can-eat feast. Equally hearty breakfasts and lunches are served. For anyone with the willpower to avoid a stomachache, it's a fun stop—the tables have checkered cloths, and there's a mini-museum of old-time kitchen and logging equipment.

SEASCAPE

Trinidad Harbor at the foot of Bay Street, Trinidad; (707) 677-3762

Meals served: Breakfast, lunch, and dinner
Cuisine: American
Entree range: $5–10 (breakfast); $7–15 (lunch); $12–20 (dinner)
Children's menu: Yes, $2.99
Reservations: Only accepted for 5 or more
Payment: MC, V

Right at the harbor in Trinidad, this place is notable mostly for its views of the pier, bay, and harbor seals right outside the window. The food is fine: good breakfasts, basic burgers, fish and chips, omelets, and, at dinner, fresh seafood.

Trinity and Shasta Counties

We're talking an area as big as some states when it comes to these two counties, and the landscapes they encompass are impressive Western mountain pine forests and big-deal rivers—the kind that inspire men to build dams.

The city of Redding is where the Central Valley meets the mountains, but it's no vacation mecca—that honor is reserved for the awkwardly named **Whiskeytown, Shasta, Trinity National Recreation Area.** Above it all towers **Mt. Shasta,** a dormant volcano whose slopes are home to five living glaciers. A mountain that has figured in legends and lore of several cultures, its snow-shrouded peak is often circled with mysteriously shaped clouds.

Family Lodging

Bridge Bay Resort

A just-okay 40-room marina motel that we nevertheless highly valued because we were just knocked out after days of fresh air and water—we simply couldn't get back in the car and cover more miles. So we extended our stay, relaxed in the air-conditioned room, and floated in the pool. You'll want to stay in this motel the night before you patio-boat or begin a houseboat vacation, or the night after you spend a day or a few days on the lake. There's a restaurant, a mini-mart, and some larger units with kitchens. Our room had a little patio area from which you could see the lake.

10300 Bridge Bay Road, Shasta Lake; (530) 275-3021 or (800) 752-9669; fax (530) 275-8365. Summertime rates $89–150.

Coffee Creek Ranch

A well-regarded family vacation ranch, Coffee Creek is located in the Trinity Alps at 3,100 feet elevation. Guests should be inclined to spend a lot of time on horseback, as that's the main activity. Participants are divided according

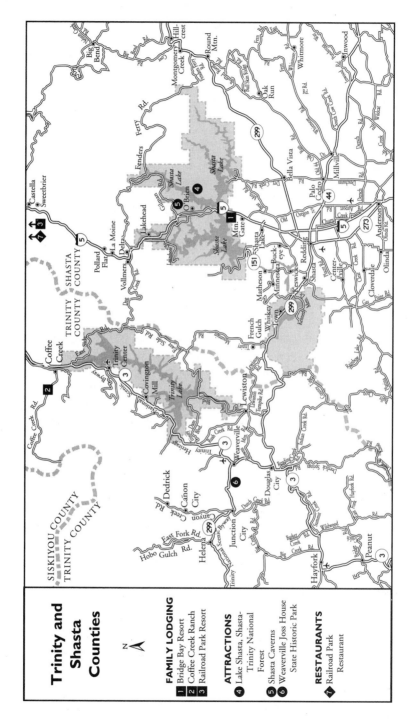

Trinity and Shasta Counties

N

FAMILY LODGING
1 Bridge Bay Resort
2 Coffee Creek Ranch
3 Railroad Park Resort

ATTRACTIONS
4 Lake Shasta, Shasta-Trinity National Forest
5 Shasta Caverns
6 Weaverville Joss House State Historic Park

RESTAURANTS
7 Railroad Park Restaurant

to ability for two rides a day, sometimes early in the morning to a destination where a hot breakfast awaits, sometimes at twilight to a hilltop for the sunset, sometimes to a swimming hole with a waterfall. Other activities include volleyball, archery, canoeing, square dancing, and hayrides. The ranch also has a pool, rifle range, and trout pond; kid programs include the Kiddie Corral, with supervised play for toddlers; games, hikes, and pony rides for 3–7-year-olds; and horsemanship, roping, and hiking programs for older kids. Fifty guests a week can be accommodated in the rustic, comfortable cabins, all with fireplaces or potbellied stoves. Riders must be five years old for all rides; no one under eight years of age is permitted on all-day trips, but lessons are available for kids age four and up.

Coffee Creek Road off Highway 3, HC 2, Box 4940, Trinity Center; (530) 266-3343 or (800) 624-4480; fax (530) 266-3597. Rates $785–900 per week for adults, $250–780 per week for children (children under age 3 stay free), $765–880 for teens; riding in summer is extra.

Railroad Park Resort

In the town of Dunsmuir just south of Mt. Shasta and near Castle Crags State Park, a collection of old freight-train cabooses are linked together to make an atmospheric family motel. The cabooses surround a pool, spa, and deck; inside the cabooses are motel rooms, each decorated differently. Also on the property are four cabins with kitchens, a restored water tower, a huge logging steam engine, and an RV campground with a creek, swimming hole, and convenience store. The train-car restaurant is a fun place to eat.

100 Railroad Park Road, Dunsmuir; (530) 235-4440; fax (530) 235-4470. Rates $70–75, plus $8 for extra person.

Attractions

Lake Shasta, Shasta-Trinity National Forest

2400 Washington Avenue, Redding; (530) 275-1587

Hours: Vary

Admission: Free; fees for boat rental; camping $25 per night

Appeal by Age Groups:

(for patio boating or houseboating on lake)

Pre-school	Grade School	Teens	Young Adults	Over 30	Seniors
★★★★	★★★★	★★★★	★★★★	★★★★	★★★★

Touring Time: Average 1 day; minimum 4 hours

Rainy-Day Touring: Not great

Services and Facilities:

Restaurants Mostly snack bars	Lockers No
Alcoholic beverages Limited	Pet kennels No
Disabled access Some	Rain check No
Wheelchair rental No	Private tours No
Baby stroller rental No	

Description and Comments   This huge man-made lake is so large that once you chug away from the dock on your houseboat, patio boat, or water-ski boat, you'll feel as if you could get lost for days. The water is cool and exhilarating for swimming; fishermen pull up 21 varieties of fish; and the slopes surrounding the lake are covered in pine forest. See Family Outdoor Adventures for more on patio boating and houseboating, page 438. For camping reservations in the national forest, call (800) 365-CAMP (2267).

Shasta Caverns

Shasta Caverns Road, O'Brien; (530) 238-2341 or (800) 795-CAVE

Hours: Summer 9 a.m.– 4 p.m., with tours every half-hour; April, May, September 9 a.m.–3 p.m., with tours every hour; off-season tours leave at 10 a.m., noon, and 2 p.m.

Admission: $15 adults, $7 children ages 4–12, free for children ages 3 and under

Appeal by Age Groups:

Pre-school	Grade School	Teens	Young Adults	Over 30	Seniors
★★	★★★★	★★★★	★★★	★★★	★★★★

Touring Time: Average 2 hours; minimum 2 hours

Rainy-Day Touring: No problem

Services and Facilities:

Restaurants Yes, snack bar	Lockers No
Alcoholic beverages No	Pet kennels Staff will care for
Disabled access No	pets on lawn
Wheelchair rental No	Rain check No
Baby stroller rental No	Private tours No

Description and Comments   We took a day off from the sun, sunburn, and water sports of Lake Shasta to descend into the cool, eerie depth of Shasta Caverns. This is not an excursion for little ones or anyone who has trouble walking—the day begins with a steep descent to a boat that takes you across Lake Shasta to board a bus that takes you, gears grinding, up a narrow steep road to the top of a mountain. In the course of visiting the cave you'll go up or down more than 600 steps. But for the energetic and hardy, it's a worthwhile look at those always-amazing underground formations, culminating in a 60-foot room of crystal-studded "draperies."

Weaverville Joss House State Historic Park

Main Street, Highway 299 West, Weaverville; (530) 623-5284 or (530) 225-2065

Hours: Memorial Day–August, daily 10 a.m.–5 p.m., with tours on the hour; December–March open on Saturday with tours on the hour

Admission: $2 adults, $1 children ages 6–12

Appeal by Age Groups:

Pre-school	Grade School	Teens	Young Adults	Over 30	Seniors
★★	★★★★	★★★★	★★★	★★★	★★★★

Touring Time: Average 1 hour; minimum 30-minute walk-through tour of Temple

Rainy-Day Touring: Adjustments made on the tours

Services and Facilities:

Restaurants Nearby	Lockers No
Alcoholic beverages No	Pet kennels No
Disabled access With assistance	Rain check No
Wheelchair rental No	Private tours Yes
Baby stroller rental No	

Description and Comments   On the road to Shasta Lake from the North Coast is a reminder that California's ethnic diversity is no new development. The Weaverville Joss House is the oldest continuously used Chinese temple in California, named by its builders "The Temple of the Forest beneath the Clouds" (an apt description of its setting). Descendants of the gold miners who built this temple still worship here in the Taoist tradition. Art objects, mining tools, and other artifacts are on display. The temple is open to the public only for guided tours.

Family-Friendly Restaurant

RAILROAD PARK RESTAURANT

100 Railroad Park Road, Dunsmuir; (530) 235-4611

Meals served: Dinner
Cuisine: American
Entree range: $10–19
Children's menu: Yes
Reservations: Suggested
Payment: AE, D, MC, V

A collection of 100-year-old train cars makes up this charming family restaurant next to the motel of the same name. Kids love the setting, and they're welcomed with a children's menu. The food is straightforward, moderately upscale dinner-house American, and there's a full bar.

Index